D1615892

*UP TO THE MOUNTAINS AND
DOWN TO THE VILLAGES*

UP TO THE MOUNTAINS AND

DOWN TO THE VILLAGES

THE TRANSFER OF YOUTH FROM URBAN TO RURAL CHINA

THOMAS P. BERNSTEIN

NEW HAVEN AND LONDON, YALE UNIVERSITY PRESS, 1977

Published with assistance from the foundation established in memory of Calvin Chapin of the Class of 1788, Yale College.

Copyright © 1977 by Yale University. All rights reserved. This book may not be reproduced, in whole or in part, in any form (except by reviewers for the public press), without written permission from the publishers.

Designed by Sally Sullivan
and set in IBM Press Roman type.
Printed in the United States of America by
Vail-Ballou Press, Binghamton, New York.

Published in Great Britain, Europe, Africa, and Asia (except Japan) by Yale University Press, Ltd., London. Distributed in Latin America by Kaiman & Polon, Inc., New York City; in Australia and New Zealand by Book & Film Services, Artarmon, N.S.W., Australia; and in Japan by Harper & Row, Publishers, Tokyo Office.

Library of Congress Cataloging in Publication Data

Bernstein, Thomas P   1937–
   Up to the mountains and down to the villages.

   Bibliography: p.
   Includes index.
   1. China–Rural development. 2. Youth–China.
3. Communes (China) I. Title.
HN737.B47   309.2'63'0951   77-76291
ISBN 0-300-02135-6

For Ellen, Anya, and Maia

CONTENTS

LIST OF TABLES

ACKNOWLEDGMENTS

This study owes much to a great many people and institutions. Funds for the initial, exploratory stage of research, undertaken in the summer of 1971, came from the Concilium on International and Area Studies, Yale University. I was able to spend the year 1972–73 in Hong Kong doing research, supported by a Junior Fellowship from Yale College, as well as by grants from the Joint Committee on Contemporary China of the Social Science Research Council and the American Council of Learned Societies and from the National Science Foundation. Later research and writing were facilitated by support from the Council on East Asian Studies at Yale and the East Asian Institute of Columbia University.

Several research assistants made indispensable contributions to this study. I would like to thank in particular my two half-time assistants in Hong Kong, HPK and YSC. HPK, a young Cantonese sent to the countryside in 1968 under the program that is the subject of this book, did a great deal of work extracting statistics from newspaper articles published between 1968 and 1972. He also compiled, and organized by topic, digests of newspaper articles which we would discuss as I translated them into English, thereby enabling me to cope with the voluminous writings on the topic. YSC, also a former resident of the People's Republic of China, did research on Chinese education, using Cultural Revolution materials. Both taught me a great deal about China. In addition, I would like to thank Erica Jen, Judith Chen, Ida Loh, and Nancy Roth Remington for doing research on the topic at various times between 1973 and 1975.

Several scholars read all or part of the manuscript and supplied detailed comments. Andrew J. Nathan and Martin K. Whyte commented on the entire manuscript. Michel Oksenberg and Ezra Vogel commented on the first four chapters, William Parish, Jr., on the last three, and Janet Salaff on chapter 4. Their comments, criticisms, and suggestions for changes are gratefully acknowledged.

I also learned from comments made by discussants and participants at various meetings at which I presented material in this book, including the New England China Seminar, the East Asian Studies Colloquium at Yale, a panel of the Association for Asian Studies, the University Seminar on Modern East Asia: China, at Columbia, and a workshop conducted by Edwin Winckler at Columbia. And I would like to thank those who supplied additional data or helped interpret data, including Roy Hofheinz, Nicholas Lardy, William Parish, Benedict Stavis, Lynn T. White, and Martin K. Whyte. Harlan Cleveland and John W. Lewis made available to me their China trip reports, and I also benefited from the oral reports of numerous other visitors.

An earlier version of chapter 4 appeared in *China Quarterly*, no. 69 (March 1977).

I would like to express my thanks and appreciation to Ruth Owen at Yale and Suzanne Nefedov at Columbia for typing the manuscript.

Also, I would like to express my appreciation to the two editors for Yale University Press, Marian Ash and Beth Kodama, who handled the manuscript.

Finally, I would like to thank my wife, Ellen, without whose support this book could not have been written, and my daughters, Anya and Maia, who put up with many abbreviated weekends. This book is dedicated to them.

LIST OF ABBREVIATIONS

CB	*Current Background*
CCP	Chinese Communist Party
CNS	*China News Summary*
FBIS	*Foreign Broadcast Information Service*
JMJP	*Jen-min Jih-pao* (People's Daily)
JPRS	*Joint Publications Research Service*
KMJP	*Kuang-ming Jih-pao* (Enlightenment Daily)
NCNA	*New China News Agency*
PLA	People's Liberation Army
PRC	People's Republic of China
RY	Returned youth (*hui-hsiang chih-shih ch'ing-nien,* "returned educated youth")
SCMM	*Selections of China Mainland Magazines*
SCMP	*Survey of the China Mainland Press*
SWB-FE	British Broadcasting Corporation, *Summary of World Broadcasts, Far East*
UY	Urban Youth (*hsia-hsiang chih-shih ch'ing-nien,* "sent-down educated youth")
YCL	Young Communist League

1 INTRODUCTION

The modernizing process characteristically gives rise to a gap between people's expectations and their satisfaction. Modernization, as many scholars have pointed out, is a process associated with changes in popular expectations and preferences resulting from the spread of literacy, increased communications, and exposure to other ways of life.[1] Modernization stimulates popular receptiveness to and interest in the idea of mobility, both horizontal and upward. Peasants want to leave their villages and move to the cities in search of a better life. People doing manual labor aspire to white-collar jobs as a way of improving their status and income. Demand for access to education increases, since secondary and higher education are the chief avenues for advancement into prestigious occupations. At the same time, however, the demand for improvement often grows faster than does the economy. The result is that many of those who move to the cities cannot find jobs, and many of those who graduate from schools cannot find employment in urban industry and administration. Pressure on the urban infrastructure grows, while unfulfilled demands and expectations create "social frustration," which is likely to be particularly serious among the educated unemployed.[2] Social frustration is a powerful stimulant to political participation which in turn may well lead to political instability. Governments faced with the problem of "overurbanization" often are neither willing nor able to regulate the flow of migrants from the villages or to synchronize the growth and character of education with the available opportunities for urban employment.[3] The pressure to acquire degrees is great, and governments find it necessary to respond positively to such pressures. In recent years, many a third-world country has come to be increasingly beset by the explosive potential of urban crisis resulting from these developments.

The People's Republic of China (PRC) has been a striking exception to the general pattern of governmental incapacity

to act.[4] For many years now the leaders of that country have
been taking vigorous steps to control the growth of cities and
to align the educational system with the economic realities of
a society that is industrializing but continues to be overwhelmingly rural in character. They have taken steps to control,
restrict, and even eliminate altogether migration from village
to city and at times have returned large numbers of migrants to
their rural homes. They have urged and demanded that peasant
youths who go to towns to be educated in secondary schools
return to farming instead of staying in urban locations searching for industrial or commercial employment. They have sought
to inculcate in urban and rural schoolchildren aspirations not
of becoming white-collar administrators but of becoming
workers, peasants, and soldiers.[5] And they have undertaken
large-scale programs of moving urbanites to the village: "China
was the first society to engineer a reverse flow to the villages."[6]
This has included the "sending down" (*hsia-fang*), both temporary and permanent, of urban cadres, the resettlement of entire
urban families in villages and in frontier provinces such as
Sinkiang, and the assignment of university graduates to rural
posts.

   This study deals with still another of these relocation programs, namely, the transfer of urban secondary school graduates to rural villages and to frontier settlements. This program,
long called *shang-shan hsia-hsiang*, "up to the mountains and
down to the villages," was practiced first on a limited scale
before the Great Leap Forward, resumed in the early 1960s,
and accelerated sharply in 1968 at the end of the Cultural
Revolution; since then it has continued with varying degrees of
intensity. According to aggregate statistics released by the
Chinese government, 1.2 million urban youths were sent to the
countryside between 1956 and 1966, and 12 million between
1968 and 1975.[7] Although recent official statistics for the size
of China's urban population are not available, if an estimate for
the urban population as of 1970 of about 125 million is reasonably accurate, it would mean that since the Cultural Revolution
about 10 percent of the urban population has been sent to the
countryside under this program.[8] In principle, the policy of
sending urban middle school graduates "up to the mountains
and down to the villages" has called for lifelong resettlement
(*yi-pei-tzu*) since about 1964. In practice, a sizable but largely

unknown proportion of the sent-down youths have been later
reassigned to the urban sector, principally to take up factory
work. However, as far as can be gathered from the evidence (see
chapter 6), for a majority of the urban youths, the transfer has
meant a permanent change from urban to rural life. This program, therefore, differs dramatically from service in the Peace
Corps, the military, or the *Arbeitsdienst* of the Third Reich in
that it is generally not of limited duration. The transfer entails
a minimum commitment of two years but for most is an open-
ended, long-term, or permanent undertaking. Indeed, one of
its goals is to transform urbanites into "new-style, cultured
peasants."[9]

Shang-shan hsia-hsiang is explicitly defined in the Chinese
press as a "revolutionary" program: "For young people to integrate with the workers and peasants is the road which the
younger generation must take to reform their world outlook, a
strategic measure for continuing the revolution under the dictatorship of the proletariat and a profound ideological revolution."[10] The program is one of the major ways of rearing
"revolutionary successors":

> What kind of people we are to produce from the younger
> generation is fundamentally speaking a question of whether
> or not there will be successors for the cause of Marxist-
> Leninist revolution . . . whether or not our descendants in
> future generations will continue to advance along the correct
> road of Marxism-Leninism and Mao Tse-tung Thought, and
> whether or not we will victoriously prevent a repetition of
> Khrushchev's revisionism in China and prevent capitalist
> restoration. . . . [Shang-shan hsia-hsiang] is an integral part of
> Chairman Mao's revolutionary line. . . . It is not simply a
> temporary measure for the relocation of a labor force, nor a
> matter of expediency, but . . . a long-term strategic policy of
> our Party. It closes the gap between city and countryside,
> between the workers and the peasants, between mental and
> physical labor, and possesses great practical as well as far-
> reaching significance for the consolidation of the dictatorship
> of the proletariat and for the prevention of capitalist restora-
> tion.[11]

What makes this program revolutionary is the idea of permanent
resettlement, the idea that educated urbanites can become peas-

ants. It is revolutionary because it runs counter to those attitudes, expectations, and demands that are characteristic of
developing countries. In his book *Choice and the Politics of
Allocation,* David Apter argues that "embourgeoisement" is a
defining characteristic of modernizing societies, meaning that
popular motivations center around strivings for upward mobility and the satisfaction of economic interests. "If a society is
in a period of modernization, the preoccupying equity principles or values of the society as a whole will be centered around
material benefits and their distribution, even if the regime is a
revolutionary one."[12] In the case of China, self-interested
aspirations for personal upward mobility within the urban sector have existed and continue to exist among urbanites. Evidence for the existence of such attitudes will be presented
throughout this study; at this point it may simply be noted
that the very fact that Chinese leaders find it essential to wage
thorough campaigns against such preferences can itself be
taken as evidence for their existence: "It is a new socialist
phenomenon for educated young people to settle in the countryside. Since it is new, not only do class enemies interfere
with it and undermine it, but the old social ideology, habits,
traditions, and concepts also have an adverse influence on it.
Shall we struggle against the old traditional concepts and
resolutely resist these unhealthy tendencies, or shall we compromise with the influence of the old habits and submit to
them?"[13]

Among the Chinese people, three kinds of widely held values
and expectations run counter to the assumptions upon which
the transfer to the countryside is based. The first, preference for
urban over rural life, is rooted in realistic perceptions of continuing urban-rural disparities. To be sure, lack of comprehensive
data makes it difficult to generalize about such matters as
urban-rural income differentials. Variation within each sector
further complicates analysis. Peasants in prosperous suburban
communes, for instance, may earn more than some urbanites,
especially those employed in cooperative street industries.
Moreover, the state has since the 1950s sought to increase rural
incomes at a faster rate than urban ones. Thus, urban wage rates
have remained largely constant since 1957, whereas peasants
have been benefiting from substantial increases in government

prices paid for agricultural products, as well as from reduced tax burdens.[14] Despite these measures, however, it does appear that major income disparities continue to exist. Sociologist Martin K. Whyte, having surveyed available data, suggests that peasant incomes have on the average been about half of those of urbanites.[15] Major differences continue to obtain between workers and peasants with respect to income security also. Workers in state-owned factories receive fixed wages; peasants on people's communes receive work points which vary annually with the size of the harvest. Workers are covered by a social security system that operates within the state sector; peasants must rely primarily on their families and secondarily on communal welfare arrangements.[16] Workers are covered by state medical services; peasants must rely on cooperative health care, the effectiveness of which varies with the wealth of the communes, though state subsidies may be provided.[17] By and large, it is fair to say that certain manufactured goods are more easily obtained in cities and that city dwellers live better in terms of consumption of such items as meat.[18] Peasants frequently work longer and harder than do workers. Villages have fewer cultural amenities, sports facilities, and places of recreation than do cities; hence village life is duller and more monotonous than city life.[19] That the transfer to the villages involves hardship, sacrifice, and deprivation is cheerfully acknowledged by the press; it is in fact regarded as one of the virtues of the program.[20]

Second, the transfer program contradicts the expectation that the purpose of education is to make possible upward mobility. Graduation from school should lead to some kind of white-collar administrative job rather than to manual labor, and, ideally, one should be able to continue one's education through the university level in order to enter the technical or administrative elite. This expectation is not merely a product of modernization: in traditional China the major task of education was to prepare students to pass the state examinations necessary both for entry into the state bureaucracy and for the acquisition of elite social status. Today, the expectation of *tu-shu tso-kuan,* "studying to become an official," is denounced vehemently in the Chinese press, which is an indicator of the extent to which such expectations are still rooted in the minds of people.[21] The transfer program is in fact regarded as one of the means by which the value underlying this expectation—namely, that white-collar work is superior to manual labor—can be undermined.

Third, the transfer program runs counter to the desire for status transmission. The program seeks to reduce or even to eliminate the capacity of parents who occupy elite positions in China's political and social structure to pass on to their offspring advantages stemming from their high status. This point applies first to the political elite, including the revolutionary generation which has been occupying high positions in the ruling hierarchies of party, government, and army. Their power, prestige, and influence made it possible for them to obtain superior educational opportunities for their children, and they also had the connections necessary for their offspring to get ahead. By making children born into high-ranking "revolutionary families" start from the rural bottom, as it were, the transfer program seeks to prevent the crystallization of a structure of privilege and power in which a large proportion of the postrevolutionary elite is recruited not from the society at large but from the first-generation elite or more generally from the emerging "New Class." It is one of the ways in which Maoist China has sought to forestall the development of Soviet-style "revisionism."[22] Whether this goal has been attained is another question (see chapters 3 and 6).

This point applies also to the "non-power elite"[23] of experts trained before liberation, including academics, managers, scientists, and engineers, who have held high positions but who are politically suspect and are more or less constantly subject to thought reform. The advantage they sought to pass on to their children was a cultured home environment and a strong motivation to excel in academic work in order to gain admission to universities, thereby securing access to elite status. The cultural gap between these intellectuals and workers and peasants was one reason why children from the former group were disproportionately represented in the student population of the universities before 1966.[24] Finally, this point applies to the "exploiting classes," such as capitalists and landlords, for whom instilling a strong motivation to succeed academically was the only advantage they could give to their children. Transfer to the countryside, together with sharply restricted access to higher education, serves to eliminate these family advantages.

Because the transfer program runs counter to several kinds of preferences, aspirations, and expectations, one would expect that those affected by the program would regard it as a form of downward mobility. Among them one ought to find a high level of relative deprivation, that is, a gap between what people expect ("value expectations") and what they can get ("value capabilities").[25] Relative deprivation is regarded by theorists as an indispensable ingredient in outbreaks of violence and revolution, and therefore one could ask about the potential for violence among those affected by the transfer program. Nor is this an idle question, since there have been episodes of violence in China in which frustrated expectations have played a role. In 1957, for instance, a riot occurred in the Wuhan area which the authorities explicitly blamed on anger over unmet demands for access to further education.[26] Similarly, more than one observer has detected the same ingredient of frustration in the youthful violence that characterized the Cultural Revolution.[27] Even if violence has not been widespread, one ought to expect that the transfer program would create problems of morale, support, and legitimacy.

But to view the transfer to the countryside merely in terms of its potential for trouble is to reckon without the very political system whose leaders have thought up the policy of sending urban youths to the countryside. The Chinese political system has powerful resources it can bring to bear on the problem of relative deprivation. It has an ideology, strong organizations, and the capacity to mobilize society and to secure participation in programs even when these are not regarded as in the immediate interests of the participants. It can use its resources to channel feelings of relative deprivation, to reduce their impact, and to provide alternative satisfactions. In the final analysis, it can prevent the collective expression of social frustration. In short, the political system can take steps to "manage" the feelings of relative deprivation which downward mobility is likely to cause.

Actually, China's leaders are not content merely with the management of social frustrations arising out of programs such as the transfer. Their most ambitious goal is to eliminate such feelings altogether by resocializing people and imbuing them with revolutionary values. In these terms, a revolutionary is one who defines the transfer to the countryside not as a form of downward mobility but as a form of service to the nation and to its goals of building socialism and communism. Chinese leaders have made intensive efforts to change popular values, to redefine social statuses so that the idea of an urbanite becoming a peasant is viewed in highly positive terms, to imbue the young with an ethic of subordination of self to the collective, the state, and the revolution. Many instrumentalities are used in these efforts to change values, including the schools, the youth organizations, and, insofar as this is possible, the family. It is very important to note that the transfer program itself is regarded as a major agent of resocialization. One of the goals which the program of "up to the mountains and down to the countryside" is designed to achieve is the purely ideological one of transforming the thoughts and values of the urban young. The youths go to the villages in order to be "reeducated by the poor and lower-middle peasants" (*chieh-shou p'in-hsia-chung nung tsai chiao-yü*), which is to be accomplished by integrating with the peasants, working with them, and coming under their influence.[28] In other words, the transfer takes place not because attitude change is assumed already to have occurred in the cities, but because the urban young are still infected with "bourgeois" thought.

Is the transfer program succeeding in its goal of resocializing the young urbanites? The evidence as it will be presented throughout this study, ambiguous as it necessarily is, suggests that in the case of many, perhaps the majority, the answer is no. This is not to say that the ethic of "serving the people" is not widely accepted among them. But it is necessary to distinguish between ways of serving the people that are congruent with one's personal preferences and ways that are not. In the 1950s, when university enrollments were expanding, one could serve the people by becoming a high-status, professional scientist, thereby combining the ethic of service with the satisfaction of personal aspirations. In the 1960s and 1970s, however, when urban opportunities were contracting (see chapter 2), the ethic of service to the people required urbanites to become peasants, which calls for the drastic subordination of personal preferences. One would assume that internalization of the former version of service to the people is easier than internalization of the latter version. Hence, youths who have internalized the new values and who display a high degree of revolutionary dedica-

tion and selflessness under conditions of acute personal disadvantage are likely to be in a minority. This point is reinforced
by the fact that the Chinese press views resocialization of urban
youth as a long-term task—a matter of generations—and by no
means as a task that has already been accomplished.[29]

As long as urban youths have not been fully resocialized, the
transfer program requires appropriate "management." How
does the Chinese political system cope with the frustrations and
feelings of relative deprivation that must be expected to arise in
the course of implementing the movement to the villages? The
measures that have been used to make the transfer work include
the following: First, reliance on pervasive political education, in
both the city and the village. Even if political education does
not result in fundamental attitude change, at least not in the
short run, it may help to legitimate the transfer by contributing
to the creation of a social climate in which the transfer is understood, is accepted as a normal rather than an extraordinary
phenomenon, and becomes incorporated into the normal range
of expectations of young people and their families. Second, by
mobilizing the basic-level organizations that link state and
society, the regime seeks to secure the participation of wide
strata of both the urban and rural communities in the implementation of the transfer. As with political education, the
purpose is creation of a social environment in which the transfer
is viewed in positive rather than negative terms. But organizational penetration also provides access to families and individuals and permits focusing of social pressures on recalcitrants.
Third, a variety of incentives are used to make rural life more
attractive to the urban youths, such as extending opportunities
to be recruited to positions of leadership in the rural political
structure as well as opportunities to make contributions to the
building of a "new, socialist countryside," both of which may
yield satisfactions and hence reduce frustration. It is a major
goal of this study to describe and analyze the policies and
practices underlying the transfer, with a view toward assessment
of their effectiveness in raising the acceptability of the transfer
program and in reducing discontent and morale problems.

The processes of the transfer and settlement of urban youth
to the villages must be seen in the broad context of the regime's
power, including the power to coerce. This power, however, is
in the background. Chinese leaders are reluctant to use explicit

and direct coercion to enforce the transfer program, and rightly
so, if they are serious about the objective of changing attitudes
and securing normative identifications with new values. As
Amitai Etzioni has suggested, reliance on direct coercion tends
to produce alienation rather than identification.[30] Coercion,
however, is in the background. The coercive capacities of the
Chinese political system have to be taken into account when
assessing the efficacy of reliance on persuasion and "helpful"
social pressures in securing compliance.[31] The link to explicit
coercion appears, for instance, in political education, which
emphasizes class struggle and the struggle between the two
lines, that is, between a right way and a wrong way. The transfer movement has been defined in ideologically fundamentalist
terms as an issue that differentiates revolutionaries from revisionists. Ultimately, such a distinction legitimates the use of
repression by the "dictatorship of the proletariat" against those
who persistently adhere to the revisionist line. Still, overt force
is rarely used.

The program to transfer urban youths to the countryside can
be analyzed in two ways, as a process and as a developmental
program. Because the transfer is so remarkably bold an enterprise, one that seeks to turn urbanites into peasants and change
deeply held values, study of the processes of the transfer—its
management and the response of those affected by it—is an in-
tellectually interesting task. But the transfer is also designed to
contribute to the attainment of developmental goals, of which
there are two. First, as already noted, the program is a response
to a problem common to modernizing nations, "overurbanization," or a disproportion between opportunities sought and opportunities available in the cities (see chapter 2). Here, the
contribution of the sent-down youths may consist simply of
reducing the burdens placed on the urban sector. Second, sent-
down youths are expected to contribute to the solution of
China's greatest problem, namely, the development of the rural
sector. According to Pi-chao Chen, the urban youths "are called
upon to be ordinary agricultural producers while at the same
time playing the role of catalysts in diffusing modern attitudes,
skills, and knowledge, and in setting up and operating modern
social infrastructures in the rural villages, all in the interests of
accelerating rural transformation."[32] Sent-down urban youths
may thus be promoting change in the villages and contributing

to the integration of the peasantry by bridging cultural and
cognitive gaps between urbanites and peasants. The transfer of
urban youths (UYs) to remote, underpopulated frontier provinces may also be significant for the national integration of the
country. Whether the UYs have actually been making these
kinds of developmental contributions and to what extent is
an empirical question, and one that is difficult to answer
because appropriate standards of measurement are lacking.
Attempts at assessment will be made in chapter 2 and especially
in chapter 5.

The transfer of urban youths to the countryside is motivated
by both developmental and ideological goals. Among the latter
are those of remaking man, of combatting elitism, and of overcoming the "three great differences"—between town and
country, worker and peasant, manual and mental labor. The
ideological goals are rooted not only in the search for ways to
prevent Soviet-style "revisionism" that was undertaken by Mao
Tse-tung in the 1960s but in the entire experience of the
Chinese revolution. The idea of bridging the gap between intellectuals and peasants, for example, goes back at least to the
early 1920s. It was advocated by Marxists such as Li Ta-chao
and by non-Marxists such as James C. Yen, the rural reconstruc-
tionist.[33] The practice of intellectuals as well as cadres going to
the villages developed on a large scale only in the course of the
communist revolution, particularly during the Yenan years.[34]
One of the assumptions out of which this practice grew was
that the city was an alien and hostile place. As Maurice Meisner
observes:

> For Mao, the city was not the modern revolutionary stage
> posited by Marxism, but a foreign-dominated stage. It was a
> situation that bred powerful anti-urban biases and corres-
> pondingly, a strong agrarian orientation; the city came to be
> identified with alien influences, the "countryside" with the
> "country." Such a perception gave rise to a more general
> suspicion of the city as the site and source of foreign bour-
> geois ideological, moral, and social corruption, a suspicion
> that lingered on long after the foreigners were removed from
> the city.[35]

Given this orientation, the idea that urban youth might need to
be "reeducated" by the peasants does not seem so farfetched.

Still another central tenet of Maoist thought underlies the transfer program, namely, that book learning cannot be considered genuine knowledge, which is acquired only when theory and practice are combined.

The fact that the transfer program is motivated by both developmental and ideological goals raises a question familiar to students of communist systems. Are the two goals congruent and mutually reinforcing or are they in conflict, so that the pursuit of one will be at the expense of the other? In his well-known study "Development vs. Utopia in Communist Policy," Richard Lowenthal suggests that while in "some respects" the two are compatible, fundamentally, they are in "stark, irreconcilable conflict": "for the sake of the final goal, the Communist regime ought to aim at creating a 'new man', a man free from the egoistic ambition and avarice characteristic of class society; yet for the sake of rapid development it must aim at educating and manipulating 'economic man', the type that has created the modern industrial society . . . by pursuing his own self-interest."[36] How the two goals relate to one another is an underlying question of this study.

SOURCES AND THEIR PROBLEMS

This study is based on three sets of sources: the Chinese media, interviews with former residents, and visitors' reports. Chinese newspapers and radio stations have for years devoted a great deal of attention to the transfer program. At the national level, the media include the two major dailies—*Jen-min Jih-pao* (*JMJP*, People's Daily) and *Kuang-ming Jih-pao* (*KMJP*, Enlightenment Daily)—Radio Peking, and the magazine *Hung-ch'i* (Red Flag). One indicator of the amount of coverage of the transfer movement in the national press is the number of articles on the subject printed in the two dailies over a five-year period (see table 1). Since the Great Leap Forward, the foreign export of provincial and local newspapers has been banned. The few that have become available sometimes shed light on aspects of the transfer that the national press may leave unilluminated.[37] In the absence of provincial newspapers, provincial radio broadcasts are a major source of data. Most of the statistical data on numbers of UYs in provinces and on recruitment of UYs to membership in the Chinese Communist

Table 1. Press Coverage of the Transfer

Articles in:

Year	KMJP	JMJP	Total
1968	88	99	187
1969	190	195	385
1970	134	105	239
1971	57	51	108
1972	125	87	212

Note: Identical articles appearing in both newspapers were counted only once, insofar as they were identified.

Party (CCP) or to positions such as village teacher or technician come from these broadcasts.

Chinese media never carry "all the news that's fit to print." Very little, for instance, is published about the basic policy decisions which implementation of the transfer movement obviously requires. Very little is made known about the planning processes of the transfer. Though the transfer is a complex administrative enterprise, the regulations that govern it are not made public and are not explicitly discussed by the media. Instead, inferences have to be drawn from incomplete and ambiguous statements in the press. What is published by the media requires interpretation, since the purpose of writing about the transfer is primarily to inspire youths to go "up to the mountains and down to the villages," as well as to stay there. The articles are full of positive models for youths to admire and emulate. The life of UYs in the villages and frontier regions tends to be depicted in heroic and highly politicized terms; problems that arise are usually resolved through hard struggle and political dedication. Nonetheless, the articles often contain a great deal of concrete information which can be utilized to construct a pattern of the way the transfer works.

In evaluating the usefulness of the official media, it is worth adding that the researcher benefits from their occasional lapses into greater frankness. For instance, in the summer of 1973, policy makers became interested in the difficulties urban youths encountered in making a living in the village. Consequently, the press ran articles that differed strikingly from previous accounts in that they bluntly detailed the root causes of these difficulties (see chapter 4). Another example concerns informal influences on the transfer such as string-pulling by high-ranking cadres. Most of the time, the press merely hints that some officials try to exert influence on behalf of their children, mainly by running stories of virtuous cadres who resisted such temptations. But in late 1973 and early 1974, publication of cases of sent-down youths who entered universities by the "back door" suddenly showed that the practice had been much more widespread than previously indicated (see chapter 6). Three years later, after the death of Chairman Mao and the purge of four "leftist" Politburo members, the Chinese press charged that the four had intended to embarrass "leading comrades of the central authorities," including Premier Chou En-lai, by publicizing the cases.[38] This suggests that contending groups who manipulate the press to advance their political fortunes have also utilized data from the transfer movement for this purpose. In the case of the "back door" material, however, the authenticity of the facts themselves has not apparently been disputed. Hence, although such data are obviously biased, the information contained in them will be used in this study unless contradicted by other evidence.

Mention must also be made of the unofficial Red Guard publications during the Cultural Revolution, some of which dealt with the transfer of urban youths to the countryside. The tabloids contained polemics denouncing the handling of the transfer by certain top-level leaders and a great many lurid exposés of abuses in the program. The materials on policies are most valuable (see chapter 2), but the exposés suffer from the opposite failing of the official press, namely, overstatement and exaggeration of the negative aspects of the transfer.

Reports of visitors to the PRC add in important ways to the data from the media. Groups of scholars have visited the PRC to study rural industry, higher education, and the green revolution.[39] Their reports shed light on the developmental aspects of the transfer. Visitors have interviewed city officials and obtained statistics that would not otherwise be available. They have secured information on the informal workings of the transfer, such as opportunities available to youths with special talents, and they have made observations about how peasants and the parents of sent-down youths react to the transfer. Valuable as visitors' reports are, however, it should be noted that for the most part the opportunities open to visitors to gather data do not add up to field research as the term is generally understood. For instance, interviews with urban youths tend to be constrained by the political setting in which they occur. That setting requires that youths disavow personal ambitions and instead proclaim their desire to serve their country and to subordinate themselves to the needs of party and state.[40] Should a youth in fact harbor reservations about these norms, it would not be "good conduct" (*piao-hsien hao*) for him or her to express these reservations to a foreign guest, except perhaps in the proper context of showing how adjustment difficulties and temptations to succumb to self-interest had been overcome. A record of good conduct is essential to advancement—to recruitment to a cadre position or nomination to attend university, for example. Given these circumstances, it is unlikely that even an opportunity to interview a sample of urban youths in the countryside would yield insights on attitudes beyond those in the press. This is not to say that such an opportunity would not be most welcome; it would yield a much richer picture of conditions and circumstances than it is now possible to obtain.

As long as proper field research is not possible, interviews with former residents of the PRC remain a major source of information. Youths from Canton sent to the countryside of Kwangtung province have been escaping to Hong Kong in considerable numbers since the intensification of the transfer movement after the Cultural Revolution. It is not known just how many of them have fled, but it is believed that for every illegal immigrant who is detected by the Hong Kong police three or four slip into the colony undetected. Sent-down youths are only one category among the refugees, and the published figures do not distinguish between them and, for example, young peasants. In 1973, by the official count, 6,139 illegal immigrants entered the colony.[41] As of 1973, 450,000 youths from Kwangtung cities and towns had been sent to the countryside of that province, since 1968.[42] If it is assumed that half of the illegal immigrants were UYs, it can be concluded that 0.7 percent of the 450,000 fled in 1973 alone. If, however, the official count is exceeded by a factor of three or four, in that for every refugee who is detected three or four are not, then the proportion of the 450,000 who fled in 1973, again assuming that half of the refugees were UYs, would be between 2 and 2.7 percent. It is noteworthy that the number of detected illegal immigrants rose in the 1970s. It was 1,700 in 1970, 3,060 in 1971, 5,100 in 1972, 6,139 in 1973, and 7,121 in 1974.[43] This increased influx aggravated the social problems that beset the crowded colony, and in late 1974 the British government adopted a policy of returning illegal immigrants to China.[44]

Observers agree that the main reason for leaving the PRC is dissatisfaction with having to remain in the countryside for life. Unmet expectations and the search for greater opportunities for personal advancement, rather than political freedom as such, seem to be the main motivations.[45] One reason why so many leave is that the penalties for trying are usually not severe. Apparently, escape attempts by urban youths are treated as a "contradiction among the people" and not as counterrevolutionary crimes. Informants report varying penalties, ranging, for a first attempt, from fifteen days' to three months' detention (*shou-liu*), followed by return to one's commune. Multiple attempts may be punished more severely with a few months of labor reeducation.[46] Although the penalties are light, however, informants believe that an escape attempt is recorded in the individual's dossier (*tang-an*), thereby reducing whatever chance he might have had for future advancement and providing him with an incentive to try again.* Aside from damaging their prospects within the PRC should their attempts fail, those who escape must also risk their lives, not so much in evading border patrols as in the long and dangerous swim to British territory.

In the summer of 1971, I interviewed eleven young people who had been sent to the countryside from Canton, and in the academic year 1972–73, twenty-two.[47] Each informant was first interviewed for two to three hours. Follow-up interviews were then scheduled; in several cases these extended over three, four, or even six weekly sessions. The interviews were open-ended, their main purpose being to learn about the individual experiences of the informants with the transfer movement, so as to acquire data on concrete conditions from those who had actually taken part in it. Informants provided data on the process of mobilization in the city, on life in the villages, in-

*Reportedly, penalties are more severe in the case of those who have occupied positions of trust, e.g., who have been cadres, teachers, party members, or youth league members. Also, penalties seem to vary with place of origin: a Shanghai youth gets three years for trying to escape whereas Cantonese are punished much more leniently. This may have something to do with the special status of Hong Kong in the eyes of the Chinese government as something of an adjunct to Kwangtung. In any event, escaping to Hong Kong is not considered a crime of national betrayal (*p'an-kuo*), in contrast to escape attempts to the Soviet Union, which are reportedly punished harshly.

cluding relations with peasants and cadres, on opportunities open to urban youths, and in general on problems of adjustment. My aim was to evaluate these materials together with media and visitors' accounts, with a view to establishing the range of conditions of the transfer and responses by the UYs.

Informants' reports do of course have to be treated with caution, especially when they go beyond the individual case and when informants offer broader judgments about attitudes and expectations of transferred youths in general. The informants cannot be considered a sample of a larger population such as all urban youth emigrés in Hong Kong, or sent-down urban youth in Kwangtung province, not to speak of transferred youths in the PRC as a whole. There being no way of securing a proper sample, I instead sought out informants who had spent a long time in the villages and who had made a serious attempt to respond to the transfer within the framework of available possibilities and opportunities before taking advantage of the Hong Kong "option." In the case of the twenty-two informants interviewed in 1972–73, an average of 34.4 months elapsed between date of transfer to the countryside and escape to Hong Kong, the range being from 7 to 72 months. Several of the informants did in fact make serious efforts to adapt to village life. They stayed between four and six years, leaving China only when it became clear to them that their prospects for advancement remained dim.* These informants contrast with those who had made up their minds already in Canton to leave the PRC at the first opportunity, as well as those who decided shortly after their arrival in the village to try to leave, affected perhaps by the "escape wind" (*t'ou-tu feng*) that has swept through some communes close to Hong Kong. In still another set of cases several years elapsed between transfer and escape, but, instead of settling down and adapting, the informants spent a large proportion of their time more or less illicitly in Canton or made repeated escape attempts. Although some of the "short-termers" provided interesting material on UY conditions in the villages, the most valuable accounts were provided by those who stayed for longer periods and who tried

*Most of those interviewed left China between 1970 and early 1973. Those who stayed in the villages for five or six years had been sent down before the Cultural Revolution, then returned to Canton for at least a year or even two, going back to the rural unit in 1968.

to adapt to rural life; their experience may have been closer to that of the UYs in the rest of China whose responses are not shaped by the special conditions obtaining in Kwangtung.

The informants were also atypical in that they came disproportionately from "bad backgrounds" (*ch'eng-fen pu hao*), that is, their families had a disadvantageous class status (*chia-t'ing ch'u-shen*), such as capitalist, landlord, or rich peasant, based on ownership of means of production in presocialist times. Or, it meant that the family head bore a negative political label such as "counterrevolutionary," "rightist," or "bad element." During the Cultural Revolution, because of the suspicion that intellectuals are tainted by bourgeois ideology, having intellectuals for parents often amounted to being considered of bad background, according to some informants. In the case of the twenty-two interviewed in 1972–73, ten came from bad backgrounds, including categories such as capitalist, counterrevolutionary (Kuomintang army officer or civilian official), landlord, and intellectual. Six came from what informants describe as "average" backgrounds, that is, one that entailed neither advantage or disadvantage, including employee or petty trader; and six came from good backgrounds, including the categories of worker, revolutionary cadre ("the best there is"), and revolutionary intellectual.

What to do about the offspring of bad-class families has long been an issue in Chinese politics. The basic assumption has been that children socialized into such families cannot be automatically trusted and treated in the same way as children from the working class or the poor and lower-middle peasantry. In principle, Maoist theory holds out the possibility that men can change their class through thought reform and good behavior.[48] For the youths in the bad categories this means that "good conduct," exemplified for instance by "drawing a line between oneself and one's family," outweighs the inherited family background. Thus the press prints examples of "sons and daughters who can be educated," who have overcome their handicap, performed well, and who consequently have been given cadre positions or even allowed to attend university (see chapters 5 and 6). But such cases seem few indeed, because class and associated political labels have in the past decade become more rather than less salient. The reason lies in Mao Tse-tung's theoretical innovation that throughout the stage of socialism classes and class struggle continue to exist, as does the danger of bourgeois restoration.[49] One of the practical consequences of Mao's injunction "Never forget class struggle" has been that those from tainted backgrounds have become the objects of renewed suspicion. Moreover, it has been in the interest of party officials to focus attention on those in society from bad backgrounds as a way of deflecting attention from themselves. The reason for this is that Mao saw a threat to the socialist revolution not only from the remnants of the old upper classes but even more so from "newly engendered bourgeois elements" in the political superstructure, who might become a "privileged stratum" and take the capitalist road, as allegedly has happened in the Soviet Union.[50] Early in the Cultural Revolution, for instance, the offspring of high-ranking cadres seeking to protect their privileged positions put forth the "theory of blood lines," an essentially ascriptive approach to class, according to which only those from good backgrounds could take part in the Cultural Revolution. The theory of blood lines was repudiated by Mao, who drew attention to the upper-class origins of senior leaders, himself included.[51] Yet, even though a behavioral approach to the class issue has been upheld, in fact, according to informants, it was their bad background rather than their conduct that determined their fate. Suspicion of them was pervasive and discrimination systematic, especially in the case of rural recruitment. The policy adopted after the Cultural Revolution of reserving university admissions predominantly for workers and peasants is only one indicator of their disadvantageous situation.

Discriminatory treatment of those with bad backgrounds results in disproportionate escapes of those who have the opportunity. Discrimination naturally affects their attitudes to the system; many an informant commented on the unfairness of penalizing children for the failings of their parents. Bad background also affects adaptation to the village. Among the informants, those from bad backgrounds tended to stay in the village a shorter time than those from average or good backgrounds.[52]

Interviewing those from bad backgrounds sheds light on their circumstances but obviously also requires care in extrapolating from their special situation to the transfer generally. It is worth pointing out that I tried to make clear to each informant the academic nature of the interview, and in general I believe that informants did not deliberately slant their reports but talked about their experiences in a reasonably dispassionate manner.

One check on the Hong Kong informants is provided by the Chinese press. By and large, virtually nothing that the informants reported could not in some way or other be confirmed in the press, if not directly then indirectly, by inference. Informants, for example, generally described living conditions in the villages as difficult, more difficult than the press normally does, but on par with data released in the summer of 1973, when a campaign to remedy deficiencies in the settlement of UYs was launched (see chapter 4). In a few instances, informants provided data that cast the transfer in a more positive light than does the press. They reported, for instance, that the state allocates a sum of money for each urban youth sent to the villages to facilitate resettlement. The press almost never refers directly to this important datum.[53] Another example concerns the exposés of abuses in the Red Guard press. Several informants who had been sent down before the Cultural Revolution felt that these accounts of persecution of UYs by rural authorities were exaggerated.[54] On the other hand they confirmed Red Guard press charges that parents' jobs were sometimes threatened to enforce the transfer.[55] Perhaps the biggest discrepancy between press and interview data pertains to leadership. As we will see in chapter 5, the press publishes a good many cases of UYs who play active and positive roles of general leadership in their villages. Informants knew of no such cases and instead stressed the difficulties of getting along with the peasants. They reported fewer opportunities for any kind of recruitment than does the press, both in their own cases and in those of the UYs of their villages. No doubt class background played a role here, as did the fact that many of them left the PRC before the intensification of recruitment.

In cases where informants and the press report the same facts, their interpretations may differ. A good example is relations with the peasants. An article may appear describing the good deed of an urban youth who walked for miles to the nearest town in order to buy medicine for a sick peasant, not just any peasant, of course, but a poor and lower-middle peasant. His deed exemplifies youths' devotion to Chairman Mao's ideal of serving the people, we read.[56] An informant who reported a similar incident explained it by pointing out that naturally an urbanite wishing to develop good personal relations with a peasant would want to do him small favors and get some in return (*hsiao-en hsiao-hui*). The motivation ascribed by the newspaper is explicitly political; in the informant's account it is apolitical and reflects the difficulties an outsider faces in trying to relate to peasants, difficulties familiar to students of peasant society. At the same time, the difference between press and informants on this point must not be exaggerated. The press reports numerous incidents in which self-interest and apolitical motivations play a role, although it always presents such incidents as something to be struggled against and overcome. Indeed, it is the frequency of such incidents that provides the link to the reports of the informants and reinforces one's impression of their plausibility. Having said this, it must still be conceded that the sources are imperfect and the possibilities of error and misjudgment great.

DEFINITIONS AND NUMBERS

In order to set the stage for the chapters that follow, we need to discuss in more detail the statistics of the "up to the mountains, down to the countryside" movement. A statistical profile of the transfer is difficult to sketch, however, because of the incomplete coverage of the published statistics and because it is not always clear what category of persons have or have not been included in them.[57] The transfer of urban youths as here defined consists of sending graduates of junior and senior middle schools to the village. Before the Cultural Revolution, the transfer also included primary school graduates who did not go on to academic or vocational secondary schools and who, unable to find employment, were sent to the villages at the age of sixteen. Since the Cultural Revolution, with the universalization of junior middle schooling in the cities, little has been heard of the transfer of primary school graduates.* Graduates

---

*Before the Cultural Revolution, the school system below the tertiary level consisted of six years of primary school, followed by three years each of academic junior middle and senior middle school. In addition, there was a separate system of secondary vocational and technical schools. Assuming a child started primary school at age seven, he or she would have graduated from junior middle school at age fifteen and from senior middle school at age eighteen. Since the Cultural Revolution, the length of schooling has been cut, but the system is described as in a state of experimentation and much variation obtains. In some places, a unified four-year middle school has been established. In others, secondary education takes five years and in some even six, the old junior and senior divisions having been retained. Since the Cultural Revolution, a major effort has been made to vocationalize the curricu-

of institutions of higher learning have normally not been included in the transfer of urban educated youth since they have fallen under the state cadre assignment system. In 1968 and 1969, however, when urban youth whose formal education had stopped with the outbreak of the Cultural Revolution in 1966 were sent to the countryside, many college students were transferred on the same basis as secondary school students, outside of the state assignment system. It is likely that many of these students are included in the statistics on the transfer of urban youth. More recently, especially since 1975, college graduates have beeen sent to the countryside as ordinary peasants, but it is by no means clear whether their status is the same as that of the UYs or whether they are included in UY statistics.[58] Other categories of urbanites have also settled in the villages, especially in the aftermath of the Great Leap Forward but at other times as well. In Anhwei, for instance, 400,000 urban youths were transferred between 1968 and 1973, but so were 600,000 cadres, medical personnel, and city residents.[59] During times of mass migration, statistical reports tend to merge these categories, so that the UYs cannot always be isolated.[60]

The most important definitional confusion is between urban and rural educated youth. The term for "educated" or "intellectual" youths, *chih-shih ch'ing-nien,* is applied both to youths whose families reside in the cities and who went to school there and to youths from peasant families who left their villages to attend secondary school, either at the commune center, where the market town is often located, or in the county (*hsien*) town. After graduation they return to their home villages. When the press chooses to be precise, the term *hsia-hsiang chih-shih ch'ing-nien,* "sent-down educated youth," is used for the urban youths, and *hui-hsiang chih-shih ch'ing-nien*, "returned educated youth" (RY) for the peasant youths. Distinguishing between these two categories is important for two reasons: first, while the RYs also have adjustment problems after their return to the village, which arise out of deep-seated expectations that education should result in an administrative position, these are different in kind from those of the UYs, who do not have the support of family and other social ties in the village. Indeed, the

---

lum of the secondary schools, but a separate system of technical middle schools continues to exist. The length of the primary schools has generally been cut to five years. (See also chapter 2.)

authorities have at times recognized the importance of this factor by permitting UYs to settle in villages in which they did have relatives (see chapter 3).

The second reason for distinguishing between RYs and UYs is that not doing so vastly inflates the numbers of the transfer. For instance, in 1957 an article appeared headlined "Over Two Million Middle and Primary School Graduates Go to Rural Areas."* A superficial reading seems to suggest that these were urbanites, but a closer look makes clear that, although some urban youths were involved, the majority of the two million were returning peasant youths.[61] From 1963 to 1965, articles appeared in various newspapers claiming that 40 million educated youths had gone to the villages, but only some made clear that this is a totally useless statistic, since it includes virtually everyone in the villages who was ever in school, including peasant youths, college graduates serving in the countryside, and urban youths.[62] Yet the 40 million figure has found its way into secondary studies of the subject.[63] Since the Cultural Revolution, the press has also not distinguished clearly between the two cases, in at least some instances. A 1973 broadcast from Shensi put the number of educated youths in that province at nearly one million. A year later, however, a *JMJP* broadcast referred to 160,000 youths from Shensi cities and towns as having settled in the villages of Shensi. It is unlikely that Shensi has absorbed over 800,000 urban youths from cities outside the province. To be sure, some youths from other parts of the country have come to Shensi, notably 26,000 UYs from Peking, who have settled around Yenan, the wartime headquarters of Chairman Mao and a place of great symbolic importance. But other cities have not reported sending large contingents to Shensi. Hence, the one million figure probably includes returned peasant youths.[64] But some confusion necessarily remains.

As the preceding remarks suggest, RYs are far more numerous than UYs. For instance, by 1962, 110,000 peasant youths had returned to their home villages in rural counties under Peking administrative jurisdiction, but only 3,000 youths from Peking city had gone to the villages.[65] Table 2 illustrates the numerical

*It is typical for statistics to come with qualifiers, such as "nearly," "over," or "well over." Just what these terms mean is impossible to ascertain in numerical terms. In most tables, therefore, they have been omitted.

Table 2. Comparison of Urban and Returned Peasant Youths

Province	Date of Report	Number of UYs	Number of RYs
Kansu	12/73	66,000	270,000
Honan	1/75	360,000	5,000,000
Fukien	12/75	240,000	1,000,000

Sources: Radio Lanchow, 12/22/73, *FBIS* no. 249, 12/27/73; Radio Chengchow, 1/15/75, *FBIS* no. 11, 1/16/75; Radio Fukien, 12/23/75, *FBIS* no. 3, 1/6/76. A rounded statistic such as the 5 million suggests that statistical reporting on rural education is less than precise.

difference between UYs and RYs who have gone to the villages between about 1968 and the dates shown.

In December 1975, two statistics were published that permit comparison of the size of the transfer before and after the Cultural Revolution: in the ten years before the outbreak of the Cultural Revolution in 1966, 1.2 million urban youths settled in the countryside; in the seven-year period immediately after that upheaval, that is, from 1968 to late 1975, ten times as many youths, or 12 million, were sent to the villages.[66] With regard to the pre–Cultural Revolution statistic, it seems that most of the urban youths were transferred after the Great Leap Forward, from 1962 on. Before then, only isolated reports refer specifically to urban youths going to the countryside, as in the instance of one report from Shenyang, Liaoning, in 1960, that spoke of 10,000 youths from factories about to leave for villages.[67] In September 1966, it was reported that "well over a million educated young people from Chinese cities, determined to take the road of revolutionization and of becoming working people, have gone to live and work in the countryside since 1962."[68] Incomplete statistics for these years give some indication of the rising intensity of the transfer in 1964 and 1965 (see table 3).

The report that 12 million youths have settled in the countryside since the Cultural Revolution also requires interpretation. Chinese reports often date the post–Cultural Revolution transfer from the publication on December 23, 1968, of Chairman Mao's call on urban youth to accept reeducation by the poor and lower-middle peasants. Does this mean that the hundreds of thousands of youths who went to the villages in the summer and fall of 1968 are not included?[69] Presumably they are, but one cannot be sure. Similarly, are the 1.2 million UYs trans-

Table 3. Volume of the Transfer, 1962–1965

Period	Number Transferred
1. Spring 1962 to early 1964	292,000
2. 1964	300–400,000
3. January–August 1965	250,000

Sources:
1. *Kung-jen Jih-pao*, 3/22/64, in *Communist China Digest*, no. 122, 6/16/64, *JPRS* 25108.
2. *JMJP* 2/19/65; and *Hong Kong Ta Kung Pao*, 2/19/65.
3. *JMJP* 9/25/65.

ferred before the Cultural Revolution included in post–Cultural Revolution statistics? Numerous press reports since 1968 have described UYs sent down before 1966, and some provincial statistics explicitly include these veterans of the transfer in current totals.[70] It thus seems unlikely that pre-1966 UYs would be separately accounted for, but again one cannot be sure. Most importantly, does the 12 million include or exclude those sent-down youths who were subsequently reassigned to the urban sector? Press and informants agree that considerable numbers of sent-down youths have been reassigned; one unconfirmed estimate is that perhaps a fourth of UYs have returned to cities and towns (see chapter 6). If those reassigned are not included in the 12 million, the total of those who have experienced re-settlement would run considerably higher; if they are included, the actual number of sent-down youths in the villages as of December 1975 would be considerably lower.

One approach to the 12 million statistic is to add up provincial statistics on UYs transferred since the Cultural Revolution. Table 4 attempts to do this for the twenty-nine provincial-level units of the PRC. These include three major cities, Peking, Shanghai, and Tientsin, all of which have sizable rural districts to which UYs have been sent. Information on the number of UY settlers is not available, however, for five of the units.

This table is also not free from ambiguity. The total of 12.3 million is within reasonable range of the 12 million national total announced in December 1975. Yet only 15 out of the 24 reports were published in that year, the rest appearing in 1973, 1974, and 1976. The transfer was stepped up sharply in 1974 and 1975 (see table 7). Since the earlier reports do not reflect the additional UY settlers, the total in table 4 should actually be lower than 12 million, particularly since data for five provin-

Table 4. UY Settlement by Province

(A) Province	(B) Date of Report	(C) Number of UY Settlers in Province	(D) Number from within Province	(E) Number from outside Province	(F) Origin of those from outside Province
Northeast					
1. Heilungkiang	12/74	1,200,000	710,000	490,000	Peking, Tientsin, Shanghai, Hangchow
2. Kirin	12/75	800,000	n.a.	n.a.	Shanghai
3. Liaoning	8/75	1,240,000	1,240,000	none	
North					
4. Hopei	12/75	400,000	n.a.	n.a.	Peking, Tientsin
5. Inner Mongolia	9/75	210,000	n.a.	110,000+	Peking, Shanghai, Tientsin, Nanking, Chekiang
6. Peking (9 counties)		n.a.	n.a.	n.a.	
7. Shansi	6/76	230,000	n.a.	50,000	Peking, Tientsin
8. Tientsin (5 counties)		n.a.	n.a.	n.a.	
East					
9. Anhwei	10/75	500,000	n.a.	n.a.	Shanghai
10. Chekiang	12/73	358,000	358,000	none	
11. Fukien	12/75	240,000	240,000	none	
12. Kiangsi	12/73	430,000	n.a.	n.a.	Shanghai
13. Kiangsu	3/75	500,000	500,000	none	
14. Shanghai (10 counties)	12/73	400,000	400,000	none	
15. Shantung	6/76	300,000	300,000	none	
Central-South					
16. Honan	4/75	360,000	360,000	none	
17. Hunan	5/75	450,000	450,000	none	
18. Hupei	late '74	810,000	810,000	none	
19. Kwangsi	12/75	334,000	n.a.	n.a.	Shanghai
20. Kwangtung	12/75	700,000	700,000	none	

Table 4. (Continued)

(A) Province	(B) Date of Report	(C) Number of UY Settlers in Province	(D) Number from within Province	(E) Number from outside Province	(F) Origin of those from outside Province
Southwest					
21. Kweichow		n.a.	n.a.	n.a.	Shanghai
22. Szechwan	11/75	1,200,000	1,200,000	none	
23. Yunnan	7/76	800,000	500,000	300,000	Shanghai, Peking, Chengtu, Chungking
24. Tibet	2/75	500	500	none	Shanghai
Northwest					
25. Kansu	2/75	100,000	n.a.	n.a.	Tientsin, Shanghai
26. Shensi	2/76	330,000	n.a.	26,000+	Peking, Nanking
27. Sinkiang	12/75	450,000	n.a.	100,000+	Shanghai, Chekiang, Wuhan, Tientsin
28. Tsinghai		n.a.	n.a.	n.a.	
29. Ninghsia		n.a.	n.a.	n.a.	Chekiang
Total of column C:		12,342,500			

Sources and Notes:

1. Radio Harbin, 12/21/73, *FBIS* no. 3, 1/4/74; and Radio Harbin, 12/21/74, *FBIS* no. 248, 12/24/74.
2. Radio Changchun, 12/27/75, *SWB-FE* no. 5104, 1/10/76.
3. Radio Peking, 12/23/74, *FBIS* no. 249, 12/26/74; and *JMJP* 8/27/75. The latter referred to 240,000 graduates who had gone to the villages in 1975.
4. Radio Shihchiachuang, 12/29/75, *SWB-FE* no. 5104, 1/10/76. The 400,000 were sent down over a period of 10 years, i.e., beginning before the Cultural Revolution.
5. Radio Peking, 9/15/75, *FBIS* no. 189, 9/29/75, is the source for column C. Data in column E were reported two years earlier, by *NCNA*, Peking, 7/20/73, *FBIS* no. 145, 7/27/73.
6. Totals of Peking UYs sent to the villages have been reported (see below, table 5), but the proportion settled in the Peking suburban counties has not been revealed.
7. *JMJP* 6/22/76.
8. Since 1973, Tientsin has administered 5 counties formerly belonging to Hopei. It is thus likely that some of the UYs listed under Hopei are actually under the jurisdiction of Tientsin.

Table 4. (Continued) *Sources and Notes:*

9. Radio Hofei, 10/28/75, *FBIS* no. 213, 11/4/75.

10. Radio Hangchow, 12/23/73, *FBIS* no. 249, 12/27/73; and Radio Hangchow, 10/30/73, *FBIS* no. 212, 11/2/73. The total number of UYs sent down by cities and towns of Chekiang was given as 438,000, of whom 80,000 were sent to destinations outside of the province.

11. Radio Foochow, 12/23/73, *FBIS* no. 3, 1/6/76.

12. Radio Nanchang, 12/21/73, *FBIS* no. 249, 12/27/73.

13. Radio Nanking 3/6/75, *FBIS* no. 46, 3/7/75. In April 1973 it was announced that a million youths from Kiangsu had been sent down, but no break-down was given by destination. Radio Nanking, 4/5/73; *SWB-FE* no. 4267, 4/10/73.

14. Shanghai has transferred about one million youths, of whom 400,000 settled in Shanghai rural counties. Radio Shanghai, 12/21/73, *FBIS* no. 250, 12/28/73; and *JMJP* 5/4/74.

15. *JMJP* 6/22/76.

16. *JMJP* 4/10/75.

17. Radio Changsha, 5/7/75, *FBIS* no. 91, 5/9/75.

18. Radio Wuhan, 5/11/73, *SWB-FE* no. 4297, 5/17/73; and Radio Wuhan, 7/29/74, *FBIS* no. 148, 7/31/74. The first report said that 600,000 youths had gone to the countryside since the Cultural Revolution; the second that in all of 1974, 210,000 would be transferred.

19. Radio Nanning, 12/21/75, *SWB-FE* no. 5095, 12/30/75.

20. Radio Canton, 12/20/75, *SWB-FE* no. 5095, 12/30/75.

21. No overall data given.

22. Radio Chengtu, 11/15/75, *FBIS* no. 225, 11/20/75.

23. *NCNA*, Peking, 7/8/76, *FBIS* no. 132, 7/8/76.

24. *KMJP* 2/11/75.

25. Radio Lanchow, 2/17/75, *FBIS* no. 36, 2/21/75.

26. *JMJP* 2/5/76; and Radio Sian, 4/29/73, *SWB-FE* no. 4286, 7/4/73.

27. Column C was reported by *JMJP* 12/2/75; the article speaks specifically of UYs from within and without the province who had settled in the last 11 years, i.e., including pre-Cultural Revolution transfers. The source for column E is Radio Peking, 5/9/73, *SWB-FE* no. 4302, 5/23/73; it refers to UYs on PLA Production and Construction Corps farms. A note in *Peking Review* 19, no. 11, 3/12/76, p. 3, includes returned youths among the 450,000.

28, 29. No overall data available.

Data in column F are found in the sources cited above as well as the following:

Shanghai UYs: *JMJP* 12/23/71 and 5/4/74; Radio Lanchow, 12/9/74, *FBIS* no. 241, 12/13/74; Radio Shanghai, 3/30/76, *FBIS* no. 64, 4/1/76.

Tientsin UYs: *KMJP* 5/6/69; Radio Urumchi, 7/24/75, *FBIS* no. 145, 7/28/75; Radio Lanchow, 6/20/75, *FBIS* no. 124, 6/24/75.

Wuhan UYs: Radio Peking, 5/9/73, *FBIS* no. 93, 5/14/73.

cial-level units are absent. On the other hand, the 1976 reports may well include some urban youths sent down in that year, who would not have appeared in the 12 million. Though the table does not establish the true size of the transfer, it does reveal some patterns that are well worth keeping in mind. Thus, it appears that most sent-down youths settle within their home provinces. Eight major cities—Shanghai, Peking, Tientsin, Hang-chow, Nanking, Wuhan, Chengtu, and Chungking—account for the interprovincial transfer of urban youths. Many, perhaps most of them have been sent to border provinces, such as Heilungkiang, Inner Mongolia, Sinkiang, and Yunnan.

Another approach to transfer statistics is to ask what propor-tion of the youth of particular cities and towns has been sent to the countryside. Precise measurement is frustrated by lack of data on relevant age groups. In the case of many cities even general population statistics are lacking. An additional problem is that large cities in China practice metropolitan government in that they include substantial rural areas within their adminis-trative jurisdictions. Metropolitan Shanghai, for instance, con-tains about 10.6 million people, of whom 5.6 million inhabit the city proper, while the other 5 million live in ten predomi-nantly rural counties, which also contain small towns and urban settlements. As of 1974, Shanghai had sent about one million youths to the countryside since the Cultural Revolution; 400,000 to the ten suburban counties and 600,000 to various provinces. Table 5, which presents data on sixteen cities, seeks to separate, insofar as this is possible, the urban population of a city (column D) from its entire population (column F). Doing so yields two percentages for the proportion of UYs in the population (columns E and G), but the first would seem to be the more meaningful of the two.

The table shows a remarkable range of variation in the propor-tions of the urban population that have been sent to the coun-tryside under the transfer program. In column E, the range is from Tsinan's 3.5 percent to Shanghai's 17.8 percent. The thir-teen cities for which column D data are available together sent 2,396,000 UYs, or 11.1 percent of their combined urban core population of 21,514,000. Data for the thirteen cities can pro-vide the basis for an estimate of the volume of the transfer for the entire urban sector. If we accept Leo Orleans's estimate that the urban population of the PRC is about 125 million,

Table 5. Sent-Down Youths as a Proportion of City Populations

(A) City	(B) Date of Report on UYs	(C) Number of UYs	(D) Core Urban Population	(E) UYs as % of Col. D	(F) Population of City Including Rural Component	(G) UYs as % of Col. F
1. Shanghai	5/74	1,000,000	5,600,000	17.9	10,600,000	9.4
2. Peking	1/73	300,000	4,000,000	7.5	7,000,000	4.3
3. Tientsin	4/73	250,000	n.a.	n.a.	4,000,000	6.3
4. Wuhan	7/74	230,000	1,900,000	12.1	2,500,000	9.2
5,6. Chungking and Chengtu	4/74	370,000	n.a.	n.a.	6,000,000	6.2
7. Canton	3/74	200,000	2,200,000	9.1	3,000,000	6.7
8. Dairen	summer '73	130,000	1,100,000	11.8	4,200,000*	3.1
9. Harbin	4/73	127,000	1,552,000	8.2	n.a.	n.a.
10. Nanking	4/74	120,000	1,700,000	7.1	3,000,000	4.0
11. Hangchow	12/75	120,000	900,000	13.3	n.a.	n.a.
12. Foochow	7/74	60,000	800,000	7.5	n.a.	n.a.
13. Nanning	4/73	30,000	400,000	7.5	n.a.	n.a.
14. Tsinan	8/74	30,000	862,000	3.5	n.a.	n.a.
15. Hu-ho-hot	1/74	29,000	300,000	9.7	n.a.	n.a.
16. Amoy	7/74	20,200	200,000	10.1	n.a.	n.a.
		2,396,200†	21,514,000			

Sources:

Column C: (1) JMJP 5/4/74; (2) "Peking's Young People Become New Peasants and Herdsmen," Peking Review, no. 4, 1/26/73, p. 4; (3) JMJP 4/19/73; (4) Radio Wuhan. 7/11/74, FBIS no. 135, 7/12/74; (5, 6) JMJP 3/26/74; (8) Ross Terrill, Flowers on an Iron Tree, p. 121; (9) Radio Harbin, 4/10/73, SWB-FE 4283, 5/1/73; (10) JMJP 4/21/74; (11) Radio Hangchow, 12/29/75, SWB-FE no. 5104, 1/10/76; (12) Radio Foochow, 7/6/74, FBIS no. 131, 7/8/74; (13) Radio Nanning, 4/6/73, SWB-FE 4269, 4/12/73; (14) Radio Tsinan, 8/16/74, FBIS no. 164, 8/19/74; (15) Radio Hu-ho-hot, 1/17/74, FBIS no. 18, 1/25/74; (16) Radio Peking, 7/6/74, FBIS no. 139, 7/18/74.

Columns D and F: (1) Harlan Cleveland, China Diary, p. 45; (2) Professor Bernard M. Frolic, York University; (3) U.S. Central Intelligence Agency (CIA), "PRC City Brief—Tientsin," July 1975; (4) CIA, "PRC City Brief—Wuhan," July 1975; Terrill, p. 235, reports 2.7 million as Wuhan's population as of 1973; (5,6) Chung-kung Nien-pao, 1973 [Chinese communist yearbook, 1973] (Taipei: Chung-kung Nien-pao Tsa-chih, 1973), p. 192; (7) CIA, "PRC City Brief—Canton," July 1975; (8) Terrill, p. 121; (9) Chung-kung Nien-pao, 1973, p. 192; (10) World Affairs Delegation, November 1975; (11) Terrill, p. 157; (12–16) Chung-kung Nien-pao, 1973; it is not clear in these cases, as well as that of Harbin, whether or not rural areas are included in the population totals.

*Includes city of Lushun (Port Arthur).

†Tientsin, Chungking, and Chengtu are excluded since column D data are missing.

subtract from that number the 21,514,000 urban inhabitants already accounted for, and calculate 11.1 percent of the resulting 103,486,000, we should then have an estimate for the UYs transferred by cities and towns other than the thirteen for which specific data are available. The result is 11,486,946; added to the 2,396,200 UYs sent by the thirteen, this yields a total of 13,883,146. Since most of the reports date from 1973 and 1974, the total should be lower, not higher, than 12 million. This result could simply be due to errors and distortions in the statistics, but it could also indicate that some unreported cities and towns send even fewer youths to the countryside than Tsinan.

The intensity of the transfer has varied considerably in the eight years 1968 to 1975 inclusive. Had the flow of urban youths to the countryside been even, 1.5 million would have settled each year. Actually, the flow was heavy after the Cultural Revolution and light in 1971 and 1972; it rose again in 1973 and climbed sharply in 1974 and 1975. Table 6 depicts numbers of UYs transferred as of the date indicated, and Table 7 depicts annual rates of transfer for the period 1968–75. In 1976, the transfer movement was apparently maintained at a level of intensity comparable to that of 1975, judging by a report published in September which referred to 14 million sent-down youths.[71]

The statistical data presented in this section give rise to ques-

Table 6. Aggregate Totals of UYs Sent to the Countryside
since the Cultural Revolution, by Date

Date of Report	Number of UYs
1. May 1970	5,000,000
2. March 1973	7,000,000
3. December 1973	8,000,000
4. January 1975	10,000,000
5. December 1975	12,000,000

Sources:
1. NCNA 5/3/70, SCMP 4655, 5/13/75. According to this article, the number of secondary school graduates sent since late 1968 or so was five times the number sent in the five years preceding the Cultural Revolution; and the number sent from 1962 to 1966 was "well over a million." Disregarding the "well over" thus yields 5 million.
2. Radio Hofei, 3/4/73, SWB-FE no. 4243, 3/13/73; the report reads "more than" 7 million since the "beginning of the Cultural Revolution."
3. JMJP 12/22/73; again, it is "more than" 8 million.
4. NCNA, Peking, 1/18/75, FBIS no. 14, 1/21/75; "nearly" 10 million.
5. Radio Peking, 12/22/75, FBIS no. 248, 12/24/75 (also in JMJP 12/23/75).

Table 7. Nationwide Annual Rates of Transfer

Year	Announced Data	Derived Data	Total
1968		1,725,000	1,725,000
1969	2,700,000		2,700,000
1970		1st 4 months 575,000 ⎫ last 8 months 492,000 ⎬	1,067,000
1971		738,000	738,000
1972	1st 8 months 400,000	last 4 months 246,000	646,000
1973		1st 2 months 123,000 ⎫ last 10 months 1,000,000 ⎬	1,123,000
1974	1st 4 months 400,000	last 8 months 1,600,000	2,000,000
1975	2,000,000		2,000,000
			11,999,000

Sources and Notes:
1. Announced Data:
   1969: *JMJP* 12/23/75; 1972: Radio Peking, 9/10/72, *FBIS* no. 179, 9/13/72; 1974: *Peking Review*, no. 19, 5/10/74 (also *KMJP* 5/5/74); 1975: *JMJP* 12/23/75.
2. Derived Data;
   a. Figures for 1968 and the first 4 months of 1970 are derived from table 6, line 1, as follows: Subtracting the 2.7 million for 1969 from the 5 million in line 1 yields 2.3 million UYs who must have been sent during the 12 months of 1968 and the first 4 months of 1970, or 143,750 per month, which in turn yields the totals specified.
   b. Lines 2, 3, and 4, table 6, are the sources for the derived data for the last 10 months of 1973 and the last 8 months of 1974.
   c. Adding all of the announced data to the derived data described in sections a and b above yields 10.4 million. If this is subtracted from the overall total of 12 million UYs, the remainder, 1.6 million, should equal the number of UYs sent in the last 8 months of 1970, all of 1971, the last 4 months of 1972, and the first 2 months of 1973, i.e., a total of 26 months. Then, 1.6 million divided by 26 months equals 61,539, which yields the totals specified (rounded off to the nearest thousand assuming a constant rate of transfer during these months. Undoubtedly the results are not very accurate. The December 1975, report, for instance, states, "More educated youths have gone to the countryside this year than in any recent year." Hence, the 2 million figure for 1974 ought to be somewhat lower.

tions: why do only a few major cities send their young people beyond the provinces in which they are located? What explains the remarkable differences between cities in the rates of transfer? Why has the intensity of the program fluctuated so greatly? The next chapter, which seeks to examine the underlying rationales for this resettlement program, may be able to shed light on some of these issues.

2 GOALS AND POLITICS OF THE TRANSFER PROGRAM

The policy of sending urban youths "up to the mountains and down to the countryside" is a response to three specific problem areas. The first is urban unemployment and growth. Second is the motivational difficulties of urban youths who have been educated in secondary schools but who can neither be accommodated in higher schools nor given white-collar jobs. The third problem area is that of rural development. Each of these requires examination in its own right; doing this will permit evaluation of the complexities involved in formulating policy for the multipurpose transfer.

URBAN EMPLOYMENT AND GROWTH

Appraising the relationship between employment and the transfer of urban youths to the countryside is difficult because of official reluctance to talk about this matter. The main publicly articulated rationales for the transfer are that it is necessary for ideological reasons and that it will spur rural development. Only rarely does a statement such as the following appear in print:

> In the cities, work must be provided every year for graduates from universities, colleges, vocational and technical schools and regular secondary schools. Since China has a planned economy, these educational institutions enroll students according to state plans. College and vocational school graduates are assigned to work in various departments of the national economy according to state needs and their specialties. As to secondary school graduates, in cities and towns, some of them are given jobs in industry, capital construction, communications and commerce so as to enlarge the ranks of the working class, while others work in the countryside to build up new socialist villages.[1]

Clearly, there is a relationship between the transfer of school graduates and urban employment. However, particularly for the 1970s, inadequate data on the number of young people who enter the urban job market every year and on the proportion that can be employed within the cities precludes a thorough test of the strength of that relationship. What follows is a review of the evidence from the 1950s to the mid-1970s.

In the 1950s, urban employment expanded rapidly, as the economy recovered from the civil war, as new bureaucracies were staffed, and as industry grew at the extraordinary rate of 19 percent per annum during the period of the First Five-Year Plan (1953–57). But already in those years, certainly by 1957, the demand for urban jobs was greater than the supply. It was estimated that during the First Five-Year Plan an average of 1.4 million new workers and employees were added annually to the labor force; about one million of them were young persons entering the labor market from within the cities each year.[2] However, additional job claimants came from the unemployed left over from preliberation times—estimated at one million as late as 1956—and from rural migrants. Between 1949 and 1957, the urban population jumped from 58 million to 92 million. Nearly half of the increase was accounted for by migration, and the rest by a birthrate of over 3 percent.[3] Controls were imposed on migration as early as 1953, and periodic campaigns were launched to return peasants who had entered cities "blindly," that is, without assurance of employment, to their home villages.[4] But clearly the net impact of migration was great. For instance, in 1954, 2.45 million persons were hired, of whom 70 percent were peasants; in 1956 the figure was 2.24 million, of whom a third were peasants.[5] The result was that as early as 1955 young city people entering the job market encountered difficulty finding employment.[6] Also, as these figures indicate, hiring in some years of the period 1953–57 was far in excess of the average annual addition of 1.4 million. In 1956, the state plan had called for adding only 840,000 new workers, but, because of expansionist optimism fueled by movements of socialist transformation then under way, over 2 million were hired.[7] The result was retrenchment in 1957, and fewer opportunities for new entrants on the job market. The decline in demand was accentuated by policy decisions to reduce the swollen staffs of the bureaucracies by transferring cadres downward (*hsia-fang*) to lower levels, including to the countryside.

It was in this context that the idea was broached that young urbanites unable to continue their education and unable to find employment in the cities go to the villages. The idea, however, was broached hesitantly; the notion that young urbanites could be called upon en masse to become peasants seemed too radical to be given high priority. Instead, the editorials that addressed themselves to the problem of employment of city youths suggested to them several possible courses of action, including staying home, studying or doing housework, or searching for jobs on their own. In addition, they called upon the relevant agencies to investigate the labor needs of agricultural collectives and to make careful plans, "persuading and arranging," for urban youths to take part in agricultural production "as far as possible."[8] The transfer to the villages was thus beginning to be viewed as a possible solution to the problem of declining urban employment opportunities, but it was not yet a major solution. In view of the statistic that, between 1956 and 1966, 1.2 million urban youths settled in the countryside, of whom "well over one million" settled between 1962 and 1966, only a few could have been transferred in 1957.[9] Indeed, the main focus of attention in these years was not on urban but on peasant youths who had gone to urban schools and who were asked to return to their home villages to become "the motherland's first generation of cultured peasants."[10]

By 1957, Chinese planners had learned that their country's urban-rural relations differed significantly from those of the Soviet Union, that China's agriculture would be unable to support a rapidly expanding urban sector, that for some time to come strict controls over urban growth would have to be imposed, and that it might be necessary not merely to return migrants to their villages but to resettle established urbanites as well.[11] The Great Leap Forward (1958–60), however, upset these prognostications. The Leap, an attempt to break through economic constraints by means of all-out mobilization of popular enthusiasm and effort, caused industrial projects to mushroom, including numerous small-scale, labor-intensive enterprises. It thus obviated the need to send urbanites to the countryside for reasons of job shortage. Quite the reverse: perhaps ten million peasants found work in the urban sector, as new workers,

including housewives, were hired on a scale vastly greater than
that of 1956.[12] But in 1960 the bubble burst and a depression
followed that made itself felt acutely in the sphere of urban
growth and employment. Unfinished projects were abandoned
and employment shrank; millions of recent migrants had to
return to the countryside.[13] Established urban residents, including families and individuals, were also sent to the countryside in
the aftermath of the Great Leap Forward, but in the absence of
detailed statistics it is hard to say how many of them were
young urbanites, graduates of schools unable to find urban employment.[14] In any event, the end of the period brought a
return to the insights of 1957. As Po Yi-po, chairman of the
State Economic Commission, put it in 1963: "We have drawn
too much manpower from the rural areas to the cities. Natural
calamities show that our urban population is greater than what
our countryside can supply. While our industry has been modernized, agriculture has not yet been mechanized. And until
the mechanization of agriculture, our urban population must be
reduced from 130,000,000 to 110,000,000."[15]

In the wake of the Great Leap Forward, the Chinese leaders
decided on major changes in development policies, symbolized
by the slogan "agriculture is the foundation, industry the leading factor." Agricultural development was assigned a much
higher priority than had been the case in the 1950s, and the
industrial sector was realigned to support the modernization of
agricultural production. The new strategy did not by any means
signify an end to industrial growth. Since recovery from the
Leap, industrial output has grown at varying rates averaging
perhaps 10 percent per year.[16] Continued industrial growth
meant the generation of additional industrial jobs, but since
industry grew at a slower rate than in the 1950s the number of
new jobs must have declined. Lack of data makes it difficult to
be precise about this. Only one projection for industrial job opportunities is available, for the years 1966–70. In 1964, T'an
Chen-lin, a Politburo member who headed the State Council's
Agriculture and Forestry Staff Office and who had responsibilities in the field of manpower planning, predicted that it would
be possible to provide 5 million urbanites with industrial jobs in
that five-year time span.[17] It will be recalled that during the
years of the First Five-Year Plan hiring averaged 1.4 million per
year; in the second half of the sixties, the rate had thus declined
by about 40 percent.

If the number of new industrial jobs had declined, the number of claimants had risen. T'an Chen-lin also predicted that 11 million persons would enter the urban labor market in the years 1966–70, that is, 2.2 million per year or more than twice as many as in the years 1953–57. High urban birthrates were the reason for the increase, a development that had caused concern already in 1957:

> Those who reach working age during the first and second Five Year Plans [1953–62] were born in the period from 1937–46. . . . The national rate of population growth was low during this period, but it has now risen to 2.2% on an average, with 3.9% in urban areas. . . . These children will reach working age during the third and fourth Five Year Plans [1963–72], and by then, the number of people looking for employment will be much greater than now.[18]

High birthrates in the 1950s were the product of peace, economic recovery, the migration of young adults to the cities, and the absence of vigorous birth control measures. The issue of planned birth had been debated in the 1950s. It was not until 1957 that a birth control campaign got under way, but it was abandoned during the Great Leap Forward. Food shortages in the aftermath of the Leap apparently had a depressing effect upon the birthrate, but with recovery it rose once again.[19] Chinese policy makers made firm commitments to birth control in the 1960s, but the Cultural Revolution (1966–68) disrupted the implementation of the program.[20] Since that upheaval, vigorous birth control measures have been put into practice in both the urban and the rural sector. In major cities, the results reported to visitors are truly dramatic: Shanghai's birthrate in 1956 was 40.3 per 1,000; for 1974, it has been put at 6.24 per 1,000 in the urban component of the metropolis.[21] Questions have been raised about both the accuracy of such reports and their generalizability, in that it is not at all clear whether the birthrate has dropped in smaller towns as well.[22] Still, given the intensity with which the planned birth movement has been pursued, it would seem probable that a significant decline has taken place in the urban birthrate. The decline has no doubt been aided very substantially by the exodus since 1968 of 12 million young people to the countryside.

If it is true that a major reduction in the urban birthrate did not take place until after the Cultural Revolution, the number

of young urbanites who reach age sixteen each year is likely
to remain at a high though perhaps fluctuating level until the
mid-1980s. Can this prognosis be translated into estimates of
numbers of urban youths for whom jobs must be found each
year? A clue is provided by school enrollment statistics given
visitors from the United States in late 1972. One figure is that
urban middle school enrollment in 1972–73 totaled about 12
million.[23] Assuming uniform distribution among five grades and
no dropouts, the 12 million yields 2.4 million graduates for the
years 1972–73 through 1976–77. However, though junior middle school education has reportedly been universalized in
"almost all the cities and towns," senior middle school enrollment is "basically universal" in only the larger cities.[24] The 12
million middle school students must therefore have been entering the job market at a much more rapid pace than is suggested
by the 2.4 million figure.* The same visitors were also told
that urban primary school enrollment totaled 22 million in
1972–73. This is a remarkable increase of 66 percent over the
mid-1950s, for in 1955, when primary schooling had probably
already been universalized in the urban sector, urban primary
schools enrolled about 13.2 million pupils.[25] Assuming uniform
distribution among the five grades and no dropouts, the 22
million yields 4.4 million graduates for the years 1972–73 to
1978–79. As indicated above, some of these children have been
entering the job market after two or three years of middle
school and the rest after completing the entire middle school
course. Although these data are crude and probably incomplete—it is not clear, for instance, where specialized vocational
and technical middle schools fit in—they do point to the conclusion that in the 1970s the number of urban youths for whom
work must be found is likely to be greater than T'an Chen-lin's
1964 forecast of 2.2 million job seekers per year for the years
1966–70.

How do these data relate to the transfer of urban youths to
the countryside in the 1960s and 1970s? For the years 1962–
66, qualitative data show Chinese officials viewing the transfer
as one solution to the problem of employment. During the Cultural Revolution, Liu Shao-ch'i, Chairman Mao's erstwhile suc-

---

*Since the Cultural Revolution, middle school graduates must be placed in either
rural or urban jobs, with the exception of those relatively few who enter the People's
Liberation Army (PLA).

cessor and chief target of the Red Guards, was charged with having "schemed and enforced the movement of 'going up to the mountain and rural areas' for the purpose of finding employment for those eliminated by the [old] educational system."[26] Similarly, Wang K'o, director of the Shanghai Department of Labor, said in 1964, "We consider that continuous mobilization of educated youths from Shanghai to join the Production and Construction Corps [in Sinkiang] is a good way of providing the young people of Shanghai with employment."[27] Yet, since only "well over one million" youths settled in the countryside in the period from 1962 to 1966, the transfer does not in fact seem to have been a major solution to the employment problem, although the actual size of the latter is not known. Perhaps it was the sluggishness of pre–Cultural Revolution bureaucracy that accounts for the small number of youths transferred. Certainly, mobilization of youths to go to the countryside has been more intense and more successful since the Cultural Revolution than it was before that upheaval. Bureaucratic foot-dragging, however, may actually have been a response to the preferences of some policy makers, who did not favor a large-scale transfer. Although Liu Shao-ch'i has just been quoted as linking the transfer with the employment problem, the low rate of transfer has also been attributed to his "sabotage."[28] According to a statement made by T'an Chen-lin in late 1966, when he had come under attack by Red Guards, "If there is a revisionist line in resettlement work, it is that Liu Shao-ch'i, Teng Hsiao-p'ing and P'eng Chen will not let more youths go to the mountains and villages. Instead, they will set up neighborhood factories in the cities and keep people there."[29] These policy makers, in other words, may not have viewed the transfer as a major solution to the employment problem, preferring instead to create additional job opportunities within the urban sector (for further discussion, see the last section of this chapter).

If the 1962–66 transfer was not a major solution to inadequate employment opportunities, the 1966–70 transfer is in sharp contrast. In 1964, T'an Chen-lin had predicted that only 5 million industrial jobs would become available in that period, leaving 6 million job claimants as candidates for transfer to the countryside. During the Cultural Revolution, the movement to the countryside was in effect suspended, but from 1968 through 1970, as will be recalled from table 7, about 5.4 million youths were moved out of the urban sector. This figure is remarkably close to T'an's 6 million and suggests that employment is a better predictor of the actual size of the transfer than the hypothesis that the main purpose of the resettlement of urban youths in 1968 and 1969 was to rid the cities of Red Guard troublemakers.

The transfer fluctuated sharply in size in the first half of the 1970s: about 700,000 were sent to the countryside in 1971, about 650,000 in 1972, about 1.3 million in 1973, and about 2 million in each of the years 1974 and 1975 (see table 7). What accounts for the fluctuations? In view of the earlier discussion of demographic trends, it is unlikely that the number of youths reaching their mid-teens could have declined in 1971 and 1972. Perhaps expansion of middle school enrollment after the Cultural Revolution temporarily reduced the number of those to whom jobs had to be assigned. Apparently, the main reason for the decline was that planners overestimated the labor needs of the urban sector, resulting in an increase in the rate of hiring, presumably in 1971 and 1972. This emerges from a classified document entitled "Outline of Education" issued in April 1973 by the Political Department of Kunming Military Region for study purposes. According to the outline,

> in planning work, due to inadequate understanding of Chairman Mao's strategic policy of "prepare against war and calamities and do everything for the people," as well as due to negligence and carelessness, the "three exceedings" and "two holes" resulted: the number of workers and employees was exceeded by so many tens of thousands, the wage bill was exceeded by so many hundred million yuan, the quantity of commodity grain was exceeded by so many hundred million catties; and there were holes in the storage of grain and cotton.[30]

An informant interviewed in Hong Kong reported that, according to a document read to workers in Canton factories in late 1972, Li Fu-ch'un, then a vice-premier active in economic planning, had taken responsibility for these errors by making a self-criticism.[31]

If retention of many school graduates in the cities was due to errors in planning, the correction of the errors meant a step-up in the rate of the transfer, which did in fact occur from 1973 on. As Liu Tzu-hou, first party secretary of Hopei, noted in April of 1973, "at present the main approach in integrating with the workers and peasants is to settle in the countryside," implying that at least in his province the majority of urban middle school graduates would be sent to the rural areas.[32] Policy makers at the national and provincial levels were deeply concerned with the transfer in 1973, in apparent preparation for its intensification in the years to come. Remedial measures designed to improve the settlement were adopted, and the country was told that the program would continue indefinitely.[33] Specific plans were formulated, as in the case of Hunan, whose leaders "worked out the province's draft plan for settling educated young people in the countryside from 1973 to 1980."[34] The plans and the reaffirmation of a commitment to the transfer program undoubtedly reflected policy makers' awareness that a gap would continue to exist, at least until the 1980s, between the number of urban youths leaving middle school and the number that could be absorbed in the urban sector.

The relationship between the transfer and urban employment is complicated by an additional variable that has thus far not been made explicit, namely, the policy makers' goal of keeping the costs of urbanization low. It has been a major objective of Chinese development strategy to economize as much as possible on urban services, including housing and transportation, as well as the wage bill.[35] This goal probably has led to the transfer of youths to the countryside even though they could have been given jobs in the urban sector. Increased labor requirements resulting from industrial expansion have instead been met in part by increasing the rate of participation among the urban population, particularly by mobilizing housewives to go to work. Visitors to Chinese cities have been impressed by the high rate of female employment, particularly in the small-scale street and neighborhood industries that have proliferated in recent years.[36] Whereas in 1957 housework was glorified in order to discourage women from seeking jobs, since then, especially during the Great Leap Forward and the Cultural Revolution, the importance of married women engaging in productive labor outside their homes has been emphasized.[37] In Shanghai, in 1957, 35.8 percent of the inhabitants were in the labor force; in 1975, the percentage had risen to 50.[38] While this may reflect changes in the age structure of the population, there is no doubt that a substantial increase in the employment of married women has taken place.[39] In addition, since the 1960s, urban employment needs have been met in part by the recruitment of peasants to work on a temporary basis in urban enterprises. These peasants work for a factory or commercial unit for stipulated periods of time but do not become workers, retaining their homes in the villages and their status as peasants.[40]

Both practices are rooted in economic considerations. Mobilizing married women to work does not require additional housing or other services (except for day-care facilities), in contrast to youths who would, in due course, establish their own households and have children. Encouraging married women to work outside the home adds to family income and hence may enable the state to keep individual wages lower than they might otherwise have to be. Similarly, peasants working in an urban undertaking get paid less than regular workers, are not entitled to state social benefits, and do not bring their families with them, thereby making possible apparently substantial savings. Although we do not know what proportion of the 12 million urban youths has been sent to the countryside because of the availability of cheaper substitutes, it would seem that the transfer has been contributing to China's development not only by helping to solve the problem of unemployment but also by helping to reduce the costs of the urban infrastructure.

The same objective of keeping the costs of urbanization down also has been achieved by adopting capital-intensive techniques in the urban sector. Visitors to Shanghai, for example, have been told that it had proved possible to increase output yet reduce the city's population not only by mobilizing women to work but also by attaining a higher level of automation.[41] Similarly, an American delegation that studied Chinese rural industry found that even county-level enterprises placed emphasis on labor-saving devices.[42] According to the Israeli economist Gur Ofer, Marxist-Leninist countries in general have sought to economize on the costs of urbanization by utilizing capital-intensive techniques in the urban sector and labor-intensive techniques in the rural sector. The result has been that, in comparison with other countries at comparable levels of development, socialist countries have tended to employ a higher proportion of the labor force in agriculture.[43] Certainly, this has been true most of all of China, which, with the possible exception of the communist countries of Indochina, has made a unique effort not only to keep peasants in the countryside but to send urbanites there as well.

Thus far the urban sector has been treated as an undifferentiated whole, which of course distorts reality. Chinese industrialization strategy has for years concentrated not only on already established industrial centers such as those in the Manchurian province of Liaoning or in Shanghai, but especially on cities and towns in the interior, where there had been little or no industry before. In line with this strategy planners have sought to limit or even to reduce the size of the largest cities, while permitting some urban places of small or intermediate size to grow. For instance, while the population of the urban component of Shanghai fell from a high of 6.4 million in the 1950s to 5.6 million in 1975, the population of Hsin-hsiang, Honan, rose from 57,000 in 1949 to 320,000 in 1965 and to 420,000 in 1975.*[44] In Honan alone, there are six or seven similar growth towns.[45] Another example was reported in 1974 by the *People's Daily,* in an article entitled "San Ming—Joyful Blossoming of a New Industrial Town," about a small county seat in western Fukien, the value of whose industrial output grew by a factor of 65 between 1958 and 1973, resulting in apparently substantial population growth.[46]

Industrial boom towns such as San Ming require an expanding labor force. It is not clear just how the demand for labor has been met. Two possibilities have already been mentioned—raising the rate of participation in the labor force of the indigenous residents, and recruiting temporary workers from nearby villages. The latter course may be particularly desirable in rapidly industrializing towns, where the provision of services is likely to lag behind the growth of industry. Another way is to transfer workers and staff from large cities to smaller towns in the interior, as has been the case with a good many Shanghai workers and employees.[47] Still another method is to recruit sent-down urban youths who have served in villages for several years to become workers in county towns (see chapter 6). And, it is quite possible that a good many peasants have been permitted

*It is not, however, wholly clear whether the Shanghai figure for the urban population refers only to the city proper or also includes the towns in the ten *hsien* that are part of the metropolis. A good deal of industry has been established in the outlying parts of Shanghai, and it is quite possible that the actual urban component is larger.

to settle permanently in such growth towns, qualifying the widespread assumption that since the Great Leap Forward no migration of peasants to urban areas has been permitted.[48] The point that emerges is simply that urban places undergoing disproportionately rapid industrialization are not likely to have to send youths to the countryside because of a shortage of jobs. If this is so, it helps explain the variations shown in table 5 in the ratio of sent-down youths to the total urban population, the range being from Tsinan's 3.5 percent to Shanghai's 17.9 percent.[49] The transfer of urban youths to the countryside is thus rooted in a complex amalgam of variables relating to the urban economy and to urban development. Inability to provide jobs for urban youths is only a partial explanation; considerations relating to urban growth and location of new industries as well as to the cost of urban infrastructure and services also enter into the planners' calculus.

EDUCATION AND THE PROBLEM OF CHANGING THE VALUES AND EXPECTATIONS OF YOUNG PEOPLE

Urban youths have been sent to the countryside not only because they cannot be absorbed by the urban economy. The transfer has also been undertaken to change the attitudes of young urbanites. As such, the transfer has been part of a wide-ranging effort to reshape the values, attitudes, and aspirations of China's youth. A major goal has been to change the aspirations of young people to move up in the social hierarchy, to obtain prestigious white-collar jobs, and to leave manual labor behind. The ideal has been that educated youths, instead of aspiring to elite status, should aspire to become ordinary workers and peasants, "with both socialist consciousness and culture."[50] This goal is rooted both in the ideological quest for "revolutionary successors" and in China's approach to development, which emphasizes mass initiative and mass participation.

To understand how the transfer to the countryside came to be viewed as a method for resocializing urban youths, it is necessary to look at the growth of the educational system and particularly at the issue of educational opportunities and the expectations generated by those opportunities. Since 1949, educational opportunities in the People's Republic of China (PRC) have expanded very rapidly at the primary and secondary levels, but only to a lesser extent at the tertiary level, as table 8 makes clear. The table shows the truly remarkable quantitative expansion of enrollments at the primary level, as well as the fact that the rates of expansion at the secondary level have been higher than at the primary level. Expansion of both stands in sharp contrast to the striking decline in higher education since the Cultural Revolution. Colleges and universities reopened in 1970, and enrollments have been rising, but as of 1974 they had not yet regained pre–Cultural Revolution levels.

From the point of view of opportunity, the pattern that emerges is that it has become progressively easier to proceed from primary to junior middle school. In 1949, there were 29 primary students for every junior middle school student; in 1957, the ratio was 13:1, in 1965, 9:1, and in 1974, for all secondary education, 7:1. The ratio of junior to senior middle school students, on the other hand, widened somewhat, from 4:1 in 1949 to 5.8:1 in 1957 and 5.7:1 in 1965. Since then, opportunities may well have increased, for, according to one report, about 40 percent of junior middle school students go on to senior middle school.[51] In the case of higher education, the pre–Cultural Revolution years saw a widening of the ratio of senior middle school students to those in higher schools from 1.8:1 in 1949 to 2:1 in 1957 and 3:1 in 1965. Since then, the gap has become a truly stupendous one of 91 secondary school students for every college student. Higher schools may now admit even junior middle school graduates; hence, the entire group is in principle eligible, assuming they all graduate and that they fulfill other requirements.

While detailed explication of these trends is beyond the scope of this study, several points may be noted. Policy makers have espoused the goal of universalizing access not only to primary education but also to secondary schooling, and in the 1950s they even spoke of ultimately doing the same for higher education.[52] As of 1974, 95 percent of children in the primary school age group were reportedly attending school so that the goal of universalizing elementary education has been substantially achieved.[53] Much progress has also been made in extending access to junior middle schools, though as of 1974 it was universal only in "almost all the cities and towns."[54] Less progress has been made in the case of senior middle schools and

Table 8. Enrollment in Primary, Secondary, and Higher Schools, 1949–1975

	1949/50	% Growth since '49/50	1957/58	1965/66	% Growth since '57/58	1974/75	% Change since '65/66
Higher schools	117,000	277	441,000	695,000	58	400,000	–42
Senior middle schools	207,000	303	835,000	(2,100,000)	(151)	36,500,000	+161
Junior middle schools	832,000	483	4,851,000	14,000,000 (11,900,000)	146 (145)		
Primary schools	24,391,000	164	64,279,000	110,000,000	71	145,000,000	+32

Sources and Notes:

All entries for 1949/59 and 1957/58, as well as the higher school figure for 1965/66, are in John P. Emerson, *Administrative and Technical Manpower in the People's Republic of China*, p. 95.

1965/66: Liu Ai-feng, "Chien-chüeh an-chao Mao Chu-hsi chih-shih pan-shih pa chung-hsiao-hsüeh ti t'i-yü kung-tso ti hen hao" [Decisively do a good job in primary and middle school sports according to Chairman Mao's instructions], pp. 8–11, is the source for the 14 million and the 110 million. The 2.1 million senior middle school enrollment actually applies to 1964/65 (Emerson, p. 95), no breakdown between junior and middle schools being available for 1965/66. The junior middle school statistic of 11.9 million is derived from the other two secondary school figures.

The higher school enrollment for 1974/75 is in "Report of the Delegation of University and College Presidents to the People's Republic of China" (unpublished). The source for the remaining 1974/75 statistics is Chun Pu, "How China Popularizes Education," p. 9.

It is possible that the 1965/66 primary school figure is too low. Emerson cites a visitor's report and enrollment of 130 million in 1964 (p. 95). Conversely, that of 1974/75 may be too high, since the Delegation of University and College Presidents was given a figure of about 130 million. The higher school enrollment for 1974/75 does not include enrollment in county, commune, and factory "colleges" established in the 1970s.

still less in higher education. Three constraints help account for the lag in the latter. First, enrollment in higher schools—as well as in secondary technical and normal schools—has in principle been planned in accordance with projections of the economy's need for specialized manpower.[55] In contrast, primary and general secondary enrollments have not been restricted by man-power planning; the purpose of expansion has been defined as that of raising the general level of culture of the society.[56] Second, the state's inadequate resources have constrained expansion at all levels. One of the goals of educational reform has been to promote inexpensive ways of broadening popular access to education, such as part-time or community-financed schools, but costs have been a particular constraint in higher education. In 1956, the per capita income of the PRC was 183 *yuan*; yet it cost 360 yuan to maintain a student in middle school for one year and 1,200 to do so in a college or university.[57] Third, expansion of higher education since the Cultural Revolution has been constrained for political reasons, as leaders have searched for a system of advanced schooling that would meet the need for trained specialists without producing a privileged elite.

The problem of frustration of expectations of secondary school students who wanted to continue their education but could not because there were no places for them arose in an acute way first in 1957. Table 8 in fact conceals a remarkable contraction of educational opportunities at the higher levels in that year. Until 1957, the absolute number of students admitted to senior middle schools, as well as to higher schools, had risen each year. Similarly, the proportion of graduates of one level who could rise to the next higher level had fallen only once, in 1955, but in 1957 it fell dramatically. Table 9 depicts these changes. The contraction of opportunities that occurred in 1957 was particularly painful at the level of college education. Previously, enrollments had increased so rapidly that in some years regular senior middle schools had been unable to supply enough graduates to satisfy the enrollment plan, and college students were recruited among outsiders, especially workers, who had taken special training programs.[58]

The downturn in 1957 provoked a great deal of public discussion. Students and their families affected by the contraction of opportunities were told that enrollments in 1956 had been excessive and hence had to be compensated for in the following

Table 9. Opportunities to Continue Schooling, 1953-1957

(1) Year	(2) Primary School Graduates	(3) Junior Middle School Entrants	(4) Col. 3 as % of Col. 2	(5) Junior Middle School Graduates	(6) Senior Middle School Entrants	(7) Col. 6 as % of Col. 5	(8) Senior Middle School Graduates	(9) Higher School Entrants	(10) Col. 9 as % of Col. 8
1953	5,945,000	818,000	8.2	395,000	161,000	40.8	58,400	71,400	122.3
1954	10,136,000	1,236,000	12.2	571,900	195,000	34.2	72,100	94,000	130.4
1955	10,254,000	1,282,000	12.5	863,000	221,000	25.6	106,000	96,200	90.8
1956	12,287,000	1,969,000	16.0	783,000	374,000	47.8	156,000	165,600	106.2
1957	12,307,000	1,603,000	13.0	1,096,400	241,000	22.0	202,600	107,000	52.8

Sources:
Columns 2, 5, 8, 9: Leo Orleans, *Professional Manpower and Education in Communist China*, pp. 32, 38, 61.
Columns 3 and 6: Ko Chu-p'o and Liu Ts'un, "Kuan-yü wo kuo chung-hsiao-hsüeh chiao-yü fa-chan chi-hua wen-t'i," [On planning the development of our country's primary and secondary education], *Chi-hua Ching-chi*, no. 10, 10/9/57, pp. 20–22.

year.[59] The same atmosphere of optimism and rapid advance that had led to excessive hiring of workers in 1956 had also, in other words, led to a further expansion of educational opportunities that was not really warranted by the country's resources. Editorials and policy makers such as Chang Hsi-jo, the minister of education, emphasized that in the foreseeable future opportunities to continue one's schooling would continue to be limited in relation to the increasing number of primary and lower middle school graduates.[60] What was to be done with those unable to continue their education? The main solution proffered was that they should take up productive labor. This raised the question of where to find jobs for them, since the contraction of opportunities in education coincided with a contraction of opportunities in urban employment, and it also raised the question of attitudes toward manual labor.[61]

Students unable to continue their education often experienced a crisis of morale because the prospect of working with their hands was distasteful to them. This problem had been raised in the media before 1957, but now it became a matter of much greater urgency.[62] It was recognized that youths had a hierarchy of preferences: at the top came continued education, preferably including university study; if that could not be attained, a white-collar job followed; after that, a blue-collar job in urban industry; and last of all, work in agriculture. As one editorial put it, an opportunity to become an engineer, a scientist, or a cadre is regarded as opening up a "big future"; having to become a peasant is regarded as opening up a "small future."[63] It was pointed out that youths had been taught these preferences in the family and in the schools. In the family, traditional concepts converged with aspirations generated by the revolution. Parents took pride in the educational achievements of their children in line with the traditional expectation that academic success brings prestige and benefit to the entire family. Those parents who themselves had been unable to get an education in the old society now wanted such opportunities for their children in the new society.[64] Parents put pressure on their children to do well on entrance examinations; poor performance was considered a disgrace. Families who held such attitudes found them reinforced in society at large; Kwangtung's first party secretary, T'ao Chu, explicitly referred to "public opinion" (yü-lun) as an obstacle to changing attitudes that put a low valuation on manual labor.[65]

The school system of the 1950s reinforced rather than combatted these attitudes. The Chinese had adopted the Soviet
model of education, or, more specifically, the system that had
emerged there in the early 1930s. This model was geared to the
training of technical specialists who could meet the industrializing economy's need for highly skilled manpower. In the
secondary schools, for instance, study was oriented exclusively
to the disciplined acquisition of academic knowledge, the aim
being to prepare students for higher education.[66] In such a
school system, the main success indicator is academic achievement; high status is allocated to those who do well and low
status to those who do not. High value is attached to mental
labor, low value to manual labor, the primacy of the working
class in the formal or official value system notwithstanding.
In China, the precommunist educational system had also been
oriented toward academic performance, and the adoption of
the Soviet model was quite congruent with this orientation.
As John W. Lewis points out, "Throughout the school system,
the curriculum was overwhelmingly geared to the cultivation
of advanced 'intellectuals' in all fields but particularly in applied
and technical science and mathematics."[67] Political study, which
might have counterbalanced the elitist attitudes fostered in the
schools by teaching students about the proletariat and the
peasants, was deemphasized in the First Five-Year Plan period,
as was student participation in manual labor. It is not surprising
that in 1957 officials criticized neglect of political and labor
education by the schools, complaining that many students did
not have a correct appreciation of the glorious nature of labor.[68] Interestingly, similar criticisms were voiced at just about
the same time in the Soviet Union by Nikita Khrushchev, and
for similar reasons, namely, that Soviet higher schools were
also no longer able to absorb all secondary school graduates,
many of whom would have to engage in manual labor.[69]

How to change the elitist attitudes toward labor and how to
replace them with new, revolutionary values have been central
concerns of Chinese leaders since the mid-1950s. They have
made a variety of efforts to bring about changes in attitudes,
of which sending urban youths to the countryside has been
only one. Indeed, it follows from the preceding paragraphs that
the school system would be a major focus of reforms.

The first dramatic attempt to change the system of education came during the Great Leap Forward. Under the slogan that education must be combined with productive labor, the authorities sought to break down the barriers between educational institutions and agricultural production. Schools and universities were to run small factories or students were to go to work periodically in factories or on communes. Whatever the particular form of participation in production, the goal was to expose students to "practice," to society, to workers and peasants. Book learning, rote memorization, and pure theory would be deemphasized. At the same time, political study would be stressed. Experts would not just be experts in their fields but would be properly "red" as well. Students would exchange their careerist ambitions for consciousness of service to the masses. Participation in production would prepare middle school students to go to work after graduation by providing them with experience and skills. Greater emphasis on political and class criteria in admission to higher schools would result in greater access by children of workers and peasants, thus dealing a blow to elitism. The same goal of increased educational opportunity, especially for peasants, would be attained by transforming the educational system into a part-time one, in which costs to the state would be greatly reduced as students contributed labor to support their school and as local communities set up their own schools. These ideas were widely put into practice during the hectic days of the Great Leap Forward, but in experimental and varied ways.[70]

During this period opportunities to attend higher schools sharply increased, temporarily reversing the 1957 situation. Enrollment in China's colleges and universities reached 441,000 in 1957/58, 660,000 in 1958/59, and 950,000—an all-time high—in 1960/61.[71] Instead of admitting 152,000 students in 1958 as planned, higher schools admitted around 300,000.[72] Senior middle school students were virtually ordered to apply for admission: "This year, in view of the demand of the nationwide leap forward, higher institutions have to enroll a greater number of students. Because the sources of students are still lacking, it is *required* [my emphasis] that all those senior secondary school students due for graduation this year [1958] who are able to study further actively apply for admission into higher institutions."[73] If in 1957 only 53 percent of that year's graduates of senior middle schools could be accommodated in higher schools, the percentage rose to 135 percent in 1958 and to 112 percent in 1959.[74] The Leap thus had paradoxical consequences: on the one hand, prodigious efforts were made to reform student attitudes toward becoming workers and peasants, but, on the other, the reality of increased opportunity often made this goal irrelevant.*

The depression that followed the Leap made itself felt in education, as elsewhere. Inadequate resources forced many locally financed schools to close down, while budgetary pressures required that cuts be made in enrollments at the higher levels of the system. As Leo Orleans put it, "Hundreds of thousands of urban youths at varying stages of completed schooling were prevented from pursuing their education."[75] Even after recovery from the Leap, possibilities for continuing one's education beyond junior middle school were narrower than they had been in the 1950s (see table 8).[76] Moreover, many of the innovations introduced in 1958 and 1959 were watered down or simply abandoned. One of the main reasons for the retreat was that educators, backed by policy makers concluded that the innovations threatened the quality of education and hence the supply of academically qualified graduates. Their concern, in other words, centered on the country's need for advanced specialists. As a result of initiatives taken in the early 1960s, the time devoted to productive labor and to politics was reduced, full-time study was largely restored, and many of the new part-time schools were closed down, while the principle of acquisition of specialized expertise through academic study was given the stamp of legitimacy by leaders such as Ch'en Yi.[77] In the case of secondary education, post-Leap policies in effect restored to the middle schools their traditional principal function of preparing students for college entrance. The values such an orientation bred among students were summed up in a caustic remark reportedly made in 1964 by Liu Shao-ch'i, himself to be blamed for the situation two years later: "And what about students from fulltime school? The general rule is that those graduated from a junior middle school despise the peasants; those graduated from a senior middle school despise the workers, and those graduated from a university despise all of them."[78]

*The burst of popular enthusiasm that accompanied the first phase of the Great Leap Forward may well have been fueled at least in part by the sudden expansion in both urban employment opportunities and education.

One consequence of the increasing disproportion between aspirations and opportunities was that the spirit of individual competitiveness among middle school youth probably increased even while the formal values of the system encouraged cooperativeness.[79] Moreover, since the quality of one's preparatory education was a critical determinant of performance on university entrance examinations, getting one's offspring into a good school also became more important. During the Cultural Revolution, Red Guards severely denounced elite middle schools that were rearing "spiritual aristocrats" and were supported by the converging interests of officials, educators, and high-ranking parents.[80] Cities such as Peking and Canton boasted several such schools, whose reputations in some cases dated back to Republican times. Such schools usually were affiliated with a nearby university, and they had excellent facilities and staff. Their index of performance was success in sending large numbers of graduates to higher schools, especially to the more prestigious universities. The principal of one Canton school, anxious to outstrip a competing school in the rate of university admission among graduates, reportedly set a goal of 60 percent admissions for 1963, 70 percent for 1964, and 80 percent for 1965, when at most a third of senior middle school graduates were able to go on to institutions of higher learning in the nation as a whole.[81] Data published during the Cultural Revolution showed that virtually no children of workers attended such schools.[82] Red Guards charged that high-ranking party officials backed these schools by devoting special attention and funds, assigning to them the role of preparing outstanding youths for university study and future leadership positions. T'ung Ta-lin, of the Central Committee's Propaganda Department, reportedly said about Peking's Ching-shan School, "Our graduates can never become men like Tung Chia-keng [a nationally publicized model youth in the movement to the countryside]. Our school must turn out secretaries of hsien Party committees, directors of propaganda departments, heads of women's federations, members of the Central Committee, premiers, leaders . . . statesmen, and soldiers."[83] And, behind the high-minded concern for the training of the talented, Red Guards detected the self-interested manipulations of elite parents seeking to preserve elite status for their children: "[The] shady element Chiang Nan-hsiang [minister of higher

education before the Cultural Revolution] managed to shove
his 'distinguished' son into the Peking University's Attached
Middle School by means of a telephone call and a note. This
boy had been rejected by his original school after repeating
several times. The teachers were instructed quite shamelessly
to teach this boy as an 'honorable political assignment.'"[84]

The need for another educational reform was widely recognized before the Cultural Revolution. There was, on the one
hand, a commitment to the expansion of secondary education;
on the other, agreement that a secondary school system that
aroused unfulfillable expectations and failed to equip students
with skills and habits appropriate for manual labor was not
tenable. Chinese leaders debated various solutions. We know
about their debates primarily from the polemics of the Cultural
Revolution, which dichotomized proposals into revolutionary
and revisionist ones in order to substantiate the thesis of the
struggle between the proletarian and bourgeois lines. For Liu
Shao-ch'i, the solution reportedly lay in work-study schools,
in which students would have become accustomed to industrial
or agricultural labor by the time they graduated. Not only
would their expectations be reduced but the low cost of work-
study schools would permit the extension of part-time secondary and even higher education to wider segments of youth.[85]
At the same time, however, Liu apparently also favored the
maintenance of full-time secondary schools in which the talented would be prepared for higher education, thereby meeting
the country's needs for academically qualified specialists. Thus
Liu opened himself up to charges of leaving the elitist aspirations of a segment of Chinese youth intact and, indeed, of
encouraging a two-track system of education, in which children
of peasants and workers were likely to end up in work-study
schools and children of the elite in full-time academic schools.[86]

Mao Tse-tung sought to tackle the elitist orientation of the
schools by reviving the revolution in education that had been
launched during the Great Leap Forward. Mao may well have
agreed with the concept of work-study schools, but he rejected
the argument that full-time and long-term academic study was
also needed in order to meet the country's developmental requirements. He was scornful of academic study as leading to
scholasticism and endangering the health of students, and he
believed that truly useful specialists and technicians could only

emerge once education was linked directly with production.[87] Among Mao's specific proposals was one that sought to change in a fundamental way the traditional role of secondary education: "After graduation from a senior middle school, one should first perform some practical work. It won't do for a person to go to the countryside alone, and he should also go to the factory, the stores, and the company unit. After performing a few years of work in this way, two more years of study will be sufficient."[88] This proposal was put into effect after the Cultural Revolution: two years of experience in production or in the PLA are now generally required before a youth is permitted to enter a higher school. This is one of the underpinnings of the transfer to the countryside. University entrance directly upon graduation from middle school tended to reinforce the traditional assumptions, values, and expectations on which secondary education was built. For teachers and administrators, high performance of their graduates on entrance tests validated their efforts as educators; for the students it was the reward for years of hard study. Performance on the entrance examination visibly and publicly separated those who succeeded from those who failed. Before the Cultural Revolution, increasingly intense efforts were made to glorify those who went to work after graduation, including those who went to the countryside. Yet this political education did not succeed in displacing the undesirable assumptions: one of the common complaints voiced by sentdown youths during the Cultural Revolution was that they were widely regarded as failures and rejects.*[89] Since the Cultural Revolution, this distinction between success and failure has been eliminated, and moreover performance in the production unit to which students are assigned after graduation from middle school has become a major criterion for entrance to higher schools. This separation between performance in secondary school and admission to higher schools should make it easier to change the dominant ethos of the former from preparation for higher education to preparation for production.

Before the Cultural Revolution, the educational system was only one part of Chairman Mao's general concern with the di-

---

*To be sure, academic failure was only one explanation for the low social esteem in which they were held. In the years immediately preceding the Cultural Revolution, class criteria were increasingly applied in university admissions, resulting in many bad-background youths being sent to the countryside who would otherwise have been qualified for higher study on academic grounds.

rection in which Chinese society would move. In the early 1960s, Mao elaborated his fundamental critique of the degeneration of the Soviet Union into a revisionist system ruled by a bureaucratic stratum anxious to preserve its power and privileges. How to prevent a comparable development in China became a central issue of the time in his mind. Youth naturally played a major role in his thinking: would they or would they not become "revolutionary successors" preserving the proletarian essence of the system?[90] As Mao sought to push his concerns to the center of the political stage, the themes of class struggle and "revolutionization" began to permeate the media and the language of public discourse. More and more political and social activities began to be defined in terms of their revolutionary purpose, and the transfer to the countryside was no exception. Much of the publicity for the intensifying transfer movement in 1964 and 1965 dwelt on the resocializing impact of going "up to the mountains and down to the villages." As one Shanghai paper put it: "You will have to wear away your nonproletarian ideas by performing ordinary farm labor."[91] Similarly, an editorial in the Young Communist League organ *Chung-kuo Ch'ing-nien Pao* (China Youth Daily) stated:

Participation in agricultural labor is . . . an important road for revolutionizing educated youths. . . . The countryside is the main center for the three great revolutionary movements for class struggle, production struggle, and scientific experiments; [it] is a place where various struggles are most intensified and complicated. By going to withstand tests in fierce struggles in the countryside, educated youths have created highly favorable conditions for promoting revolutionization of themselves. . . . To revolutionize themselves, educated youths must first turn themselves into laborers. Going to share the bitter and the sweet with the laboring people in the countryside, educated youths can gradually cultivate the habit of doing labor eagerly, establish a correct attitude towards physical labor, [and] reform their nonproletarian thoughts . . . an important guarantee for preventing themselves forever from being corrupted.[92]

This quote sums up as well as any the process of resocialization which the transfer to the countryside is supposed to entail.

Although the rhetoric of revolution permeated pre–Cultural

Revolution China, the actual progress made in changing those parts of the superstructure that shaped attitudes and beliefs, such as the school system and the cultural media, was much too slow to suit Chairman Mao's sense of urgency. He became convinced that many of his colleagues were in effect sabotaging his program for the suppression of revisionism. One of the sources of the Cultural Revolution thus was Mao's belief that it was necessary to purge the superstructure, including the political, cultural, and educational systems, of bourgeois power-holders and influences. China's urban secondary and higher school students became the major instrument for this purpose. At the same time, it is clear that for Mao the mobilization of the young to rebel against the authorities defined as bourgeois had more than an instrumental purpose. In the process of rebelling, the values of the students, hitherto shaped by bourgeois intellectuals in control of the schools, would undergo a fundamental transformation, for "successors to the revolutionary cause of the proletariat come forward in mass struggles and are tempered in the great storms of revolution."[93] As it turned out, Mao's hope in this regard was not realized. Instead of becoming dedicated revolutionaries, the Red Guards took to fighting among themselves, and in the process brought violence and chaos to many cities. One source of the factional strife was desire for advancement, especially for positions in the political structure that emerged during the Cultural Revolution, a desire that participation in the revolutionary struggles was supposed to eliminate.[94] The fighting in China's cities in 1967 and the first half of 1968 disillusioned Chairman Mao, who reportedly expressed his disappointment personally to Red Guard leaders in the summer of 1968.[95]

Following this abortive experiment in revolutionary resocialization, the transfer to the countryside came into its own in the form of an intensive mass campaign. In December 1968, Mao Tse-tung issued his most widely quoted instructions on the subject: "It is very necessary for educated young people to go to the countryside to be reeducated by the poor and lower-middle peasants. Cadres and other city people should be persuaded to send their sons and daughters who have finished junior or senior middle school, college, or university to the countryside. Let's mobilize. Comrades throughout the countryside should welcome them."[96] For the next two years, the transfer to the countryside was defined virtually exclusively in terms of this goal of reeducation. Its purpose was both to change attitudes acquired while students attended schools dominated by bourgeois thought and to change the attitudes that had brought about violence during the Cultural Revolution.

Removing fractious Red Guards from the cities so as to restore order and stability was clearly also a major goal of the transfer in the wake of the Cultural Revolution. In the official rhetoric this latter goal was subsumed under the ideological goal of reeducation, but some people in China associated the resettlement with the reform through labor that is imposed by judicial agencies on political and criminal offenders. Thus, Lin Piao, who became Mao's successor after the Cultural Revolution but who was purged in 1971, is said to have "slandered" the transfer as "a disguised form of labor reform" (*pien-hsiang lao-kai*).[97] However, if the main purposes of the transfer immediately after the Cultural Revolution were to reeducate and to restore order, its scope was apparently restrained by economic manpower considerations. This emerges from the earlier mentioned finding that the number of youths sent to the countryside from 1968 to 1970, about 5.4 million, approximates the forecast made by T'an Chen-lin in 1964 of 6 million persons in 1966–70 for whom there would be no urban jobs. Red Guards must have numbered far more than 6 million—in the autumn of 1966, 11 million of them paraded before Chairman Mao in Peking—hence by no means were all of them indiscriminately swept out of the cities and towns of China.[98]

Since the Cultural Revolution, educational institutions have been subjected to major changes, one of the results of which, it is hoped, will be graduates who are "revolutionary successors." Many of the innovations tried out during the Great Leap Forward have been put into practice, especially regular participation in labor and intensive political study. Efforts have been made to reshape the curriculum of secondary schools in order to provide practical knowledge; instead of mastering chemistry in the abstract, students are to learn how to apply chemical fertilizer, thereby also preparing themselves for life in the village. (Questions can, however, be raised about the extent to which urban schools have actually been teaching skills useful in the village; see chapter 5.) Judging by visitors' accounts and the press, the messages transmitted to the students, both by elementary and secondary schools, now emphasize much more than in the past the goal of integration with workers, peasants, and soldiers. The goal of entry into production, rural or urban, is being made a normal part of children's educational experience. As previously noted, direct transition from secondary to higher school is generally not possible, while the institutions of higher learning themselves have also been transformed with a view to eliminating the elitist expectations that higher education would otherwise encourage.[99]

The new educational system, it should be stressed, is still defined as in a state of experimentation. The reason for continuing flux is that the educational system has not yet succeeded in reconciling the competing demands placed upon it, that is, the demand that it produce "cultured workers and peasants" and the demand that it supply the country with well-trained scientists and engineers. Bitter political conflict has in fact centered around attempts to "reverse the verdicts of the Cultural Revolution" by restoring greater emphasis on academic excellence—by reinstituting entrance examinations or by allowing talented youths to bypass the production requirement that intervenes between middle school and college.[100]

Despite the "revolution in education," one of the articulated goals of the transfer to the countryside continues to be the "reeducation" (*tsai chiao-yü*) of urban youth. To be sure, since the early 1970s, other goals, particularly that of rural development, have also been stressed in the program. But the theme that urban youths should "humbly accept reeducation from the poor and lower-middle peasants" has remained central in the media, and the question is, why?[101] It may be that continued mention of reeducation merely serves ritualistic purposes, or that it has been redefined, standing less for profound value change and more for the acquisition of specific work skills in the village. It seems likely, however, that reeducation continues to be necessary because the new educational system has not in fact succeeded in thoroughly instilling new attitudes, perhaps because secondary education, no matter how diluted by politics, labor, and practice, inherently stimulates aspirations for upward mobility. Moreover, it is also likely that the other agency of socialization, the family, mentioned at the outset of this section, has not been fundamentally changed and that the "wrong" kinds of attitudes and expectations are still being transmitted there. In the next chapter, which deals with mobilization in the cities for the transfer, mention will be made of the tenacity with which old values continue to be held by members of urban families, which suggests, from the point of view of Chinese leaders, a continuing need for efforts at resocialization and hence a continuing rationale for the transfer to the countryside.

RURAL AND FRONTIER
DEVELOPMENT

In 1964 an editorial in the *China Youth Daily* described the transfer of urban youths as part of a broader flow of human resources from the urban to the rural sector designed to help develop agriculture:

> Agriculture is the foundation of the national economy. To transform thoroughly the "poor and blank" aspects of our countryside and to build a socialist, new countryside is an unprecedentedly great undertaking. Our party and state are now concentrating on aiding agriculture. Thousands upon thousands of cadres, technicians and educated youths are going in an unending stream to the countryside. Going to the rural and mountainous areas, the educated youths are showing their talents in places where the motherland needs them most. . . . In the countryside . . . it is necessary . . . to bring about technical innovations . . . so as to realize mechanization, electrification, chemicalization and universal building of water conservancy projects in the 20 or 25 years to come. . . . Cultured youths with socialist consciousness are urgently needed in building a socialist new countryside.[102]

These same themes—the need of the village for youths with "cultural and scientific knowledge" who will popularize literacy, science, and modern health practices, who will help change "outdated habits and customs," and who will bring "an inspiring new atmosphere to the countryside"—have been articulated again and again in the Chinese media in recent years.[103] The intent is clear: urban youths should make positive contributions to rural development; the program is not merely designed to achieve ends distinctive to the urban sector. But questions arise: just how important are the sent-down youths to the rural development effort? How central is the development goal to the workings of the transfer program?

When policy makers consider how to fill the perceived rural need for youths with midde school education, they are likely to think first not of urban but of rural youths, that is, of peasants who have attended middle schools outside of their villages, subsequently returning to them. As noted in the previous chapter, *hui-hsiang chih-shih ch'ing-nien,* the returned educated peasant youths (RYs), are far more numerous than sent-down urban youths (UYs). In Fukien, as of 1975, there were 240,000 UYs and one million RYs serving in the countryside. Opportunities to attend middle schools have broadened greatly for rural youth in recent years. In 1972, two-thirds of the country's middle school population of 36 million reportedly came from the rural areas, which would mean that, in that year alone, twice as many rural youths were attending some kind of middle school as were sent to the countryside in the years 1968–75 (24 million versus 12 million).[104]

Chinese leaders were aware of the crucial importance of retaining the services of educated peasants within the villages long before the transfer of urban youths became a major issue. Teng Tzu-hui, head of the Rural Work Department of the Central Committee in the 1950s, wrote about the problem in 1954, as did Mao Tse-tung a year later in connection with the socialist transformation of agriculture: "All people who have had some education ought to be very happy to work in the countryside if they get the chance. In our vast rural areas there is plenty of room for them to develop their talents to the full."[105] The latter of these two sentences has become one of the most widely disseminated quotations for the mobilization of urban youth to go to the villages. Yet what Mao was writing about in 1955 was not urbanites but peasant youths who, having gone to school, chose to remain in the village, utilizing their knowledge for the advancement of producers' cooperatives as bookkeepers and work point recorders.

As long as migration to the cities was possible, educated peasant youths tended to leave, or, rather, not to return after completion of their education, in accord with the universal pattern that the educated leave the countryside for the superior attractions of city life. Teng Tzu-hui, writing in 1962, reported that in Shan-yin county, Shansi, 9,975 youths had graduated from primary school since 1949; 9 remained in the village. In the same time span, the county produced 1,554 junior middle school graduates; not one remained in agricultural work within the village.[106] In 1957 a *People's Daily* editorial complained that there were very few graduates of junior middle schools in the villages and virtually no graduates of senior middle schools. Peasants who had attended middle schools—virtually all of which were then located in the urban sector—either continued their education or found employment in industry.[107] It is no wonder that the return of educated peasants to their villages was viewed as an issue of major importance.

Motivating educated young peasants to stay in the village presupposed a change in their attitudes and expectations not dissimilar to that required of urban youth. The traditional peasant attitude toward education was that it permitted an escape from the labor of farming: "Those who farm need not read books and those who read needn't do farm labor."[108] Education was considered the route of escape from farming into officialdom.[109] These attitudes have been reinforced by the attractions of the cities as places with higher living standards and higher rewards. Indeed, as in other developing countries, the very process of education has raised peasants' awareness of the urban world.[110] Changing such attitudes has required intensive political education of the rural communities. Many a newspaper story recounts how a peasant, having returned to his village to take up farming upon graduation from school, was met with ridicule and contempt for having failed to make it into the administrative system or stay in the city, and only gradually did he find acceptance.[111] It might in fact be suggested that the transfer of urban youth is intended to have a demonstration effect upon rural youth: if it is legitimate and proper to subject urbanites to the drastic step of moving them to the village, how can ruralites ever expect to leave the countryside?

Surely, however, sent-down urban youths are not merely of symbolic importance to rural development. Their numbers, after all, are not insignificant, even if they are less numerous than the returned youth. Furthermore, the quality of their education may well be higher than that of the educated peasants, though this advantage could be outweighed by the greater familiarity of peasant youth with rural conditions, and moreover it is likely to be more difficult to motivate an urban than a rural youth to stay in the countryside (see also chapter 5). On balance, it would seem fair to conclude that educated peasant youths are of primary importance to rural development; urban youths of secondary importance.

The other question that can be raised concerns the centrality of the rural development goal to the transfer program. One way of approaching this question is to look at settlement patterns. In principle, urban youths have an advantage over rural youths in that they can be deployed "where the motherland needs them most," whereas returned peasant youths by definition go back to their home areas, regardless of developmental needs.[112] Do UY settlement patterns in fact maximize this advantage? Presumably, the motherland needs them most in the least-developed, poorest, backward parts of the country, that is, either in the western and frontier provinces, or in the remote, mountainous parts of provinces in China proper as opposed to the more advanced, richer, and more developed areas in the plains. The evidence on this point, however, is mixed: a number of youths have in fact been sent to backward, remote, poor areas, but a good number have also been sent to more modern-ized, advanced, and prosperous areas. Shanghai youths may serve as an example: 600,000 have settled outside of Shanghai, a great many among them in such frontier provinces as Heilung-kiang, Inner Mongolia, Sinkiang, and Yunnan; 400,000 how-ever, have settled in the ten suburban counties of Shanghai, an area that has been subjected to modernizing influences for over a century and is in one of the most prosperous parts of the country. Does the motherland really need them "most" in the Shanghai suburbs, or could it be that goals other than maximiz-ing their impact on rural development enter into settlement decisions?

Beyond the case of Shanghai, evidence is available—not con-clusive, to be sure—suggesting that many UYs have been sent to more modernized areas. From 1968 to 1972 the two national dailies, *Jen-min Jih-pao* and *Kuang-ming Jih-pao,* carried ar-ticles on the settlement of urban youths in which 312 coun-ties were mentioned, though usually without data on the actual number of youths involved. These 312 counties can be com-pared with those counties not mentioned, using the China County Data Bank at Harvard's East Asian Research Center.[113]

It turns out that the counties mentioned in connection with UYs tended to be somewhat closer to their provincial capitals than those not mentioned, indicating settlement in less remote and hence presumably more modernized places.[114] Similarly, the counties mentioned were somewhat lower in altitude than those not mentioned, that is, they tended to be located in the plains rather than in the presumably more backward mountainous areas.[115] Finally, the counties mentioned tended to have been penetrated by railroads slightly earlier than those not mentioned, indicating earlier exposure to modernizing influences.[116] These findings are not conclusive, if only because press mentions do not necessarily reflect actual settlement patterns. Also, conditions within counties differ and these are not reflected in the comparison.

Evidence is also available from Kwangtung province showing that UYs have tended to settle not in the poorest villages, where presumably they are needed the most, but rather in more prosperous ones.[117] According to informants, the ten work points accumulated by an adult male per day may be worth only 0.3 or 0.4 *yuan* in an average year in a mountainous Kwangtung village. In contrast, in a rich village in the Pearl River Delta, the ten work points may be worth 1.2 or even 1.5 yuan, 0.7 to 1 yuan being considered a daily income that is neither large nor small. The worth of ten work points in the production teams in which my informants settled ranged from 0.4 to 1.2 yuan but clustered around 0.8 to 1 yuan, that is, in the middle range. Two sociologists, William Parish and Martin Whyte, obtained data indicating that UYs in Kwangtung tend disproportionately to settle in prosperous, more developed villages. Parish and Whyte differentiated between villages in which sent-down youths made up less or more than 3 percent of the adult population. They constructed a household livelihood scale, incorporating data on radios and bicycles owned by peasant households, as well as machinery owned by production teams. Table 10, based on data from 36 villages, shows clearly that fewer UYs tended to reside in villages that ranked low on their household livelihood scale. Similarly, Parish and Whyte constructed a collective economy scale, using data on rice yields, the value of work points, and brigade machinery for 39 villages, of which 23 ranked low and 16 high. In three-fourths (74 percent) of the low-ranking villages, UYs made up less than

Table 10. Settlement of UYs in Poorer and Richer Kwangtung Villages

UYs as % of adult population	Rank on Household Livelihood Scale			
	Low		High	
	No. of Villages	%	No. of Villages	%
Under 3%	14	82%	9	47%
3% and over	3	18%	10	53%
Total	17	100%	19	100%

Source: Data collected by William Parish, Jr., and Martin K. Whyte, in connection with their forthcoming book *Village and Family in Contemporary China.*
Note: Although the villages could not be randomly selected, a significance test was nonetheless performed: Chi-square = 4.7598
$$DF = 1$$
$$P < 0.05$$

3 percent of the adults, whereas this was the case in only half of the high-ranking villages.[118]

Although the data are not conclusive, undoubtedly, a substantial number of UYs have ended up in wealthier, more highly developed villages.[119] Why? One possible answer is that the initial reasoning about needs is wrong. It could be that it is precisely those villages that are already fairly advanced that need sent-down youths. The process of modernization entails differentiation of functions. Hence it should be the more modernized villages that are most in need of teachers, paramedics, or agricultural technicians. While this may be the case, there is little evidence to show that more modernized villages have in fact experienced a need for the services of sent-down youths. Indeed the opposite could well be the case, for such villages are likely to have more peasants with middle school education than do poor and remote villages (see chapter 5).

Another explanation for this pattern is that it reflects China's distinctive approach to rural development, namely, its labor-intensive character. In the urban sector, Chinese strategy seeks to economize on labor; in the rural sector, the emphasis is on practices that increase the demand for labor. Innovations such as double- or triple-cropping have increased the demand for labor, as has encouragement of sideline enterprises, the establishment of workshops and factories within the communes, and the intensive mobilization of manpower to work on farmland capital construction projects, such as landscape modification (terracing and leveling of hillsides) or construction of drainage tunnels and other irrigation facilities. Multicropping often leads to labor shortages in the peak busy season even in densely populated villages; mechanical implements such as rice transplanters are designed to alleviate this shortage.[120] In these circumstances, it is not inconceivable that sent-down youths could help meet a need for additional laborers. Since diversification has probably gone furthest in the suburban villages, this putative need may help explain why a good many UYs can be found there. Thus, visitors from the United States to Red Star Commune, outside Peking, where UYs made up 7 percent of the population of 82,000, were told that the youths were welcome because the labor situation was "very tight."[121] Such explicit confirmations, however, are quite rare.

Some of the more developed and prosperous villages are likely also to be densely populated and to have a very low ratio of arable land to labor. Such villages might well be unable to absorb more than a few newcomers even when the most labor-intensive practices are used. Judging by reports of both informants and visitors, density of population and land-labor ratios do limit the assignment of UYs, and it appears that in fact few have been sent to villages where the marginal product of their labor might be close to zero.[122] In the Parish-Whyte study, even though they discovered a tendency for villages outside of the thickly populated Pearl River Delta to host fewer UYs than did delta villages, they also found that the percentage of UYs was affected by land-labor ratios. They compared 12 villages with a land-labor ratio of under 3 *mou* per laborer with 19 villages with higher ratios. (Six *mou* equal one acre.) The proportion of UYs was over 3 percent in only 2 of the 12 low-ratio villages but in 9 of the 19 high-ratio villages.[123]

Because it is not all that clear just how critical the needs of the more modernized villages are for UYs—either as laborers or as "modernizing agents" such as teachers—a third explanation for the settlement of UYs in such villages can be suggested: the main criterion for deciding on places of settlement may not be development needs at all but the capacity of a village to absorb newcomers.[124] Its prosperity, in other words, becomes the key criterion. Very poor villages are unable to sustain migrants; hence, transfer program administrators are more likely to pick wealthier villages, though presumably keeping in mind their ability to provide urban youths with some sort of useful employment. More broadly, it can be suggested that assignment patterns are likely to be influenced by a variety of nondevelopmental goals. The decision to send UYs to villages able to absorb them may well be reinforced by the goal of advancing their adaptation to rural life, since UYs are likely to adjust more easily to prosperous than to poor villages.[125] The goal of adaptation is also attained more easily if urban youths are sent to places close to home, such as suburban communes or communes within their home county, and to nearby places where differences in dialect, climate, food, and customs are not too great.[126] Still another goal that may influence assignments is that of reeducation: in principle, reeducation can take place wherever there are poor and lower-middle peasants, whether or not a developmental need exists. And there is the goal of reducing administrative burdens. In table 4 it was shown that, except for urban youths from eight cities, UYs are settled within their home provinces. Confining interprovincial transfers to a few cities conforms to China's decentralized administration. Most provinces are evidently asked to take care of their own urban youth problem and not to impose a coordinating burden on the center. These goals, it should be stressed, are not incompatible with UYs' making significant contributions to rural development (see chapter 5 for details), or with the official intent that such contributions should be an outcome of the transfer. But the existence of these other goals does challenge the hypothesis that rural developmental contributions are at the very center of the transfer.

Virtually nothing is known about settlement decisions, that is, the ways in which urban and rural, provincial and national officials interact in reaching such decisions.[127] At times, nondevelopmental needs may be of such urgency that they override other considerations. A possible instance was in 1968 and 1969, when millions of Red Guards were sent to the countryside, in part to restore order in the cities, and at a time when the administrative system had been battered by the Cultural Revolution. It is possible that rural destinations were simply not planned very carefully in those days. Informants report that a good many Canton youths were sent to thickly populated Pearl River Delta counties, but that this practice did not last beyond the 1968–69 transfer campaign. Since then, decision-making processes have been normalized, but the weight given to rural development needs is still not altogether clear.

Thus far discussion has focused on only one set of sent-down youths—those sent to the more advanced, prosperous places. As noted earlier, many UYs have also been sent to poor, under-developed places, both within their home provinces and in distant frontier regions, where the need for them is more clear-cut. How is this possible if local prosperity is so important? State aid is the answer. The preceding pattern assumes that the state provides no help to the communes beyond the settlement fee which it allocates in order to get the youths started in their new environment. Once it is used up, the UYs must live off the local economy. Settlement in poor places requires a more sub-stantial flow of outside funds. The state has evidently not been willing or able to supply enough funds to make it possible to settle all UYs in those places where the need for them may be greatest. When the state does allocate funds, it channels them primarily to state institutions, that is, to state farms operated by national, provincial, or county government agencies, or farms operated by the Production and Construction Corps (PCC) of the People's Liberation Army (PLA). State and army farms are expected to strive for self-sufficiency and self-reliance, but their investment funds come from the state, and if their incomes are too low to pay the fixed wages which the workers receive, the state budget makes up the difference. Hence, state and army farms have apparently been the major instrumentali-ties for the settlement of UYs in places too poor to sustain them out of local resources. The Kwangtung data presented earlier, it should be noted, pertained only to settlement on people's communes, cooperative institutions independent of the state budget. Similarly, the county comparison reflects primarily settlement on communes, since the press does not mention counties when writing about army farms and does so only infrequently in the case of state farms. Both sets of data, moreover, originate from the late 1960s or early 1970s. Since then, a policy of extending state aid to communes may have made it possible to settle more UYs on poor communes. In the last few years the practice has developed of setting up youth teams and youth farms (*ch'ing-nien tui, ch'ing-nien ch'ang*) within communes, but separate from the regular subdivisions of team and brigade, and settled on reclaimable, marginal land. These units have received various kinds of material assistance from the state. In Kiangsi, where 1,400 such youth teams have been set up, the state extended loans to them amounting to 6 million yuan in 1974 and 1975 for the purchase of chemical fertilizer, oxen, seeds, and farm tools.[128] This innovation may permit large-scale settlement of UYs on poor and remote communes, thereby enhancing their developmental relevance.

State and army farms have been set up in most provinces of China.[129] Their purposes vary from the growing of specialized crops such as fruit or sugarcane (in areas close to Canton, for example) to livestock raising and forest management. One of their main purposes has been to reclaim land. Remarkably, land can apparently be reclaimed even in places where one would assume that possibility long since to have been exhausted. Out of the 400,000 sent-down youths in the Shanghai suburbs, 150,000 serve on state farms; their achievements include having "opened up thousands of canals and ditches and reclaimed tens of thousands of mou of fine crop fields."[130] Many state and army farms, however, are located in the more remote areas. In Kwangtung, for instance, a number of state farms have been set up in the underpopulated north, while army farms have been established on Hainan, a large island suitable for the development of rubber plantations. Although the data are incomplete, it appears that state and army farms are concentrated heavily in the frontier provinces. In Heilungkiang, where efforts have been under way for many years to open up large tracts of wasteland to cultivation, 400,000 out of 1.2 million UYs were serving on army farms in 1974.[131] Another report spoke of eighty state farms with 150,000 UYs engaged in land reclamation in the northern part of the province, above the fiftieth parallel; these are probably not the only state farms in that province.[132] In Inner Mongolia, as of 1972, about 100,000 out of 180,000 UYs served on army farms, and in Sinkiang at least 100,000 out of 450,000, but probably many more have been serving on state farms.[133] In 1975 "nearly 100,000" of Yunnan's 400,000 UYs served on state farms within the province's "farmland reclamation system"; the number serving on army farms had not been published.[134]

Several factors account for the settlement of urban youths in frontier provinces. First, provinces such as Heilungkiang or Sinkiang autonomous region are underpopulated. Their needs for labor are quite clear-cut and they have in fact, long been the destinations not only of urban youth but of other migrants as well.[135] As Saifudin, first party secretary of Sinkiang, put it in 1975, aid from the interior, "particularly in terms of labor" has in the past "constituted one of the important conditions for carrying out large-scale economic construction projects. . . . It will still be necessary in the future."[136] Moreover, Inner Mongolia, Sinkiang, Yunnan, and Hainan are in part inhabited by national minorities, and increasing the Han component in their populations has implications for the national integration of China. Finally, setting up army farms in frontier provinces, particularly those bordering on the Soviet Union and Outer Mongolia, is at least in part motivated by another nondevelopmental consideration, national defense. Establishment of military colonies in Inner Asia, it is worth noting, is rooted in China's traditional practice. The army farms establish the Han-Chinese presence close to the borders as well as among the minority nationalities in Sinkiang or Inner Mongolia. The construction projects of the PCC are relevant to military needs; they include not only opening new land for cultivation but also building roads. The army farms are staffed by regular as well as demobilized soldiers, while urban youths who become "fighters" (*chan-shih*) on army farms receive some military training.[137]

PERSPECTIVES ON POLICY FORMULATION

Making policy on the transfer of urban youths to the country-side is a complex matter, because, as we have seen, the transfer is undertaken not just for one but for several reasons. The number of participants in the policy process is correspondingly large. With regard to institutional participants, a broadcast made in 1976 shows that a wide range of units is involved: "Special groups and offices have been set up from the Central Committee down to the local party committees at all levels to study and solve new problems that arise with the movement of educated youth to the countryside. Related government departments make appropriate arrangements and find over-all solutions."[138] At the national level a "Small Group to Guide Youth Going to the Agricultural Villages" was formed within the Central Committee in 1964, together with a Settlement Office, while a similar unit functioned in the State Council, in Premier Chou's office. A Red Guard article referred to both offices together as *Chung-yang an-pan* (Central Assignment), headed by T'an Chen-lin and Chou Jung-hsin, then an assistant secretary of the State Council. Central Assignment drafted a joint decision on the mobilization of urban youth to go to the countryside, apparently in 1965.[139] Such a draft decision must have been based on inputs from other agencies in party and government, including the State Planning Commission, and the Ministries of Labor, Education, Agriculture, State Farms and Land Reclamation, as well as Defense. Less is known about the structural arrangements in Peking since the Cultural Revolution. Some of the ministries have been abolished, and others, such as the Ministry of Education, were reconstituted only in 1975. At least some functions of the ministries that have disappeared have been assumed by other central units. Thus, in place of the Ministry of Labor, the State Planning Commission has a Labor Bureau, whose staff members have written on the transfer of urban youths.[140] In 1976, a broadcast referred to the State Council's "Office in Charge of Work concerning Educated Young People," which suggests that there has been institutional continuity since the period before the Cultural Revolution, and possibly continuity in personnel as well.[141]

China's political system is decentralized to a considerable degree and hence policy formulation is not a matter for Peking only. Within the framework of basic policy set in Peking, provinces undoubtedly exercise a fair degree of autonomy in the handling of the transfer, since, as noted, a large proportion of urban youths are sent to rural destinations within their home provinces.[142] Agencies and officials at the subprovincial administrative levels—in the rural areas, the prefecture, the county, and the commune with its two subdivisions of production brigade and team; in the urban areas, the city and borough, as well as the street and residential administrations—should also be included as participants in policy formulation. To be sure, their task is to implement the transfer, but the way in which the lower-level officials do so affects policy formulation, if only because higher-level policy makers may have to react to the problems that arise in the course of implementation. Finally, the masses too influence policy formulation in that their attitudes, preferences, and reactions are gauged as the policy is revised and amended. Policy makers are influenced by implicit or explicit assumptions about what is or is not acceptable to the masses, and what the masses can be brought to accept.

The interactions between individual policy makers, administrators, and their agencies that produce policy outcomes are hidden from view. Because of our ignorance, care must be exercised in attributing particular outcomes to particular influences. We do not know, for instance, whether the settlement of a proportion of the sent-down youths in fairly prosperous areas or within their home provinces reflects pressure from the public, officials' perception of the existence of popular demands, resource constraints, or administrative convenience.* Little is known about the preferences of the agencies that participate in the policy process. To be sure, the agencies in charge of administering the program have an impact on the way it is run. Thus, Red Guard critics assailed the officials of Central Assignment, as well as lower-level cadres, such as Chung Ming, the head of Canton's Assignment Office, for distorting Mao's revolutionary line on the transfer of urban youths. These officials were said to have been more concerned with solving the concrete problems of the settlement than with the ideological goals of the program.[143] But it is not possible to verify whether the officials in charge have acquired a vested interest in the program and hence exert pressure for its maintenance. This may well be the case, but, in the absence of explicit evidence, a bureaucratic politics analysis of transfer policy formulation is not really feasible.

How much support has the program commanded among China's leaders? At the top of the hierarchy, Mao Tse-tung undoubtedly gave the program strong support, since it exemplifies approaches to societal transformation and development commonly associated with his name. Specifically, Mao at times intervened in the particulars of transfer policy. Examples include his famous pronouncement of December 1968 that urban youths should be reeducated by the peasants, and his response in April 1973 to the plea of a Fukien teacher for help in coping with the hardships caused by the transfer, a response that ini-

---

*With regard to the question of popular attitudes, it is worth reiterating that the transfer is a revolutionary program that runs counter to deeply rooted popular assumptions. Hence, if the policy makers simply responded to popular feelings as they are, or as they were when the program was launched, there would have been no transfer at all. The problem for the policy makers is how to devise a policy that will reduce or even eliminate grievances but will also attain the objective sought.

tiated a substantial remedial effort (see below and chapter 4). Premier Chou En-lai also spoke out in favor of the program. During the Cultural Revolution, in early 1968, when the transfer movement had come under attack from sent-down youths, Chou En-lai vigorously defended it: "Going to the mountain areas and the countryside is an idea of Chairman Mao's, whose aim is to direct our attention to the rural areas and to the masses, to change the abnormal and uneven state of the semi-colonial economy, to effect the transition to socialism and then achieve a more balanced development.[144] Shortly after he succeeded Mao Tse-tung to the chairmanship of the party Central Committee in October 1976, Hua Kuo-feng made a public commitment to the continuation of the program.[145] Its long survival could thus be attributed to the backing it has received from China's key leaders.

Judging by the way the program has been treated in the Chinese media, however, it has been controversial indeed. According to some statements, the program has been under almost continuous challenge by those espousing the bourgeois-revisionist policy line, in opposition to Chairman Mao's proletarian-revolutionary line:

> The rustication of millions of educated youth . . . is a deep-going socialist revolution which will inevitably encounter frenzied resistance by the bourgeoisie in the party. Such resistance, exemplified by Liu Shao-ch'i's theory of going to the countryside to make a name and Lin Piao's theory of reform through forced labor in disguised form, has never ceased. . . . When the right deviationist wind to reverse verdicts was prevalent last summer [1975], Teng Hsiao-p'ing and the right deviationists were impudent enough to openly attack the great movement to rusticate educated youth and oppose this revolution.[146]

A polemic of this sort leaves many questions unanswered: Did Liu come under attack at the time he put forth a careerist approach to the transfer or was this approach denounced only after he had fallen from grace? Was Lin's likening of the transfer to labor reform a casual remark or did it signify advocacy of substantive alternatives? Did Teng advocate abolition of the program as a whole or only modification of its principles and practices? Interpretation of such polemics is complicated, moreover, by the rapid changes in the fortunes of high-level leaders. The article just quoted was part of a political campaign waged in the spring of 1976 against Teng Hsiao-p'ing. Teng, who had been purged during the Cultural Revolution, had been rehabilitated in 1973, only to fall from power once again in April 1976, after the death of Chou En-lai. His downfall was engineered by a group of leftist Politburo members. Shortly after the death of Chairman Mao in September of 1976, that group (Wang Hung-wen, Chang Ch'un-ch'iao, Chiang Ch'ing, and Yao Wen-yuan) was itself purged and vilified as the "gang of four." They were denounced as sham leftists who had actually been bourgeois conspirators. Many of their "crimes" were detailed in the press. And among these "crimes" were "sabotage" and "undermining" of the settlement of educated youths in the countryside.[147] This sequence of events would seem to suggest that issues such as the transfer are merely manipulated by contenders for power and do not play an important role in their own right.

However, a closer look at specific charges aired in connection with the purges of certain leaders suggests that some policy makers have raised real issues about the costs and benefits of the program, that there has been some ambivalence about the program and perhaps even real opposition. One such issue concerns the impact of the transfer program on the country's requirements for highly trained manpower, and it involves Teng Hsiao-p'ing. In 1976, he was charged with having "represented going up to the mountains and down to the villages as an obstacle to the four modernizations."[148] In January 1975, Chou En-lai had set before the country the task of accomplishing the "comprehensive modernization of agriculture, industry, national defense, and science and technology before the end of the century, so that our national economy will be advancing to the front ranks of the world."[149] In the opinion of some educational officials, including Chou Jung-hsin, the newly appointed minister of education, the attainment of this ambitious goal was in jeopardy because of the deficient state of training of advanced scientific and technical manpower. They criticized the low quality of the student body in the higher schools as well as the focus on the application and popular dissemination of knowledge. They argued that more attention had to be paid to research in order to make possible future technical and scientific advances not only in industry but also in agriculture.[150] Teng Hsiao-p'ing evidently supported these critical assessments, resulting in a challenge to educational policy, one designed to "reverse the verdicts" of the Cultural Revolution, as subsequent denunciations charged.

Teng Hsiao-p'ing saw in the transfer to the countryside an important reason for the poor quality of higher education. Partly because of the long interval between graduation from secondary school and entry into a higher school, China's colleges and universities were preoccupied with remedial teaching. In order to improve the quality of the students, Teng proposed modification of the principle that middle school graduates must first go into production before being allowed to enter colleges or universities. In proposing a return to the principle that the most able middle school graduates should continue their education immediately, he contravened one of the most basic changes brought about by the "revolution in education," one that has provided a major foundation for the transfer to the countryside. To his opponents, this proposal and others in the realm of education threatened basic political values. After Teng's purge, the idea of exempting an elite of the able from the transfer or its equivalent (service in a factory or the PLA) was bitterly denounced as part of a plot to restore the bourgeoisie to power.[151]

The full circumstances of the 1975–76 controversy over educational policy and the transfer have not yet become known. It is possible that Teng may have reacted against initiatives to radicalize the educational system further by extending the principles of the transfer movement to college graduates. In the summer of 1975, the press publicized the sending of university graduates to the villages as ordinary peasants, rather than as state cadres, thereby further reducing their status and raising questions about their developmental role. Teng was in fact charged with having "viciously attacked . . . college graduates becoming peasants as 'ultra-left,'" that is, as leaping ahead to practices appropriate only to the stage of full communism. [152] Whatever the circumstances, Teng and the education officials raised some fundamental questions about the negative impact of the transfer on the quality of higher education. At issue, it might be added, is not only that remedial training must be given to sent-down youths chosen for higher study in order to enable them to do college-level work but also that, as a result of the transfer system, the most talented youths may not in fact always be chosen for advanced training. These issues, it should be noted, have not been resolved by the purge of the "gang of four" and the cessation of the campaign against Teng in the fall of 1976. To be sure, the "gang" has been denounced for blatant anti-intellectualism and opposition to academic study.[153] But substantial changes in the educational and transfer systems had not, as far as one can tell, been instituted as of early 1977. Whether and how these questions will be resolved remains to be seen.

If the transfer program has been challenged because of its impact on advanced education, the question can also be raised whether it has been attacked as a way of challenging underlying developmental priorities. The transfer is a symbol of the priority given to rural development, and it can in fact be seen as part of a flow of urban resources to assist the rural sector. One wonders whether some policy makers might not see the transfer as the product of a strategy that does not maximize China's potential for rapid advance in the modern urban sector. They might reason that, if China were to accept long-term foreign loans and import Japanese and Western technology on a larger scale, the rate of growth in the modern sector could be accelerated such that it would no longer be necessary to send so many urban youths to the countryside. To such policy makers the transfer may be only an expedient necessitated by urban unemployment that would disappear were large scale industrial development accorded higher priority, and were it not constrained by the needs of the agricultural sector or by reluctance to expand foreign economic commitments. These questions have indeed been issues in Chinese politics but there is little evidence that the program has actually been attacked on these grounds.[154] Perhaps the oft-repeated claim that the program is necessary for the modernization of the rural sector is designed to rebut an argument that the young people, or at least some of them, could more fruitfully be used in the urban sector. Affirmation that the young urbanites are needed in the countryside may also, however, be directed at critics who may be questioning just how significant the rural contributions of the sent-down youths really are. As noted in the preceding section, the need for their services varies, as does the worth of their contributions, and probably there has been a good deal of debate on how to maximize their utility in the countryside. Whether the issue of their rural use has led to conflict among policy makers is not very clear, however.[155]

Another policy issue pertains to the social costs of the program. In the cities, numerous organizations must devote a great deal of time and effort each year to the task of securing compliance on the part of youths targeted for the transfer and their families. A good many families affected by the program are unhappy with it. Their anxieties may well complicate the task of mobilizing their support not only for this program but for the attainment of other goals as well. Moreover, some of the youths have illegally returned to the cities and have spawned something of a crime problem (see chapters 3 and 6). In the villages, cadres and peasants have to cope with sent-down youths who have problems adapting to rural life. Some officials in the countryside have complained that the transfer program creates an "extra burden" for them. This perception has been widespread enough to elicit comment from the journal *Red Flag*.[156] Particularly when the developmental contributions of the UYs are not all that apparent, it is not unreasonable for ruralites to see them in this light. This may be so especially when the young urbanites are "hard to control," as has indeed been the case in at least some instances (see chapter 4). It is in fact possible for the transfer to aggravate rural-urban cleavages rather than to narrow them, as is the official intent. During the Cultural Revolution, Red Guards protesting against revisionism in the program charged that policy makers and administrators had defined its purpose as ridding the cities of delinquents, failures, and bad-class elements, that is, those unable to qualify for higher school or factory work. They quoted T'an Chen-lin as having said in 1963 that "to solve the problem of employment of city youth and wipe out the sources of gangsters and juvenile delinquency and exterminate the sources of revisionism the support of construction of agricultural villages is better than employment mobilization."*[157] These definitions, so the charges went, communicated themselves to rural cadres and peasants, who resent-

---

*The Red Guard newspaper that quoted T'an failed to define the meaning of "employment mobilization." Conceivably, it refers to an alternative to the transfer, such as the provision of employment by street industries, a solution suggested by some policy makers, as noted in the first section of this chapter.

ed treatment of the countryside as a dumping ground for urban rejects, and who consequently looked down on the UYs and mistreated them.[158]

Direct evidence showing that the urban and rural social costs associated with the transfer have significantly influenced policy formulation is lacking. Still, it may have been this factor that prompted Liu Shao-ch'i, Teng Hsiao-p'ing, and P'eng Chen to advocate a partial alternative to the transfer in the form of employment for youth in street industries, as charged during the Cultural Revolution. This factor may also have led policy makers to consider whether the program should not provide for guaranteed return to the urban sector. A rotation system would eliminate much of the popular unhappiness with the program but rob it of its revolutionary significance. The rotation issue has indeed been considered by policy makers. It was not apparently until about 1964 that the national government committed itself to a permanent transfer program.[159] In Kwangtung, according to informants, youths were sent to the countryside in the early 1960s with a promise of guaranteed return after three years made by First Party Secretary T'ao Chu, a promise severely criticized as revisionist during the Cultural Revolution. In 1976, Teng Hsiao-p'ing was charged with having advocated a policy of "returning to the cities after two years in the countryside."[160] Moreover, unnamed "leading comrades" were accused of supporting this idea.[161] All these tidbits of information raise questions, not only about the extent to which policy makers have been influenced by perceptions of social costs, but also about the extent to which some policy makers have thought it possible to provide employment for the sent-down youths within the urban sector.

Sensitivity to the social costs of the program may well be rooted in skepticism about the central underlying assumption on which the program is based, namely, that it is in fact possible to reshape human motivation. Unless the policy makers share the ideological faith that this can be done, they may view the enterprise with a considerable measure of doubt. That this has been the case emerges from charges made during the Cultural Revolution. Liu Shao-ch'i is quoted as conceding that educational policy ought to be aligned with the aspirations of youth for upward mobility, and T'an Chen-lin is quoted as fundamentally doubting whether urbanites can be turned into peasants:

The existing mode of production being what it is, who is willing to be in the rural district? All want to go to the cities. One who sweeps the ground in a city can earn 30–40 yuan a month, while in the rural district one can earn no more than 200–300 yuan a year. Among those present at this meeting, who is willing to be a peasant? Even if one raises his hand expressing the wish to be a peasant, he can only do so reluctantly. This is a fundamental question.[162]

T'an believed that only after the countryside had advanced to the level of the cities, only after the disappearance of rural-urban disparities, would urbanites be willing to accept life in the countryside: "Many people are unwilling to work in rural areas and want to return to the cities. They will be ready to stay in the countryside in the future when rural construction is completed because of the clean air in rural areas and the possibility of having electric lighting, asphalt-paved roads, and foreign-style buildings."[163]

T'an's critics compared this vision to Khrushchev's promised land of goulash communism.[164] In this context, then, a revolutionary is one who believes that an urbanite can be made into a peasant; a revisionist, one who does not. It need not necessarily follow that the revisionist therefore opposes the transfer; after all, an earlier quote showed T'an as quite in favor of sending urban youths to the villages.[165] But it may have been this skepticism that has motivated some policy makers to look for partial alternatives to the program or for ways to expand opportunities to return to the urban sector.

The revolutionary optimist rejects the pessimism of the revisionist skeptic. Where the latter sees a problem, the former sees a challenge: "Shall we struggle against the . . . traditional concepts . . . or . . . submit to them?"[166] Revolutionaries value the transfer precisely because its implementation requires a long-term struggle for the new:

The great communist ideal is urging us on. Revolutionary young people must break out of the confines of bourgeois right, put down their roots in the countryside, take up farming as their lifetime career, [and] make the vast . . . socialist motherland more beautiful. . . . Many outstanding young people have done just that. . . . While they are engaged in the struggles of the day, they are thinking of the struggle for the current century and the next. They regard every step they

take as part of the effort gradually to create the conditions under which the bourgeoisie can neither exist nor rise again.[167]

More broadly, leftists may support the program not only because of its desired value-transforming impact, but also because
it can be linked to the cause of combatting embourgeoisement
in the society at large. The transfer is a radical program; it requires a radical environment in which to thrive. For example,
the more reliance is placed on material incentives and the more
wage and status differentials are allowed to widen in the urban
sector, the more acutely may sent-down youths resent the gap
between themselves and those who have made it in the cities.
Conversely, further restrictions of "bourgeois right" may reduce
the gap and hence raise the acceptability of the transfer. Similarly, the more the status of university graduates is raised, the
greater the gap between them and the middle school graduates
serving as peasants in the villages. Indeed, it has been suggested
that one purpose of the 1975 campaign to send college graduates to the countryside as ordinary peasants was to "reduce the
distance" between the two groups.[168] Additional equalizing
measures can thus be justified on the grounds that such a program makes them necessary. Perhaps this line of reasoning is
persuasive to some of those who support the program on developmental grounds, leading them to support leftist policies.

   In the months since the fall of the "gang of four," the ideological goals of the program have been reaffirmed. Sending
urban youths to the countryside has continued to be regarded
as of "far-reaching historic significance" for the narrowing of
the "three great differences" (between town and country,
worker and peasant, manual and mental labor), as well as for
the restriction of bourgeois rights and the consolidation of the
dictatorship of the proletariat.[169] This continuity may indicate
that the leaders now in charge believe strongly in the vision of
an egalitarian society and a new man. This may be the case,
though their ideological commitments are likely to be linked
closely to the belief that the program continues to be necessary
on developmental grounds. These leaders probably regard invo-
cation of ideological values as essential in order to keep the
program going. Mobilization of ideological values serves to
legitimate the program and is a form of pressure on critics or
opponents. The purge of the leading leftists may well have
given encouragement to officials skeptical about the transfer,

just as it probably raised expectations among Chinese at large that the transfer policy might now be ended. Reinvocation of the major ideological symbols serves notice to the country that opposition to the policy will not be tolerated. As the first party secretary of Kiangsi province, Chiang Wei-ching, put it at a rally of sent-down youths held in January 1977: "Following the wise leader Chairman Hua by persisting in settling educated young people in the countryside . . . means adherence to Chairman Mao's proletarian revolutionary line. Whoever hesitates about it hesitates about Chairman Mao's revolutionary line. Whoever lacks confidence in it lacks confidence in Chairman Mao's revolutionary line. Whoever opposes it opposes Chairman Mao's revolutionary line."[170]

If it is true that ideological pressures play an important role in sustaining the transfer, it can be asked whether such pressures have influenced the management of the program. In Chinese practice, reliance on normative power has often been accompanied by strong opposition to reliance on personal or material interests, since appeals to self-interest detract from the goal of building a selfless new man. And indeed, during the Cultural Revolution, policy makers and administrators were vehemently criticized for appealing to individual interests in order to raise acceptance of the transfer. Liu Shao-ch'i in particular was denounced for holding out to youth opportunities for further schooling and for advancement:

If junior middle school graduates are always asked to go to the countryside to be peasants, they would be unwilling to go. If, after arriving . . . they can go to school, say, the part-work, part-study or part-farming, part-study schools, they may be willing to go.[171]

After tilling land for three to five years . . . and after acquiring three qualifications, you may become a hsien [county] cadre and then a cadre at the provincial level and by then you may go to the Central Committee.[172]

Similarly, instead of taking seriously Chairman Mao's goal of integration of intellectuals and creating "the most favorable conditions for the fulfillment of the ideal of communism," the bureaucrats of Central Assignment were condemned for concerning themselves with such prosaic matters as equal pay for equal work, private plots for UYs, exemption from taxes, provision for housing, and the question of marriage.[173]

Ideological intolerance toward material incentives creates difficulties for the program, since effective implementation requires dealing with people as they are and not only as they might be. After the Cultural Revolution, individual incentives were deemphasized, and it proved impossible to rely mainly on political education in coping with problems of individual motivation. Hence, in the 1970s, renewed stress was laid on the material conditions of the transfer, one article in 1973 declaring that "the young people must first enjoy peace physically before they can have peace of mind."[174] In that year, a remedial campaign sought to correct deficiencies in the program with measures strikingly similar to those adopted by Central Assignment and denounced as revisionist during the Cultural Revolution (for details, see chapter 4).

This time, however, despite the continued affirmation of fundamentalist principles, such policies did not come under public attack, and it is in fact remarkable that since then many statements reasserting the revolutionary goals of the program have also referred to the necessity of coping with concrete material problems encountered by urban youths.[175] The source of this tolerant spirit was Chairman Mao himself. As mentioned earlier, in October 1972, a primary school teacher in Fukien sent him a letter in which he described the plight of his son, who had settled in a village in that province, but who was unable to make a living. His father consequently had to support him. Fearing what would happen to the son after his death, he appealed to the chairman for help. In April 1973, Mao responded with a gift of 300 yuan and a promise that something would be done about the situation, since there were many similar cases.[176] It can be assumed that it was Mao who set the wheels in motion to improve settlement conditions. A national conference held on this topic was convened in 1973 by none other than Hua Kuo-feng.[177]

The policy of sending urban youths "up to the mountains and down to the countryside" has thus been presented to the Chinese people as one that is inseparable from the country's goal of building a new, socialist society, but also as one that is implemented in a flexible and pragmatic way. This image of ideological fundamentalism combined with a problem-solving approach is best conveyed by a quote from an article commemorating the first anniversary of Chou En-lai's death:

> Premier Chou regarded educated youths going to settle in the countryside as a strategic measure for training worthy successors to the proletarian revolutionary cause, building socialist new villages and narrowing the three major differences . . . and he gave meticulous care to the young people. He personally called various discussion meetings among educated youths, listened to their opinions, helped solve their difficulties and showed great concern for their development.[178]

Whether China's leaders have in fact been able to make the program work satisfactorily is a question that can be answered only by a detailed examination of the workings of the program.

3 MOBILIZING URBAN YOUTH TO GO TO THE COUNTRYSIDE

The next four chapters of this study deal with various aspects of the transfer at the local level. In this chapter, the focus of attention is on mobilization processes within cities, the purpose of which is to secure the compliance of youth with the demand that they "go up to the mountains and down to the villages." This entails first some discussion of the appeals and pressures that are brought to bear in the course of mobilization campaigns. Next, on the hypothesis that compliance will be much greater if the values embodied by the transfer program are shared by urban inhabitants, an effort will be made to assess what is known about attitudes of urbanites toward the program. Because of evidence that the transfer continues to provoke a conflict of preferences and interests, I will also try to assess the degree to which it is possible for those affected by the program to influence the decisions associated with the transfer. This possibility arises because of variation in the volume of the transfer. While there are cases of entire graduating middle school classes going to the countryside, thereby eliminating choice, the more common pattern is that only a proportion of the graduating class is assigned to rural service. Choice also exists with regard to rural destinations.

ORGANIZATIONS, APPEALS, AND PRESSURES

Sending urban youths "to the countryside is a long, arduous task."[1] It is regarded as so important that it cannot simply be handled by specialized administrative agencies, such as the city assignment offices or the bureaus of labor or education. It is a task which the key leaders of the city must take charge of, or, as a statement from Kwangtung put it, "at present, party organizations at all levels must strengthen leadership and continue to push ahead the vigorous mass campaign of settling educated young people in the countryside. It is necessary to put rustication work in an important place on the agenda of CCP (Chinese Communist Party) committees. The number one and two men must take up this work personally and grasp typical examples well. The cadres in charge must concentrate their time and energy on this work."[2] Mobilization entails activation of the urban political and administrative infrastructure, with particular emphasis on those organizations in which officials and inhabitants regularly interact. Aside from the mass organizations, the trade unions, women's federations, and the Young Communist League (YCL), the three most important organizational units in transfer mobilization are the schools, the neighborhood or street offices of the government together with the residents' committees, and the places of employment of the parents:

> All localities should . . . bring into full play the enthusiasm of schools, neighborhoods and units in which parents are working. Schools, neighborhoods and parents should maintain close ties and coordination. Schools should be responsible for educating students to firmly take the road of integrating with workers and peasants and mobilize them to voluntarily register for settlement in the countryside. Neighborhoods and units in which parents are working should see to it that the work on the part of the parents is well done.[3]

Since the Cultural Revolution, as the middle schools in the cities have come closer to enrolling all of the appropriate age group, the schools have been at the center of the mobilization process. It is in the school that each graduating middle school student is assigned to a production unit, either industrial or agricultural, or to the People's Liberation Army (PLA). Before the Cultural Revolution, when "social youths" who had left school but had not found urban employment were a major target of the transfer, the street organizations played a more direct role in making job assignments. Since then, their role in mobilizing youths to go to the countryside has continued to be important. The residential units have access to the families within their jurisdictions and they maintain contact with the youths after they have left school and before they actually leave for the villages. Because of the reduction in length of schooling, some young people graduate from middle school at age fifteen or even earlier. They apparently are permitted to live at home until their sixteenth birthday. In the case of older youths, a hiatus of several months, typically from July to October, elapses between graduation and departure. The residential organizations are charged with involving youths in preparatory activities for the transfer during this interim period, and with seeing to it that they show up at the appointed departure time. Parents' work units have been regarded as of primary importance in the mobilization process, in recognition of the crucial role that parental attitudes play in securing compliance with the program.

As the mobilization campaign gets under way, intensive efforts are made to convince the youths and their families of the virtues of the transfer, and to create a social climate of supportive enthusiasm for this cause. The media devote much attention to the transfer, the "advanced deeds" of model UYs are studied especially in the schools, publicity is given to the applications of early volunteers for the transfer, and, particularly in recent years, to instances in which high-ranking cadres are sending their own children to the countryside.[4] Parades, rallies, and mass meetings are held. City leaders who address these meetings stress the ideological importance of the transfer, relating it to other campaigns currently in progress, as in 1974 to the movement to criticize Lin Piao and Confucius. Meetings may be addressed by peasant cadres from suburban communes who report on their experiences in reeducating UYs, by sent-down urban youths who are visiting their home town to report on their rural life, or by members of an urban "comfort team" (wei-wen t'uan) of parents and cadres who have visited UY settlements in distant parts of the country and who report on their accomplishments.[5] These types of reports permit the depiction of the transfer in fairly concrete and realistic terms relevant to the audience, but within a setting of approval and support for the transfer. Meetings are followed by intensive study and discussion within the three crucial units—school, residential organization, and work place—with the focus on youths and families targeted for the transfer.

The propaganda on behalf of "going up to the mountains and down to the countryside" consists of formal appeals communicated through the media, at meetings, mass demonstrations, and other public gatherings, as well as informal appeals communicated when mobilization becomes a matter of small group meetings or face-to-face contact. Formal appeals tend to consist of revolutionary-ideological and patriotic appeals to support national construction. In the first case, youths are called upon to be worthy revolutionary successors who wage a struggle for the right ideals and against the wrong ones, who repudiate the exploiter class's ideals of chasing after fame, wealth, promotion, and status, and who see their personal futures not in terms of a comfortable career but in terms of helping to realize the great goals of the revolution: "Revolutionary young people who have aspirations should be farsighted. They should keep the great objective of communism in view [and] see their personal future closely in light of the future of the state and the destiny of mankind. They have a future beyond comparison."[6] The patriotic appeal to take part in national construction often is linked to the need to build up the frontier provinces as well as the remote, mountainous, underdeveloped regions of the deep interior. Youths should go to those places where the motherland needs them most. Such appeals play on the old theme of national "wealth and power" (*fu-ch'iang*): "We must help all our young people to understand that ours is still a very poor country, that we cannot change this situation radically in a short time, and that only through the united efforts of our younger generation and all our people, working with their own hands, can China be made strong and prosperous within a period of several decades".[7] The two appeals are often mixed. Youths are told that they should "look far into the future, shoulder heavy responsibilities, be ready to pay a certain price, and be ready to work hard for a long time in order to change the poor and blank state of our motherland and to eliminate the system of exploitation of man by man."[8]

Both types of appeal call for sacrifice and for willingness to bear hardship and privation. The revolutionary-ideological appeal, however, tends to emphasize withstanding of hardship as a positive value in itself. What counts is having the right attitude of "fearing neither hardship nor death." The appeal to take part in construction, in contrast, especially when linked to the theme of rural modernization, contains a promise of personal benefit. In the early 1960s, the promise was quite explicit; going to the village to contribute one's scientific and general knowledge was the "revolutionary and glorious path to position and fame."[9] After the Cultural Revolution the self-denying

theme of bearing hardship for reasons of revolutionary purity
dominated, but in the 1970s, as the theme of youth "making
still greater contributions to rural modernization"[10] gained in
prominence, an implicit promise of recruitment and gains in
status went with it:

> Han Chih-kang . . . was an educated youth who came from
> the city. After working arduously for more than ten years, he
> and the poor and lower-middle peasants succeeded in building
> the poverty-stricken and back-ward Peima brigade into a pros-
> perous socialist new village. . . . Later he was posted as deputy
> secretary of the CCP Hsing-p'ing Hsien Committee and worked
> with more remarkable results. In May of this year [1973] he
> was . . . selected to be secretary of the YCL Shensi Provincial
> Committee.[11]

Informal persuasion may simply reinforce the formal messages,
but it may also go much further in appealing directly to individual interest. Before the Cultural Revolution, mobilizers,
sometimes including state farm cadres visiting Canton to hire
unemployed youths, would paint attractive pictures of life in
the countryside and of the opportunities open to young settlers,
especially in distant places such as Hainan.[12] According to informants, this was credible to youths whose only rural experience had been helping to harvest crops in prosperous suburban
communes during summer vacations. After the Cultural Revolution, however, such informal appeals were generally not made.
The reason, informants say, is that during the Cultural Revolution the difficult conditions under which UYs lived on state
farms and in communes had been extensively publicized, thus
depriving this appeal of credibility. Thus, post–Cultural Revolution informal communications coincided with formal messages,
which stressed the virtues of withstanding hardship.

Appeals to personal advantage are not necessarily made on the
initiative of a low-level cadre or teacher but may also reflect
formal but unpublished directives or lower-level personnel's perceptions of the intent of higher-level officials. The material incentives, including promises of quick promotion, which T'an
Chen-lin, Central Assignment, and some provincial party committees offered to the UYs, according to Cultural Revolution charges, may have been communicated in this manner.[13]
Certainly, little mention of such incentives was made in the
press, though relevant directives could have been published in

the local press, of which only a fraction is available to the outside world.

The question of return to the city highlights the relationship between formal and informal appeals. In formal communications, the youths and their families are told that the transfer is for life. The ideological quest for spiritual transformation demands that urban youths do not go to the countryside with the attitude of time servers:

> Each educated youth must decide whether to strike true or false roots in the village. When educated youths go to the village, they must establish an attitude of persisting in the village for life, becoming revolutionaries with an iron resolve to serve the peasants (*t'ieh-hsin wu-nung ti ke-ming che*). They must decide that they will not just hurriedly pass through the village. To go down to the countryside for three years is rather easy; what is hard is to strike roots for life.[14]

The ideological goal means that it is wholly illegitimate for mobilizers to play upon the return theme in order to secure compliance. Yet, in fact, return possibilities have been informally communicated to the youths and their families. This has not necessarily violated transfer policy, which has usually been more flexible than is suggested by the "for life" theme. As noted in chapter 2, until about 1964, youths in Kwangtung were guaranteed the right to return, their household registrations being retained in the cities (*hu-k'ou pao-liu cheng*), a practice that may have been in conformity with national policy. As far as is known, reassignment of sent-down youths to the urban sector did not take place in the two-odd years before the Cultural Revolution and in the two years after that event. Even then, however, the "for life" theme was played down or tacitly contradicted in informal communications. In one pre–Cultural Revolution instance, an informant was told by a teacher that he would be able to take the university entrance examinations in his second year in the village, though in fact his production team did not permit it. In 1968, informants with good class backgrounds and good political records were given to understand that their stays in the countryside would not necessarily be permanent. Since about 1970, a minority of the sent-down youths has been permitted to return. Administrative directives that specify rules of eligibility such as good conduct exist, but, in contrast to the early 1960s, no promises and no guarantees of return have been given. These directives have been made known to urbanites through China's internal communications system, that is, through announcements conveyed to the masses orally or in writing but not published in the press.[15] Reassignment possibilities have also been communicated to students by their teachers.[16] The press, even though it never mentions return in connection with urban mobilization, has carried articles dealing with reassignment of youths already in the countryside (see chapter 6). Youths and their families are thus made aware in various ways that the formally propagated "for life" principle does not necessarily correspond to reality. Unquestionably, this awareness facilitates transfer mobilization, since the major objection to the program is the principle of lifelong settlement. The resulting gap between rhetoric and reality must not, however, be exaggerated. For most, the "for life" theme is a realistic description of the transfer, since only a minority of sent-down youths has apparently been reassigned. Belief that the transfer is temporary makes it easier to secure compliance, but disappointment of that belief may cause long-term problems in the rural areas. Hence, the theme of permanent resettlement cannot be abandoned.

Some urban youths sign up for the transfer on the basis of the appeals alone. Among them are those who are thoroughly committed to the cause and who genuinely and wholeheartedly believe in the revolutionary and patriotic construction appeals. Informants agree that in their schools a number of youths did volunteer to go to the countryside out of essentially pure political commitments. Such youths left the city with their minds at ease (an-hsin). But informants estimate that the proportion of such youths does not run above 15 percent. In addition, however, youths may volunteer for other reasons, such as the desire to be independent of their parents, the excitement and sense of adventure that accompanies the prospect of travel to distant parts, the desire to remain a member of their school group, or awareness of the concrete advantages that accrue from volunteering. With regard to the last, the fact of having been an early volunteer is apparently noted on the youths' dossiers and hence may influence future opportunities, such as recruitment to some position within the village or eventual return to the urban sector. Also, volunteers may choose among the destinations to which their school sends its students. Among these factors, judging by informants' reports, volunteering for the purpose of securing an advantageous settlement place is quite frequent; it reflects the perception that the transfer is inevitable and thus one ought to obtain the best possible deal. In some cases, motivations may be mixed. Two of my informants had been active Red Guards strongly imbued with Maoist values. They volunteered in 1968, believing it to be the duty of intellectuals to integrate with the peasants. One of them spurned an opportunity to remain in Canton as a political instructor in his middle school. Both, however, say that they did not take the "for life" theme very seriously in 1968. When it turned out to be true in their cases, they escaped to Hong Kong.

Most of my informants stressed that they and a majority of their classmates were reluctant to go to the village, essentially for three reasons: the material attractiveness of urban life and work, reluctance to be separated from their families, and the feeling that they could serve their country more effectively by studying in a university or working in a factory than by becoming peasants, thereby wasting their education. These attitudes are by no means confined to refugee informants, since the press has also confirmed their existence. For instance, in the case of the last-mentioned of these attitudes, Yang Hsing-wu, a student in Tan-tung, Liaoning, reportedly " 'thought that since he would have to go to the countryside anyway, there was no point in studying.' Consequently he did not do well in class." In this as in other press cases, political education reportedly led to a change in attitude.[17]

Appeals by themselves do not suffice to secure enough volunteers for the transfer to the countryside. Candidates for the transfer and their families must also be subjected to pressures. As noted earlier, the three organizations of work unit, school, and residential unit provide opportunities for "penetrating education." In the schools, the authority of teachers and YCL cadres can be utilized, as can pressures from the peer group, to which teenagers are likely to be highly susceptible. Members of the residence committee can drop in for a friendly chat or a "heart-to-heart" talk, such visits recurring daily until compliance is achieved. The family members can be asked to take part in a study class (*hsüeh-hsi pan*) in which appropriate thoughts of Chairman Mao are discussed.[18] Factory party and trade union organizations may set up a special *shang-shan hsia-hsiang* office that organizes small groups of family heads (*chia-chang hsiao-tsu*) and launches an intrafactory campaign on behalf of the transfer (in one Shanghai plant, 135 such groups were set up between 1973 and 1975).[19] These activities sometimes take place in an atmosphere of intolerance toward deviants. Mass vigilance toward enemy sabotage may be raised and "revolutionary mass criticism" aimed at "erroneous" ideas about the movement to the countryside. Transfer mobilization may include the dealing of "blows to a handful of class enemies and new bourgeois elements who had vainly tried to undermine and obstruct the task of settling the educated young people in the rural areas."[20] The pressures are intensified when transfer mobilization is coordinated with other campaigns, such as the movement in 1968–69 to purify class ranks, in which case compliance with the transfer was at least implicitly a criterion of whether or not one had drawn a line between oneself and the class enemy.[21]

In such a campaign, the line between pressures of a psychological sort and administrative coercion may be thin or blurred. Thus, although it is not legitimate from the regime's point of view, parents may be threatened directly if their children do not comply. Kwangtung's T'ao Chu was criticized during the Cultural Revolution for having voiced such threats as "If your sons and daughters do not apply for agricultural support, your jobs will be in danger," and "If your children do not engage in agriculture, all political consequences are your responsibility."[22] Several informants reported that their compliance in fact was motivated by fear for their parents' job security. In the cases reported by the informants, threats to dismiss parents were not carried out (although in one instance, as long as the informant evaded the transfer, his parents were not allowed to work but instead had to participate in a study class without pay). But such threats were effective particularly in cases of bad-class families. It is worth noting that in these cases compliance with the transfer took place because of the strength of family ties, as youths agreed to go to the countryside to spare the family difficulty.

From the point of view of the targets of mobilization, differentiating between pressures and coercion is not the pointless semantic exercise it may seem. Several informants differentiated between the two. They thought that mobilization accompanied by careful explanations, study, and friendly persuasion served to make the transfer more acceptable than mobilization that consisted merely of an order to leave the city or of summary transfer of a youth's household registration to a commune. Early in the Cultural Revolution, in September 1966, a case of forcible mobilization occurred, when a large number of bad-class youths were in effect deported to the countryside without accompanying persuasion and education. This case was viewed as illegitimate and improper: a real effort should have been made to elicit a positive response among the youths.

The appeals and pressures generated during the mobilization campaign lead to the compliance of a majority of those slated for the transfer. Compliance, however, is not universal, as even press data show. In Hofei, Anhwei province, for instance, 15,000 UYs were sent to the countryside in the period from late 1968 to the spring of 1969; this was 90 percent of those who should have gone. By contrast, in the first half of 1973, when 4,000 youths were sent, the compliance rate had been raised to 97 percent.[23] Similarly, 1,444 youths of family members working in a Tientsin factory were slated to go to the countryside between 1968 and early 1973. The compliance rate was 97 percent.[24] In the spring of 1974, a Kirin conference on UY mobilization noted that "it is also necessary to do a good job in the mobilization of the graduates of previous years who should have gone to the countryside but still have not done so," while a broadcast one year later reported the departure of 6,000 youths from Changchun who had "graduated in 1974 or earlier."[25] If the 3 percent evasion rate is typical, it would mean that as many as 360,000 youths—3 percent of twelve million— have at one time or another succeeded in evading the transfer, at least temporarily.[26] In addition, a good many urban youths have illegally returned to cities and towns. Together, the two groups constitute a considerable social problem for the authorities (see chapter 6).

How can youths evade the transfer? One way is to remain illegally in the cities as hei-jen, "black persons," without household registrations. Such individuals cannot obtain ration cards for staples such as rice and they lack regular employment. Some manage to live off friends and relatives for long periods of time. Others sustain themselves by engaging in petty crime or in black market activities. Still others, however, succeed in staying not in situations of complete illegality but more or less with the tolerance of the neighborhood organizations. In principle, the residents' committees should cooperate closely with the schools in seeing to it that youths assigned to the countryside actually leave. In practice, however, as several informants reported, particular street organizations may not be very strict in pursuing youths who have failed to leave on the appointed date, and more generally in enforcing population controls. One informant spent three years in Canton after having failed to comply. In his case, not only did the street organizations take a relaxed attitude, but so did his mother's work unit. (He finally left, he says, in order to be able to escape to Hong Kong.) The strictness of the street organization varies with campaigns. When a recruitment campaign is in progress, evasion is much more difficult, but, once its peak has passed, a youth who has succeeded in sitting out the campaign, by getting "sick," for example, may then be tolerated by the street cadres.* Several informants reported that they succeeded in delaying their transfer by a year or more, using pretexts such as illness in the family, or, in one case, simply telling the street cadres that it was "not convenient" (pu fang-pien) to leave at the time. One informant knew of a youth who failed to respond to the mobilization effort and in the end was permitted to stay permanently. Pressure and persuasion not having produced results, the street administration gave up, considered the case to be closed (suan-le), and assigned the youth to a job in a local service station (fu-wu chan), that is, a cooperative whose employees get paid less than those in state-owned enterprises and are not entitled to state social security benefits. The informant concluded that, since force was not considered the proper way to secure compliance, the street organizations had no choice except to allow him to stay. Of course, the informant added, this person's recalcitrance would become part of his record and it is unlikely that he would ever obtain a better-paying job in a state-owned factory or become a cadre.

These examples of evasion suggest that the urban neighborhood units have been a weak link in transfer mobilization. Efforts have been made to upgrade the quality of their work among the young people and their relatives. But even when a street or-

---

*One informant who lived in Shanghai reports that household checks were made when important visitors came, such as a foreign head of state, but that normally neighborhood committees did not make household checks very thoroughly.

ganization makes special efforts to persuade youths to leave, the results may be paltry. In 1975, for instance, the party branch of a Canton residential area set up a political school to educate the "130 or so educated young people living in this district," presumably transfer evaders or illegal returnees. Study was tailored "to the fact that some young people did not understand well the great significance of the settlement of educated young people in the countryside." The instructors also held "heart-to-heart talks" with them and their parents. In two months, out of the 130 youths, "seven educated young people" went "spontaneously . . . to the countryside to make revolution."[27]

One response to the weaknesses of the neighborhood organizations has been to experiment with increasing the role of industrial enterprises in the transfer. In 1973, some enterprises were assigned responsibility for seeing to it that the offspring of their workers who were assigned to the countryside actually went, thereby reducing the role of the neighborhood units.[28] Another response has been to organize urban militias. One of their key tasks has been to strengthen the residential units. In Harbin in 1975, for instance, one-third of the militia groups were on mobile patrol assignment; two-thirds functioned as the "backbone" of neighborhood committees. Militia members attached to the street organizations spent a lot of time working with young people, organizing after-school activities of a political and recreational nature. In Harbin neighborhoods, they reportedly brought about a "drastic change" in the social climate, by leading young people to repudiate "feudal, capitalist, and revisionist trash."[29] Most descriptions of the militia's activities have not specifically mentioned the transfer program but instead suggest that the militia has been designed to create a social milieu favorable to the program's implementation. The militia's task of "dealing blows to lawbreakers" and safeguarding social security may be deemed a response to social misbehavior caused in part by the transfer, in the sense that evaders or illegal returnees may have to turn to crime to get along, but also in the sense that the prospect of being sent to the countryside may have increased the rate of youthful misbehavior in general.[30]

Formation of urban militias, it is worth adding, has been attributed to the four radical leaders who were purged following the death of Chairman Mao in September 1976. Allegedly, the "gang of four" regarded the militias, a paramilitary force, as a potential counterweight to the regular military, the PLA.[31] This may well have been the intent of the "gang." But the case for widespread organization of urban militias must have rested on evidence of social disorder, at least part of which has been caused by the transfer program.

Evasion of the transfer suggests that some urban youths are willing to defy the system and that in their case the normal incentives and sanctions of the mobilization process are not enough to elicit compliance. Most youths, however, comply, not with great enthusiasm, but essentially because they calculate that it is better to stay within the opportunities and constraints offered by the system. As one of the informants put it, "it is a special characteristic of the Chinese people that most would go along with a policy such as the transfer (*sui ta-liu*)." But at one extreme a few enthusiastically support the policy while at the other a few obstinately resist it.

THE CONFLICT OF VALUES

The fundamental reason why mobilization is an arduous undertaking is that the goals of the transfer conflict with the preferences of many urban inhabitants, who continue to attach high value to more orthodox definitions of individual success than becoming a peasant. This was so certainly before the Cultural Revolution but evidence is available that suggests the persistence of the same value conflict since. Before the Cultural Revolution, ideas in conflict with those of the transfer were articulated quite openly in urban society, not only within the family, but among neighbors and friends as well: "When some young intellectuals want to go to the rural and mountain areas, their neighbors, relatives, and friends will make fun of them, ridicule them, and even obstruct them, saying: 'You have studied all these years in vain,' and 'It is a pity that young girls go to till land.'"[32] A similar point is made in the following quotation from a letter to the editor of *Chung-kuo Ch'ing-nien Pao* by a girl who had not passed the entrance examinations for higher school:

> Now I am on life's crossroads, not knowing whither I shall go. Even though the party gives young intellectuals definite direction—to the rural areas—and there are model young intellectuals as Hsing Yen-tzu, Wang P'ei-chen, Tung Chia-keng and Hou

Chun . . . I still have many practical problems to solve before deciding to follow this road.

My father is in Nanking. My mother is a store clerk and my elder brother a college student. My mother hopes that I can find a light job in Nanking and marry a good high-ranking intellectual, at least a college student. My brother introduced me to a college teaching assistant. Many relatives often praised my mother for raising her children so well and intentionally made such comments in front of her, 'Don't let this bright pearl of yours drop into a heap of ashes.' The people in our neighborhood are very snobbish. When well-to-do people called on us, they showed great admiration and flattered my mother saying, 'Your daughter need not worry about marrying a talented and wealthy husband.'

This girl went on to say that a classmate had encouraged her to go to the village, but "if I insist on going . . . it may arouse my mother's disapproval and my brother's anger"; she asked the editor's advice on what to do.[33] In another case, when a politically active parent, a primary school teacher, encouraged his child to go, he came under pressure from relatives and friends who said that he was "hardhearted" and did not love his own child. The remarks caused the teacher to waver in his convictions, though only temporarily.[34] As one newspaper story pointed out in 1962, since "most parents cherish the ambition to see their children rising in position and fame,"[35] they pressure them to work hard in order to pass the college entrance examinations; "if [they] fail . . . [they] will have to undertake the hard work in the country."[36] Because "one who is successful in college entrance examinations will become a dragon and one who fails . . . will become a worm," parents have exerted "public pressure" on school administrators to emphasize preparation for the entrance tests.[37] Teachers who agreed with these priorities sometimes discouraged bright students from volunteering for the transfer, encouraging them instead to compete for admission to higher schools.[38] The boldness with which even teachers articulated old values may have been strengthened by a certain ambivalence and tentativeness displayed in the media about the new values in the early 1960s, though far less so by 1965 or 1966. Thus, as late as early 1964, *Chung-kuo Ch'ing-nien Pao* (China Youth Daily), carried a lengthy debate between proponents and opponents of the transfer. Opponents were able to state their case, namely, that going meant a waste of talent and of education and hence was not in the country's interest, under headings such as "going to a higher school promises a greater future than doing farm labor," or, "it is a waste for bright students to be sent to the farm."*[39]

With the approach of the Cultural Revolution, and especially after it, hesitant affirmation of the new values gave way to wholehearted and uncompromising commitment in the media. Transfer mobilization, moreover, has become much more thorough and intensive, and as such much more centrally a part of urban life. Hence, reinforcement of the old values from those in positions of authority has been less prevalent than it was before the Cultural Revolution. Yet, despite these changes, the degree to which occupants of official roles have been behaving in accord with the new prescriptions must not be exaggerated. Earlier it was noted that the urban street organizations are not necessarily airtight agencies of control. Perhaps the reason for this is that street cadres also share an underlying skepticism about the new values, so that when pressure from above is relaxed they become more receptive to pressures from below and hence less zealous in enforcing the transfer.

In the case of the schools, teachers and school administrators have undoubtedly been giving more thorough backing to the transfer than was the case before the Cultural Revolution. But when the political situation permits it, some teachers revert to articulation of old values, demonstrating that they have not as yet accepted the redefinition of their professional role implied by the revolution in education and the transfer system. In the first half of 1973, educational policy shifted for the first time since the Cultural Revolution in favor of tightening academic standards. Applicants to higher schools had to pass entrance examinations reminiscent of those administered before 1966. This change, which came under attack in the fall of 1973 during the campaign to criticize Lin Piao and Confucius, pleased middle school teachers in No. 6 Middle School in Tan-tung, Liaoning. "Some of them said elatedly: 'If it goes like that, teaching will then be meaningful,'" whereupon they set aside time for lessons to enable sent-down youths to prepare for the tests.[40] In the

---

*Inadequately intensive mobilization by the Youth League for such causes as the transfer probably was one reason for the de facto dissolution of the YCL during the Cultural Revolution.

town of Chi-hsi, Heilungkiang, a teacher took advantage of the new situation and openly voiced antitransfer sentiments, as the following exchange shows:

> Some time ago, my classmates wrote criticism articles in which they expressed a determination to go to the countryside after graduation in order to repudiate with concrete deeds Confucius' fallacy "only inferior men do farming." The teacher in charge said to us at a class meeting: "All of you have said that you are going to the countryside after graduation. Now, has anyone made a firm promise to do so? If so, stand up and let us see." I felt this was a challenge to the younger generation and stood up to announce resolutely: "I promise that I will go to the countryside after graduation." He said: "Yours is not a good case. Your home is in the suburbs. You are on grain ration in the countryside. You simply have to go back even though you are not willing." I asked him: "Are you citing such a case to prove that nobody is taking the brilliant road indicated by Chairman Mao?" He said flamboyantly: "Such is the case—we cannot but admit it." Not only did he in theory oppose educated youths going to the countryside but he even warmly encouraged those students who wanted to leave the school to look for jobs.[41]

Furthermore, schools have been known to offer the children of high-ranking cadres urban assignments, in implicit recognition of their true preferences.[42] In one such case, a cadre's son, himself a good Maoist, rejected an offer of factory employment. The article quotes "some people" as calling him "stupid" for having made his decision.[43] The press, in fact, quite frequently refers to "some people" as expressing opinions that run counter to the official norms. Typically, a cadre may be advised by "some people" to take steps so that his offspring can stay in the urban locality or at least go to a favorable destination.[44] These instances suggest that ihtensified transfer mobilization may have succeeded in reducing the amount of antitransfer articulation that goes on within institutions as well as in society at large, but that a good deal of communication at variance with the official message still takes place.[45]

Evidence supplied by the press suggests that reluctance to abide by the transfer system continues to be found in many urban families, even after the intensive efforts to change popu-

lar values during and after the Cultural Revolution. An article
written in 1971 by members of Shanghai's "Up-to-the-Moun-
tains-Down-to-the-Countryside Office," for instance, grouped
the heads of families of that city into two kinds: in the first
group were those parents who thought of the transfer as an external demand coming from party and government (*yao wo
sung*); in the second were those who themselves wanted to send
their children to the countryside (*wo yao sung*). Those in the
first group regarded their offspring as their "personal property,"
not the "people's property." They proceeded from their personal interests, hoping to keep the children by their side, or, if
that proved impossible, to have them sent to a nearby village, or
at least to a place with good conditions. Such parents were passive toward the transfer movement; they were individualistic
and "slighted agriculture and emphasized industry." Parents in
the second group thought of their children as having been raised
by the party and by Chairman Mao to be revolutionary successors, and they felt that not sending the children would be a
form of disloyalty to the chairman. Hence, they took a leading
role (*tai-t'ou*) in the transfer. While the authors of the article
did not estimate the size of each group they implied that the
first group was not small.[46]

Parents express two sets of concerns. One is about the difficulties the transfer may cause both for the youth who is sent to
the countryside and for the family members left behind. The
press quotes parents as worrying about the hardships their children will encounter, especially when they are sent at a young
age, sixteen or seventeen, when they are female, and when they
are sent to places bereft of the buffering comforts of particularistic ties. As one Peking father said: "I have never been in
Inner Mongolia before. It is far, far away. We have neither a
kinsman nor a friend there. The child will find it unbearable
especially when he gets sick. Many students are staying. Let us
see about it and talk about it later."[47] Belief that life in the
rural areas is "bitter" may be deeply rooted. In 1975, the deputy party secretary of a Canton factory wrote in the *People's
Daily* that he had not wanted to send his children to the village
because of the hardships, which he remembered, having himself
migrated to Canton only after liberation. The media had evidently been unable to convince him that rural life had improved
since 1949, for it was not until he himself spent a year in a com-

mune that he became convinced that, while rural life was still harder than urban life, substantial improvements had taken place.[48] For the families left behind, the departure of the young may upset the family division of labor and create difficulties in the care of sick or aging family members, a frequently mentioned issue.[49] Faced with such concrete problems, not all parents have as yet revised the old proverb of *yang erh fang lao*, "raising children to guard against old age," to read *yang erh fang hsiu*, "raising children to guard against revisionism."[50]

The second set of parental concerns is about the status and career implications of the transfer. Some parents fear that their offspring have few or no prospects for advancement in the countryside.[51] Or, even if they do see such possibilities, they perceive the transfer as a form of downward mobility and cavil at the thought of their children starting out again at the bottom: "It would be 'a great pity' to send Yung-hung, the first middle school graduate in the family for generations, to the countryside."[52] The perception that the transfer is a form of downward mobility is prompted not only by noncommunist values but also by the official status hierarchy of postliberation China. After all, the leading class in society is the industrial proletariat, whereas the poor and lower-middle peasants are only the closest ally, to be led by the proletariat. Consequently, some workers' families are not happy with the prospect of their offspring becoming peasants. "Workers' sons and daughters are of good family origin. There is no reason to send them to the countryside."[53]

When the press discusses unfavorable family attitudes toward the transfer, it is usually presented as a conflict within the family, in which some members are for and some against the transfer, and in which the "good" side wins out after lengthy family discussions and study of appropriate ideology. Articles depicting such family conflict are quite numerous, though no clear patterns of the direction of the conflict emerge. Sometimes the youths want to go to the countryside but the parents are opposed and the youths convince the parents.[54] Sometimes it is one or both of the parents who play the mobilizing role, as in the case of the daughter of a PLA commander who felt that, since "I am still young, it is better to let me continue with senior high school or to let me join the army." The father studied Mao's Thought with her and she went to the countryside.[55] In other instances opposition to the transfer comes from one of the parents—typically, but not always, the mother.[56] If there is a pattern in the latter cases, it is that the parent with the most significant political involvements plays the role of mobilizing the other parent, who is less political and hence believes more strongly in the old values. In the case of the father from Peking who did not wish to send his son to Inner Mongolia, it was the mother, a propaganda team member, who supported the son's going and convinced her husband by recalling their sufferings in the old society. In other cases, however (which probably are less likely to be reported in the press), no one in the family is willing to uphold the new values.[57] It need not be assumed that in such cases the family decides overtly to defy the transfer demand. Rather, if no possibilities exist for securing exemptions or otherwise influencing the transfer decision, the family may decide to comply, albeit reluctantly, on the grounds that not doing so is too costly.[58]

The Chinese leaders have responded to the continued existence of the old values among many urbanites by persisting with the program. Repeated mobilization, in which "revolutionary public opinion" (ko-ming yü-lun) supportive of the transfer program is created in a "big way," will, they hope, whittle away at the old beliefs and attitudes.[59] Sometimes their efforts to bring about value change come in highly concentrated form. The 1973–74 movement to criticize Confucius is a good example of a campaign in which there was an open confrontation between the old and the new values and in which the search for converts was pressed with some intensity. The anti-Confucius campaign lent itself to the denunciation of such sayings as that of Mencius's "Those who labor with their minds govern others; those who labor with their brawn are governed by others," or such popular sayings as "While his parents are alive, the son may not go abroad to a distance."[60] Unquestionably, however, the task is a long-term one; it cannot be accomplished overnight.

Given the ambiguous nature of the evidence, it is hard to say whether the proportion of urbanites who believe in the new, revolutionary values is increasing. But there are indications that, even if many urbanites have not been converted to the new values, their attitudes have not remained unchanged. The intensification of the movement to the countryside has, it seems, had an impact on values and attitudes. Before the Cultural Revolution, there was still considerable snobbishness about blue-collar work, in that some youths from educated homes refused assignments to factory work.[61] As the transfer intensified, the value attached to factory work rose. "Those assigned to a factory are in high spirits and elated and those assigned to rural and mountain areas are a cut below others."[62] My informants strongly stressed the desirability of a factory job; some noted that they would not have escaped to Hong Kong had such a prospect been in the offing. For an intellectual's daughter, marriage to an urban worker is considered a good match, judging by informants.* The movement to the countryside has thus served to raise the status of the industrial working class in the eyes of the urban populace; ironically, its status may now be more in conformity with the official values than may have been the case in the past. The idea of an educated person working on the land also seems to be viewed less in terms of disgrace and humiliation than formerly, simply because the practice is so widespread. It is not possible to predict whether these new attitudes will in due course become fully internalized or whether they will remain only as long as the policies and practices that induced them continue in force, but their existence is itself worthy of note.

INFLUENCES ON THE CHOICES OF
LOCAL DECISION MAKERS

If each year all youths graduating from middle schools were sent to the countryside, the task of the local authorities would simply be to secure universal compliance. But their task is frequently more complex. In any one city or town, only a proportion of a given year's graduates may be sent; hence the authorities are confronted with the task of making a fundamental decision about each individual: should the youth be sent to the countryside, given employment in a factory or commercial unit, or sent to the military? The scope for choice varies with the intensity of the transfer. Nationally, the scope for choice was low in 1968 and 1969, rose in the early 1970s, and then declined again, especially in 1974 and 1975 (see table 7).

*Staying in the city is not the only consideration here. Informants with the Cultural Revolution in mind suggest that it is no longer as desirable as it once may have been to be an intellectual or a cadre, since both have come under severe attack. See also chapter 4 for a discussion of UY marriages.

If the findings in chapter 2 are accurate, however, some scope
for choice has always existed, at least at the national level, even
in the years of the most intensive transfer.[63] Particular cities
and towns, moreover, may not follow the national pattern.
Table 6 showed substantial variation between cities in the ratio
of sent-down youths to the urban populations. Some places
have consistently sent virtually all their school graduates to the
countryside, even when the national rate of transfer was low.
Ying-k'ou, Liaoning, did so in 1971 and has apparently continued to do so ever since.[64] In order to offset the Ying-k'ou
rate of 99.5 percent in 1971, some other urban place or places
must have had a correspondingly low rate. Other cities and
towns report having come close to universal transfer in high-in-
tensity years, such as 1974 and 1975. In mid-July 1974, Wuhan reported that about 100,000 students would graduate
from middle schools that year; in August, it was reported that
the same number would be settling in the countryside in 1974.[65]
Several Liaoning cities, including Lüta, Tan-tung, Liaoyang, and
Fuhsin, as well as Ying-k'ou, reported virtually universal transfer in 1974 and 1975.[66] Similarly, in 1975 thirteen town-level
administrative units in Kirin sent all their graduates to the countryside.[67] On the other hand, Canton sent only about 80 percent of its graduating class in 1975, but this is a substantial
increase over 1972, when only about 50 percent were transferred.[68]

Apparently a decision is made each year for each city and
town allocating members of the graduating middle school class
to the three modes of employment. From the vantage point of
an individual school, an official of Wusong Middle School,
Shanghai, described the choices to be made, in 1975: "'The
state informs the school how many people are needed in agriculture, industry, military affairs, or the border region. We then
meet the parents and the students themselves to discuss how to
distribute the jobs according to the needs of the state. The
needs of the state conform to the wishes of the students so that
the two things are identical.' But even he admitted that 'education' is often needed to fill the quotas."[69] If it is true that many
students prefer not to be sent to the countryside, and if therefore not enough youths volunteer to fill the rural quotas, to
whom, then, do the mobilizers direct their "education"? What
criteria guide them in deciding to pressure one youth to go
while permitting another one to stay?

In making selections, the discretion of the decision makers is limited by rules and regulations, but the extent of the formal limitations is not clear. According to informants, rules govern the granting of exemptions to handicapped and to those in poor health, as well as to those whose families are in financial difficulty and need them for support. Rules also govern the number of children in a family that may remain in the city. In the early 1970s, when the rate of transfer was low, some informants report that, if one sibling had already gone to the countryside, the others were eligible to stay. In 1973, when decisions were made to intensify the transfer, this rule was apparently changed such that only one sibling was allowed to remain. In one Canton school, the hundred-odd students who were assigned to factory work in 1973—about 10 percent of the graduates—reportedly came for the most part from one-child families.[70] If this rule is widely applied, it would mean that, when the rate of transfer is high, the decision makers have little or no leeway to hand out urban assignments on other grounds.*

Decision makers have been known to assign youths to urban jobs or to the PLA for reasons of achievement or status.[71] With regard to achievement, one can distinguish between political, academic, artistic, and athletic achievement. In the case of the first, informants usually report that a good political record—but also a good class background—is an informal requirement for assignment to factory work and especially to the PLA. In principle, a youth who has compiled an impressive record of political activism and leadership is of course not exempt from the transfer. Indeed, activists are expected to be the first to volunteer for an unpopular assignment. Yet, among the activists are some who have made a calculus of personal benefit. In Peking in 1968, for instance, a "few comrades" of school Red Guard organizations were said to "mobilize other people to go to the countryside and mountainous area, but they have another plan for themselves. They feel that since they are the responsible persons of the mass organizations, they should be 'taken care of.' How should they be 'taken care of'? To tell the truth, they want to stay in the city and are unwilling to lead the life of ordinary peasants."[72] In some cases these calculations in fact paid off. In Canton, according to informants, it was the Red Guards from

*Permitting one child to remain at home could conceivably lead to further reductions in the urban birthrate, if parents who dislike the transfer program decide in response to have only one child.

the winning East Wind factions who in 1968 were appointed study instructors in the schools or given some other political position in the city and who therefore won exemption from the transfer. Conversely, youths whose political attitude is poor are likely to be selected for the transfer, on the grounds that they are in particular need of reeducation by the poor and lower-middle peasants.

Before the Cultural Revolution, academic achievement, as reflected in performance on university entrance examinations, was grounds for exemption from the transfer. In the years immediately preceding the Cultural Revolution, however, students from bad class backgrounds were often required to go to the countryside regardless of how well they did. Since the reopening of the higher schools in 1970, even high achievers have in principle not been able to continue academic study beyond middle school; yet, various functional needs forced erosion of this principle even before it came under high-level challenge in 1975. For example, as China's contacts with the outside world broadened in the 1970s, the need for interpreters and teachers of foreign languages, especially English, became acute. Visitors learned that a "small number" of senior middle school graduates have been allowed to proceed directly to higher schools in order to study languages; other were able to find immediate employment as primary school teachers in cities after their graduation from senior middle school.[73] Opportunities for continuous study have been extended to a few students of scientific and technical subjects, presumably those in which a critical manpower shortage has existed. Visitors in Canton were told in 1972 that a "small number" of middle school graduates were being sent directly to higher institutions.[74] Scholars who visited China during the Lin-Confucius campaign, which sought to check the erosion of the principles of the Cultural Revolution, learned that at such institutions as Peking University thought was being given even then to future enrollment of students in mathematics and physics directly from secondary school.[75] There is also a possibility that the research institutes of the Academy of Sciences have recruited outstanding middle school students, providing for them some kind of academic apprenticeship; possibly, the PLA has done likewise to train scientists and technicians for its weapons development programs.[76] All this suggests that academic achievement, at least in certain fields and to a limited extent, has exerted some influence on transfer decisions, though evidently not enough to satisfy those policy makers who in 1975 sought large-scale entry of the talented from middle schools directly into higher institutions.

Talented youths in such fields as interpreting, athletics, music, theater, and acrobatics may be protected from the rigors of the transfer by their affiliation with an institution that plays a part in the transfer decisions. The case of two young interpreters who accompanied an American delegation in the PRC illustrates this point. Apparently because they were talented linguists, these young men had joined the staff of Luxingshe, the China Travel Service, before they were sent to the countryside. As staff members, they went to a state farm with links to Luxingshe, where they spent six months laboring as well as studying English. After this stint in the countryside they returned to Peking to work for their organization.[77] Clearly, the conditions under which they were transferred contrast sharply with those of ordinary urban youths, who do not have ties to a similar urban institution and whose return is therefore not guaranteed.

In the case of artistic or athletic talent, Chinese cities, especially large ones such as Shanghai, have an intricate network for the identification and recruitment of promising children.[78] The All-China Sports Federation (ACSF) maintains branches in cities and towns, which work closely with coaches in the schools. When an outstanding athlete graduates from middle school, affiliation with the ACSF may protect him or her from being caught up in the routine processes of the transfer. Sports officials play a role in the decisions and will press for assignments that permit outstanding youths to continue training and competing. An aquatic sports official, whom I interviewed while accompanying an American swimming team on a visit to the PRC in 1973, stressed that first-class swimmers were not exempt from being sent "up to the mountains and down to the villages." However, an effort is made to send them to places with appropriate facilities and also to inform their work units as well as the local ACSF branch. Since not all Chinese villages contain Olympic-size swimming pools, this suggests that an excellent swimmer is likely to be sent to a suburb with easy access to an urban sports complex, or simply to be given an urban job assignment.[79] Indeed, it seems likely that a large proportion of the talented in such fields as music, theater, and acrobatics are recruited directly from school by the appropriate organizations.[80] For a talented youth, then, cooptation by an achievement-oriented organization does offer opportunities to escape from the transfer, or at least to mitigate its impact.

How does status affect mobilization? Low social status—a bad class background—has with few exceptions been a major reason for being sent to the countryside.[81] High social status, such as a working-class background, may be a necessary but cannot be a sufficient condition for being allowed to stay, especially if the rate of transfer is high and the individual lacks a record of political commitment.[82] Still, when an enterprise recruits middle school graduates for apprenticeships or other training programs, the children of the plant's workers and employees may enjoy an advantage. This could occur if the enterprise recruits from nearby middle schools, given the practice of urban planners of locating work site, housing, schools, and other facilities as closely together as possible. Thus, the Shanghai Diesel Engine Factory gave "some preference" to middle school graduates living nearby.[83] It is not clear whether in such cases the school in question is assigned a lower-than-average rural transfer quota. Little is actually known of how quotas for the transfer and for local employment are distributed among the schools. Informants' reports show considerable variation in the proportion of students not sent to the countryside in 1968, the range being from 1 to 15 percent, 5 to 10 percent being typical.[84] But data do not suffice to establish a relationship between retention rates, the location of the school, and the composition of the student body. Quite possibly, opportunities have existed here for the exercise of informal influence.

The main status issue, one that has received much attention in the press, has arisen in the case of offspring of high-ranking cadres. High parental status has itself often sufficed to win the youth a desirable assignment in that it has not been necessary for the cadre actively to use personal power to influence the decision. As cases cited earlier showed, decision makers have made assignments on the implicit assumption that of course the child of an important person should receive appropriate treatment.[85] In another such case, the daughter of a county party secretary in Kiangsi graduated from senior middle school and the "department concerned" assigned her to a team doing cultural work, taking into account her special talents and preferences (*t'e-*

chang and *ai-hao*).[86] In still another one, the son of a county party secretary in Kwangsi hoped that on graduation he would be given a factory job, and indeed the school assigned him to one.[87] In both these cases, as reported in the press, the fathers decided that cadre offspring should not enjoy special privileges and had the decisions reversed. These cadre fathers acted in accordance with the new values, as did the parents in a number of similar instances. Their cases show that, because high cadre status is itself a source of influence on the transfer decision, cadres must take positive steps to resist temptations and not to fulfill traditional expectations of how officials should behave. This is also illustrated by the case of a county cadre who was in charge of military affairs; his daughter, a senior middle school graduate, wanted very much to join the PLA, and he did not oppose her wish until he had been enlightened by Chairman Mao's Thought. Then he commented, "Why is it that all comrades feel that my daughter's joining the army is the acceptable thing to do (*k'en-ting ti shih*)? Doesn't this show clearly that in the eyes of the masses I am a personage with special privileges (*t'e-shu jen-wu*)?"[88]

Some cadres, however, have tried to exert direct influence, going by the "back door" to win exemptions for their offspring. In the fall of 1973, when the campaign to criticize Lin Piao and Confucius got under way, the press bluntly and unequivocally acknowledged that some cadres were wielding behind-the-scenes influence, as shown by the following three quotes, from Kansu, Kiangsi, and Anhwei (my italics):

Some comrades have gone so far as to take advantage of their positions or connections to keep their sons and daughters in urban areas or have them transferred from the countryside.

Leading cadres should set an example by sending their children to the countryside and resolutely correct the *wrong tendency* of avoiding sending their children to the countryside.

[A Hofei party secretary:] At one time some cadres in Hofei Municipality, corrupted by bourgeois ideology, engaged in the unhealthy practice of "going by the back door. . . ." On the question of educated young people going to the countryside, I have never practiced favoritism, *no matter who has come to see me.*[89]

Cadres have exerted influence both to prevent their children from being sent to the countryside at all and to have them reassigned after having spent some time in a village. Given the campaign pattern of transfer mobilization, it would seem likely that the latter has been more pervasive than the former. When the campaign is in full swing, cadres come under very heavy pressure to play model roles in sending their own children to the countryside, and many find it advisable to comply with this demand. But, when the focus of attention has turned to other matters, cadres can then take advantage of their connections to have their offspring reassigned. In the most famous of the reassignment cases, the father, a high-ranking military official, simply telephoned the "departments concerned," resulting in his son's admission to Nanking University (see chapter 6 for a full description of the case).[90]

As the foregoing examples show, the press publicizes numerous cases of cadres who have sent their children to the village, who have withstood the temptations to secure special favors for their offspring, and who have set a personal example. It is noteworthy that in a good many such cases the cadres are reported as making sacrifices that are not demanded of the masses, such as sending down additional children even though the older ones have already gone to the countryside, rejecting offers of exemption because of illness in the family, or even encouraging a handicapped son or daughter to go.[91] The most prominent of such cases is that of the new chairman, Hua Kuo-feng. In November 1976 a front-page story in the *People's Daily* told how he had encouraged his youngest daughter to leave Peking and settle in a village, even though policy would have permitted her to remain "by his side" as the last of his offspring.[92]

The leadership has attached importance to the transfer of the children of leading cadres for general ideological reasons—it is one way to ensure a circulation of elites, so that "revolutionary successors" will not be recruited via the path of inherited claims to privilege and status—and because it helps make the transfer system work. Nothing is more likely to destroy what enthusiasm for the transfer exists, especially among the idealistically committed, than the perception that it is not being handled fairly and equitably. Such perceptions were at the root of some of the grievances voiced against the "revisionist assignment system"

during the Cultural Revolution.[93] Fairness in handling the transfer probably increases its acceptability among those not highly
committed to the new values. Some informants who were sent
down in 1968 during the massive movement to the countryside,
which was much more egalitarian than pre–Cultural Revolution
practices had been, convey this impression. As the transfer became more selective in the early 1970s, it is likely that the rate
of favoritism rose, stimulating cynicism on the part of those not
favored. Certainly there has been recognition of the important
role played in mobilization by the personal example of leading
cadres who send their children.[94] In a Hofei factory, for instance, because the children of two leading cadres did not take
the lead in signing up, the rest of the youths also lagged behind;
it was not until the two cadres were publicly criticized at a mass
meeting that the campaign gained momentum. The Hofei City
Party Committee found out that a party secretary in one of the
city's plants had used influence to secure his daughter's admission to a school, probably a technical school run by an enterprise to train skilled workers. The committee felt that if the
correct principles were not applied in this case it would entail a
loss of the power to persuade (*shuo-fu li*).[95] For this reason
alone it is likely that the Chinese leadership is quite serious in
enforcing the rule that high-ranking cadres' children must also
take part in the transfer.[96] Yet, securing compliance with this
demand has been and continues to be problematic in the case
of cadre parents who are in fact in positions of power and influence that permit them to affect the opportunities open to their
children.[97] The transfer demand entails a confrontation between the new values and the natural desire of parents to help
their offspring get a good start in life, a confrontation that can
be poignant indeed in the case of parents who themselves sacrificed a great deal for the revolution.

Comparison of the cadre cases with those of the academically
talented highlights the conflicting role played by ideology. In
the case of the cadres, the norms that pressure them to comply
with the transfer are ideological in nature. To the extent that
cadres respond to them, to that extent the increase in the fairness and equality of the transfer makes it easier to send urban
youths to the countryside and hence contributes to the success
of the program. But, to the degree that ideological norms pre-

vail, a discriminating treatment of the talented is made impossible, and as a result the country's advanced sector may be
deprived of its brightest products.

INFLUENCES ON CHOICE
OF DESTINATION

Once a decision has been made to send a youth to the village,
a destination must be chosen. The nature of the destination is
naturally also of great interest to those affected; hence, the
question of exerting influence on this matter arises. If the transfer is inherently unequal because some youths are retained in
the city and some are not, it is also unequal with respect to the
destinations of those youths selected to go "up to the mountains and down to the villages." Two such inequalities need to
be mentioned. The first is inequality of distance of settlement
from home. Some youths are sent to nearby suburban communes or state farms; others are sent to places as far distant as
Hainan from Canton or Heilungkiang from Shanghai. In the
former cases, UYs can visit their families frequently; in the
latter, visits are possible at best only once a year. Assignment to
a suburban commune permits continued contact with urban cultural life; settlement in a remote, mountainous village with poor
communications to the outside world may entail cultural
deprivation. From this vantage point, the 400,000 Shanghai
youths sent to the ten suburban counties of Shanghai Municipality are better off than the 600,000 sent to Sinkiang,
Heilungkiang, or Yunnan.

The second inequality is in the wealth of the communes and
their subdivisions (brigades and teams) to which UYs may be
sent. As noted in chapter 2, urban youths have generally not
been sent to extremely poor communes in places where the
local economy simply cannot support migrants. Within this limitation, however, there is still considerable variation in wealth
among the communes on which youths have been settled. The
prosperity of the unit to which urban youths are sent is a major
variable in the transfer system. It involves choices that are important to the youths and to their families. Other things being
equal, it is easier to adjust to life on a relatively prosperous
commune than on one at the lower end of the income scale.

In addition, it is also necessary to choose the type of produc-

tion unit in which a youth will work, that is, a people's commune, a state farm, or a PLA Production and Construction
Corps farm.* From the youth's point of view, these differ significantly. State and PLA farms offer greater material security
to the youths, since workers are paid a regular wage, receive free
medical care, and do not need to worry about arrangements for
daily living, such as the cooking of meals. But living conditions
on state or PLA farms, especially in remote areas, can often be
primitive, tough, and trying. Life on these farms, moreover, particularly those run by the PLA, is highly disciplined, semimili-
tarized, and collectivized. The communes, by contrast, offer
less material security but also less discipline and more freedom
of choice as to whether or not to work steadily. Urban youths
on communes depend on work points the worth of which varies
annually with the harvest, but also with the work grade classifi-
cation given to the youths, which in turn is related to the effort
they are willing to put in. The choices of how to structure one's
life are greater on communes but so are the risks. (However, as
will be discussed in the next chapter, substantial efforts have
been made in recent years to regularize UY life on communes.)

Truly committed, revolutionary youths may genuinely ask to
be sent to places where "hardships are greatest." Such youths
may ask to go to a distant border province, attracted by the collective life, the pioneer spirit, the patriotism, and the military
features of the PLA farms. Informants report that in 1968 a
good many leftist Red Guards, including the children of cadres,
chose to serve on army farms on Hainan Island. Youths who
closely identify with the revolution may ask to be sent to villages around the town of Yenan, the wartime headquarters of
the CCP, and in fact over 20,000 youths, mostly from Peking,
have settled there. As one group of Peking middle school students put it, "The people of Yenan have made outstanding contributions to the Chinese Revolution. We want to inherit and
develop the spirit of Yenan." Their request was approved both
by the authorities in Peking and by Yenan prefecture.[98] In such
cases, the volunteering may be done in groups; group spirit and

*Although Production and Construction Corps farms are administered by the PLA,
UYs sent to them are not considered regular soldiers. The latter are recruited through
a national conscription system. Since only a fraction of the vast pool of eligible
manpower is needed, the PLA is able to pick the cream of the crop and, by all accounts, being chosen for service in the armed forces is considered highly desirable.
While army farm workers are called "fighters" (*chan-shih*) and, as noted earlier,
receive some military training, their social status is lower than that of regular soldiers.

perhaps group pressures may reinforce the collective commitment to go "up to the mountains and down to the countryside"
without thought of material advantage.

The dominant impression from my interviews, however, is
that many youths do assess the costs and benefits of particular
destinations in material and personal terms. The press reinforces
this impression. It is news when young people renounce calculations of self-interest, as in the case of two Canton middle school
classes, all of whom volunteered, declaring that "they would
not pick posts and localities and would not bargain."[99] Preferences vary, but perhaps the most widespread is simply for a
place of settlement that is close to the home town, permits
maintenance of continuous contact with the family, and is reasonably prosperous. Informants reported that they and most of
their classmates did not want to go to Hainan, essentially because of the island's distance from Canton, aggravated by cum-
bersome communications. Counties in northern Kwangtung had
a reputation for poverty and backwardness, which inclined
youths not to want to settle there. However, youths from low-
income families, which would not be able to send them money,
reportedly did not mind going to a state or army farm in a distant or poor place such as Hainan, because of the economic
security. According to an informant who attended a Shanghai
school in 1968, this reason prompted some of her classmates to
ask to go to Inner Mongolia and Heilungkiang. Among her classmates, Anhwei was thought of as a very poor place; when
natural disasters struck, Anhwei peasants could be seen begging
in the streets of Shanghai. Much discussion evidently takes place
within families and among friends about the advantages and disadvantages of particular destinations, and numerous considerations enter in. Some of the Shanghai informant's classmates, for
instance, thought that going to the far north was not so bad because the harsh winters meant that one would have to work for
only half the year. Others thought of Kiangsi as advantageous
simply because of the warmer climate. One of her classmates, a
YCL activist, volunteered to go to Yunnan as a member of the
first group of fifty Shanghai youths to settle there, apparently
enticed by the prospect of being trained as a leadership cadre
for army farms scheduled to be established or expanded. One
Canton informant reports that Ta-wang state farm, though close
to Canton, was feared as a destination because of outbreaks
there of schistosomiasis, the snail-borne disease.[100] Informants

who had already decided, while in Canton, to try to escape to Hong Kong naturally preferred a destination as close to the colony as possible.

The major tactic open to youths who want to influence the choice of destination is to volunteer early in the mobilization process. Assigning units such as Canton schools have typically had three destinations to which the students in that school are sent, including Hainan PLA farms and several communes in counties of varying distances from Canton. Often early volunteers were able to obtain their first choice. To be sure, constraints operated, in that class background and political record influenced the probability of getting the preferred destination. In 1968, Red Guards who had taken part in the armed struggles (*wu-tou*) of the Cultural Revolution, particularly if they came from the losing Red Flag factions, were reportedly sent to army farms on Hainan, where they could be more easily controlled.

Providing even a limited opportunity to choose among destinations would seem to be a tactic that facilitates transfer mobilization. If the transfer is perceived as inevitable, choice of destination provides an incentive to make the best of it and to come to terms with the program. It is not, however, clear whether all cities and towns have permitted the exercise of choice.

In the 1968 mobilization, Canton youths had considerable opportunity to manipulate the destination decision to their advantage. One way of doing so was to make use of a policy then in force in Canton called *k'ao-ch'in k'ao-yu*—"depend on relatives and friends"—which permitted youths to go to a village in which they had relatives and friends, including previously transferred classmates. In principle, inquiry was to be made to verify the claim and to secure the consent of the commune in question, but in the chaotic days of the mass transfer in 1968 and early 1969, when administration was still confused, a good many students were able to go to preferred places simply by lying about their personal circumstances. As some informants reported, assignments were made by PLA propaganda team members assigned to the schools who were unfamiliar with conditions in Kwangtung. Without adequate records, students who feigned political enthusiasm were able to manipulate the situation to their advantage. According to the informants, the k'ao-ch'in k'ao-yu practice was abolished in 1969 because of these abuses.[101] It need not be assumed that the deceptions practiced by some of those who were sent down in 1968 are typical; they no doubt reflect the demoralized state of some urban youth at the tail end of the Cultural Revolution.

Exercise of influence by cadres on destination decisions has not received the publicity devoted to influence on the transfer decision and on reassignment. Nonetheless, such influence may well have been exerted. The press does print cases of cadres who had been "advised" by "someone" to send their children to a more convenient nearby destination rather than to a far-distant one.[102] Possibly, influence is reflected in the destinations assigned to particular schools in which numerous offspring of high-status parents are enrolled. Visitors in 1973 to No. 31 Middle School in Peking, where 30 percent of the students came from families of cadres or employees, were told that those graduates who were sent to the countryside—30 percent in 1970, under 30 percent in 1971, and over 50 percent in 1972—all went to a commune in a suburban county of Peking, in years when many other Peking youths were sent to provinces such as Yunnan or Shensi.[103] Another foreigner, who visited a prosperous fish-breeding brigade in the suburbs of Changsha, Hunan, in 1975, met sent-down youths who mostly came from families of cadres, doctors, and college teachers. The visitor was struck by the "manifest embarrassment" to which discussion of these backgrounds gave rise.[104]

ASSESSMENT

Given the continued commitment to the policy of sending youths "up to the mountains and down to the countryside," it would seem to be in the interests of this cause to devise approaches to the transfer that would maximize the urban population's acceptance of and cooperation with the transfer. Ideally, the transfer ought to become a part of the normal and routine expectations of urban life, as probably has happened in the case of other aspects of Chinese socialist practice. And indeed, much is being done to bring about such a state of affairs. For example, urban children are being conditioned for life in the countryside at an early age, beginning with songs in nursery schools and continuing through middle school with teachings about the countryside and study of model heroes of the transfer. This undoubtedly contributes to the transfer's becoming a part of the normal expectations of the younger generation.[105] Yet, at the same time, the overall impression conveyed by the process of mobilization in the cities is that sending urban youths to the countryside has not really been normalized or routinized. The reasons for this are twofold. First, the program continues to be characterized by value dissonance in that substantial numbers of urbanites do not appear to have accepted the values on which this program is based. Second, the very practices of the transfer have often militated against its becoming a normal part of urban expectations. From the point of view of the inhabitants, the transfer must often have appeared as an uncertain, unpredictable, and perhaps arbitrary affair. Urban parents have not been sure whether their children would be sent down, whether they would be able to manipulate or influence such vital decisions as choice of the destination, or whether their children would eventually be able to return. Added to these uncertainties must be awareness of the inequalities involved, inequalities that may well aggravate feelings of relative deprivation. Rhetoric contending that it does not matter where one is sent or what one does if only one serves socialism cannot disguise the striking disparities between those who go and those who stay and between those who are sent to a nearby place and those who are sent far away. It is not surprising in this light that Chinese statements about mobilization stress the difficulties and note that the "end of the struggle is not yet in sight."[106]

The Chinese leadership has been wrestling with these problems. Efforts have been made to devise new policies and approaches designed to enhance the acceptability of the transfer and to facilitate popular adjustment to its demands. In the summer of 1974, innovative practices in an industrial city in Hunan, Chu-chou, received nationwide publicity and praise as a model for resettlement from which other localities should learn.[107] Chu-chou's innovation was to forge links (*kua-kou*) between urban and rural units in the surrounding county of Chu-chou. A unified transfer plan was drawn up by the city in cooperation with the communes, which greatly reduces uncertainty and provides assurance that Chu-chou youth will not be shipped off to far away places:

The plan for sending educated youth up to the mountains and down to the countryside from 1974 to 1980 has become a household word. The leaders of a factory know how many middle school graduates there will be in a given year and in which commune they will settle; the rural . . . cadres . . . know how many educated youths will come in a given year and from which units they will come; the parents know in which commune their son or daughter will settle after graduation from middle school.[108]

The Chu-chou model emphasizes not only predictability and certainty but also continuous involvement of urban institutions in the implementation of the transfer on the rural end. Formerly, urban units had participated in the mobilization of youths to go to the countryside, but not very systematically in follow-up activities. The most extensive follow-up work in the cities has been done with the parents of sent-down youths, in order to influence positively the content of letters to their children. Much attention has continued to be devoted to this issue.[109] Similarly, each year many cities have sponsored organized activities for visiting UYs, in order to prevent their coming under undesirable influences while on home leave.[110] But most urban units, such as factories, have done little to help with the settlement itself.[111] In Chu-chou, however, factories themselves help set up "support-agriculture points" (*chih-nung tien*) in those communes to which the children of their work force are sent following graduation. Before the youths arrive, cadres from the particular urban unit contact their rural counterparts in order to prepare for their coming. The urban unit helps with the construction of housing or with the transport of building material. Cadres from the urban unit are permanently and continuously involved with the solution of settlement problems of the UYs. They live with the sent-down youths, reporting back to the urban unit as well as to the parents. Because of the establishment of these linkages between urban and rural units, the youths are not completely cut off from the urban sector. The Chu-chou articles do not mention reassignment to urban employment—the "for life" theme appears in them as well—but the maintenance of ties between the UY groups in the villages and particular urban units may facilitate return.[112] Chu-chou is a growth town, and as vacancies arise they could well be filled from among its sent-down youth. Even if this does not happen, the participation of urban units in the management of the settlement may reassure the families of the sent-down youth. It is thus not surprising that the *People's Daily* hailed the Chu-chou model as a new

way of reducing urban-rural differences. A commentary positively chortled that the innovations "combine rather well the
long-run with the immediate interests of the masses. Hence all
sides welcome them: the sent-down educated youths are free
from worry, as are the parents, and the poor and lower middle
peasants are happy too."[113]

To what extent has the Chu-chou model been emulated elsewhere? Since it came to national prominence, many more urban
units, particularly industrial enterprises, have become involved
with the transfer program. This applies not only to mobilization
of youths to go to the countryside, but also to participation in
the settlement. To be sure, urban-rural ties are woven more
easily when UYs settle in the nearby countryside, as in Chu-
chou, rather than in distant places. But new practices have also
been devised to overcome barriers of distance. In some cases,
urban enterprises have been assigned distant rural communes or
state farms as destinations for the children of the work force,
enterprise cadres going along to participate in the settlement.[114]
Indeed, the dispatch of urban cadres to help lead the sent-down
youths in the countryside has become a widely adopted practice,
as will be shown in more detail in the next chapter.

With regard to the predictability that is one of the chief char-
acteristics of the Chu-chou model, it is doubtful whether a similar degree of advance knowledge about the transfer can be
achieved elsewhere. Urban manpower needs are likely to be different from year to year in different cities. The press does not
give the impression that in other cities young people have similar advance knowledge about whether they will be sent to the
countryside. Nor can the certainty of Chu-chou youths that
they will be sent to the surrounding countryside be emulated
easily everywhere. Not all suburban areas can absorb new settlers, and it is, after all, one of the purposes of the program to
send urban youths to the frontier provinces. Thus, Shanghai has
kept sending its young to Heilungkiang, Inner Mongolia, Yunnan, and, in 1976 for the first time, to Tibet, as well as to the
suburban counties.[115] This is not to say that an increased effort
may not have been made to settle more youths in the nearby
villages. In Peking, for instance, according to an overseas Chinese
visiting relatives in 1973, parents had complained about the in-
equities of sending some youths to far-off places, some to the
suburbs, and still others to city factories. Reportedly, parents
were told that the transfer would be made more uniform in ap-

plication. Judging by press reports, incomplete to be sure, in 1974 and 1975 Peking youths were in fact sent to the suburban counties of that city.[116]

This discussion suggests that certainty may enhance the acceptability of the transfer, but only if there is certainty of a preferred outcome. A completely predictable, certain, and equitable transfer system would be one in which all youths are sent to far-off rural destinations, for life. Such a system would eliminate all choice but, in the view of many urbanites, would also be the worst outcome. Hence, the problem of securing compliance might well substantially increase. For many urbanites, the best transfer system would be one in which all go to the nearby countryside and all are allowed to return after a fixed time span. Such a system evidently is not possible, for economic and ideological reasons. Thus, policy makers seem to have settled on flexible practices that fall between the worst and the best system. As a result, there are many uncertainties, which have prevented the program from becoming fully institutionalized. The uncertainties entail other costs: they provide opportunities for corrupt practices on the part of cadres seeking exemptions, for example. Conversely, the uncertainties also make possible informal practices that exempt some of the talented from the transfer. And, the uncertainties mean that for many urbanites the least-preferred outcome does not materialize, hence raising the probability that they will reconcile themselves to their situation.

4 ADAPTING TO RURAL LIFE:
PROBLEMS AND REMEDIES

The objective of the settlement of urban youths in the country-side is that they should take root (*cha-ken*) in the villages, feel at home and at ease (*an-hsin*) in their new environment, integrate with the peasants, themselves become cultured peasants, and make contributions to rural development. It is recognized that attainment of this goal is not easy and that it can take place only through a process of struggle to overcome difficulties, in which the UYs are "tempered" (*tuan-lien*), and in which they grow and mature, ultimately becoming worthy "revolutionary successors." Concretely, one of the struggles that UYs must wage is against a drop in morale that seems to affect many, if not most, sooner or later after arrival in the rural areas, including those who volunteered and who arrived with a sense of excitement and enthusiasm. A mix of factors is responsible for this initial adjustment crisis. To begin with, there are the hardships of rural life, as illustrated by what the father of one UY wrote in *Red Flag*: "For some time after her arrival Yung-hung showed enthusiasm and vigor in her work. But not long afterward, she began to write in her letters about the rural hardships. . . . 'When I go out of my house, I have to climb slopes. When I go to the fields, I have to cross hills. I rise very early in the morning and do not return until it is dark. . . .' Shortly afterward, Yung-hung wrote again, saying that she wouldn't have gone to the mountain area had she known life there was so hard."[1] Youths may be daunted by the prospect of having to get used to the strenuous physical labor (*ch'ien-k'u lao-tung*) which peasants do routinely and for which agricultural labor during school holidays does not seem to have been adequate preparation.[2] Youths may be discouraged by the generally lower standard of living, and they may well experience something of a culture shock in making the transition from more modernized to less modernized circumstances, especially if their new rural home is isolated and remote from major cities. They may encounter barriers of dia-

lect or even language in communicating with the peasants;
peasant customs and peasant particularism may pose obstacles
to integration, as may lower standards of sanitation (such as the
limited availability or complete absence of certain toilet articles),
and the contact with dirt which agricultural labor entails. "Fear
of dirt" (*p'a ang-tsang*) is a frequently recurring theme in articles
describing the settlement.[3] Then there is the monotony of a
rural life (*tan-tiao*) that seems to offer little beyond a routine of
working, eating, and sleeping, interrupted only by political
study and an occasional cultural event. And there is the reduction in status which the transfer entails, illustrated by the story
about a youth who settled in a suburban commune of Nanning
and who was mortified by children chanting after him: "Here
comes the middle school student who carries nightsoil."[4] In his
case, Chairman Mao's Thought taught him the dignity and worth
of agricultural labor no matter how seemingly menial. But, as
long as old values still play a role in people's thinking, the idea
of educated youths doing farm labor and of urbanites subjected
to "reeducation" by the peasants raises a problem of status and
hence affects adaptation.

Even when UYs succeed in overcoming their initial difficulties
in adapting to life in the countryside, it does not necessarily
mean that their adaptational difficulties have been permanently
resolved. Youths who have adapted in the short run may over
the long run experience new crises of morale, which arise essentially out of the indeterminate, long-term nature of the transfer.
If an urban reassignment does not seem to be in the offing,
some urban youths may suffer from chronic dissatisfaction with
their rural life. Such youths have not reconciled themselves to
the proposition that the settlement is for life. Their basic complaint is that the village does not offer an appropriate "future"
(*mei-yu ch'ien-t'u*)[5] and their feelings of relative deprivation are
made vivid and concrete by the knowledge that their schoolmates who were not sent down are enjoying the comforts of
city life.[6]

Whether or not an urban youth will adapt to rural life, overcoming both the initial and the long-term adjustment crises, is a
function of several variables. It is a function first of his own underlying motivations, which are presumably a function of his
personality, and his expectations and commitments as shaped
by his socialization experience and by factors such as his class
background. The youth, however, is not a free agent; his motiva-

tions do not exist in a vacuum. They are affected by his environment, including his particular living and working conditions, the opportunities open to him in the village, the nature of the UY peer group with which he lives, his relations with cadres and peasants, as well as his relations with the family and friends he left behind in his home town. To what extent does his environment reinforce what willingness there may be on his part to adapt to rural life and to what extent does it reinforce his dissatisfactions?

The role played by his environment is shaped at least to some degree by what the regime does or does not do. As already pointed out, the settlement of urban youths is a revolutionary program that runs counter to "normal" expectations; it is not a self-sustaining program but one that requires continuous support on the part of the political system as a whole. If it cannot be taken for granted that the UYs will automatically behave in accord with official expectations, it also cannot be assumed that the actors in the youth's rural environment—local cadres and peasants—will behave as the higher-level policy makers and administrators would like them to behave. Local people may have their own perspectives and interests which may frustrate the goal of reeducation of the UYs, that is, of reshaping their motivations in the direction of adaptation to the countryside. Thus, the degree to which interactions between UYs and locals are monitored, shaped, and supervised becomes an issue in its own right.

The structure of this chapter reflects interest in the role played by the rural environment of the sent-down youths. The first part of the chapter, "Urban Youths and the Rural Communities," will show that the environment has often not contributed as much to UY adaptation as is in principle possible. Cadres have not always provided the necessary guidance and supervision; relations between peasants and sent-down youths have not always been free of friction. The second part of the chapter, "Remedial Measures," discusses policies and practices adopted beginning in 1973 to improve the relationship between the UYs and their rural environment, in the hope of increasing the rate of adaptation. The two parts are to some extent separated in time. The first is based largely on data from the late 1960s and early 1970s, when the villages had to cope with the influx of several million young people in the wake of the Cultural Revolution. The problems that arose in those years became agenda items for policy makers in 1973 and for the remedial campaign that followed.

URBAN YOUTHS AND THE RURAL COMMUNITIES

Providing Guidance and Supervision

It is widely recognized that when urban youths arrive in the villages they cannot be left to themselves. They need guidance and supervision. The need for guidance is made explicit in the concept of "reeducation"; the purpose of their life in the countryside, after all, is to be resocialized, and the poor and lower-middle peasants are in principle their teachers. The need for guidance emerges from the realities of the settlement as well: UYs experience adjustment difficulties and morale crises; they need help to overcome these. They arrive in the villages unfamiliar with the local scene and often inexperienced in rural ways. They must learn production techniques and may not even know how to distinguish the five grains from weeds. Many of them are immature and dependent, not having lived an independent life before; they must learn how to arrange their daily lives—how to cook and how to budget.[7]

Urban youths sent to communes are settled in various ways. Where land is available or can be reclaimed, large, self-contained UY settlements may be established. Where it is not, small groups of youths, ranging from three to fifteen, may be settled within the production teams according to the principle of "scattered insertion" (*fen-san ch'ou-tui*), living among the peasants but not with them, in a house or houses built using the state's settlement fee, provided in part for this purpose. Because of variation in settlement patterns, the structure of guidance also varies. When UYs are inserted into production teams, normally a commune-level cadre is put in charge of UY work, as is a cadre on the brigade level. In addition, ordinary peasants may be assigned to work with UY groups settled in their teams. Hsiang-yang commune in Tien-chang county, Anhwei, for instance, absorbed 230 Shanghai youths in 1970 and 1971. The men were organized into fifteen groups and the women into twenty-five, and they were distributed among forty production teams. The May 7 Work Department of the commune took charge of the settlement, and May 7 leading groups were set up at each of the three levels of the commune. Next, 120 peasants "who are politically reliable and ideologically progressive and who follow the correct style of work and are enthusiastic about youth work" were assigned to the leading groups. Some of these peasants worked directly with the UY groups as "political instructors, instructors in production or personnel in charge of daily life management."[8]

Numerous cases published in the press illustrate the model role that local guidance should play. Guidance should not be sporadic lest problems crop up and go unsolved. It must be ongoing because of the likelihood that UYs will waver in their commitment to stay and will develop morale difficulties. Peasants and cadres should adopt a patient, nurturing approach toward the UYs, combining political education with attention to the concrete details of the settlement, such as living arrangement.[9] Undoubtedly, in a proportion of cases of commune settlement, steady guidance has been provided.[10] But data from both press and informants suggest that in a good many other cases guidance has left something to be desired. One reason for inadequate attention has been that some local leaders believed that the UYs would not be staying for long anyway but were only "guests passing by" (*kuo-lu k'e*), for whom not much need be done.[11] This impression, which runs counter to the "for life" theme of the transfer, probably has been created because some UYs have been sent back to urban locations and also because other urbanites have come to the village only temporarily, as in the case of cadres going to May 7 Cadre Schools. The press has found it necessary to remind rural cadres that the nation's commitment to the transfer system is permanent and that resettlement should not be viewed as a mere "stop-gap measure."[12]

An apparently widespread pattern has been for cadres and peasants to get involved with UY settlement when the youths first arrive, but to disengage once the UYs have settled down. When they first arrive, attention must necessarily be paid to them and their concrete problems, such as housing and work assignments. But once these pressing tasks have been taken care of and the youths are formally integrated, cadres can turn their attention to other, more important matters.[13] As one informant reports, at first the cadres were helpful and talked with the UYs every day, but later on cadres treated them like peasants, the only special program for the youths being periodic political study at the brigade level. In other instances, local authorities made intensive efforts to reeducate UYs—holding ongoing study programs for them, or pairing off each UY with a committed peasant or cadre for the purpose of improving his thinking—but after a while cadres and peasants began to weary of such intensive involvement. Two years of reeducation are enough, it was thought, so why continue time-consuming special efforts?[14] The result of such a lapse into indifference can be virtual cessation of communication between UY settlements and the local commune units. Thus, party committee members of Ch'angling *hsien* (county), Kirin, found that "some commune and production brigade cadres had no knowledge about what was occurring in specific localities" where UYs had settled.[15] Or, as *Red Flag* complained in 1971, "In a few places (*ko-pieh ti-fang*) the educated youths receiving reeducation have not been called for a single meeting for more than a year, nor are their conditions understood in a penetrating way. It is feared that the comrades in charge of youth work in those places do not know what sorts of political demands these youths have, what their difficulties in livelihood are, what changes have taken place in their thinking, and how much or how little progress they have made."[16]

When guidance and supervision of UY groups are inadequate, the autonomy of the urban youths is increased, raising the possibility of behavior that undermines rather than promotes adaptation. A laissez-faire approach to UY groups provides opportunities for the development of what might be called countersolidarity, in which membership in a UY group, or a subgroup within a UY collective, reinforces rather than combats maladaptive attitudes and behavior. If guidance is strong, the group should function in accordance with the principles of preemptive solidarity: a leader identifies activists or well-motivated UYs and mobilizes them to aim group criticism and group pressures against backward UYs, a process that in turn pressures UYs in the middle, who waver in their thinking, to behave in more positive ways.[17] What is striking about the informants who were settled on communes is that their groups were generally not characterized by preemptive solidarity, in which activist members seek to influence the backward and wavering youths. Instead, informants described a pattern in which cleavages developed between activist and backward youths. The two subgroups had little to do with one another. In one instance, the backward youths reacted with fear and avoidance toward those who worked hard and showed a positive attitude. In another case, each group looked down on the other. In still another case, those of good class background lived in a different house from those of bad class background, without meaningful interaction between them. In still another instance, two of ten UYs in a production team were hard-working and had a good attitude. The less devoted majority asked the two not to work so hard since it made the rest look bad. The two, one of whom was the informant who reported the case, did not comply. The backward majority did not, it should be noted, apply sanctions, such as ostracizing the two activists; reportedly, relations continued to be good. But the two activists also did not attempt to influence the rest to do better in the village. The press has confirmed the existence of such cleavages.[18] In one case, a UY group consisted mainly of activists, but instead of "helping" a backward fellow-UY they simply refused to have anything to do with him, even seeking to have him expelled from the group.[19] In another instance, tensions between advanced and backward UYs were caused or aggravated by peasant cadres who strongly favored the former over the latter.[20]

In some cases entire UY settlements in the villages may be characterized by countersolidarity. Instead of cleavages developing between backward and advanced UYs, a group may altogether lack activists, and, as awareness of one another's disaffection spreads unchecked, all UYs in the group may become bitterly resentful against the transfer. The development of such common countersolidarity is facilitated by the fact that UYs in one commune usually come from the same city and in a village often from the same school.[21] Internal cleavages that originated in the cities, such as membership in opposing Red Guard factions, or even differences in class background, may lose their salience and heal, being displaced by common feelings of solidarity vis-à-vis the peasants.[22] Cases of groupwide countersolidarity have certainly existed. During the Cultural Revolution, when opportunities for open articulation of group interests arose, some rural UY units coalesced in common opposition to local power-holders.[23] Since then, common countersolidarity seems to have been the basis for some mass escapes to Hong Kong from communes in the southern part of Tung-kuan hsien, where the "escape wind" (t'ou-tu feng) infected virtually all UYs in some brigades. Similarly, examples of collective assertions exist, in

which UYs in a production team or even brigade jointly seek redress of grievances, in cases of discrimination in work points or
the provision of inadequate housing.[24] While such examples of
entire UY groups characterized by countersolidarity can be
cited, however, the dominant impression conveyed by the informants is that such whole-group countersolidarity was impeded
by the continued existence of cleavages among the UYs. Informants agree that Cultural Revolution cleavages rapidly disappeared, but they stress the salience of class cleavages among
the UYs as well as those between active and passive or backward
UYs.[25] The latter point suggests that, in a given UY unit, at
least a few will usually make a more or less serious effort to
adapt to village life, but such activists do not necessarily seek to
influence their backward fellows.

From the point of view of the political system, inadequate
guidance opens up the UYs to influences that undermine the
settlement. One of the main themes that permeates the press is
how fragile the determination of the UYs to take root really is,
and how easily it is upset when UYs are not subjected constantly to the "right" kinds of influences.[26] If supervision is relaxed,
the youths may withdraw into their own world, as in one instance where UYs spent their evenings playing poker (p'u-k'o)
and reading "bad books."[27] Or they may become susceptible to
the influence of rural class enemies, as landlords or rich peasants
allegedly undermine the settlement by developing friendly relations with UYs. In such cases, a class enemy may make sympathetic remarks such as, "It is truly hard for educated youths to
be sent down to the village," or "There is no future in the village" for UYs.[28] Expressions of concern may be accompanied
by gifts of vegetables or fruit. According to press reports, such
interactions have sufficed to turn some UYs from an active to a
passive state and have in some cases incited them to return illicitly to their home town.[29] The following quote, describing
Hai-ch'eng county, Liaoning, where as of 1972 an unusually
large number of UYs had settled, hints at the possibly serious
consequences when spontaneous influences are permitted to
spread among UYs:

> Since 1968, more than 28,000 young intellectuals from
> Anshan, Yingkou and the urban areas of Haicheng County
> have settled down in the countryside. At first, some county
> party committee members did not fully understand the far-

reaching strategic significance of Chairman Mao's teaching that "it is very necessary for the educated young people to go to the countryside to be reeducated by the masses of poor and lower middle peasants," thinking that "what the young intellectuals only need is a place to live and work in the countryside." When problems with the young intellectuals broke out, these same comrades thought that the "young intellectuals are difficult to control" and that the "young intellectuals are disobedient." As a result, they looked upon [them] as a burden and neglected to conduct ideological education among them. Seeing this opportunity, class enemies began to create disturbances, trying to win over the young people by doing them small favors and poisoning the young people's minds with the bourgeois way of living and other reactionary ideas.[30]

Laissez-faire approaches to the UYs and to their group life have also adversely affected their capacity to earn a living and therefore their adaptation to life in the countryside. In 1973 the press confirmed what a good many informants have reported, namely, that many UYs have not been self-sufficient (*tzu-chi*) but have been unable to earn a living in the countryside. Thus in Chi county, Hopei, which was singled out as a model case illustrating the problem as well as solutions, the majority of UYs settled in Tung-shih-ku commune had not been self-sufficient in 1970; similar data were not supplied for the rest of the county.[31] Youths who were not self-supporting have depended on their parents for remittances, and this was one of the defects of the transfer program to which top-level leaders paid attention in 1973. Among the reasons for the absence of self-sufficiency were two that were aggravated by lack of guidance: urban youths often have been free to work fewer days than the peasants, and their groups have often not been organized to benefit from subsidiary production.

Lack of supervision enlarged the scope of individual choice for the UYs. Those lacking in motivation to work steadily, especially when able to depend on remittances from their parents, could decide on their own whether or not to show up for work. In Tung-shih-ku commune, UYs worked on the average one-third fewer days than did the peasants; other press reports suggest considerable year-to-year variation in numbers of days worked by the UYs, depending on the intensity of mobilization.[32] Thus, in one brigade in Chi county, UYs worked an average of 205 days in 1971, but 269 days in 1972, the brigade leaders having addressed themselves to the problem. Informants report having been quite free to make decisions on this matter. About a third of the informants who served on communes say they worked very hard, more or less on par with the peasants. But the others took off a great deal of time, typically by overstaying leaves in Canton. During the busy season, one youth made it a practice to show up for the early morning shift, sleep through the early afternoon shift, and then show up again for the evening shift. In such cases the production teams, rather than "strengthening leadership," would react by issuing rations to the UYs for each day actually worked, rather than in advance, as is normally done. Otherwise, the UYs would run deficit accounts, earning less than the cost of their rations, and hence constituting a burden on the local community. In the process, UYs often required a reputation for laziness, which did not improve their relations with the peasants.

Subsidiary undertakings such as raising pigs and poultry, growing fruit trees, cultivating private plots, and doing handicrafts are a most important source of income for peasant households. In many instances, urban youths have not benefited from this source of income.[33] As commune members, youths were assigned private plots and in principle were able to engage in subsidiary productive activities. But in practice few did so. Informants report that they were too tired to cultivate a private plot after working on the collective fields all day, or that they simply lacked the interest and motivation to do so. The problem, however, was not just a motivational one but a structural one: UY groups were insufficiently collectivized to permit the introduction of a division of labor, in which work on sideline production would be rotated among group members and the proceeds shared by all. In other words, UY units needed a system comparable to that of peasant households, whose division of labor permits some family members, especially women and children, to engage in sideline activities. The remedy—to be discussed more fully in the second part of the chapter—has been to promote the establishment of collective households (*chi-t'i-hu*), an old idea that dates back to the mid-1960s but was not sufficiently widely promoted until 1973 or so. An added consequence of this individualism was that each youth had to cook for himself, after a day's work in the collective fields.[34] Infor-

mants say that collective cooking was difficult to practice because the financial situations of UYs differed, as some received
funds from home and others did not, some worked hard and
others did not. Similarly, when a youth got sick, the groups
often were inadequately organized to provide care. Needless to
say, the consequent hardships did not increase the chance for
successful adaptation.

It need not be assumed that all UY settlements on communes have been characterized by lax leadership and guidance.
Certainly the press has carried a good many cases where consis-
tent leadership was in evidence, and where group organization
of the UYs followed the model of preemptive solidarity and was
also highly collectivized.[35] Two informants knew of UY groups
in neighboring villages that were quite progressive and where
activists must have played leadership roles. Probably laxness has
tended to be greatest in those cases in which very small groups
of three or four UYs were placed in production teams and
where the need for direct leadership of UY groups may not have
seemed so apparent. Larger UY settlements necessarily required
more formal organization and leadership structures in order to
function. This may explain why one of the remedial measures
aimed at strengthening leadership over the UYs has been to concentrate UYs into larger settlements.

Settlement on state and PLA farms provides a comparative
perspective to settlement on communes, especially in those
practicing the insertion system. State farms and PLA Production and Construction Corps farms have exercised much stricter
discipline and organizational supervision over the UYs. On two
PLA farms, as reported by two informants, UYs were organized
along military lines in a hierarchy of squad, platoon, company,
and regiment. Discipline was strict; youths did not have choices
over matters such as whether or not to show up for work.
Cadres, moreover, made an effort to break up cliques, groups,
and close friendships. If a youth had an argument with his company commander (lien-chang) and several of his friends came to
his assistance, the commander might then diagnose a "small
bloc" (hsiao chi-t'uan) and see to the transfer of its members to
different units. Moreover, cadres sought to mobilize group pressures in order to increase the commitment and enthusiasm of
the backward UYs. In neither case, however, were these measures completely effective. While an activist playing a leading

(*tai-t'ou*) role did sometimes have influence by virtue of his example, backward or less-committed UYs often sought to avoid
contact with activists, or sometimes made subtle fun of them
even while fearing them because of their power to report laggards to the superiors. Moreover, when UYs held the position of
squad, platoon, or company commander—the last being the
highest position to which UYs reportedly could rise—they could
come under informal pressures from below to understate output
in the case of a desirable commodity such as peanuts or to overstate norm fulfillment, as in the case of tasks such as clearing
land of tree stumps. The informants note, however, that explicit
collective countersolidarity did not develop; controls were too
strict. In 1970, for instance, one of the PLA farms set individual
norms at a very high level and no one was able to fulfill them.
The sanction for failure to fulfill norms, a cut in wages, was not
enforced because it would have affected everyone. Yet the UYs
had not made a collective decision not to fulfill the norms. This
case suggests, however, that countersolidarity among UYs on
PLA farms can develop and take on at least latent forms, not
because of the absence of strict guidance or supervision, as on
communes, but because of common interests created by harsh
demands for performance from the higher levels, which can
override the cleavage between those who are active and those
who are backward.*

Peasants and Urban Youths

Peasants are taught to welcome the new arrivals, but beneath
the warmth of the welcome, peasants assess the urban youths in
terms of the costs and benefits associated with their settlement.
Potential costs to the locals include the time and effort that
cadres and peasants may have to devote to UY problems. Some
of them have the "erroneous perception" that this constitutes
an additional burden on them.[36] The UYs may impose a burden

*In this case, the conflict between UYs and the leadership was apparently not
resolved. According to the informant, the norms were not reduced, nor were wages
as a whole cut, but after some time the wages of several lazier UYs were cut as a way
of putting pressure on the rest. It is worth adding that the informants did not evaluate the quality of the PLA regulars assigned to the Production and Construction
Corps farms in high terms. Some, very impressed with their own status (*liao pu ch'i*),
looked down on local workers and the UYs; some had committed errors and their
assignment to the farms was a form of punishment; others were inexperienced, and
in general, they tended to be "commandist" and toughly unrelenting in demanding
hard work. Older workers, in contrast, were apparently more favorably regarded;
they were loyal to the party but also good in working with the UYs.

on the local community simply by virtue of their presence as urbanites whose values, customs, and expectations may be different and as youths some of whom are quite unwilling to be in the village. Certainly peasants and village cadres have expressed apprehension at the prospect of "sly" or "cunning" city slickers in their midst, or, after the Cultural Revolution, of Red Guards who might be hard to handle and who might easily rebel.[37] The settlement may also impose material costs on the community if urban youths consume more than they produce. It is reasonable to hypothesize that, if these costs are very high, peasant attitudes toward the newcomers are likely to be negative and relationships characterized by strains and tensions. Conversely, if the costs are perceived as being not too high, and if they are balanced or even outweighed by benefits accruing from the settlement, relationships are likely to be good. Benefits might consist of UY contributions to village development projects or services rendered to the local community.

Policy makers have been sensitive to the burdens which the settlement might impose on the peasants and have sought to reduce these. For example, the goal of integration with the peasants (*chieh-ho*) does not mean that UYs must impose a burden by living with peasant families. Despite occasional rumblings to the contrary, such as criticism of "power holders" during the Cultural Revolution who allegedly prevented UYs and peasants from living more closely together,[38] policy makers have defined "integration" as compatible with separate living arrangements, in order to avoid strains resulting from UYs "disrupting the family life of the masses."[39] None of my informants lived with peasant families. One knew of a Canton youth who had done so, but the arrangement had not worked out because the youth "was not a relative."

While physical integration is not required, it is worth noting that the practice of settling a large proportion of urban youths in villages within their home provinces and often close to their home towns does reduce barriers of custom and dialect. Conversely, when UYs are sent to distant areas, particularly those inhabited by national minorities, they tend to be settled on state or army farms, in which there is less need to communicate with the surrounding rural population.[40] To be sure, the press has published some notable cases of UYs who settle in minority villages, learn the language, and achieve a remarkable degree of social integration. Some have even lived with minority families, as reported from some Mongol communes.[41] But such cases are balanced by accounts of Han youths encountering considerable difficulty because of unfamiliarity with the local language and customs.[42] One informant lived in a Hakka village, but since he spoke only Cantonese and some Mandarin his contact with the villagers was necessarily limited.

The definition of the transfer as entailing the "reeducation" of UYs by the poor and lower-middle peasants can also be regarded as an attempt to prevent a burden from being imposed on the peasants. As early as 1957, an editorial warned that peasant resentment could be aroused if educated urbanites flaunting their cultural superiority were sent to the villages to teach modern ways to the country bumpkins.[43] Subjecting the young urbanites to reeducation is a way of raising the status of the peasants vis-à-vis the urbanites and of reducing UY status in the eyes of the local community: it is the youths who come to learn from the peasants; it is they who must adapt to rural ways, and it is only when they have proved their worth to the local community that their status may be raised, such as through recruitment. The reduction in status which results from the elevation of sometimes semiliterate peasants to the position of teachers of graduates of urban upper middle schools is, at least in some cases, bitterly resented by the UYs. The idea that intellectuals should learn from peasants rather than peasants from the intellectuals was a major reason why one informant who had been politically active in the Red Guard movement found life in the village unbearable. Another one, who had taken part in the struggle meetings against Wang Kuang-mei, Liu Shao-ch'i's wife, during the Cultural Revolution, said, after all "we were the masters" (*wo-men shih chu-jen*). Informants note that peasants are in fact more likely to accept the UYs if they are deferential, ask peasants for advice, and do not display an air of superiority. Thus, if the conscious lowering of UY status below that of the peasants makes the transfer more acceptable to the peasants, it also makes it more difficult for at least some UYs to adjust to village life. Raising the acceptability of the UYs to the peasants entails costs that are borne by the UYs.

Policy makers have also sought to reduce or even eliminate the material costs which the settlement of urban youths might impose on a local community. The purpose of the state settlement fee, which until 1973 was 230 *yuan* for each youth but was raised in that year, reportedly to 480 yuan, is to enable the communes to absorb the UYs without having to pay for the costs associated with the initial settling in. It is not expected, for instance, that UYs will be able to earn a living on a par with that of the peasants in the first six months of their stay, since they lag behind the peasants in strength and endurance and need time to acquire the skills and knowledge to perform agricultural routines. Hence, part of the settlement fee is used to pay for the UYs' rations during the initial phase of their stay. Similarly, the settlement fee is supposed to pay for the construction of simple housing, the purchase of small tools, and other necessities. Actually, the settlement fee has not always been adequate for these purposes, leading in some cases at least to the local community's having to assume additional financial burdens. With regard to housing, it is known that some brigades have chipped in funds of their own in order to build adequate accommodations, causing grumbling among the peasants, who often have also been asked to contribute their labor for building UY houses (see below in this chapter). Conversely, however, the state settlement fee has in some cases been of benefit to the recipient team or brigade. In communes close to Hong Kong, UYs have sometimes escaped even before the settlement fee was used up, thus leaving the local unit with a net gain, and providing one reason why rural cadres do not seem to mind if UYs leave. The same point apparently applies to youths who leave their rural posts by illicitly returning to their home town. And cases have been reported of basic-level units that have diverted the settlement fee from its intended uses, using it instead to buy chemical fertilizer or to make some other investment, thereby creating a community benefit at the expense of the UYs.[44]

From the peasants' point of view, UY settlement costs exceed benefits when UYs are perceived as additional consumers of a constant pie. Peasants may resent UYs when the man-land ratio is high to begin with and additional labor power is simply not needed. Thus, in one Hopei village, the peasants grumbled that adding people without adding land would result in reduced individual incomes, while in another, which had a manpower shortage, the welcome was warmer.[45] When UYs are settled separately on communes, the land chosen is normally marginal or virgin land. Yet some peasants might wish to reclaim the land themselves. Tensions over competing claims to land have not

apparently been reported in the press, but in one case, in Huai-
te county, Kirin, where 10,000 UYs have settled, the county
party committee ordered production teams to put 3–5 *mou* of
good land at the disposal of UY collective households for the
purpose of conducting scientific experiments.[46] Perhaps in this
part of the Northeast, land is not scarce; if it is, however, one
wonders what the reaction of the peasants was. Peasants may
also feel deprived if the quotas for the sale to the state of surplus grain and other commodities remain unchanged despite the
arrival of additional consumers. It is not in fact clear what
policy is. One informant reports that the sales quota is reduced
to allow for the additional rations that have to be distributed.
But, he added, the peasants do not like this because it means a
reduction in their cash income. Other informants, however,
thought that the sales quota is not reduced, on the assumption
that additional laborers would lead to additional output.

While UYs do not control such elements of the peasants' cost-
benefit calculus as the availability of land, their response is
crucial to what may be the most important cost-benefit variable
in the peasants' perceptions, namely, whether or not they make
an effort to pull their weight, or whether they are merely consumers of local resources. This is not a matter of precise measurement. The key is whether they are seen as making a genuine
effort to adapt, to work hard in the fields, to contribute their
fair share, and not to be a burden to the local community. If
UYs exert themselves, do their best to adapt to the hardships of
village life, and work alongside the peasants steadily and persistently, the chance of acceptance by the peasants increases.[47] Informants agree that peasants' attitudes toward them were
shaped in large part by this variable. The fact that a good many
UYs simply lack the motivation to try hard is an important explanation for strained relations between them and the peasants.

If in addition to pulling their weight the youths, collectively
or individually, also make positive contributions to the village,
relations with the peasants are likely to improve still further. A
youth group may benefit the local community by constructing
a small dam, reclaiming a piece of hitherto infertile land, undertaking a project such as the electrification of a village, or
improving locally used seeds by "scientific experiments." Individual youths may contribute to the local community by becoming barefoot doctors or teachers. These contributions will

be discussed in detail in chapter 5, but it is worth noting that the press has in recent years given much publicity to this topic. Undoubtedly, a proportion of the UY population in the rural areas has been contributing to rural life in these ways, and presumably the peasants have appreciated this.

Still another way in which good relations can develop is on the level of individual UYs and individual peasants. Genuine friendships based on personal compatibility may develop, and some marriages between peasants and UYs may take place (see below). In some cases, sent-down youths will cultivate what is essentially an exchange relationship with a peasant, in which good relations are based on the trading of small favors. The small favors performed by informants for peasants consisted primarily of buying in Canton certain goods difficult to obtain in the villages, such as soap, lightbulbs, toothpaste, and medicine, but also of writing letters for peasants, and in one instance of repairing radios, watches, and electric motors free of charge (the latter being of course a service to the community as a whole); in another instance a youth took a peasant family's children to Canton to sightsee. Peasants reciprocated with gifts such as peanuts, a chicken, vegetables from their private plots, a New Year's present, or the loan of a bicycle. The press also prints examples of UYs performing services for peasants, but, as noted in chapter 1, it interprets such transactions as altruistic acts in which UYs display their class feelings for the poor and lower-middle peasants. Similarly, the press describes peasants or cadres who go out of their way to make the transfer a success by helping an individual UY in need, whether physically ill or beset by morale troubles.[48] But in addition the press voices uneasiness over the direction which the development of personal relations can take. This is shown by the numerous examples of class enemies who cultivate good relations with UYs in order allegedly to undermine the settlement.[49]

It is not possible to ascertain the proportion of UY-peasant relationships that are good because peasants perceive the UYs as in some way beneficial to them or at least as not imposing costs on them. Informants report that good relations developed primarily between individual UYs and individual peasants but in only a few cases between UY groups as a whole and the peasants, and that only a small minority of UYs enjoyed a good relationship with the peasants. Press reports would suggest that the proportion of good relationships has been considerably greater, but enough material has appeared to suggest that indifferent or bad relations have been a major problem.

Peasants and cadres react in a variety of ways toward UYs who do not make positive efforts to work hard and to adapt—with disappointment, exasperation, resentment, distrust, or simply incomprehension. In one case, reported from Chi-yuan county, Honan, the peasants had welcomed the UYs "like relatives." But after a while relations cooled. The UYs, afraid of hardship and ill at ease (*ching-hsü pu-an*), said and did some wrong things, unspecified in the article. The peasants concluded that "these city people are hard to handle," and "we country bumpkins can't handle these foreign students" (*yang hsüeh-sheng*). Like most press reports, this story had a happy ending: commune cadres taught both urban youths and peasants how to get along better, and it turned out, furthermore, that a class enemy had undermined their relations.[50] Several informants agreed that initially village cadres were helpful and showed concern for the UYs, but relations gradually cooled as the UYs failed to reciprocate and as they caused trouble and contributed little, from the cadre point of view. Local resentment of burdensome UYs is often based on incomprehension of the motivation of the urban youths. Cadres and peasants may not understand that some UYs simply do not want to be in the village in the first place, that they may in fact be unable to endure the labor and hardships that peasants are accustomed to from childhood on, and that some of them, if unable to cope with life in the countryside, are likely to act in improper ways. One informant quoted a county cadre as saying that he simply could not understand why so many UYs were infected by capitalist ideology. Unable to understand UYs who perform badly, local cadres may then react with such measures as issuing rations to UYs only for days actually worked. But even this may not improve UY behavior. Then, as one informant pointed out, what else can they do to you after they have deducted your rations? Exasperation and annoyance can turn into open distrust, all the more since some UYs in fact commit petty offenses such as stealing chickens from peasants.[51] As a Hong Kong Chinese wrote after visiting his home in Hupei: "Some of the people advised me not to become too familiar with 'hsia-feng' youngsters who accompanied me from Wuhan; the reason being that they might cheat me or steal my money. I asked whether they disliked the 'hsia-feng' students; they said no, but they did not trust them."[52]

Tensions between UYs and peasants could erupt into open hostility and conflict if an opportunity arose. During the Cultural Revolution, for instance, in some villages peasant mobs ganged up on UYs accused of being troublemakers and, according to charges in the Red Guard press, beat and even killed some of them.[53] The more normal situation since the Cultural Revolution, according to informants, is for poor relations to take the shape of mutual aloofness. In such cases, UYs and peasants have little or no contact with one another other than the minimum required by meetings and work. The youths may retreat into their own world and compensate for their bad relationship with the peasants with attitudes of superiority and disdain.[54] One group of UYs even put up a sign in front of their house saying "unauthorized persons keep out" (*hsien-jen mien-chin*) in order to prevent the peasants, whom they regarded as unclean, from visiting.[55] It need not be assumed that cases of bad relations are in the majority, however. Probably most UYs do try at least for some time to fit in and avoid causing offense, even if they do not make special efforts to develop good relationships.*

Implicit in the preceding discussions is an important point that needs to be spelled out further because of its significance in obstructing UY integration into the village. I have argued that peasant acceptance of the UYs hinges on the degree to which UYs make an effort not to be burdens on the local community. Yet there is also evidence suggesting that, even if the UYs do make the requisite effort, the peasants do not necessarily then accept UYs as full-fledged members of the local community. Informants who tried hard to cultivate good relations with peasants report that they were not fully accepted, that barriers between them and the peasants remained, that peasants did not treat them as one of "us."[56]

Peasant particularism has manifested itself not only in exclusionist attitudes toward outsiders but also in discriminatory treatment with regard to allocation of goods and especially with regard to work points.[57] In the case of work points, if an adult

---

*As we will see in chapter 6, hope for reassignment to the urban sector, which usually requires assent by the rural unit, is an important factor leading to adaptive behavior, but when prospects for reassignment are perceived as dim this incentive loses its force.

male peasant is adjudged by team members to be a full labor power (*lao-li*) and is given work grade 1, permitting him to earn ten work points per day, male UYs may be put into grade 2, or even 3 or 4, reducing the number of work points they can earn to the level of women or children. In Tung-shih-ku commune, Chi county, Hopei, because compensation was "unreasonable," the average UY male got two points less and female UYs one point less than their average local counterpart.[58] In villages in which work points are awarded for the completion of particular jobs, UYs may be regularly assigned to less remunerative work. When the UYs first arrive, their generally lower ratings are justified, since many UYs in fact lack the strength and endurance of peasant laborers. But, as their skills and endurance rise, UY work ratings should increase. In many cases this has not happened, as production teams failed to make the requisite adjustments. Some UYs have therefore done the same work as the peasants but have earned less. One informant took part in a work group engaged in felling trees. He worked at the same pace as the peasants but received fewer work points because he could not broadcast seeds. Peasants can broadcast seeds, he could not. Therefore he could not earn as many work points as peasants even when engaged in other tasks.[59] Another informant, a former Red Guard activist who had volunteered to go to the village, reports that he worked as hard as the adult peasants, doing first-grade labor, but was given a fourth-grade rating. "They exploited me by three degrees," he complained, adding that he was unable to earn more than 10 yuan per month. Discrimination, as illustrated by this case, is especially damaging to the morale of those who are well motivated and who try hard to adapt to rural life. Not all production teams, it is important to point out, have discriminated against UYs. About half of the informants who lived on communes report that their work grades and work points were fair and reasonable, given the actual amount of work they put in. But discrimination has been pervasive enough to be regarded as a major reason for UY inability to earn a living and consequently for a nationwide campaign launched in 1973 to guarantee the urban youths "equal pay for equal work" (see below).

When it comes to participation, peasants have also not always been willing to accept UYs as equal members of the community. In principle, UYs, when they join a production team, become commune members and have the right to take part in meetings. In practice a good many of them have abstained from involvement in village affairs. Reluctance to participate may be motivated by the UYs' own lack of interest in becoming integrated, but also by the UYs' perception that peasants resent the participation of outsiders. In the press, UYs have been portrayed as reluctant to suggest innovations, for fear the peasants would turn on them as interfering troublemakers if the suggestion backfired.[60] When one sent-down youth criticized cadres for not taking part in manual labor, the cadres considered it a rebellious act, until appropriate study convinced them that the UY actually had a right to take part in the criticism campaign.[61] Urban youths have been reluctant to take part in class struggle campaigns especially in single-surname villages, since peasants did not seem to think it appropriate for an outsider to criticize a relative, even if he was a class enemy.[62] A *Peking Review* article provides an illustration from Kwangsi: "When two girl students among us joined the peasants in their struggle against local class enemies, someone threatened them: You are not familiar with our place yet. Why do you mind other people's business? You girls mustn't go too far. The girls were somewhat uneasy on hearing this."[63] As a model case, this story naturally ended with the UY girls in fact taking part in class struggle and, with the help of leadership, successfully overcoming the opposition. But this is by no means the only bit of evidence of local resentment at UYs who poke their noses into "others' business."[64]

Peasant relations with the UYs, it should be clear by now, have varied considerably. Just as some UYs make strenuous efforts to adapt and others do not, so also some local communities seem more accepting of the UYs than others. In some places (see chapter 5), UYs have been able to play active participatory and even leadership roles; in others, they find it difficult or even impossible to achieve acceptance. It is not possible to determine the distribution of the cases, but can an explanation be offered for the range of variation? One possible explanation would cite level of rural modernization: the more traditional and backward a village, the more likely it is to have a particularistic and discriminatory attitude toward the outsiders, whereas the more modern or advanced a village is, the more likely it is for peasants to base their approach to the UYs on universalistic criteria. This hypothesis makes a good deal of intuitive sense. It finds support in the distinctions that one informant drew between urban and rural life: "It is easy to become integrated into a factory; everybody is habituated to that kind of life. But the peasants' way of life is different. Living standards are lower, as in housing, food, medical care, labor. But human relations also differ; it is hard to get used to."

While the hypothesis is plausible, it has not been possible to test it with the available data, that is, to find out whether, in those cases in which UYs tried hard to adapt but met with a discriminatory response on the part of the peasants, the level of modernization was a major factor. One problem is that the peasants' treatment of the UYs is also a function of political leadership. Political leadership (as well as organization) influences the behavior of both the UYs and the peasants. If village cadres behave according to the official norms, discrimination against the UYs cannot occur; they will then be treated not in accordance with the peasants' particularistic values but more in accordance with the regime's universalistic ones.* If village cadres behave in accordance with the values and perceptions of their fellow peasants and take or ratify decisions to discriminate, it follows that higher-level leadership has neglected or failed to influence them to act in accordance with the "correct" norms. When peasant and official values conflict, village cadres must be reminded that they are not only peasants but also communist leaders whose duty it is to educate the peasants to abide by the official prescriptions. The role of political factors—leadership, organization, political education—in making the transfer work may thus be at least as important as socioeconomic factors, if not more so. The decisive role of politics is of course an article of faith of the regime; some of the interviews reflect this as well. Three informants had settled in Po-lo county, about 120 kilometers from Canton. These informants did not encounter discrimination. Relations with the cadres were "more regulated" and there were no abuses; work points were given according to actual work performed. Relations with the peasants seemed to be fairly good; cadres encouraged the peasants to help the UYs. For their part, the UYs also were not "wild" (*yeh-man*); there were no mass escapes. Po-lo is apparently a fairly poor county, with few local factories, but it was politically progressive—a

*To be sure, these have their ascriptive components as exemplified by the treatment of those from bad class backgrounds.

model in the study of Mao Tse-tung Thought. Strong politicization, two of the informants argued, made a difference in the
way the settlement there worked; this contrasts with the reports
of informants from less politicized areas.* If this is so, then it is
not surprising that one of the remedial measures to improve the
workings of the transfer has been to "strengthen leadership."

REMEDIAL MEASURES

Remedial measures designed to improve the adaptation of urban youths to rural life should in principle be in progress all the
time. That is, as experience is gained with the settlement, as
problems arise and are uncovered, remedies should be tried and
put into practice. In fact, at various times measures have been
taken at the national or local levels to effect improvements in
the settlement. But it was not until 1973, nearly five years after
the onset of the mass transfer of urban youths to the countryside in the wake of the Cultural Revolution, that a sustained
campaign to correct deficiencies in the program was launched.
As noted in chapter 2, the initiative came from Chairman Mao
himself, to whom a Fukien teacher had succeeded in communicating word of the difficulties encountered by sent-down
youths. The need for remedial measures was no doubt reinforced by decisions taken in 1973 to speed up the rate of transfer and to draw up specific plans for the implementation of the
program in the next seven years. Indeed, one of the reasons for
inadequate attention to the settlement on the part of local leadership had been the perception that it was only a short-term
program.

Reexamination of the program entailed taking a searching
look at major aspects of the settlement, ranging from the efficacy of leadership to the adequacy of the resources committed
to the transfer program. Some remedial measures were taken in
1973, but others only later. That is, high-level interest in the
transfer led to a search for new approaches and to the singling
out of innovative local experiments as models for nationwide
emulation. A good example is provided by the Chu-chou model,

*Of course, the difference was not great enough to motivate the informants to
adapt to rural life on a permanent basis. In their cases, it is worth adding, bad class
background was a factor in prompting escape. One of the informants had actually
become an activist and a teacher but found further upward mobility blocked because
of her class; hence she ultimately left the PRC. Indeed, because it was a model
county, the class line may have been enforced more strictly.

mentioned at the end of chapter 3, which came to public notice
in June of 1974 and heralded a new emphasis on separate settlement of sent-down youths rather than on inserting them into
production teams. An important feature of the remedial campaign was its concern with highly concrete, material issues, even
while the ideological goals of the transfer were strongly reasserted. The following quote, from an article that criticized "localities where work has not been done adequately or has been
done with poor results" gives an illustration:

> Livelihood problems of the educated young people are chiefly
> concerned with food, housing, daily necessities, labor, medi-
> cine and marriage. They must be arranged properly. Their
> problems regarding food grain, vegetable plots and firewood
> supply must be solved rationally. Effort must be made to run
> well the collective messhalls for educated young people. Their
> problems of housing must be solved in practical ways. . . . Care
> should be taken of the young women's physiological charac-
> teristics, concern should be shown for the young people's
> health and attention paid to the prevention and treatment of
> diseases and to the proper running of cooperative medical ser-
> vices.[65]

The remainder of this chapter examines various remedial measures designed to improve the settlement of urban youth.

Improving Leadership

In late summer and early autumn of 1973, following a national conference on urban youth settlement reportedly convened by Hua Kuo-feng, many provinces held meetings on the
subject.[66] One of the conclusions that these conferences reached
was that the management of the youths required more sustained
and institutionalized leadership. As an editorial from Kweichow
put it, "Leadership at all levels must absolutely not regard the
task of setting educated young people in the countryside as a
temporary measure. . . . Instead of grasping this task sporadical-
ly, they must grasp it constantly, repeatedly, and through to the
end. They must not cast educated young people aside as soon as
they have sent them to the countryside."[67] At the levels above
the commune, especially the county, a party secretary was to
take charge of UY work. Hitherto, as in Ming-shui county,
Heilungkiang, UY work had been entrusted to a specialized de-

partment (*yeh-wu pu-men*) on the assumption that this would suffice and because "central tasks are heavy."[68] Because the leading members of the party committee failed to deal with the settlement, problems arose. Consequently, as a Hunan conference on the settlement concluded, "CCP committees at all levels must . . . include this work [UY settlement] on their agenda and assign a secretary to take charge of it. The regional, municipal, and county CCP committees must set up leadership groups for the settlement of educated young people in the countryside, with the participation of responsible comrades concerned, and establish competent offices."[69] At the commune, brigade, and team levels, emphasis has also been placed on allocating responsibility for UY work to specific cadres who are members of a party committee or branch, so that UY matters can be readily brought to the attention of the key leader of the unit. A model was provided by one Anhwei brigade, whose *ch'ou-tui hsiao-tsu* (small group to deal with those inserted into the brigade) was headed by a CCP branch deputy secretary, and which assigned members of the branch to do ideological work with the UYs on a rotating basis. Each production team in the brigade assigned one person to take charge of UYs in the team. The party branch committee met once a month to discuss UY "thought problems." At the end of the year, the conduct of each UY in the brigade was evaluated.[70] Assignment of specific responsibilities and placing UY affairs on the committee's agenda were thus designed to block the drift into indifference and neglect that seems to have occurred on a wide scale when responsibility for UYs was diffused or assigned to minor cadres.

Judging by appraisals published two years later, the effort to secure ongoing attention to UY settlement problems on the part of the rural leadership hierarchy has not been fully successful. Thus, in June 1975, *Red Flag* voiced complaints similar to those heard two years previously.[71] In Hupei province, "party committees at all levels" were told in 1975, in words virtually identical to those used in 1973, to put settlement work on their agendas. "The first secretaries must frequently check up on this. The secretary-in-charge must take specific responsibility."[72] In Hopei, "some leading cadres . . . have not paid sufficient attention to this work" nor taken "prompt and effective measures."[73] Repeated prodding is essential to secure attention to a program which a good many rural cadres continue to view as a

burden and evidently as of marginal importance to them. This is
not to say that it is impossible to obtain the requisite level of
involvement. Thus in Anhwei in 1975, the "leading bodies . . .
have further increased their understanding . . . and done an increasingly better job" in the settlement.[74] A national appraisal
published in December 1975 was also positive: "better settlement work has been done this year than ever before."[75] But administrative interest in the transfer program is clearly not of the
same order as is concern with, say, the annual harvest.

Perhaps because rural leaders have been somewhat reluctant
to devote time to the settlement program, large numbers of
urban cadres were mobilized to assume this burden in 1974 and
1975. In 1974, when nearly 2 million UYs went to the countryside, 40,000 cadres went with them, a ratio of 1 cadre to 50
UYs.[76] In 1975, when 2 million youths were sent down, "more
than 60,000 cadres" were assigned to the program, that is, 1 for
every 33 youths.[77] In 1969–70, 1,600 cadres accompanied
"several hundred thousand" UYs from Shanghai to the rural
areas; in the first half of 1974, 1,900 cadres escorted 68,000
UYs from cities and towns in Szechwan to rural destinations in
that province.[78] Reports from other cities and provinces show
that sometimes the ratio of cadres to UYs is far below the
national average, for example, 1 to 13 in Wuhan or 1 to 15 in
Fukien.[79] In contrast to the earlier period when cadres merely
escorted UYs to their rural destinations, since 1974 cadres have
stayed with them for prolonged periods of time, in emulation of
a practice publicized by the Chu-chou model. After perhaps a
year or so of rural service, they are rotated back to their home
towns.[80] Much stress is laid on their outstanding qualities; the
vast majority are party members and quite a few occupy responsible positions in the cities. In Hupei, "it is necessary to select
outstanding cadres to lead the young people. They must include
a certain number of women cadres. . . . The selection of cadres
to lead the young people can be combined with the sending
down of cadres for participation in labor. . . ."[81]

The main assignment of the urban cadres is to lead UY groups.
Sian cadres, for example, have taken charge of four tasks: they
(1) organize UY political study, (2) lead UYs to become "steeled"
in the movements to criticize Lin Piao and Confucius, as well as
in class and line struggle, (3) organize them to become a "contributing force" in the movement to learn from Tachai, and (4)
closely concern themselves with the management of the UYs'

livelihood (*sheng-huo kuan-li kung-tso*).[82] The urban cadres are to be closely integrated into the local administrative and political structure, functioning under the "unified leadership" of the local party organs: "In accordance with the needs of the work, they should be absorbed into the leading groups of the counties, districts, communes and brigades for the specific purpose of looking after work concerning educated young people who have settled in the countryside".[83] Depending on the number of such cadres in any one locality, their presence would seem to reduce at least to some degree the burden of UY management that falls on the local cadres. Their presence may thus help to realize the intent of the policy makers that constant and ongoing attention be paid to the UYs.

Data are as yet insufficient to assess the actual role played by the urban cadres in promoting UY adaptation. To the degree that they in fact supply ongoing guidance to UY groups, these groups may come to function more effectively along the lines intended, with less development of countersolidarity. Their leadership may enable more UYs to earn a living, both because these cadres may mobilize them to work harder and more steadily and because they may oversee the structural changes needed to enable UY groups to engage in sideline production (see also below). In leading UY groups, the urban cadres may be more effective than rural cadres, for in the cases reported they come from the home towns of the UYs. The *t'ung-hsiang* ("same locality") feeling they may share, which by definition is lacking in UY relations with the rural people, may provide a basis for solidary interaction. Indeed, it is one of the duties of the urban cadres to maintain ties with the home towns by reporting to urban units as well as to parents of sent-down youths. This continuing linkage may serve to reassure parents and hence positively affect UY adaptation.[84] Conversely, it is conceivable that the presence of the urban cadres could undermine adaptation. Urban cadres apparently are rotated back to their urban homes; UYs stay for life, at least in principle. This difference between UYs and urban cadres could aggravate UY feelings of relative deprivation and thus breed resentment.

Changing Settlement Patterns

The reexamination of the program resulted in a distinct shift in policy in favor of concentrated as opposed to "scattered" (*fen-san*) settlement, and in favor of a more strictly organized collective group life. The purpose was to make the development of countersolidarity less likely and to make it possible for groups to make a proper living. Central regulations called on local authorities to make a choice between different organizational forms:

> In settling educated youths in the countryside, consideration should be given to local conditions. Youth centers consisting of at least 10 persons may be set up within production teams. Educated youths may be settled on farms and forest and livestock farms practicing collective ownership which are run by counties, communes, or production brigades. . . . In areas where there is waste land to be reclaimed, youth farms and youth teams practicing collective ownership may be set up under the supervision of local production brigades or teams.[85]

All these forms imply greater concentration. Even in cases of insertion of youths into production teams, policy now called for a minimum of ten persons to form a "collective household" (*chi-t'i hu*) or a "youth point" (*ch'ing-nien tien*). Judging by reports from various provinces, concentrated settlement has been promoted on a wide scale. In Fukien, "those places where no youth points have been established should concentrate the widely scattered educated youths and establish youth points. Help should also be given to the youth points to establish strong leading groups."[86] In Szechwan the new policy emphasis led to the organization of 10,000 youth points by the middle of 1974; few such units had evidently been in existence previously.[87] In 1975, Kwangtung too stressed collective settlement; policy statements called for "minimizing" the dispersal among production teams of the 80,000 youths to be settled that year.[88]

Chu-chou provided a national model for separate settlement. The county had an estimated 2 million *mou* of undeveloped hill and mountain lands, at least some of which could be put to productive use.* In an effort to do so, the communes set up agricultural, forest, and tea farms (*nung-, lin-,* and *ch'a-ch'ang*) attached to either a commune or a brigade. As of 1975, 600 such farms had been set up; 12,000 sent-down youths had settled on 420 of them (an average of 29 youths per farm), together with some local peasants and urban cadres:[89]

> The agricultural, forest, and tea farms of the communes and

*Six *mou* equal one acre.

brigades are established according to the principle of "three-level ownership with the team as the foundation." Within the boundaries of a brigade, the adjoining mountain lands which individual production teams cannot cultivate on their own are cultivated jointly as a farm operated by the brigade. . . . Part of the income of the farms is allocated to the owners of the land, part to accumulation by the farm, and part to compensate the labor contributed by the production teams. Educated youths settled [on these farms] have their household registration with a production team. They spend most of their time studying and laboring on the farms. During the busy season they return to their production teams to work. . . . Several times a month they also go back to their teams to take part in meetings with the commune members, to study with them, so as constantly to maintain close ties. Like other commune members living on the farms, they share in the distribution of [income] of the teams to which they belong.[90]

Relations with the indigenous collective units vary; in one case reported from Kiangsu, a UY collective farm was set up as an independent accounting unit, but apparently the more common pattern is for youth collectives to be attached to one of the communal subdivisions.[91]

The trend toward more widespread establishment of separate youth settlements reduces the degree of integration of urban youths into the peasant communities. Undoubtedly, this reflects awareness on the part of the authorities that close contact between the urbanites and the peasants can easily lead to friction. Moreover, even close contact that does not give rise to tensions may not be desirable; witness press sensitivity to the development of informal but corrupting relationships between urban youths and "backward" peasants or class enemies.[92] Official approval is given to the development of warm human relationships between urban youths and peasants, provided, however, that the peasants in question reinforce rather than undermine the transfer program. Separate settlement reduces opportunities for the development of close informal relations but has the advantage of permitting interactions between urban youths and peasants to be formally organized, as at meetings or joint work projects.

A major reason for the shift to concentrated settlement forms is that they make it "easier to strengthen leadership and orga-

nize study in a unified way."[93] Small groups of three or four
UYs have tended, as noted previously, to be left to their own
devices, thereby providing opportunities for spontaneous and
improper behavior. Establishment of a larger collective household within a production team has required provision of leadership, usually in the form of an experienced peasant or urban
cadre who serves as an "instructor" (fu-tao yuan) or "head of
household" (hu-chang).[94] Larger, separate units necessarily require articulation of even more differentiated leadership structures. In Huai-an county, Kiangsu, for instance, a commune
decided in 1970 to settle forty UYs on separate, barren land.
Two cadres and four peasants from the commune were assigned
to the UY collective and a three-in-one leading body of cadres,
peasants, and UYs was set up: "The cadres shared the same
quarters and messhall, worked and studied with the poor and
lower-middle peasants and educated young people, and took
good care of the young people. Under the guidance of the
cadres and the poor and lower-middle peasants, the educated
young people displayed the revolutionary spirit of arduous
struggle and relied on their own efforts in building a farm."[95] It
seems unlikely that, under these circumstances of face-to-face
guidance and supervision, countersolidarity could easily have
developed among these urban youths. In Hai-ch'eng county,
Liaoning, where it will be recalled that lax leadership had given
rise to "problems and disturbances" among the 28,000 UYs
who had settled there as of late 1972, concentrated settlement
was viewed as the answer:

> Special groups have been organized and special personnel as-
> signed at county, commune and brigade levels to keep a firm
> grip on the reeducation of young intellectuals. . . . Further-
> more, some 1,911 youth centers have been set up by represen-
> tatives of the poor and lower-middle peasants, brigade cadres,
> and production team cadres to help the young intellectuals
> temper themselves. To strengthen leadership . . . the county's
> party committee has incorporated the 1,911 youth centers
> into 67 youth centers with the production brigade as the basic
> unit. YCL branches and groups have been established in 85
> percent of the youth centers and some youth centers have
> formed party groups.[96]

Two years later, the number of UYs in Hai-ch'eng county had
grown to 48,000 and a broadcast spoke of "youth commu-

nities," suggesting that some of the 1,911 youth centers have
been physically amalgamated into even larger settlements.[97]

Whatever the form of settlement, a major goal was to collec-
tivize living arrangements, in order to raise the capacity of the
UYs to earn a living. In the absence of collective arrangements,
youths individually were supposed not only to work on the
fields of their production unit but also to engage in sideline
activities, cultivate a private plot, and cook their own meals.
UYs unable or unwilling to do all this suffered loss of income as
well as the discomforts of having to eat in a makeshift manner.
By the same token, those who did carry out all these tasks had
no time left for political study or participation in social activities, points of particular concern to the press.[98] Concentration
of sent-down youths into larger settlement groups has made
possible the introduction of a division of labor among the UYs,
according to which some are assigned in rotation to tasks such as
operating mess halls and sideline undertakings such as the raising
of pigs and vegetables. The division of labor makes possible a
more settled and stable pattern of life.[99] Income generated
from sideline operations boosts their capacity to be self-sufficient and make a living in the countryside. In the case of one
separately settled youth collective in Huai-an county, Kiangsu,
40 percent of its income came from diversified undertakings, including the growing of mushrooms and medicinal herbs, the
operation of a repair shop, and the raising of ducks, chickens,
and hogs. As a result, "the income and living standards" of the
UYs have been raised, and a "solid material foundation" has
been laid for these UYs "to take root in the countryside."[100]
Well-run youth collectives have growing assets, as pigs and other
products are sold to the state. The collective savings make possible expansion of facilities as well as a richer political and
recreational life: books are bought, subscriptions taken out, and
sports equipment acquired.

Despite these advantages, the pooling of resources and rotating
of assignments that are characteristic of collective living can give
rise to conflict among the UYs unless guidance and supervision
are provided. In one brigade in Kuei-yang county, Kwangsi,
sixty-nine UYs had been organized into ten "collective hearths"
(chi-t'i tzao). Because of inadequate leadership, "disunity" arose
among some of them when they exceeded their budgeted living
expenses and when UYs quarreled over assignments. Once the
party branch had provided "help" in the form of tightened lead-

ership, the advantages of the collective hearth system became apparent: the youths were learning the "spirit of collectivism," they were able to take part in political and social activities, and they raised their own pigs, poultry, and vegetables. Their incomes rose not only because of sideline production but also because the UYs worked more on the collective fields of the brigade than they had before.[101] This last point deserves emphasis, for the theme that increased guidance results in increasing the number of days worked runs through the remedial literature. More sustained work can be the product simply of greater control, such as the imposition of "work checks" (*lao-tung k'ao-ho*) or of requirements that UYs put in a minimum number of days per month (22 in a case from Anhwei), but it can also be the product of collectivized group life.[102] When a UY collective pools resources, each member acquires a stake in the performance of the other members. This interest can be mobilized by the leaders of the collectives and can result in group pressures being aimed at those UYs who otherwise would have chosen not to work so hard. It is this consequence of collective interdependence which the press seems to have in mind when it refers to the "growth of habits of collective life."[103]

The establishment of youth collectives was so central a part of the remedial campaign that it can probably be assumed that youth collectives have become much more widespread, although it is not possible to determine the proportion of UYs in communes who live a collective life. As a result of this change, it is likely that more UYs are becoming self-sufficient and able to earn a living independently of their families, thereby furthering the cause of adaptation to rural life. At the same time, little information on UY incomes has been released. In one commune in Huai-te county, Kirin, where UYs had been organized in collective households early on, the average annual personal income of the UYs rose from 186 yuan to 262 in 1971 but fell slightly to 255 yuan in 1972.[104] It is not clear whether income from the sideline operations of the collective households is included in these figures, nor how these compare to the per capita income of the peasants of that commune. The 1972 income figure comes to 21.25 yuan per month, which is slightly higher than the 16–20 yuan per month reportedly paid on state farms until 1972 or 1973. It is reasonable to assume that many more UYs have become self-sufficient, but it is not possible to estimate the proportion.

Allocating Additional Resources

The remedial campaign sought to make the urban youths self-sufficient, thereby lightening the "burdens on society and on the families."[105] Yet the remedial effort itself was costly in that it required additional resources. Such resources originated from the state, the urban units, and the rural communes. The state increased the settlement fee paid for each urban youth, reportedly from 230 to 480 yuan, apparently making it possible to support a youth for a full first year, not just for six months.[106] Pay on state farms was increased to 30 yuan per month—an important measure, since the old wages had necessitated parental subsidies for clothing and incidentals.[107] In addition, as noted in chapter 2, in one province, Kiangsi, 6 million yuan in loans have been extended to UY settlements in order to get them started. Undoubtedly, this is not the only such case.

Urban industrial and other units that have taken part in the settlement, following the Chu-chou model, have contributed the time of their cadres, as well as tangible resources, particularly for housing. The resource implications of the urban-rural linkages were highlighted at a settlement conference in Kirin, at which it was "pointed out . . . that in popularizing the experience of Chu-chou Municipality, rural communes and brigades should not seek to cooperate with only those big and financially or materially well-off urban units, while urban units should not cooperate only with well-to-do communes and brigades."[108] Presumably what had happened was that the rural units wanted to extract the maximum from the urban ones and the urban ones wanted to minimize their commitments. As for the communes and their subdivisions, they have been asked to contribute the time of cadres and peasants to UY affairs, to contribute labor for the construction of housing, and to do better preparatory work.[109] A new regulation was also apparently put into effect in 1974 requiring communes to guarantee UYs a minimum annual wage of 200 yuan, provided they worked for at least 250 days per year. If the cash value of their work points was less than the minimum wage, a subsidy would be paid to make up the difference. Conversely, higher work point earnings would be paid as usual. It is not, however, clear whether the supplement was to come out of the resources of the communes or their subdivisions, or out of the state sector, that is, from the county governments.[110] If implemented generally, this reform would

begin to meet the grievance of those who worked steadily but
earned a pittance because their work point ratings were too low
(see the next section).

Housing has been a key claimant on resources. As noted in the
first part of this chapter, the state settlement fee was not always
adequate to pay for housing, resulting either in inadequate or
substandard housing for sent-down youths or in the local community's having to contribute funds of its own.[111] For instance,
a brigade in Yi-ch'eng, Shansi, invested 5,700 yuan for UY
housing.[112] The reaction of the peasants was not recorded. In a
small brigade of only eighty households in Feng-jun county,
Hopei, UYs from Tangshan arrived in 1965, giving rise to a debate about housing. "Some comrades" proposed that only as
many houses be built as state funds permitted, even if UYs
would have to be crowded in a bit. The party secretary opposed
this view on the grounds that the UYs were going to remain for
a long time and hence would need proper quarters. Apparently,
his view carried the day, for five years later, when an additional
group of UYs was assigned to the brigade, "some comrades"
noted that in 1965 the production teams had had to raise additional money to build houses for the youths. This time, they
argued, it would not be necessary to build more houses and the
state fee could be invested in agriculture. The party secretary
opposed the proposal to divert the settlement fee, arguing that
in a few years the UYs would want to get married; hence they
would eventually need additional living space. His views prevailed and ten more houses were built, eleven having been constructed in 1965.[113] The story hints at the conflicts that can
arise over resource allocation and suggests that villages lacking
so properly motivated a party secretary may well have made
different decisions.

The policy of concentrating UYs, and particularly of establishing separate settlement, increased the demand for housing, and
this may explain why the settlement fee was more than doubled.
In addition, administrative agencies above the communes have
contributed resources for the solution of the housing problem.
In Szechwan UY housing was defined as "a long-term item of
capital construction."[114] A provincial conference was held in
1973 on the financial problems of UY settlement, in which the
county authorities were evidently asked to supply building materials, for the same report goes on to say that "Chichiang
County CCP Committee has provided 300 cubic meters of tim-

ber for the educated youths to build houses."[115] When eight hundred UYs were to be settled in Pa-yen county, Heilungkiang, the county's Department of Building Materials drew up a supply plan for the forty-eight projected youth points, thereby insuring the availability of wood, bricks, tile, sand, stones, and glass.[116] In a case reported from Yung-teng county, Kansu, the party committee, having found that a brigade had not built houses for new UYs, "immediately consulted the brigade party branch and sent special personnel to transport timber from a place 200 li away."[117]

Urban participation in the settlement has focused on housing. In Chu-chou, in an eight-month period in 1973, 957 new houses were built for the sent-down youths. "When building materials were in short supply, the factories made available their scrap materials. When transport could not be found, the factories sent their trucks to help out."[118] Similar assistance by urban industrial units has been reported from elsewhere.[119]

The increased availability of state and urban resources has not meant a repudiation of self-reliance and local self-help as solutions to the housing problem. Not only is it expected that the basic-level units assume responsibility for actually building the houses, but accounts also stress the desirability of using local building materials and other resources. In cases in which youth collectives prosper and accumulate their own funds, these may be tapped for expansion and improvements.[120]

Appraisal of the results of the remedial campaign to build adequate housing is hampered by inadequate data on the proportion of UYs who have benefited from improved housing. In a good many instances, much progress has been made. Chi county, Hopei, a model case for the diagnosis and cure of settlement problems, built 1,189 houses for UY groups, for an average of 0.8 rooms per UY. Construction in Chi county, moreover, anticipated future UY marriages: a UY couple will receive 1.5 rooms, which is more or less the equivalent of what the local peasants have.[121] In Anhwei, where 400,000 UYs had settled as of May 1974, "45,000 new houses" have been built, but it is not clear what the time period is. In four specifically mentioned communes, "each educated youth" has a private room. "Each group of educated young people has its own walled compound with a kitchen, wells, a toilet, pig sties and vegetable gardens."[122] All this suggests that in many places vigorous action has been taken. Nonetheless, newspaper stories published after the remedial campaign continued to treat housing as a problem, and not one that affected only new arrivals. Thus in November 1975 the *People's Daily* reported that a county party committee member in Ssu-hui, Kwangtung, uncovered inadequate housing conditions in four communes. The committee immediately sent building materials in order to remedy the problem.[123] To the extent that adequate living quarters have been provided where this had not been the case previously, to that extent the cause of adaptation to rural life has been advanced.

Securing Redress of Grievances

Some of the difficulties encountered by sent-down youths in the villages were due to discriminatory treatment. The remedial campaign addressed itself in no uncertain terms to violations of UY rights. Provincial conferences held in 1973 issued demands for equal treatment: "It is necessary to implement the policy of equal pay for equal work between the educated young people . . . and the local commune members and between men and women."[124] Similarly, they demanded an end to misappropriation of the settlement fee: "Funds and material supplies allocated by the state for the settlement . . . should be put under strict control. . . . No unit or individual should be allowed to use these funds or supplies for other purposes."[125] Physical abuse of UYs was also condemned: "As for class enemies and criminals who have persecuted and done harm to the educated youths, we must use the dictatorship of the proletariat to punish them according to law."[126] The public media did not detail instances of "persecution" or "harm." Materials circulated within China that have reached the outside world indicate that severe punishment of rapists of female urban youths was an important component of the remedial campaign.[127]

How can redress of legitimate UY grievances be achieved? One approach is for the UYs themselves to take the initiative. They can lodge complaints with higher-level authority. But higher-level officials have not always responded, at least not before the Cultural Revolution, judging by Red Guard accusations of extreme bureaucratic insensitivity among them: "There were 77 youths on the Ta-p'ing Farm at Kueiyang. After coming to this farm, 26 of them contracted diseases. Over 80 percent of the young women were insulted and raped. The farm manager, the Party branch secretary and the *hsien* committee cadres 'played a leading role' in this regard. The youths sent 27 reports on this matter to the administrative district and provincial committees but received no answer."[128] Informants say that it is possible to lodge complaints with the higher levels, such as the commune cadre in charge of UY affairs, who has the right to require remedial action within the framework of prevailing policies and principles. One informant felt that this cadre was able to help with "small questions" concerning livelihood and labor, but not with big questions relating to return to the city. Other informants cast doubt on the effectiveness of complaining, noting that the higher-level cadre may refer the complaint back to the team or the brigade, that is, to the very cadres against whom it was lodged. Since village cadres can retaliate in subtle ways, as with work assignments, UYs are likely to be cautious in voicing complaints. The press has reported on the reluctance of UYs to offend or criticize local cadres for fear of jeopardizing opportunities for reassignment, which depend on a favorable recommendation from one's unit.[129] "Even Chairman Mao can't change that," one informant concluded in commenting on the informal power of basic-level cadres.

What are the possibilities of collective redress of grievance? In the early stages of the Cultural Revolution, UYs on some communes and state farms confronted cadres collectively, subjecting some to mass criticism and struggle meetings, and checking accounts to see how the settlement fee was spent. As we shall see in chapter 6, however, sent-down youths who sought to confront the rural power structure during the Cultural Revolution generally fared badly, which was one reason why many of them returned to the cities during that upheaval. In Chinese society as a whole, mass criticism during the Cultural Revolution may well have made cadres more cautious in misusing their powers, but in the case of UY-cadre relations this does not seem to have been so. Instead, after the Cultural Revolution, in 1968 and 1969, some rural cadres retaliated against returning UYs who had criticized them in 1966 during the first stage of the Cultural Revolution, while in other cases, UY-cadre relations were worse than they had been before.[130] Since the Cultural Revolution, occasional reports have surfaced of collective articulation of grievances that resulted in remedial action. A group of five UYs in a brigade in Han-chiang county, Kiangsu, had been living in an inadequate house. They demanded that the revolutionary committee of the brigade see to the rapid completion of construction of a larger house, threatening that they would spend the nights in the county town more than 20 *li* away. (One *li* equals half a kilometer.) The brigade cadres responded that their threat violated Chairman Mao's teachings, but that their request for improved housing was a reasonable one.[131]

If UY initiative in seeking redress of grievance can have results, it does seem that the main burden for insuring proper treatment of the UYs falls on higher-level officialdom.[132] Sending higher-level officials down to the grassroots to investigate (*tiao-ch'a*) or inspect (*chien-ch'a*) is a well-established practice in China, and one which recognizes that the upward flow of communication through regular channels is not adequate to keep the higher levels informed.[133] Higher-level cadres inspecting conditions in the villages are in a position to push for immediate remedial action. When the official in charge of UY work of Ta-hsien Special District, Szechwan, visited a commune, he found that three UY girls were badly housed and had not been given work tools and kitchen utensils. He also found that some new arrivals had not been issued the oil and grain allowance which the state stipulated they should. This cadre felt that these shortcomings jeopardized the settlement and hence asked the commune to correct these conditions.[134] In another case, in Hopei, the commune deputy party secretary went to investigate conditions in a production brigade and found UYs poorly housed, whereupon he personally led the brigade to construct ten new houses.[135] In this case, the commune party committee generalized from the deputy secretary's discovery of a housing problem in one brigade and adopted countywide remedies. When higher-level investigation teams visit villages, the purpose is to compile information that can be used by policy makers up to the central level. Investigation reports are undoubtedly an important source of information on problems that require remedial action, as the frequent references in this chapter to the case of Chi county, Hopei, suggest.

When higher-level authorities become aware of the need for remedial action, it does not necessarily follow that vigorous action will be taken. According to an informant, in 1970 a document was issued by the State Planning Commission, reportedly approved by Mao Tse-tung, which instructed local leaders to end discrimination. The county cadres accordingly organized a countywide meeting for the UYs, at which the document was read to the UYs and they were asked to voice complaints.[136] The youths complained about bad housing and unfair work points. With regard to housing, the county cadres met with brigade cadres separately, and it was decided that additional housing should be built. The cadres in the informant's brigade were not happy with this decision, but the brigade chief did ask UYs to cut wood, make bricks, and transport sand from the nearby East River, and also assigned some peasants to the construction task. Progress was slow, however, and ceased when a shortage of bricks developed. At the time the informant left in the summer of 1971, the construction project had not been completed. With regard to work points, the results were similarly inconclusive: brigade cadres responded to UY complaints with the charge that the UYs did not work hard enough. The informant's brigade chairman did discuss the issue with the ten chairmen of the production teams, who also accused the UYs of not putting in enough work, and who recommended that they work hard in order to gain a good reputation, so that when the team general meeting set work point ratings in the following year theirs would improve. The informant concluded that the center's policy had been correct but that it had not been implemented correctly locally. The impression emerges that there was simply not enough pressure from the higher levels to secure a change and to overcome the latent sympathy of the county cadres with the point of view of the village cadres.*[137]

In 1973, in contrast, policy makers decided to make redress of UY grievances a focus of a major campaign to promote UY adaptation to rural life. National and provincial conferences, editorials, and model cases referred to discrimination or other abuses, thereby greatly raising the salience of this issue for officials in the rural administrative hierarchy, who were told in unambiguous terms to "conduct a strict and comprehensive inspection" and take corrective action.[138] The underlying assump-

*The complex interactions between higher-level investigators, local cadres, and UYs are also illustrated by an informant who served on a PLA farm. He reports that local cadres employed such stratagems as selecting activist UYs to represent each squad in talks with members of investigating work teams. Also, while the work team was "squatting" in the company, life for the UYs was at its best, especially with respect to the quality of food. He reports that ordinary UYs were afraid to voice frank complaints, which usually concerned living conditions such as food but also cadre work methods. Cadres were not happy when blunt complaints were made by UYs to the work teams, but at the same time, cadres were afraid to retaliate. If the regimental command learned of the retaliation, it would lead to the transfer of the company commanders (lien-chang). The informant added that soon after the work team left, the food situation would revert to its normal unsatisfactory state.

tion was that cadres of the production teams and brigades could not be fully trusted to report accurately and eliminate shortcomings on their own. Indeed, instead of relying on outside inspection, control over the disposal of the settlement fee in one commune in Anhwei was taken away from the basic-level cadres; "funds for the settlement of young intellectuals are appropriated and accounted for under the unified command of the commune."[139] It can be assumed this was not the only case of centralized control over these funds.

It seems plausible to assume that the pressure applied in 1973 on rural leadership to take remedial action did bring about improvements in many, perhaps most places. If remedial action required the exertion of considerable pressure from above, the question arises of what will happen when pressure is reduced— when new priorities and new issues claim the attention and time of higher-level officialdom. As the focus on UY grievances fades, old abuses could recur and new ones might take their place. It is in this light that the large-scale despatch of urban cadres takes on added significance. The urban cadres presumably are less subject to the shifting campaign priorities than their rural colleagues. Moreover, their status gives them access to the local hierarchy as well as to the urban one from which they came. They are therefore in a better position to press for redress of grievance than the UYs themselves. Their very presence may have an inhibiting effect on local decisions to discriminate and on individual cadres who might be tempted to misuse their positions for personal gratification.[140] That such considerations may have been in the minds of policy makers is suggested by the sequence of decisions in which a remedial campaign launched in 1973 with a focus on the rural leadership was followed in 1974 by a campaign to send more urban cadres to the countryside with the UYs. Perhaps the policy makers have recognized that the rural political and administrative system cannot by itself be expected to insure treatment of the UYs in conformity with national norms.

An illustration of the potential role of urban cadres as defenders of sent-down youths comes from Ch'ien county, in Shensi. A brigade in that county had "not grasped tightly" the construction of houses for the UYs. The urban cadres attached to the UYs, all of whom had come from Sian, got together with the brigade cadres, studied with them Mao's saying that "con-

cern should be shown for the maturing of the younger generation," and helped them raise their awareness of the importance
of UY living conditions. Consequently, the party branch secretary led commune members in "very quickly" building seven
new houses.[141] Other such cases of intervention have not come
to light, however. Therefore, it remains to be seen whether the
urban cadres have in fact been playing this role. It is worth
noting that in 1975 and 1976 occasional broadcasts again referred to the need to deal "heavy blows" to those who "perse-
cute" educated youths or "interfere with [their] livelihood."[142]
The remedial campaign undoubtedly resulted in a substantial reduction of instances of discrimination and abuse, but the problem of protecting them from abuse and securing redress is, at
least to some degree, an ongoing one.

Facilitating Marriage

If UYs experience difficulty adapting to rural life, marriage
would seem to be a remedy. Marriage of a UY to a local person
can be said to constitute a complete form of integration into
the village. Marriage among UYs would seem to promote adaptation in that it entails settling down to a stable life. However,
official approval has been given only since 1973. Previously,
the predominant approach was that the UYs "should be advised
to postpone marriage."[143] The reason for the negative approach
was that the state policy of delayed marriage took priority over
the special issue of UY adaptation. In order to limit births,
women in the cities are not supposed to get married till age 25,
men till age 28. In the villages, the approved ages are apparently
lower, 23 and 25 respectively. Since urban youths are normally
sent to the countryside at age 16 to 18, UY marriage as a
positive policy issue did not arise until quite recently, as the generation sent to the countryside before and after the Cultural
Revolution reached the age at which marriages could be officially
sanctioned.* The remedial campaign also addressed itself to the
question of marriage: "under the conditions of encouraging late
marriage, care should be taken to solve their marriage problems

---

*It is not clear whether policy calls for sent-down urban youths to abide by the
urban marriage age or the rural one. In any event, informants had heard of marriages
among UYs and between sent-down youths and locals whose ages were below the
recommended rural ones. More generally, as reported to me by Professor Martin
Whyte, of the University of Michigan, he and William Parish found that the average
rural female in Kwangtung marries at age 20 or 21; the male at about age 24.

. . . to teach them to continue the revolution after they get married . . . to handle correctly the relations between work, study, and family affairs," and also to practice planned parenthood.[144]

When UYs marry locals, the predominant pattern reported by informants and the press is marriage of UY females to local males. The opposite rarely happens, because it conflicts with the traditional patrilocal pattern of rural marriage in which the girl comes from outside the village, and because UY males usually do not have the resources to set up an independent household. When a UY male does marry a local person, special reasons are likely to obtain. In P'ing-lu county, Shansi, for instance, a young man from Tientsin married a local woman, but he had been elected party secretary of his brigade in 1970 and moreover had risen to deputy secretary of the county party committee. As an upwardly mobile cadre, he was no doubt a good catch.[145] Marriage between UY females and local males offers advantages to both sides but also some disadvantages. Informants report that peasants regard the arrival of potential marriage partners as one of the good points of the program; in some villages, they have been referred to as "sent by the state" (*kuo-chia fen-lai ti*). In a good many Kwangtung villages, traditional marriage customs still prevail, the male's family having to pay bride money as well as stage expensive feasts. Marriage to an urban girl makes it possible to escape from these obligations. On the other hand, an urban wife may not be able to work as hard as a local one, and apparently there has been some disenchantment with such marriages.[146] From the point of view of the urban girl, marriage to a local offers the prospects of security, stability, and status, particularly if the partner occupies an important position in the village. The main drawback of such a marriage is of course that it means making a permanent commitment to village life, precluding the possibility of eventual return to the city. In cases publicized in the press of young women who insisted on marrying locals, opposition from parents and others was in part based on this factor.[147] According to informants, the attraction of city life has led some sent-down girls to marry city workers. Even though regulations do not permit the wife or the children to move to the city, such marriages are advantageous: visits are possible, the wife benefits from the higher urban wage rate, and policy on residence may eventually change. Such calculations also are behind marriages that informants heard about between

UY girls originally assigned to villages quite distant from Canton and peasants in the suburbs of that city.

During the campaign to repudiate Confucian ideas, marriages between UYs and peasants were publicized as dramatic instances of breaking with the traditional Confucian value that assigns high status to the educated and low status to the uneducated. Pai Chi-hsien, for example, the daughter of a Peking worker and the first college graduate in her family, settled in a Hopei village in Ts'ang county after graduation from Hopei Normal University in 1968. (Her college education, in other words, was probably incomplete, having ended in 1966 with the outbreak of the Cultural Revolution.) In 1970 she married a peasant who had only gone to primary school, and with whom she had fallen in love while he taught her farm work. The decision to marry was a difficult one and the case was publicized because she waged a struggle within herself as well as against the hostile attitudes of others. She was aware that the marriage would end hopes of ever returning to Peking. Her father opposed the marriage: "Marrying a peasant and living in the countryside all your life, what future will you have?" She was scorned by "some people with outdated ideas" who said that it is a "pity a Peking-born college graduate married a peasant." One teacher reportedly referred to the marriage as a "scandal." Even in the village, while the poor and lower-middle peasants were said to have approved her decision, others thought she was being stupid, marrying a country bumpkin. Pai refuted all these objections and persisted in her decision. She eventually became a teacher in the commune middle school.[148] Other such cases have received press publicity, including one in which two girls on a PLA farm in Hunan married youths of the Miao nationality, thereby breaking with the old values and promoting the new ones.[149]

Marriages in which both partners are UYs have encountered difficulties. This emerges from an investigation of such marriages in Hai-ch'eng county, Liaoning, which was undertaken by the county party committee on the initiative of a letter sent by UY married couples. As of November 1974, out of a total of 48,000 UYs then in the county, 1,631 (3.4 percent) had married.[150] The investigation showed that "cadres of some production brigades in Wang-shih commune felt that 'since the sent-down educated youths have gotten married and have left the youth points, there is no need to be concerned about them anymore.'"[151] As a result, "they paid very little attention to the political study and livelihood conditions of these educated youths, thereby causing some of the married sent-down educated youths to waver in their thinking and not to be at ease in the village." This neglect contrasted with the concern shown by cadres in another commune, who encouraged the married youths to study politics and take part in collective labor, helping them to solve problems of housing and child care. Because Hai-ch'eng did not have child care facilities—apparently, only prosperous suburban communes in China have been able to establish them—UY mothers necessarily had to stay home and care for their children, unless cadres helped devise ad hoc solutions such as locating a peasant woman to take care of the child. But the countywide problem "most in need of urgent solution" was that of housing for UY couples. The recommended solution was that houses in production teams formerly occupied by UYs who had been resettled in brigade-level youth teams should be assigned on a priority basis to married UY couples, although new housing would have to be built as well. This shows that, in contrast to Chi county, Hopei, UY couples in Hai-ch'eng county were unable to continue living in the youth settlements but had to live among the peasants at large. Lacking the support of the youth collectives and not having relatives in the village, poorly integrated into the peasant village (having left the youth points, the married UYs were afraid to take part in "struggle" for fear of offending the peasants) and lacking an adequate economic foundation, the UY families found it hard to manage, thus creating a new problem for the authorities. Informants, who had heard of only isolated instances of UY intermarriage, in contrast to the more frequent occurrence of UY-peasant marriages, assessed the problems of intermarriages in terms similar to the Hai-ch'eng investigation. Unless parents provide substantial assistance, a UY couple will have difficulty setting up a proper household even when both partners work. A single male UY who works industriously can support himself but he usually will not be able to earn enough to support a wife and children. Peasant marriages are based on the social and economic foundations of established family life; UY marriages lack such foundations, and, until more is done to provide appropriate substitutes, marriage among sent-down youths cannot be considered an obvious measure to improve their adaptation to rural life.

Few statistics on UY marriages have been published, but it is not clear whether those that have pertain to marriages among UYs or also to those between sent-down youths and peasants. Two provincial figures have been published. In Kirin, as of December 1975, 50,000 out of 800,000 UYs (6.3 percent) had gotten married, and in Liaoning, as of May 1976, 80,000 out of 1.2 million (6.7 percent).[152] Subprovincial rates may vary considerably, as shown when the 3.4 percent rate in Hai-ch'eng county, Liaoning, quoted above, is compared with the 11.5 percent rate in Ch'ang-t'u county, Liaoning (115 out of 1,000).[153] In Chi county, Hopei, as of the summer of 1973, 13 percent, or 124 out of an apparent total of 952 UYs, had married, but no provincial totals have been released.[154] Since marriages are supposed to take place only among the older age groups, the percentages ought perhaps to be calculated against UY totals reported several years ago. In the case of Liaoning, 700,000 urban youths were serving in the villages in 1973.[155] This base would raise the marriage rate to 11.4 percent.

Quite possibly these low rates are due to the difficulties that UY marriages must confront. They may also, however, be due to the fact that many sent-down youths have not yet reached the age of marriage, particularly if the urban marriage ages of 25 and 28 are applied, as may well be possible in self-contained UY settlements. That is, a female sent to the countryside at age 18 in 1968 would only have become marriageable in 1975; a male would have to wait until 1978. Testing the hypothesis that the transfer leads to a lower rate of marriage than would have been the case had the young people not been sent down clearly requires much more data on age distributions, especially in the light of partial reassignment to the urban sector, and on marriage rates among the UYs' counterparts not sent to the villages. Possibly the policy makers regard the transfer as a measure to lower the rate of marriage and hence the birthrate, not just in the cities but generally. If it is their goal to discourage UY marriages, this would clearly conflict with the goal of furthering adaptation to rural life; but probably this is not the case. According to an article published in 1976 from Ch'ang-t'u county, Liaoning, commune party leaders recognized that when UYs marry and settle down (chieh-hun an-chia) it is a sign of their determination to take root in the countryside. Hence, UY marriages "deserve encouragement and support."[156] This suggests that as more UYs grow into full adulthood the marriage issue will become more and more salient and will prompt policy makers and administrators to commit more resources to facilitate such marriages.*

Improving Political Education

Policy makers attach great importance to political education as a remedial measure, since many of the problems that arise can be attributed to the "erroneous" ideas, values, and conceptions held by those who participate in the process of implementing the settlement of the UYs. As long as not all participants have internalized the new ideas, it is necessary to keep on studying them in order to make everyone aware of what is right and what is wrong. UYs, therefore, "must give prominence to study and constantly arm their minds with Marxism-Leninism, Mao Tse-tung Thought," in order to raise their consciousness and capacity to take part in the "great struggle" of settling in and building the countryside.[157] By the same token, cadres and peasants must also study the ideological rationales of the transfer movement.[158]

The form and content of political education of the UYs varies but consists in the main of periodic study sessions organized specifically for the UYs. Informants report weekly or monthly meetings for UYs held at the brigade level and annual meetings for all UYs in a commune, which lasted three to four days but in other cases two weeks. The themes raised in the UY study meetings correspond to those stressed in the current political campaigns—criticism of revisionism and the style of work in 1972, criticism of Lin Piao and Confucius in 1973 and 1974. But an effort is made to tailor the general themes to the specific concerns of the UYs, that is, to promote their adaptation by making them feel more "at ease" in the countryside. For instance in 1970 and 1971, when a good many UYs were given urban assignments, political study focused strongly on the morale problems of those not reassigned, and the criticism of revisionism was closely linked to discussion of what the correct

*The use of the term "urban youth" (UY) in this book obscures the fact that many of the young urbanites had as of the mid-1970s reached full adulthood. It is worth noting, however, that the Chinese press continues to refer to *hsia-hsiang chih-shih ch'ing-nien*, "sent-down educated youths," even when writing about a person who has been in the village for ten or twelve years and who must be close to thirty years of age.

"ideals" (*li-hsiang*) of youth should be and how they should view their future (*ch'ien-t'u*).[159] In general, study of theory and current political themes aims at getting UYs to see their own particular situation in the perspective of the great goals of revolutionary transformation and socialist construction of the countryside. Successful communication of this perspective will presumably motivate UYs to see their own deprivations as insignificant in comparison to the great cause of which they are a part.

Peasant participation in UY political education is strongly encouraged. When peasants lead study sessions, the emphasis is not on theoretical concepts but on the communication of emotion-laden material. Poor peasants will talk about their suffering in the old society, contrasting "past bitterness with present sweetness" (*yi-k'u ssu-t'ian*). They will detail the story of their families and describe the history of the revolutionary struggle in their village, as well as that of the class struggle and the struggle between the two lines.[160] The following quote, from an article by a Shanghai girl settled on a Heilungkiang army farm, illustrates the emotional impact which yi-k'u ssu-t'ian is supposed to have: "The company invited uncle Lin, an old poor peasant to teach us to recall past bitterness and think of the present sweetness. In the most wicked old society, uncle Lin's father was tortured to death by the landlord, his mother was starved to death and his elder sister was sold off. When I heard his story I shed tears of grief and anger. I will never forget the class sufferings and will always bear in mind the blood feud. I will love the new society and Chairman Mao more!"[161] To heighten their awareness of the miseries of the old society, UYs may eat a "recall-past-bitterness meal," consisting of wild vegetables, tree bark, and coarse grain.

The urban youths are also supposed to be educated politically through participation in villagewide political campaigns, such as "struggle-criticism-transformation" (*tou-p'i-kai*), as well as through informal contact with the peasants. The model of "re-education" calls for individual peasants to maintain informal contact with UYs, in which they expose UYs to correct teachings and values, while setting an example to the UYs through their practice of a revolutionary life style of devoted, unselfish work and plain, frugal living. And in principle the UYs' entire rural experience, especially participation in production, is supposed to have an impact on their politically relevant attitudes and values.

Though viewed as a remedy for crises of UY adaptation, political education itself has been the focus of remedial action. To begin with, the village environment does not always support intensive and ongoing political education. The degree of politicization of Chinese villages varies; in a good many, interest in explicit political ideas is low.[162] As a result, when responsibility for UY reeducation was diffused among village cadres and the peasants as a whole, little was accomplished. Judging by informants, informal contacts between UYs and peasants were rarely, if ever, infused with political content. Similarly, material presented earlier showed that the frequency of meetings for UYs declined as cadres reduced their involvement with the UYs, while the quality of the study meetings themselves was often low and characterized by formalism and superficiality.[163] One of the reasons for concentrating UYs and for collectivizing their group life has been to improve political education. Reorganizing UY groups into formally structured collectives with designated leaders, including urban cadres, is supposed to lead to the establishment of a definite study system (hsüeh-hsi chih-tu). Existence of such a system has come to be one of the indicators of how well the unit functions.[164] Whether the new approach will make political education more sustained and systematic or whether study in the UY collectives will fall victim to routinization remains to be seen, but, at least for the time being, conditions for improvement have been created in a good many communes.

It has been a major assumption in the Chinese media that political education has a causal effect upon UY adaptation: "Not every one of the educated youths at Kuanchiatun production brigade [Faku county, Liaoning] has great ability. When they first came to the countryside they had various shortcomings and weaknesses. As Chairman Mao has pointed out, many of them demonstrated subjectivism and individualism. Their thoughts were usually vain and their actions irresolute. How did they make such quick and extensive progress? It was due to the reeducation they received from the poor and lower-middle peasants."[165] The press carries numerous examples of UYs whose flagging morale is revitalized by political education in the form of a chat with a cadre and a session of yi-k'u ssu-t'ian with a peasant.[166] Typically, the morale crisis consists of hankering for return to the city. For instance, some UYs who had left Sian in 1968 had come to feel six years later that they were entitled to "graduate" from the rural school and go back to their home town. The cadres in charge—in this case from Sian— used every opportunity to study with the UYs, using such materials as Mao's "Orientation of the Youth Movement"; the result was that their determination to stick it out in the countryside and make revolution the rest of their lives was firmed up.[167]

If political education is to contribute to adaptation by changing UY attitudes, the persuasiveness of the messages needs to be examined. It could be suggested that recalling past bitterness has persuasive power because it taps the traditional respect in which older people are held in China, motivating the UYs to "come up to the expectations of the elder generation."[168] Informants, however, disagree on two grounds. First, since the UYs were born after liberation, it is not possible for them to assess the accuracy of stories of "past bitterness." Second, UYs tend to be concerned not with the past but with the future, especially their own; tales of an increasingly distant past are not relevant to them. If such views are widespread, perhaps political education that focuses on the future possibilities inherent in rural modernization would be more effective. Informants expressed skepticism on this point also: they were not impressed by the degree of rural modernization achieved in southern Kwangtung and in general they thought of modernization in urban terms, attributing their transfer to the lagging industrialization of China, specifically of Canton.

If political education does not change the thinking of those who have not adapted, what does it do? It seems plausible to suggest that political education is important in two ways. In the case of those UYs who are committed to the transfer, political education may play a reinforcing role in providing explanation, rationalization, and legitimation. For those who have not adapted to rural life, political education may be important not by dint of the messages that are transmitted but by dint of what the presence of political education signifies. Ongoing and sustained political education is evidence of well-functioning UY collectives and can thus be taken as an indicator of social control, of the presence of a "strict political atmosphere."[169] It signifies that the political system plays a visible and concrete role in the daily lives of the UYs. It means that the daily discourse among UYs is more likely to take place in terms supportive of the transfer, and it means that there will be fewer opportunities for dissident UYs to express their dissatisfactions without some kind of a protransfer response. The presence of sustained political education is an indicator of an environment which constrains UYs to behave as if they had adapted, and to make the best of the settlement.

The remedial measures sought to accomplish two goals. The first was to create a rural environment in which UY behavior would be more effectively shaped and constrained, thereby reducing freedom to behave in maladaptive ways. The second was to improve living conditions in order to make it possible for the sent-down youths to lead tolerable lives in the countryside, the hope being that as a result more UYs would come to terms with their situation and adapt to it. Assuming that the changes have been carried out everywhere, the remedial measures have undoubtedly created more favorable conditions for UY adaptation than existed before their implementation.

The remedial measures demonstrate the capacity of the Chinese bureaucracies to learn and to devise new approaches to the management of the transfer of urban youths to the countryside. What is remarkable about some of the remedial measures was their concreteness and their explicit concern with the material conditions of the sent-down youths. It is remarkable because the concern with material improvements came at a time when the country as a whole seemed to be turning left in the second half of 1973, with the onset of the campaign to criticize Lin Piao and Confucius. A turn to the left is usually taken to signify reduced concern with material interests. In this case, increased stress on the ideological rationales of the transfer movement was combined with detailed and specific emphasis on material improvements. Another noteworthy aspect of the remedial measures is that they convey a sense of skeptical realism about the possibilities of UY-peasant integration. Rather than singlemindedly insisting on settlement of UYs within peasant villages, policy makers initiated a partial disengagement of UYs from the peasants by stressing separate settlement, where possible.

Urban youth adaptation does not hinge only on the implementation of the remedial measures discussed in this chapter. Some of the other factors that bear on this issue can only be mentioned in passing, since survey data to demonstrate the extent of their relevance are not readily available. One factor is the personal background variables of the sent-down youths. It could be hypothesized that UYs from good class backgrounds adjust more easily than those from bad class backgrounds, although impressionistic evidence suggests that this is by no means always the case. Maladjustment of working-class youths, for example, may occur because some of them have high expectations of what society should do for proletarians, while their rural supervisors may well expect more from them because they come from good backgrounds.[170] Or, it could be hypothesized that UYs from poorer families adjust more easily than those from better-off families.[171] And, there are the many variations in urban and rural conditions. It is possible, for instance, that youths from small towns adjust more easily than those from large ones, since the former are closer to rural life than the latter. UYs sent to relatively poor areas are likely to adjust less well than those sent to prosperous areas, and those sent to areas close to their home towns, where familiarity with custom and dialect obtain, may adjust more easily.[172] Another factor that bears on adjustment will be discussed at length in the next chapter, namely, opportunities to make meaningful and possibly satisfying contributions to rural society. Once those topics have been discussed, the topic of adaptation can be raised once more in the last chapter of this book, in connection with the issue of return to the urban sector.

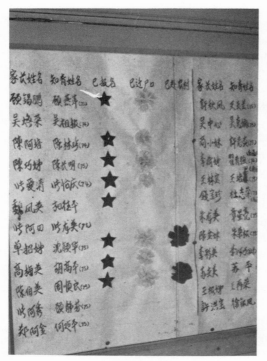

Photograph of a poster taken in early 1976 in a silk factory in Wusih, Kiangsu, showing the extent to which the different stages of the transfer process have been completed in individual cases. The first column on the left shows the name of the family head, the second, the name of his son or daughter, with the year of graduation from school added in parentheses. In the third column, a star is awarded to those who have "already signed up," that is, to eight out of twelve names. The fourth column shows whether the individual's household registration has already been sent to the rural destination, and the fifth, whether the individual has already departed for the village. It shows that only two of the eight have already done so. Courtesy of W. L.

Festive arrival of Peking school graduates in Yenan, the cradle of the revolution, early in 1969. Source: *China Reconstructs,* June 1969.

An army farm in Heilungkiang. Source: *Chih-shih ch'ing-nien tsai pei ta-huang* [Educated youths in the great northern wilderness], ed. Heilungkiang Sheng-ch'an chien-she pu-tui cheng-chih pu (Political Department, Heilungkiang Production and Construction Corps), p. 72.

(*Above*) Harvest time on an army farm in Heilungkiang. Source: *Chih-shih ch'ing-nien tsai pei ta-huang*, p. 61.

Members of a Heilungkiang army farm working on a water conservancy project. Source: *Chih-shih ch'ing-nien tsai pei ta-huang*, p. 46.

Members of an army farm in Heilungkiang engaging in political study during a work break.
Source: *Chih-shih ch'ing-nien tsai pei ta-huang,* p. 15.

"Li Pen-fu, a poor peasant in the old society, tells the new commune members his bitter family history, teaching the vital importance of the proletariat holding firmly to power." The tablet in the background reads: "Compare past bitterness with present sweetness; do not forget [your class] origins." Source: *China Reconstructs,* November 1968.

Young people on a Heilungkiang army farm read model letters sent by parents to provide encouragement. Source: *Chih-shih ch'ing-nien tsai pei ta-huang,* p. 117.

Ch'i Hsiao-tung, the fifth of the model youths described in chapter 5. Source: *China Reconstructs,* October 1976.

(*Below*) "Still another group of outstanding youths gloriously joins the Chinese Communist Party." Source: *Chih-shih ch'ing-nien tsai pei ta-huang,* p. 140.

Members of an army farm in Heilungkiang working on breeding superior seeds. Source: *Chih-shih ch'ing-nien tsai pei ta-huang,* p. 74.

"Learning the hows and whys of tractors at a state farm's spare-time college," on Hainan Island, Kwangtung. Source: *China Reconstructs,* September 1976.

Doing survey work for the construction of a new branch farm of the Production and Construction Corps in Heilungkiang. Source: *Chih-shih ch'ing-nien tsai pei ta-huang*, p. 31.

Building a new camp. The banner reads: "Bring wasteland under cultivation and reap a harvest in the same year." Source: *Chih-shih ch'ing-nien tsai pei ta-huang*, p. 28.

5 RECRUITMENT OF URBAN YOUTHS AND CONTRIBUTIONS TO RURAL DEVELOPMENT

The previous chapter focused on urban youths as ordinary members of communes, "fighters" on PLA farms or workers on state farms, who spend their days doing agricultural labor and taking part in political study. With the passage of time, however, a process of differentiation takes place among them. For some UYs the ordinary routines of rural life do not change, but for others additional activities come to supplement and in some cases partially replace agricultural labor. Some UYs become political activists, some come to occupy formal positions of leadership, and some are selected to perform specialized tasks such as teaching or the provision of paramedical services. The first part of this chapter is devoted to an assessment of patterns of recruitment to such posts.

Recruitment is also closely related to the question of the kinds of contributions UYs have been making to rural development, a topic to which the second part of the chapter is devoted. To be sure, UYs have not contributed to rural life only when they have been given specialized posts or when, as has happened in some cases, they have served as leaders of production teams or even of brigades. The labor that all of them perform presumably constitutes a contribution in its own right. Their contributions, in fact, often come in collective form, as when a youth collective undertakes a construction project, when a UY group engages in a "scientific experiment," or when a group exerts influence on a village to utilize an innovation such as improved seeds. In such cases the contributions go beyond those made by specifically recruited individuals. The topics discussed in both parts of this chapter bear not only on the theme of rural change but also very importantly on the problem of UY adaptation to rural life. Recruitment to specialized positions or tasks may promote adaptation by raising the status of the UYs; contributions may do so by giving UYs a sense of satisfaction, worth, and accomplishment. But the most important goal of this chapter is to marshal empirical evidence to assess the hypothesis that the transfer program has developmental significance not only for the urban but also for the rural sector.

RECRUITMENT

Measurement of the extent of UY recruitment—a task made frustratingly complex by inadequate statistics—requires drawing distinctions between political and cultural-technical roles, major and minor roles, and recruitment that leads to movement out of the rural units in which UYs serve versus recruitment that does not. With regard to the first distinction, membership in such organizations as the Young Communist League (YCL), and the Chinese Communist Party (CCP) can be regarded as recruitment to political roles, as can becoming an activist in political study or in the movement to criticize Lin Piao and Confucius. Political recruitment also includes election to positions of general leadership and management, such as chief of a production team or secretary of a brigade party branch. Cultural-technical roles consist of service in a specialized post or activity: teacher in a team- or brigade-operated school, "barefoot doctor," agricultural technician, electrician, carpenter, or radio repairman. With the expansion of rural education and of peasant access to medical care since the Cultural Revolution, and with the gradually increasing technical modernization of the village, an expansion in the number of cultural-technical posts has taken place, and UYs have filled some of them.

Because UYs are recruited to a wide range of posts, memberships, and activities, some of which clearly are more significant than others, a distinction must be made between major and minor roles. Four criteria can be used to differentiate between the two. First, a role may be regarded as major if the post or activity takes up a substantial part of the working day; it is minor if it occupies only one's spare time.[1] A UY who serves as a teacher in a daytime school clearly has a more significant job than a UY who teaches night school. Second, a major role is likely to raise the status of the incumbent significantly in the eyes of the community; a minor one does so only to a limited extent. A UY who provides a needed service by becoming a barefoot doctor is likely to be more highly regarded than one who is a participant among many in scientific experiment groups. Third, occupying a major role may make it possible to influence the rural community in differing but meaningful ways; a minor one affords fewer such possibilities. An urban youth who becomes head of a production team obviously exerts more influence than one who becomes an activist in the movement to criticize Lin Piao and Confucius. And finally, a role may be regarded as major if the posts, memberships, or activities are finite or limited in number, and if the recruitment process is highly selective. In some cases, recruitment to minor roles takes place by self-selection; UYs simply volunteer to engage in some activity. In contrast, election of a UY to head a production team is a weighty decision. Similarly, it is much easier to join the YCL than the CCP.

Minor roles, it should be emphasized, are not unimportant. Identification of the number of UYs who serve as activists may well provide an indicator of the proportion among them who are willing to make an effort to adapt and to do well in the countryside. Measurement of the extent of political activism among the UYs also provides an indicator of the size of the pool from which occupants of major roles are likely to come, since evidence of political activism is normally a prerequisite for both major political and cultural-technical recruitment. Moreover, while minor roles may be "minor" in relation to particular individuals, they may well be of considerable collective significance. An example might be a UY scientific experiment group that scores a success in adapting an improved variety of seeds to local conditions.

As the preceding point indicates, it is difficult to apply the major-minor distinction to all cases. Much subjective judgment is necessarily involved.[2] In making the distinctions, if a particular post or activity fits one of the four criteria for major recruitment, it is assigned in most but not all cases to the major category. Table 11 provides illustrations.

The third distinction, between recruitment that entails movement within the rural units in which UYs serve and movement out of these units altogether, is very important, since aspirations to move out of the rural units may influence UY attitudes toward mobility within the units. Mobility within the units includes jobs and positions at one of the three levels of the commune, or within a state farm or PLA farm. It includes not only the positions already outlined but also assignment to work

Table 11. Recruitment to Major and Minor Roles

	Major	Minor
Political	Brigade secretary Team chief YCL branch secretary CCP member Cadre	YCL member Mao Tse-tung Thought propagandist Study guide Activist in movement to criticize Lin and Confucius Activist
Cultural-technical	Barefoot doctor Teacher in daytime school Agricultural technician Tractor driver Electrician Carpenter Team accountant	Participant in scientific experiment group Night-school teacher Storekeeper Work point recorder Cashier

in commune- or brigade-operated factories or to serve as sales personnel in supply and marketing coops situated within the commune. Movement out of the rural units, which is treated in chapter 6 under the heading "reassignment," typically entails joining the PLA, assignment to a factory job (either in the county town or a more distant city), or assignment to study in an institution of higher learning. In the last case, the distinction is blurred, for some higher schools are now located within communes, and, furthermore, UYs who leave the village to go to college are supposed to return to their rural units upon graduation. Assignment of college graduates, however, is a complex matter, and it is not at all clear whether UY college graduates in fact return to the countryside, and, if they do return, whether they go back to their original units, say, a brigade within a commune, or whether they are assigned to work at higher levels, such as in the county town. This aspect of UY mobility will be treated in chapter 6. The distinction between intra-unit and extra-unit mobility is also blurred in the cases of successful UYs who are elected to party or revolutionary committees of a county or even a prefecture, but who retain their posts within the commune. Such cases are treated in this chapter.

Before discussing trends and looking at quantitative data, it is useful to present a few cases of successful UYs, models publicized in the press, who illustrate the possibilities that are open at least in principle to sent-down youth:

1. *Chu K'o-chia* graduated from a Shanghai junior middle school in 1969 and volunteered at age seventeen to go to Yunnan, where he settled in a T'ai minority village in Meng-la county. He learned T'ai as well as carpentry and tool repair, thus making contributions to the village. After some time, Chu responded to a request from an Ai-ni minority village located on a nearby mountainside, but part of the same brigade, to come and teach school. He agreed to leave the relative comforts of the T'ai village, participated in the construction of the school, and learned Ai-ni in order to be able to teach, while performing such other services as making clothes and cutting hair. Chu played the role of a general innovator, helping to introduce tractors to the village and taking part in the construction of a small hydroelectric station. While on home leave in Shanghai he acquired knowledge of electrical work. In 1972, he refused an opportunity to enter a university in order to stay with the Ai-ni. Chu rose rapidly in the political hierarchy. It is not clear when he joined the YCL, but by 1972 or 1973 he had become a member of the Yunnan provincial YCL standing committee. Similarly, he apparently joined the CCP only in April of 1973 but was elected an alternate member of the Tenth Central Committee in August of that year, the only urban youth to have attained such high status. (Another "educated youth," Hsing Yen-tzu, was elected a regular member of the Tenth Central Committee, but she in fact returned to her native village as long ago as 1958, having completed her studies in Tientsin.[3]) Although it is not clear whether Chu has continued to live in the Ai-ni village, as of 1975 he continued to live in the brigade, having become deputy secretary of his brigade's party branch. In early 1974, he served as deputy leader of a youth delegation to Japan. A year later he was elected to the National People's Congress, China's parliament, as well as to its Standing Committee. In October 1975 he was one of a dozen outstanding educated youths to attend a national conference on rural development.*[4]

2. *Hou Chün* graduated from a Peking senior middle school in 1962 and went to Pao-ti county, Hopei. Early on she was active and played leadership roles in a variety of undertakings, including organizing a night school, a broadcasting station, a wall newspaper group, and a Mao Thought propaganda group. She joined a scientific experiment group, of which she became the head in 1965, and which contributed to the transformation of her brigade from a grain-deficient to a grain-surplus one. Already a well-known model before the Cultural Revolution, she reportedly resisted an offer by Chou Yang, a leading official in cultural affairs who was purged during the upheaval, to take her out of the village and make her a professional writer. During the Cultural Revolution she was attacked by people "hoodwinked" by enemies and was denounced

---

*It is possible that Chu's spectacular rise to the national level was due not only to his achievements but also to connections with the powerful. Chu K'o-chia came from Shanghai, the political base of the "gang of four" purged in October 1976. The "gang" has in fact been accused of sponsoring certain sent-down youths as a way of building a network of support. However, as of January 1977, Chu's name had not apparently been mentioned in connection with the "gang," nor had other prominent UYs noted in this chapter. (See also the last section of chapter 6.)

as an evil influence, but in the end she was supported by the poorer peasants. She played a leading role in persuading fellow UYs to stay in the village even after three or four years' service. Ultimately, probably after the Cultural Revolution, she became party secretary of her brigade, as well as chairman of the brigade's revolutionary committee while serving concurrently as vice-chairman of the commune's revolutionary committee as well as of the county party and revolutionary committees.[5]

3. *Tung Liang-ho* graduated from a Peking senior middle school in 1965 and was sent to Chi county, Hopei. He worked hard at mastering agricultural skills, played an activist role in mobilizing fellow UYs to construct a pigsty and raise poultry, while resisting temptation to join the army or attend higher schools. In order to contribute to peasant health care, he studied acupuncture. He joined the CCP in 1970, was made brigade party branch deputy secretary in 1971 and secretary in 1972. As a brigade leader he went to a backward team and led its transformation into an advanced one, working closely with the team's cadres. In 1973 he came to serve concurrently as secretary of the commune party committee.[6]

4. *Chin Shih-ying* volunteered at age sixteen, even before graduation from junior middle school, to accompany her brother Chin Hsün-hua from Shanghai to Heilungkiang in May 1969. Three months after their arrival her brother sacrificed his life trying to save collective property and became a national model UY hero, having left a diary in the style of Lei Feng, a famous model soldier. His sister emulated her brother in heroic work and in "modestly receiving reeducation." By the fall of 1970, when she met Chairman Mao at the National Day celebrations, she had become YCL branch secretary as well as vice-chairman of the brigade's revolutionary committee. She joined the CCP in 1972 and was immediately elected a member of the party committees of the county and the prefecture. She retained her YCL membership and secretaryship, and was elected in May 1973 to serve as deputy secretary of Heilungkiang's YCL provincial committee.[7]

5. *Ch'i Hsiao-tung* was sent in 1968 from Tientsin to K'o-erh-ch'in-yu-yi-ch'ien Banner (county) in Kirin, in the steppe close to the border with Outer Mongolia, where she lived in a Mongol sheep-raising commune. She learned Mongolian and became involved with the task of breeding a superior variety of sheep. In 1970 she was made head of her brigade's breeding station and she spent four years working at this task, while also fulfilling other veterinary duties. Her work was successful, and in 1973 she joined the CCP, becoming in February 1974 deputy secretary of the commune party committee. By then her duties had changed, for, having joined the commune's mounted militia unit in 1973, she organized the study and training of brigade militias, working with the head of the department of armed forces. Acting on behalf of the commune party committee, she helped set up cultural offices and night schools in brigades to which she went "squatting on a point." Ch'i also refused several opportunities to take up factory work or attend university. In January 1975, she attended Kirin and Tientsin representative congresses of advanced UY collectives and activists.[8]

These model cases show that it is in principle possible for UYs to serve as generalist leaders of peasants, to overcome such seeming barriers as sex and ethnic differences (Han UYs in minority settlements), and to rise to positions of high status if not power. These cases also show that the "ladder of success" is quite varied. Some of the models became involved in a variety of political and cultural-technical activities simultaneously; others moved through different kinds of roles sequentially. Several of them made clear their commitment to stay in the village by refusing offers of reassignment—a point that will be raised again in later sections of this chapter.

Trends and Findings

Recruitment of UYs was emphasized fairly strongly before the Cultural Revolution, was deemphasized for several years afterward, and has received a great deal of attention since the early 1970s. Before 1966, the prospect of recruitment was used as a stimulus to induce urban youths to volunteer for the transfer. This purpose was apparent in reports such as the following, which appeared in the Shanghai press in 1964:

> Of the 200 Shanghai young people who went to Hupeh in 1958 and settled down at Tatunghu State Farm, 160 have become cadres and technicians. Nearly 90 per cent of the 91 young people of Shanghai who went to the YCL Farm in Kiangsi during 1955 have become cadres and technicians. Over 15% of the educated youths who went to Sinkiang Production and Construction Corps last year have been rated "five-good" workers. . . . In various communes and production teams in the suburban areas, many educated youths do accounting work; many youths have been praised by aged peasants to be "reliable accountants," "good cadres" and "good housekeepers." All this is very encouraging.[9]

After the Cultural Revolution, the main problem was absorption of fractious Red Guards in the countryside, and reeducation was therefore stressed much more than recruitment. Moreover, the political climate was not propitious for recruitment drives, since the alleged schemes of Liu Shao-ch'i to corrupt youth with incentives, including career mobility, were being denounced.[10] But as time passed and as some UYs proved themselves by working hard and "humbly receiving reeducation," the issue of recruitment came to the forefront. The fall of Lin Piao provided an opportunity to denounce him for having obstructed the utilization of UYs in technical capacities. Making use of their talents, particularly in the case of "those who have been trained in the countryside for years and whose thinking has been transformed," became an important theme in the press, as UYs were asked to make greater contributions to the modernization and transformation of the countryside.[11] Recruitment, furthermore, was an important theme of the 1973 campaign to remedy deficiencies in the transfer system: "It is necessary to cultivate educated young people, admit those with membership qualifications into the party and the [YCL] and promote the outstanding ones to leadership groups at all levels, so as to give full play to their active role in the three great revolutionary campaigns."[12] The increasing attention devoted to recruitment is reflected in press coverage of UYs (see table 12).

Many but not all provinces have released data on UY recruitment. Because the data have not been published at the same time, it is difficult to establish a single cross-sectional profile of provincial recruitment. Table 13 presents data on thirteen provinces that published figures in 1973, together with a national report released in December 1973. The table also includes data on six other provinces that reported on recruitment only in other years, either before or since 1973.

Table 12. Press Coverage of Recruitment

(1) Year	(2) Number of Articles on Transfer	(3) References to Political Recruitment	(4) Column 3 as % of Column 2	(5) References to Cultural- Technical Recruitment	(6) Column 5 as % of Column 2
1968	187	34	18.2	12	6.4
1969	385	110	28.6	94	24.4
1970	239	173	72.4	128	53.6
1971	108	94	87.0	46	42.6
1972	212	183	86.3	155	73.1

Notes: Column 2 is taken from table 1. The results of the table were arrived at in the following way. Each article was examined for mention of UY recruitment. References to a particular role were counted only once per article. For instance, if an article contained several references to UYs joining the CCP or the YCL, only two mentions were recorded—one for the CCP and one for the YCL. The results were then separated into political and cultural-technical recruitment. Both major and minor roles are included; see tables 18–21 for differentiation between them. References to the recruitment of returned educated peasant youths were excluded, as were references that could have applied either to them or to UYs.

Table 13. Recruitment of Sent-Down Youths by Province

(A) Date of Report	(B) Province	(C) No. of UYs	(D) CCP Members		(E) YCL Members		(F) Members of Leading Groups, or Cadres		(G) UYs in Cultural-Technical Posts	
			No.	%	No.	%	No.	%	No.	%
1. 12/71	Kwangsi	150,000	200	.13	7,000	4.7	9,000	6.0	n.a.	
2. 11/72	Inner Mongolia	180,000	4,387	2.40	34,545	19.2	5,277	2.9	n.a.	
3. 12/72	Szechwan	800,000	980	.12	25,390	3.2	19,163	2.4	n.a.	
4. 1/73	Shensi	140,000	400	.29	7,000	5.0	8,900	6.4	n.a.	
5. 3/73	Hunan	260,000	978	.38	26,900	10.3	32,760	12.6	36,100	13.9
6. 5/73	Kirin	420,000	2,400	.57	48,000	11.4	11,000	2.6	n.a.	
7. 5/73	Yunnan	400,000	4,000	1.00	47,000	11.8	200	.05	n.a.	
8. 5/73	Kwangtung	450,000	4,000	.89	60,000	13.3	20,000	4.4	n.a.	
9. 10/73	Honan	300,000	1,190	.40	36,700	12.2	16,800	5.6	n.a.	
10. 10/73	Hopei	200,000	1,900	.95	17,000	8.5	10,400	5.2	30,000	15.0
11. 11/73	Shantung	110,000	1,100	1.00	11,000	10.0	6,000	5.5	1,000	.9
12. 12/73	Chekiang	348,000	1,000	.29	27,000	7.8	10,000	2.9	35,000	10.1
13. 12/73	Fukien	160,000	1,000	.63	20,000	12.5	6,067	3.8	n.a.	
14. 12/73	Kiangsi	430,000	1,800	.42	31,000	7.2	18,000	4.2	n.a.	
15. 12/73	Liaoning	700,000	6,000	.86	80,000	11.4	20,000	2.9	60,000	8.6
16. 12/73	Heilungkiang	900,000	18,000	2.00	190,000	21.1	19,400	2.2	n.a.	
17. 12/73	NATIONAL	8,000,000	60,000	.75	830,000	10.4	240,000	3.0	n.a.	
18. 5/74	Anhwei	400,000	2,000	.50	49,000	12.3	20,000	5.0	n.a.	
19. 12/74	Kansu	100,000	1,000	1.00	18,000	18.0	3,000	3.0	n.a.	
20. 12/75	Sinkiang	450,000	5,600	1.24	47,000	10.4	23,000	5.1	n.a.	

Sources and Notes: In all cases the data on a particular province come from a single report. Some provinces have issued statistics on the number of UYs at one time and on recruitment at another. Such reports have not been used in order to avoid distortion that would arise because of rapid changes that can occur in the base totals of UYs.

1. Radio Nanning, 12/21/71, *FBIS* no. 1, 1/3/72. The cadre statistic is incomplete since it excludes the team level.
2. Radio Hu-ho-hot, 12/22/72, *FBIS* no. 251, 12/29/72. These statistics are made up of two sets, one for communes and one for UYs on army farms. See below, table 15, for a breakdown. The cadre statistic is incomplete, since it excludes those at the squad and platoon levels in the Production and Construction Corps units.
3. Radio Chengtu, 12/21/72, *FBIS* no. 248, 12/22/72.
4. Radio Sian, 1/18/72, *FBIS* no. 14, 1/19/73.
5. Radio Changsha, 3/11/73, *FBIS* no. 50, 3/14/73. Column G consists of teachers, barefoot doctors, mechanics, etc.
6. Radio Changchun, 5/3/73, *SWB-FE* no. 4291, 5/10/73.
7. Radio Kunming, 5/4/73, *SWB-FE* no. 4293, 5/12/73. Although the cadre statistic is said to apply to all levels, it must be the product of an incomplete count.
8. Radio Canton, 5/3/73, *SWB-FE* no. 4304, 5/25/73. The cadre statistic does not include the team level.
9. Radio Chengchow, 10/9/73, *FBIS* no. 196, 10/10/73.
10. Radio Shihchiachuang, 10/11/73, *FBIS* no. 204, 10/23/73. Column G consists of teachers, barefoot doctors, agricultural technicians, and accountants.
11. Radio Tsinan, 11/4/73, *FBIS* no. 215, 11/7/73. Column G consists of instructors, teachers, barefoot doctors, agricultural technicians, and tractor operators.
12. Radio Hangchow, 12/23/73, *FBIS* no. 249, 12/27/73. Column G consists of barefoot doctors, teachers, and accountants.
13. Radio Foochow, 12/22/73, *FBIS* no. 249, 12/27/73.
14. Radio Nanchang, 12/21/73, *FBIS* no. 249.
15. Radio Shenyang 12/22/73, *FBIS* no. 249.
16. Radio Harbin, 12/21/73, *FBIS* no. 3, 1/4/74.
17. *JMJP* 12/22/73.
18. Radio Hofei, 5/4/74, *FBIS* no. 92, 5/10/74.
19. Radio Lanchow, 12/22/74, *FBIS* no. 250, 12/27/74.
20. Radio Urumchi, 2/17/76, *FBIS* no. 34, 2/19/76.

These data raise questions of interpretation. In terms of the distinction between major and minor recruitment, columns D and E (CCP and YCL) are clear, but what about columns F and G? Members of leading groups refers to UYs who serve on revolutionary or party committees or in other leadership groupings such as a party branch. Sometimes the press simply reports the same total under the heading of "cadre." Column F can thus be considered as indicative of major political recruitment. The numbers, however, are sometimes misleading since some reports include all levels of the rural hierarchy and others do not. In the first case, for instance, that of Kwangsi, the total is incomplete since production team cadres are excluded (see notes to the table). Moreover, even when all levels of the hierarchy are included, the number may be misleading, since, as the biographical sketches of model UYs showed, some hold positions at several levels simultaneously, probably resulting in double counting. Cultural-technical positions (column G) are usually reported in the form of a list of jobs, but this varies in inclusiveness from report to report: Hopei's list includes teachers, barefoot doctors, agricultural technicians, and accountants, but Fukien's omits agricultural technicians. Two years later, a Fukien report did include the last-mentioned job, along with several additional ones.[13] It is not clear whether UYs had not as of 1973 become agricultural technicians in Fukien or whether the count was sloppy. Undercounting may well be responsible for the low cultural-technical total in Shantung or the low cadre total in Yunnan. An additional source of distortion is the inclusion in cultural-technical data of extraneous political categories. Liaoning listed five cultural-technical jobs, as well as "red propagandists," a minor political role which inflates that province's cultural-technical recruitment to an unknown degree. It is not possible to correct for these distortions, which necessarily introduce an element of uncertainty into the analysis.

What, then, can be learned from table 13 about recruitment of sent-down youths to major roles? The data show that fewer UYs joined the CCP than became members of leading groups and, for the five provinces for which data are available, fewer became members of leading groups than obtained cultural-technical posts. In the case of Yunnan, the only exception, it can be assumed that the count was incomplete. That more UYs served on leading groups than were recruited to the CCP means that UYs have tended to obtain secondary leadership posts such as deputy chief of a production team or member of a brigade revolutionary committee rather than the most important posts. Although a substantial expansion of party membership has taken place since the early 1960s—nationwide, from 17 million in 1961 to 28 million in 1973—it appears that, at the level of the production team, only the team chief is likely to be a party member.[14] Mere youthfulness, it is worth noting, is in principle not an obstacle to major recruitment, since policy has emphasized in recent years that leadership posts should be awarded to a "triple combination" of the young, the middle-aged, and the old. The press points with pride to communes in which a third or so of the key posts are held by youths in their twenties.[15] The finding that major cultural-technical recruitment tends to be larger than major political recruitment may reflect advancing modernization, which should result in a more rapid proliferation of cultural-technical roles than of political ones. In addition to reflecting local needs, however, this finding could also reflect UY preferences, a question to be discussed below.

Is it legitimate to arrive at a cumulative total of major recruitment by adding the three categories (columns D, F, and G) together? In the case of CCP members, the answer is no, since they are likely to be members of leading groups and may well also be holders of cultural-technical posts. Adding members of leading groups to holders of cultural-technical posts also results in some double counting, since a team or brigade accountant is surely a member of his unit's leading group. Nonetheless, adding these two categories together is the only way of arriving at an estimate of major recruitment as a whole. In the case of the five provinces that have published data for both categories, addition of the two sets shows that, out of a total of 1,618,000 UYs serving in these provinces, 241,260 UYs or 14.9 percent held major political and cultural-technical jobs. An alternative way of arriving at a combined total is to add the national percentage of membership in leading groups, three percent, to the percentage of UYs in the five provinces holding cultural-technical jobs, 10.0 percent, for a total of 13 percent. Despite the many shortcomings in the data, the finding that major recruitment ranged between 13 and 15 percent may perhaps be regarded as a plausible "ballpark" indicator.[16]

In evaluating major political and cultural-technical recruitment, it would be desirable to know what proportion of all such roles are filled by sent-down youths. In the case of major cultural-technical recruitment, national- or provincial-level comparative data are apparently absent altogether. In the case of political recruitment, we know that in 1963 there were 1.5 million commune cadres and 20 million "leading cadres" at the brigade and team levels.[17] The 240,000 UYs who were members of leading groups as of 1973 thus constituted a mere 1.1 percent of the communal cadre force, assuming of course that the 1963 figures are still valid. Since a proportion of the UYs serve on state and army farms, the 1.1 percent is actually too high. If the main goal of the transfer is defined as infusion of villages with new leaders and with "catalysts of change," this finding, when combined with the point that only 13–15 percent of UYs have been recruited to major positions and memberships, must inevitably appear disappointing. If, on the other hand, the transfer is viewed as a process in which UYs face difficult problems of adaptation, then the result could be viewed as a substantial achievement and as evidence that a proportion of the UYs—small, to be sure—has done well in the face of difficult circumstances.

Table 13 depicted cross-sectional recruitment. Table 14 shows changes over time for the nation as a whole and for five provinces. Let us look at major recruitment. Nationwide, absolute increases took place in membership in the CCP and in leading groups. But the rate of arrival of newcomers was greater than the rate of recruitment; hence, slight percentage reductions can be observed. Similar percentage reductions can also be seen in provincial data. In Liaoning, for instance, the number of holders of cultural-technical posts increased by 47,000, or 58 percent, between the summer of 1974 and the summer of 1976, but the proportion of Liaoning UYs in that category declined from 11.3 percent to 10.3 percent. Liaoning's case does conform to the expectation voiced in the press that, as time passes, more UYs should be recruited. Thus, in the same two-year period, UY party membership increased by 12,600, or 121 percent, and the UY cadre force doubled. These increases were large enough to offset the rise in the number of sent-down youths in Liaoning, thereby leading to growth in the percentage of UYs recruited in the two categories.

But what accounts for the absolute reductions in major recruitment observable in several provinces? Column E, membership in leading groups, shows reductions in Inner Mongolia, Honan, Hunan, and Kwangtung. In Honan and Hunan, party membership first declined, then rose again. And in Honan, a truly spectacular drop took place between 1973 and 1975 in the number of holders of cultural-technical posts. It is worth adding that other cases of absolute reductions in recruitment have been reported as well. In Kirin, for instance, there were 9,000 UY party members in January 1975, but only 3,000 in December.[18]

The simplest explanation for the absolute reductions is changing data-gathering procedures. In Hunan, the drop in membership on leading groups between March and September 1973 was an artifact of changing inclusiveness, since the March report included UY cadres at the production team level but the September one (and the May 1975 one) did not. In Honan, however, the drop in cultural-technical recruitment cannot be explained by inclusion and exclusion of certain jobs; rather, the drop probably was due to more careful differentiation between UYs and returned educated peasant youths.[19] The 1975 reports speak of five million returned youths and 360,000 UYs, and the May report specifically applies the recruitment statistics to the UYs alone. Of course the round figure 100,000 may only have been some official's estimate in the first place.

Another possible explanation is that the absolute reductions were due to reassignment to the urban sector of veteran UYs, that is, youths sent to the villages in 1968 and 1969, who were recruited in, say, 1971 or 1972, and subsequently sent to a higher school or an urban factory. Newcomers, not as yet eligible for major recruitment, would not have shown up in the statistics. Reassignment of successful UYs has in fact been a touchy issue (see below). It is a plausible explanation, but direct evidence linking the reductions in the table to reassignment is lacking.[20] Still another explanation for the drops or the very slow growth observable in some cases is routine turnover in positions. Elections for team and brigade positions, for instance, are held annually and biannually; upon expiration of their terms, some UYs have no doubt returned to full-time farming. A combination of these factors probably accounts for the absolute and relative reductions in recruitment.

Discussion of the data in table 13 led to the conclusion that, as of 1973, somewhere between 13 and 15 percent of UYs had

Table 14. Changes over Time in Recruitment

(A) Date of Report	(B) No. of UYs	(C) CCP Members No.	%	(D) YCL Members No.	%	(E) Members of Leading Groups No.	%	(F) Holders of Cultural-Technical Posts No.	%
National									
1. 12/73	8,000,000	60,000	.75	830,000	10.4	240,000	3.0	n.a.	
2. 12/74	10,000,000	70,000	.70	1,480,000	14.8	290,000	2.9	n.a.	
Liaoning									
1. 11/72	1,000,000	5,800	.58	19,000	1.9	n.a.		n.a.	
2. 12/73	700,000	6,000	.86	80,000	11.4	20,000	2.9	60,000	8.6
3. 8/74	720,000	10,400	1.40	158,000	21.9	33,000	4.6	81,000	11.3
4. 7/76	1,240,000	23,000	1.85	339,000	27.3	66,000	5.3	128,000	10.3
Inner Mongolia									
1. 12/72	180,000	4,387	2.40	34,545	19.2	5,277	2.9	n.a.	
2. 9/75	210,000	7,400	3.50	53,000	25.2	3,200	1.5		
Honan									
1. 1/73	240,000	1,072	.45	22,334	9.3	n.a.		100,000	42.0
2. 10/73	300,000	1,190	.40	36,700	12.2	16,800	5.6	n.a.	
3. 1/75	360,000	835	.23	58,354	16.2	11,884	3.3	40,900	11.4
4. 4/75	360,000	3,200	.90	58,300	16.2	11,800	3.3	40,900	11.4
Hunan									
1. 3/73	260,000	978	.38	26,900	10.3	32,760	12.6	36,100	13.9
2. 9/73	280,000	940	.34	26,900	9.6	13,785	4.9	n.a.	
3. 5/75	450,000	950	.21	52,400	11.6	16,400	3.6	44,000	9.8

Table 14. (Continued)

(A) Date of Report	(B) No. of UYs	(C) CCP Members No.	%	(D) YCL Members No.	%	(E) Members of Leading Groups No.	%	(F) Holders of Cultural-Technical Posts No.	%
Kwangtung									
1. 3/73	450,000	4,000	.89	60,000	13.3	20,000	4.4	n.a.	
2. 5/75	560,000	4,000	.71	70,000	12.5	15,000	2.7	n.a.	

Sources:

National:
1. *JMJP* 12/22/73.
2. *JMJP* 12/23/75.

Liaoning:
1. Radio Shenyang, 11/15/72, *FBIS* no. 226, 11/29/72.
2. Radio Shenyang, 12/22/73, *FBIS* no. 249, 12/27/73.
3. Radio Shenyang, 8/5/74, *FBIS* no. 154, 8/8/74.
4. Radio Shenyang, 7/13/76.

Inner Mongolia:
1. Radio Hu-ho-hot, 12/22/72, *FBIS* no. 251, 12/29/72.
2. Radio Peking, 9/15/75, *FBIS* no. 189, 9/29/75.

Honan:
1. Radio Chengchow, 1/6/73, *FBIS* no. 9, 1/12/73.
2. Radio Chengchow, 10/9/73, *FBIS* no. 196, 10/10/73.
3. Radio Chengchow, 1/14/75, *FBIS* no. 11, 1/16/75; Radio Chengchow, 1/16/75, *FBIS* no. 12, 1/17/75.
4. *JMJP* 4/10/75.

Hunan:
1. Radio Changsha, 3/11/73, *FBIS* no. 50, 3/14/73.
2. Radio Changsha, 9/25/73, *FBIS* no. 192, 10/3/73.
3. Radio Changsha, 5/7/75, *FBIS* no. 91, 5/9/75.

Kwangtung:
1. Radio Canton, 5/3/73, *SWB-FE* no. 4304, 5/25/73.
2.. Radio Canton, 5/8/75, *FBIS* no. 91, 5/9/75.

been recruited to major posts or memberships. In table 14, columns E and F can be added in the cases of Liaoning, Honan, and Hunan for the years 1975 or 1976, data on CCP membership again being excluded because of overlap. The result is a rate of major recruitment in the three provinces of 15 percent (307,100 out of a total of 2,050,000 UYs) as of 1975 or 1976. Recruitment since 1973 thus does not substantially change the point that only a small minority of UYs have become holders of major posts and memberships. Perhaps it is not surprising that the press continues to issue calls for "active" recruitment.[21]

Since a large-scale influx of newcomers lowers the percentages of major recruitment at least temporarily, a more meaningful mode of assessment might be to lag the percentage calculations. In Liaoning, for instance, if the 1976 data for membership on leading groups and cultural-technical recruitment were calculated using the 1973 UY base of 700,000, the rate of major recruitment would be 27.7 percent. In Honan, using the 1975 recruitment data and the October 1973 base, the result is 17.6 percent, and in Hunan the May 1975 recruitment data and the March 1973 base yield a figure of 23.2 percent. Such calculations, however, require much more accurate data on inflow of urban youths as well as on the extent of outflow than is available.[22]

Membership in the Youth League is the chief indicator of minor recruitment in national and provincial data. Tables 13 and 14 show that YCL membership has always been larger than CCP membership. It has also outstripped cadre recruitment in the great majority of cases and has frequently exceeded cultural-technical recruitment. These findings are not surprising since the YCL is by definition an organization for young people.[23] How does YCL membership among UYs compare with other categories of youth? Again, comparative indicators are hard to come by. In 1964, 13 percent of rural youth was enrolled in the league, but this was considered much too low and a vigorous recruitment drive was started.[24] While it is not known what proportion of rural youth had been admitted to the league as of 1974, the enrollment that year of 14.8 percent of sent-down youths would seem to be on the low side, judging by the standards of 1964. In 1973, 28.3 percent of all of Liaoning's youth—1.7 out of 6 million—had become league members, in contrast to only 11.4 percent of Liaoning's sent-down youth.[25]

Nearly three years later, in the summer of 1976, 27.1 percent of that province's UYs had been admitted, but it is not known how much the provincial membership as a whole had increased.

Youth League data both overstate and understate the actual extent of minor recruitment among UYs. On the one hand, a good many YCL members may already have been counted in the major category as members of leading groups or holders of cultural-technical posts. On the other hand, because youths must demonstrate evidence of activism before they can join the Youth League, the number of activists ought generally to be larger than the number of YCL members in any given unit. In March of 1975, for example, 20,000 of 200,000 UYs in Hopei were members of the YCL, but 40,000 were classified as "Marxist theorists" and 20,000 as "advanced producers, labor models, and backbone elements in the movement to criticize Lin Piao and Confucius."[26] The extent of double counting among these categories cannot be determined, but it is clear that the number of activists exceeded the number of YCL members. Non-YCL activism, however, is rarely aggregated at the provincial level. If we assume that for every YCL member there ought to be at least one other political or cultural-technical activist, the national YCL percentage of 10.4 percent would yield an estimate of minor recruitment of around 20 percent for December 1973 and 28 percent for the end of 1974. These estimates clearly suggest that sent-down youths have had substantial and increasing opportunities to take part in political and cultural activities—as political study guides, newspaper readers, radio broadcasters, night-school teachers, or participants in scientific experiment groups.

The finding that 13–15 percent of UYs have been recruited to major political and cultural-technical roles and 20–30 percent to minor ones conceals wide variation among provinces, as a glance at tables 13 and 14 shows. These variations are not accounted for by the time of publication of a provincial report. That is, one would expect the lower figures to cluster in the early period, the higher ones in the later period. But this does not explain why, at just about the same time in 1972, 2.4 percent of Inner Mongolia's UYs had joined the CCP but only 0.12 percent of Szechwan's. Variation between provinces, moreover, is accompanied by variation within provinces, as shown by recruitment data available for a few prefectures, counties,

communes, and communal subdivisions.[27] Among the factors
that might explain variations in recruitment there is one for
which some statistical evidence is available: recruitment into
the CCP and the YCL is high in several of those provinces that
host sizable PLA Production and Construction Corps units.
Inner Mongolia is a telling case, as shown in table 15. The difference is clear and unambiguous with regard to CCP and YCL
membership, but apparently it does not hold for membership
in leading groups. Data on cultural-technical recruitment are
lacking. The CCP-YCL difference also holds for Sinkiang, as
shown in table 16. For Heilungkiang, data published in December 1974 on all UYs in that province can be juxtaposed with
army farm data on UYs published ten months later. Evidently
a veritable explosion had occurred in recruitment on army
farms, since the number of CCP members in them exceeds the
total for all of Heilungkiang ten months earlier (see table 17).
Since we do not know how much recruitment on communes
grew in the ten months, firm conclusions about the difference
cannot be drawn, but undoubtedly the point that CCP-YCL
recruitment on army farms is larger than on communes holds
in Heilungkiang as well.[28]

What explains the difference? One possibility is that UYs
serving on the army farms are an especially well-motivated
elite, who are therefore more likely to qualify for CCP membership than UYs settled on communes, but the evidence for

Table 15. Recruitment on Communes and Army Farms in Inner Mongolia

Type of Unit	No. of UYs	CCP Members No.	CCP Members %	YCL Members No.	YCL Members %	Members of Leading Groups No.	Members of Leading Groups %
1972							
Army farms	100,000	3,847	3.80	28,277	28.3	2,702	2.7
Communes	80,000	540	.68	6,318	7.9	2,575	3.2
1975							
Army farms	200,000	6,500		40,000		640	
Communes		930		12,900		2,600	

Sources:
1972: Table 11. The report did not mention state farms. The data on leading
       groups are incomplete in the case of army farms, since the platoon and squad
       levels are excluded.
1975: Radio Hu-ho-hot, 8/31/75, *FBIS* no. 183, 9/19/75. The report speaks of
       leading groups at all levels; the drop in numbers in the case of the army
       farms is not explained.

Table 16. Recruitment on Communes and Army Farms in Sinkiang

Type of Unit	Date of Report	No. of UYs	CCP Members No.	%	YCL Members No.	%
1. Army farms, Sinkiang	5/73	100,000	2,000	2.00	20,000	20.00
2. Army farms, Tarim Basin, Sinkiang	5/74	60,000	1,862	3.10	13,500	22.50
3. Communes	12/72	200,000	950	.48	2,300	1.15
	11/73	200,000	3,000	1.50	9,000	4.50

Sources:
1. Radio Peking, 5/9/73, SWB-FE no. 4302, 5/23/73.
2. Radio Peking, 5/5/74, FBIS no. 91, 5/9/74.
3. Radio Urumchi, 12/22/72, FBIS no. 4, 1/5/73; and Radio Urumchi, 11/11/73, FBIS no. 223, 11/19/73. As in the case of Inner Mongolia in table 15, it is not clear whether state farms are included in the data on communes.

this proposition is inconclusive.[29] Another possible explanation is that UY recruitment on army farms is facilitated by the fact that there UYs are the major target group for recruitment, whereas on communes UYs must compete with local youths for the attention of recruiters. This suggests the hypothesis that recruitment is likely to be greater when UYs are settled separately from peasant villages than when the UYs are integrated into the villages, since peasant leaders will tend to prefer local youths to outsiders. If correct, this hypothesis might help account for the policy, noted in chapter 4, of promoting separate and more self-contained UY settlements within the people's communes. A full test of the hypothesis is not possible in the absence of data on all categories of recruitment and data that discriminates between types of settlement, including integrated settlement within production teams, youth farms or youth points attached to production teams or brigades, as well as state and army farms.[30] But even if it cannot be tested, the hypothesis is worth mentioning, since it suggests that the attitude of local cadres and peasants is an important determinant of UY recruitment.

Local Attitudes

Policy makers encourage the recruitment of UYs, but leaders in the communes seem to have considerable leeway on this issue. If no UYs at all are recruited, higher-level officials may well intervene, but there is no evidence of a quota system or a requirement that a certain percentage of UYs be recruited.

Table 17. Recruitment in all of Heilungkiang and on Army Farms

Date of Report	Unit	No. of UYs	CCP Members		YCL Members		Members of Leading Groups	
			No.	%	No.	%	No.	%
1. 12/22/74	Heilungkiang	1,000,000	20,000	2.0	200,000	20.0	17,000	1.7
2. 9/18/75	Heilungkiang Army farms	400,000	35,500	8.9	130,000	32.5	13,000	3.3

Sources:
1. *JMJP* 12/22/74.
2. Radio Harbin, 9/18/75, *FBIS* no. 183, 9/19/75. Another broadcast, from Peking, puts the number of UYs on army farms at "over 300,000." See *NCNA*, Peking, 9/10/75, *FBIS* no. 183, 9/19/75.

Local attitudes, therefore, can make themselves felt. Chapter 4 showed that a good many peasants harbor latent or manifest distrust of the UYs; reluctance to recruit UYs to positions of local responsibility should therefore be expected. And indeed, the press has quoted peasants as expressing anxiety over the risks of entrusting responsibilities to urban youths. They might "rush into calamity," "make trouble," and "become cocky." These fears can be overcome by UYs who establish their trust-worthiness by hard work and good conduct, as well as by doing well in taking on minor activist responsibilities.[31]

However, local people may continue to oppose UY recruit-ment even when the UYs in question are otherwise eligible, simply because they regard the urban youths as outsiders, as transients whose commitment to the village is not permanent. It is this attitude which the press held responsible for the fact that in Liu-ch'eng county, Kwangsi, where 5,100 UYs had settled since 1969, only one had been permitted to join the CCP as of mid-1973, and he actually joined only after having been transferred to factory work. Some local cadres felt that training UYs for party membership was like "planting trees that will give others shade."[32] Similarly, in a Kirin brigade, because the UYs were regarded as "pigeons likely to fly away anytime" (fei-ke p'ai), party members were reluctant to invest the requisite time and effort in recruiting them, even though ten out of the fifty UYs in the brigade had taken the initiative to apply for party membership.[33] The cost consciousness of the peasants also noted in the previous chapter comes to the fore here: why expend time and effort in cultivating UY leaders when the benefit may go to someone else? In the case of cultural-technical recruitment too, costs arise in that some kind of formal or informal on-the-job training may have to be supplied, most obviously in the case of barefoot doctors. If UYs are perceived as lacking in commitment to stay, the ob-vious corollary is preference for local youths, who have family ties in the village, whom everyone has known from childhood on, and who are seen as more likely than UYs to be of perma-nent benefit to the local community.[34]

When attitudes unfavorable to UY recruitment prevail, out-side intervention may be essential. In one such case, an urban youth complained to the county party committee about the reluctance of village party branches to recruit UYs. The county committee sent an investigator to find out why recruitment was lagging and organized the basic-level cadres to study policy on the matter.[35] In the Kirin case, however, it was the party branch members themselves who became aware of the discrepancy between the correct norms and the attitudes of some local party members. The branch organized study of Mao's Thoughts designed to inculcate the concept that the purpose of recruitment is to strengthen the party as a whole and not merely to serve the interests of a particular unit.

Sent-down youths who wish to be recruited must demonstrate that they are "at ease" (an-hsin) in the village. Informants stress that this was the most important criterion for selecting urban youths. Peasants measured an-hsin by the willingness of UYs to work hard, by the efforts they made to cultivate good relationships with the peasants, and especially by the frequency of absences from the village. Youths who ran off to Canton all the time or kept overstaying home leaves were not considered an-hsin and would not be recruited. In this connection it is worth recalling that several of the model youths whose careers were summarized above refused opportunities to leave the village. Turning down opportunities to do factory work or go to a university is no doubt a convincing demonstration of unselfish devotion to the local community—but one that can, as in the model cases, be accompanied by substantial upward mobility within that community.

As might be expected, local needs influence the attitudes of cadres and peasants toward UY recruitment. A village might well experience a need for someone to provide a cultural-technical service. Chu K'o-chia, the model youth in Yunnan, responded to such a felt need when he moved to the Ai-ni village to teach school. But it does not follow that urban youths are always the only available candidates to meet these needs. Other people may well be available to fill such posts as village teacher, barefoot doctor, agricultural technician, or team accountant, especially returned educated peasant youths (RYs) who have attended middle school at the commune center or the county town and then gone back to their home villages. Nan-an county, Fukien, recruited 1,400 teachers to staff village schools set up since the Cultural Revolution as follows: 54 percent of the teachers were poor and lower-middle peasants "with high political consciousness and a certain cultural level," 15 percent were demobilized or specially assigned PLA soldiers, and 31 percent were "returned educated youths who had labored for more than two years and conducted themselves well."[36] Perhaps no urban youths had been sent to this county; in any case, examples can be cited of others in which substantial members of UYs did become teachers.[37] A visitor learned that about a fourth of the 10,000 UYs in Shun-te county, Kwangtung, became teachers, and in Hui-ning county, Kansu, 1,620 out of 5,000 UYs (32 percent) served in this capacity.[38] The point is that a particular locality may not necessarily depend on city youths. The degree of backwardness is likely to play a role: villages in which few peasants have gone to middle schools are likely to depend more on urban youths than villages where education has made greater inroads. As noted in chapter 2, a substantial proportion of urban youths has been sent to the more modernized areas, where their services may well be less in demand. Indeed, one informant, who had served as a cadre in a village near Wusih, Kiangsu, a prosperous and advanced area, reports that teaching positions there were filled by graduates of regular normal schools, obviating reliance on middle school graduates such as UYs lacking pedagogical training.

Discussion of needs reinforces the point that recruiters tend to have a choice as to whether or not to pick UYs. Two factors in addition to those already discussed may influence their choices. The first is that particularism is not equally strong in all villages. Whether due to politicization or the effects of modernization, the fact is that in some villages peasants simply do not object to an outsider playing a significant role in their lives. One informant who became a teacher reports that local youths were not jealous. They felt that UYs were new community members sent by Chairman Mao, who, if they had good records and good working ability, could indeed be recruited.[39] The local youths objected only to lazy UYs. The second factor is that peasants may prefer to have outsiders take on certain tasks even if qualified locals are available. An informant who served as grain depot manager for his team provides an example. At harvest time he spent his evenings registering in-coming grain and dividing it into portions slated for distribution to households, for payment of tax, and for sale to the state. The peasants were glad to have him take on this task since they preferred to devote evenings to their private plots and sideline undertakings. More importantly, it is not inconceivable that peasants might turn to a capable outsider and elect him to a post such as team chief. Some villages are beset by troubles, such as strife between different surname groups, which may make it difficult for any local to serve as team leader. As William Parish notes, "In teams with perennially bad harvests and bad social relations, the problem can be finding someone to serve rather than getting rid of a bad leader."[40] The press has publicized cases of UYs who became team chiefs and who effectively led the peasants in struggling against both economic and social backwardness. In such cases an urban youth may have had to be accepted because he or she enjoyed higher-level backing, but it is at least in principle possible that peasants saw benefit in such an appointment (see the section on leadership and influence, below). And finally, the demands and the low material rewards of basic-level posts may in at least some cases make locals willing to share them with outsiders.

Aggregate statistics are not available to determine how, in the final analysis, rates of recruitment of UYs compare with those of local youths and especially of subgroups such as returned educated peasant youths. However, various indicators, including informants' reports, suggest that RYs are in fact likely to be in a more advantageous position when it comes to recruitment. Ying-ch'ien Middle School in Shang-yu county, Kiangsi, graduated 135 peasant youths in 1970. Among them, 15 joined the PLA and 25 were assigned to factory work. The remaining 95 returned to their villages and were recruited as follows: 11 (11.6 percent) joined the CCP, 42 (44.2 percent) the YCL, 56 (59 percent) became cadres or members of leading groups at the team and brigade levels, and 26 (27.3 percent) were assigned to cultural-technical posts.[41] It would be almost impossible to find a comparably high level of recruitment in all four categories among a similar group of UYs.[42] Moreover, it may be the case that RYs tend to be recruited more readily to major political positions than UYs. An example comes from a commune in Shensi, where two youths, one a returned youth and one an urban youth, both joined the CCP. The RY was subsequently made deputy team chief and distinguished himself in leading antidrought work. The UY was made a theory instructor and, while continuing to do agricultural labor during the day, taught Mao's Thoughts and literacy at night. Although both were party members, the RY occupied a major post, the UY a minor post.[43] One case does not prove much, but content analysis of the press suggests the difference is real in the case of political recruitment. Newspaper articles on educated youth in the countryside deal for the most part with UYs but also contain material on returned youths. If the references to political recruitment of both are divided into major and minor categories, as in table 18, it turns out that a consistently higher proportion of the references to recruitment of RYs are to major recruitment than is the case with UY references. An even more striking difference between returned and urban youths emerges if, as in Table 19, the five most important leadership posts in the commune are singled out, namely, party secretary of the brigade branch and of the commune party committee, chairman of the brigade or commune revolutionary committee, and chief of the production team.

These data would seem to suggest that UYs are less likely than RYs to be found in general leadership positions, particularly those that require the highest level of organizational, managerial, and leadership capacity, as well as ability to get along with the peasants. But it is also worth noting that references to UYs' holding the five key positions doubled between 1969 and 1972, whereas in the case of the returned youths, little growth is seen. Since 1973 a considerable number of articles have appeared describing UYs serving as team chiefs or brigade secretaries, and these materials suggest that a growing number of UYs have been occupying the main leadership posts (see the discussion of leadership and influence below). On balance, however, and taking into account the statistics presented earlier on party membership, the absolute number of such UYs is likely to be very small. It probably continues to be true that urban youths tend to be more acceptable in secondary leadership positions than in the most important ones.

With regard to cultural-technical posts, comparison of refer-

Table 18. Press Coverage of Recruitment of Urban and Returned Youths

Year	Number of Articles	References to Political Recruitment of UYs			References to Political Recruitment of RYs		
		Number	Major	Minor	Number	Major	Minor
1968	187	33	17 (51.5%)	16 (48.5%)	29	25 (86.2%)	4 (13.8%)
1969	385	102	40 (39.2%)	62 (60.8%)	17	11 (64.7%)	6 (35.3%)
1970	239	165	68 (41.2%)	97 (58.8%)	22	17 (77.3%)	5 (22.7%)
1971	108	72	36 (50.0%)	36 (50.0%)	14	13 (92.9%)	1 (7.1%)
1972	212	133	96 (72.2%)	37 (27.8%)	22	22 (100%)	0

Notes: The references to political recruitment of UYs come only from people's communes, which is why the total number in the third column is smaller than the figure in table 12.

Table 19. Press References to Five Key Political Positions
Held by Urban and Returned Youths

	Urban Youths		Returned Youths	
Year	Total No. of References	References to 5 Key Positions	Total No. of References	References to 5 Key Positions
1968	33	0	29	7 (24.1%)
1969	102	3 (2.9%)	17	2 (11.8%)
1970	165	5 (3.0%)	22	6 (27.3%)
1971	72	4 (5.6%)	14	4 (28.6%)
1972	133	8 (6.0%)	22	6 (27.3%)

ences to major and minor recruitment does not yield substantial differences between UYs and RYs (see table 20). If five key posts are singled out—teacher, barefoot doctor, agricultural technician, operator of machinery (mainly tractors), and accountant—the content analysis shows far less striking differences between UYs and RYs than was the case with the five key political posts (see table 21). If it is indeed true that in major cultural-technical recruitment the advantageous position of returned youths disappears, one of the reasons could be that UYs tend to be more acceptable to locals in specialized roles than in general political ones. In the former, interaction with the peasants can be more confined to the specific task for which the UY is recruited. A lesser degree of integration into the village may suffice to enable the UY to carry out his task satisfactorily. To be sure, this explanation conflicts with the official line which regards integration with the peasants as a key condition for effective performance of specialized tasks. Other factors, such as UY preferences and qualifications, might also explain the absence of a differential between returned and urban youths, as well as the finding that major cultural-technical recruitment of UYs is larger than major political recruitment.

UY Attitudes toward Recruitment

From the viewpoint of urban youths, is recruitment a desirable good, a positive incentive that stimulates them to do well and to adapt to village life? Given UY complaints reported in chapter 4 about the monotony of agricultural labor and about their low status in the village, is the answer not obviously yes? In fact, UY reactions to recruitment opportunities are actually quite complex; a variety of motivations and preferences enter in. To begin with, some UYs evaluate rural recruitment not so much in terms of its local payoffs as in terms of its impact on

Table 20. Press Coverage of Cultural-Technical Recruitment of
Urban and Returned Youths

	References to Cultural-Technical Recruitment of Urban Youths			References to Cultural-Technical Recruitment of Returned Youths		
Year	*Number*	*Major*	*Minor*	*Number*	*Major*	*Minor*
1968	12	7 (58.3%)	5 (41.7%)	19	10 (52.6%)	9 (47.4%)
1969	89	37 (41.6%)	52 (58.4%)	19	12 (63.2%)	7 (36.8%)
1970	122	75 (61.5%)	47 (38.5%)	14	8 (57.1%)	6 (42.9%)
1971	37	20 (54.1%)	17 (45.9%)	13	4 (30.8%)	9 (69.2%)
1972	120	55 (45.8%)	65 (54.2%)	9	4 (44.4%)	5 (55.6%)

Notes: As in table 18, references to political recruitment on state and army farms have been deducted from the numbers given here.

Table 21. Press References to Five Key Cultural-Technical Positions
Held by Urban and Returned Youths

	Urban Youths		Returned Youths	
Year	*Total No. of References*	*References to 5 Key Positions*	*Total No. of References*	*References to 5 Key Positions*
1968	12	6 (50.0%)	19	10 (52.6%)
1969	89	33 (37.1%)	19	10 (52.6%)
1970	122	62 (50.8%)	14	6 (42.9%)
1971	37	16 (43.2%)	13	3 (23.1%)
1972	120	45 (37.5%)	9	3 (33.3%)

their ultimate goal of returning to the city. This goal has led some UYs to respond favorably to recruitment opportunities, in order to build up a good record and win reassignment. For example, the leaders of a commune outside of Shenyang had "constantly to correct the erroneous thought" among UYs that "in the first year you join the League, in the second, the Party, and in the third, you go to work in a factory."[44] Seeking to earn reassignment by "gold-plating" can, however, backfire. A female UY in a Heilungkiang commune worked hard and was active in politics, ultimately being elected head of her production team. Then she witnessed the reassignment to factory work or university study of several fellow UYs who had evidently not done as well as she had. Disappointed, she came to feel that "those who are advanced suffer loss" (*hsien-chin ch'ih-k'uei*).[45] Some sent-down youths have refused offers of recruitment in order to avoid making a long-term commitment to the village. In one case, two UYs whom the peasants asked to serve as teachers refused on the grounds that accepting entailed a commitment to stay that could adversely affect their chance to return to the urban sector.[46] In another case, a female UY, elected by the masses to be head of a women's team, was reluctant to accept the job, since it might "nail her to the village" (*ting-tzu nung-ts'un*).[47] These are by no means isolated cases.[48] Some urban youths feel that even ordinary factory work in the urban sector is preferable to becoming a village-level cadre or teacher. For others, it is the hope for a career based on higher education which causes them to reject opportunities for local recruitment. One informant scorned the idea of becoming a barefoot doctor, saying that he wanted to be a professional physician, not a half-trained paramedical.[49] Another informant, who had landed an artist's job working for county government, in the end escaped to Hong Kong, since she wanted to develop her artistic talents in a higher school. Such reactions, which suggest that in at least some cases recruitment does not lead to adaptation, confirm the suspicions of local people that some UYs lack a fundamental commitment to the villages and hence are not worth recruiting.

Even when aspirations to return to the city are not the governing motive, the inherent attractiveness of positions within the village may not be all that great. Several informants appraised cadre jobs as undesirable. Rewards are few and demands are great. Serving as a cadre takes up one's evenings since team cadres are expected to put in a full day's field work. Mobility prospects for team cadres have generally been low, a point singled out by an informant who observed that it is not difficult for UYs of good class background to become team cadres, but that it is much more difficult to rise to positions in the brigade and especially the commune, where cadres serve as full-time administrators. Moreover, team cadres not only get blamed by the higher levels when things go wrong but are also reproached and criticized by the peasants.[50] The marginal status of many UYs in the villages undoubtedly makes service as a village leader a delicate task with many pitfalls. If, as noted in chapter 4, some UYs are reluctant to participate in the discussion of village affairs as ordinary commune members, it follows that they would be even more reluctant to serve in positions that by definition require active assertion of one's point of view. The press confirms the existence of these reactions by printing articles that depict UYs given major responsibilities as fearful of offending peasants or of losing face by making mistakes.[51]

Negative or unenthusiastic reactions to recruitment opportunities are by no means universal among UYs. Data from both press and informants suggest that many UYs do want to be recruited and are disappointed if recruitment is not forthcoming.[52] In the case of political positions, one informant, who had become an activist in the study of Mao's Thought, acknowledged that serving as a cadre brought no material advantages but did raise one's status (*ti-wei*) and reputation (*ming-yü*)—both powerful desiderata from the UYs' point of view.[53] Another informant worked hard, showing good conduct, and was selected to visit neighboring brigades and communes to talk about her advanced experience in applying Mao's Thoughts to her daily life. But a further rise on the ladder of political activism—attendance at a Canton congress of activists in the "Living Study and Application of Mao Tse-tung Thought"—was denied her, reportedly because of her undesirable class background. Had this ascriptive criterion been disregarded, she might well have striven hard to become a political leader. For its part, the press runs many examples of UYs who seem satisfied with the positions they hold.

Do UYs who do want to be recruited prefer cultural-technical to political jobs? The press, constrained by the assumption that politics is in command, does not carry much explicit information on UY preferences; but informants did indeed express a preference for cultural-technical work. At the top of their list came skilled and technical work. Informants wanted to be electricians, carpenters, radio repairmen, technicians, or mechanics. Peasants, they reported, respect such work, and, as previously noted, informants with skills such as radio repair found it easy to cultivate good relations with them. Preference for skilled and technical work was connected not only with future prospects within the village but also with hopes for reassignment to factory work, if not in Canton, at least in the county town or a commune factory. The informants who served on communes, however, knew of virtually no one who actually became a skilled worker or technician, except for one who became a carpenter. Informants who served on state farms reported that there were limited opportunities to do skilled or technical work. One Production and Construction Corps regiment of 2,500 UYs had about 100 UYs who worked with mechanical equipment of various kinds such as tractors or trucks, and these jobs were much sought after. For the most part, informants serving on communes reported UYs becoming teachers in brigade schools as well as barefoot doctors. In individual cases, including their own, UYs served as accountant, midwife, commune broadcaster, county artist, work point recorder, and storekeeper.

One advantage of holding a position such as teacher or barefoot doctor is that it necessitates partial exemption from field labor, in contrast to team cadre jobs which in principle are not exempt. Holders of such posts, moreover, may earn more work points than they would doing only field labor, as in the case of a female informant, whose work points rose from 7 to 9 per day while she taught school, only one short of the 10 points given a full (male) labor power. UYs holding teaching jobs, however, must behave in a more disciplined manner than ordinary youths, in such matters as Canton visits, and for some informants this was a disadvantage. Teaching, it is worth noting, was not regarded as a highly satisfying occupation. Informants complained that the status of teachers had been lowered by the Cultural Revolution, and that teaching peasant children could be a rather frustrating task.[54] Still, such jobs as teaching, while not as attractive as skilled or technical work, were sought after. Informants observed that their brigades needed only a few teachers and barefoot doctors and that therefore there were few openings.

Does recruitment further UY adaptation to rural life? Inadequate as they are, these materials suggest that adaptation does not always follow, most obviously not in the cases of informants who themselves had been recruited and who subsequently went to Hong Kong. In the cases reported in the press of UYs who perceived recruitment as a way of earning an urban reassignment, adaptation also did not result. Such cases are balanced by others of UYs who were recruited and who turned down subsequent reassignment opportunities and of UYs who seem to serve contentedly in rural positions. Among the informants, moreover, some aspired to be recruited but were disappointed, because of either inadequate opportunities or the barrier of class status. While policy maintains that unusually good conduct makes possible recruitment of those from undesirable backgrounds, informants report cases of UYs who did well and wanted to be recruited but were denied the opportunity to serve because of their class status.[55] Less inflexible class practices might well have increased the rate of adjustment among these young people. By and large it seems reasonable to conclude that recruitment reinforces the determination to adapt of those UYs who are predisposed to make efforts to do so.

As noted in chapter 4, UYs come to the village with differing degrees of determination to overcome the difficulties that face them, and for those willing to make efforts to adapt, the possibility of assignment to a major position may well act as a significant incentive. Actual recruitment may then strengthen and reinforce their commitment to stay, and eventually, though not necessarily, it may turn into a permanent commitment.

Even though it does not work in all cases, expansion of recruitment opportunities promises to increase the rate of adaptation of sent-down youths. Probably this is true of both political and cultural-technical recruitment, although it would seem that occupation of technical roles offers the best chance of making rural life meaningful, exciting, and satisfying. Whether opportunities to do cultural-technical work will substantially increase in the future beyond the level of the mid-1970s remains to be seen, however. On the one hand, China's leaders have committed themselves to achieving "basic mechanization" of agriculture by 1980 and all-round modernization by the end of the century. Specialized cultural-technical roles therefore ought to proliferate. As new chairman Hua Kuo-feng put it in 1975: "We must train a mighty contingent of people for mechanized farming, people who are both workers and peasants and well versed in modern techniques."[56] On the other hand, despite technical modernization, China's agriculture is likely to retain much of its labor-intensive character. It is noteworthy in this regard that some informants complained that even when a commune employed electric power, tractors and other machinery, as well as chemical fertilizer, only a few skilled workers and technical specialists were needed.[57] As the use of modern inputs increases, this may well change. But as a commune modernizes, expansion of education for peasants is likely further to limit (as it evidently already has) opportunities for sent-down youths, except in areas of separate settlement. Thus, while some increase in the number of major cultural-technical jobs held by UYs is likely, a dramatic rise may not be in the offing.

Opportunities to Learn Cultural-
Technical Skills

As an area modernizes and more cultural-technical positions become available, an obstacle to the recruitment of UYs may arise in the form of a shortage of youths qualified to fill these positions. The informants who were so eager to do skilled and technical work would for the most part have had to be trained first. In the last few years, more opportunities to acquire skills have become available in the rural areas, and this section seeks to survey and evaluate them.

First, however, a comment is in order concerning the educational attainments of urban and rural youths and the role of urban schools in preparing youths for village work. That urban youths are better educated than their rural counterparts seems obvious if the UYs are compared with rural youths who have attended only primary schools in their teams or brigades. Most of the UYs are secondary school graduates, either of the junior or senior middle schools or of the unified middle schools widely established since the Cultural Revolution. Not all peasant youths educated in brigade schools have actually completed primary school, since there seems to be a considerable dropout rate. To be sure, brigade schools have in many cases also begun offering one or two years of middle school.[58] If the level of village-educated youths is generally inferior to that of the urban youths, the same cannot be said as unequivocally if UYs are compared with returned peasant youths, who are also graduates of middle schools. Were data available, it might well show that UYs do have an edge over them, in that more UYs than returned youths may have completed senior middle school. UYs from major cities such as Peking, Shanghai, or Canton will also have received a qualitatively superior education than returned peasant youths educated in middle schools located at the commune center or in a county town. Schools in major cities are likely to have better facilities and the students will have been exposed to a wider range of cultural stimuli.*

If the academic level of UYs is indeed somewhat higher than those of RYs; the advantage that this gives them in terms of qualifying for village positions is limited. General educational achievement is directly convertible into only a few rural jobs

---

*In assessing the educational attainments of sent-down youths, another factor that must be taken into account is the interruption of education during the Cultural Revolution. Youths whose secondary education stopped in 1966 were often declared graduates in 1968, just prior to their despatch to the village, even if they had completed only one year, say, of senior middle school. This discrepancy between pretense and reality probably contributed to the difficulties of urban youths of the Red Guard generation in adjusting to the countryside. Peasants have been known to grumble about urban middle school "graduates" who knew less than primary school graduates.

even when political and morale criteria have been met. One of these is team accountant (bookkeeper). Another job is teacher in a locally run (*min-pan*) school. Teachers for these schools have often been appointed simply on the basis of completing middle school, preferably senior but also junior middle school. But for most other types of cultural-technical work the main requirement is not so much a certain level of abstract knowledge as the capacity to apply it, which requires concrete technical skills, and it is on this score that UYs often have problems. For example, in 1970 a group of 17 youths from Changsha, Hunan, settled in a brigade in Hui-t'ung county, a remote mountainous region of that province. The peasants, evidently impressed and delighted with the arrival of the educated youths, entrusted them with the task of building a hydroelectric power station and a dam—both small-scale projects of the kind that have proliferated in China. The Changsha youths, however, had no idea how to go about these assignments. Then the brigade bought some chemical fertilizer and asked them to apply it. Again the youths failed: they wasted the fertilizer and damaged the crops. When the UYs first arrived, they held an attitude often found in the cities: "Had we known we were going to be sent to the village, we wouldn't have bothered to study."[59] Now, their failures made them realize that knowledge was important even in the village and that they in fact needed additional, applied knowledge. For its part, the brigade party branch realized that the UYs needed to study not only politics but also technical subjects. Hence, the youths began studying two nights a week and for a full day each month. After studying appropriate manuals and acquiring skills in design and measurement, they were able to build the hydroelectric station.

The complaint that secondary school graduates had studied chemistry but could not use chemical fertilizer or that they had studied physics but did not know how to repair an electric motor was a commonly voiced criticism of education before the Cultural Revolution, which stressed theory but not practice.[60] The example just cited of the difficulties encountered by post–Cultural Revolution graduates suggests that the "revolution in education" has not had an equally strong impact everywhere. Some urban secondary schools have achieved substantial results in vocationalizing their curricula in ways relevant to agriculture. Yenan Middle School in Tientsin, for instance, teaches courses centering on agriculture, so that the teaching of biology is related to the concrete problems students may encounter in the village, such as management of experimental plots. Physics classes concentrate on solving problems connected with rural electrification.[61] In twenty-five schools in Foochow, Fukien, the senior middle school students spend six months of every year in rural branch schools, half of their time being devoted to labor and half to study. Students relate such subjects as physics or chemistry to agricultural processes.[62] But these may be exceptional cases. It is difficult for schools to teach both basic theory and application when the overall length of schooling has been cut, and in the urban setting it is easier to relate the curriculum to nearby industrial undertakings.[63]

During the campaign to criticize Lin Piao and Confucius, inadequate implementation or erosion of Maoist educational ideals came under fire, but at the same time, the campaign prompted some cities to set up short-term study programs to teach youths concrete skills useful in the villages.[64] The No. 2 Middle School in Nanning, Kwangsi, for example, organized 24 two-week courses in eleven subjects, offered to the 900 students about to graduate from its junior and senior divisions. The specialties included woodworking, electrical work, horticulture, veterinary medicine, plant protection, "civil engineering and projects," use and repair of agricultural machines, rural accounting (including use of the abacus), and installation and repair of radio diffusion networks as well as radio receivers. The teachers were drawn from a wide variety of Nanning's enterprises and higher schools. The students acquired a "preliminary mastery" of the "basic knowledge" of their specialties.[65] These short-term classes seek to compensate for the apparent absence in the regular curriculum of vocational training for students to be sent to the village.

Until more urban schools prepare their graduates better, many of them will continue to arrive in the village unprepared to assume most types of cultural-technical positions. Since county school inadequacies have also come under fire, it may be that peasant youths who attend middle school outside of their villages have also not been taught technical skills.[66] This might account for the finding in tables 20 and 21 that RYs are not mentioned more frequently than UYs as occupants of major cultural-technical posts. They still have a competitive advantage in that they are more familiar with local conditions and adapt more easily to life in their home villages than UYs. But both urban youths and returned peasant youths require training after they come to the villages in order to qualify for cultural-technical work.

In the last several years, a significant expansion in opportunities to learn cultural-technical skills in the rural areas has taken place compared to the late 1960s and early 1970s. It is not that opportunities were wholly absent—the advances in rural health care, for instance, necessitated establishment of a large-scale program to train barefoot doctors—but the range of formal training opportunities was much smaller than it has since become.[67] Learning of cultural-technical skills took place largely through informal on-the-job arrangements, apprenticeships, learning by doing, and individual and group study within the villages. The times were not propitious for widespread formal technical study. After the Cultural Revolution, political re-education of UYs was emphasized, and cultural-technical study was suspect simply because Liu Shao-ch'i had advocated making the transfer acceptable by providing youths with a chance to further their education in the village.[68] When policy shifted in the 1970s toward greater emphasis on UY contributions to rural modernization, renewed interest in cultural-technical study was reflected in denunciations of Lin Piao for having "peddled such trash as 'it is no use to study' and 'techniques are of no use,'" or the idea that "politics can oust anything," thereby negating the "red and expert" formula.[69] Still another obstacle to the establishment of part-time schools for UYs was disbelief on the part of some rural officials in the permanence of the transfer program.[70]

Formal study programs organized by counties, communes, army farms, and urban institutions began to be organized on an isolated basis from 1971 on, and much more frequently since 1973.[71] One of the earlier efforts took place in a regiment of the Heilungkiang Production and Construction Corps, whose party committee launched a drive to set up "red and expert" evening schools in its subordinate companies in November 1971. Within a year, two-thirds of the companies had in fact done so. Technical courses included agricultural machinery, agriculture, animal husbandry, forestry, medicine, and public health. Both basic principles and application were taught, but the weight of instruction was on application. Thus during the wheat harvesting season the course on machinery taught prevention of breakdown of machinery, and during the slack season, techniques for the maintenance of machinery. Teachers giving technical instruction included old workers and technicians with practical experience; they learned as they taught. Positive results were reportedly attained:

> Among the 55 youths of the 16th Company . . . that attended evening schools, 13 . . . learned how to operate and maintain machinery correctly, two became drivers of Tungfanghung tractors, three learned to drive combines . . . one learned the technique of electric welding, two learned to shoe horses, three learned how to make "5406" and "920" bacterial fertilizer, two learned to crossbreed wheat, four learned how to make Bordeaux mixture and liquid sulphur mixture as well as how to cure fruit plants, ten learned how to give injections to pigs, one became a veterinarian, and one learned how to operate oil presses.[72]

In 1975 the Chinese press devoted much attention to agricultural colleges situated in counties, communes, and even brigades, which enroll peasants as well as sent-down youths. The model institution is Ch'ao-yang Agricultural College in a remote Liaoning county by that name. The goal is to train students to become "new peasants with socialist consciousness and modern agricultural scientific techniques and knowledge." The emphasis is on short-term training classes: from its establishment in 1970 to 1975, Ch'ao-yang trained 10,000 technicians while graduating only 167 regular students. Students do not transfer their household registrations and remain members of their communes. They return to their brigades and teams as peasants without coming under the nationwide job assignment system for college graduates, thus eliminating the prospect of upward mobility beyond the rural sector from higher education.[73] Elsewhere, the proliferation of "communist labor universities" in rural areas—Hopei has set up ninety such schools enrolling 20,000 students—is primarily geared to spare-time study within the basic rural units.[74] In the fall of 1974, for instance, ten state farms in the Shanghai suburbs pooled resources for a spare-time college for 3,000 students; some 300 teachers were recruited from among cadres, old peasants, technicians, and urban youths. Classes met two or three evenings a week, with the course of study lasting about a year. Offerings included politics, Chinese language, management of crops, foundations of industry, water conservation, cattle breeding, and revolutionary literature and art.[75]

In addition to schools within the rural areas, correspondence courses offered by urban colleges and universities have since 1973 become an important source of rural educational opportunity. Higher schools in cities such as Harbin, Shanghai, Wuhan, Kunming, and Chengtu have started to offer correspondence courses, primarily but not exclusively for UYs. In Harbin, a correspondence school was organized in November 1973 by that city's UY office and the Department of Education. Run by a revolutionary committee that includes UY representatives, the school recruited 136 teachers from Tung-pei Agricultural College, the Provincial Agricultural Machinery Institute, and the city Department of Science and Technology. Participating communes and state farms set up "leading groups" for correspondence study and, as of June 1974, 3,300 study groups made up of 15,000 UYs and RYs were enrolled, spending two hours a week during the busy season and four hours in the slack season on their studies, under the supervision of locally recruited study guides. The general curriculum consists of politics, Chinese language, and mathematics, while specialized study includes politics, vegetable cultivation, and rural electrical work, with courses on machinery, cattle breeding, and veterinary medicine in preparation.[76]

Together with the expansion of opportunities to learn in the rural areas has come an expansion in the supply of books and study materials. During the remedial campaign of 1973 the attention of publishing houses and of the Hsin-hua Bookstore network was drawn to the needs of UYs in this regard.[77] The experience of Shanghai publishers, who put out twenty kinds of books for self-study, was publicized, and in various parts of the country steps were taken to equip UY settlements with libraries and reading rooms.[78] By October 1973, three-fourths of Heilungkiang's Production and Construction Corps companies had set up reading rooms as had two-thirds of the UY settlements on communes, the rather remarkable implication being that until 1973 little had been done to meet UY needs for political, cultural, technical, and scientific reading matter.[79] The Hsin-hua Bookstore in Shu-yang county, Kiangsu, dispatched seven mobile supply units to UY settlements, helping them set up reading rooms, and paying special attention to the supply of technical books appropriate to a particular locality's crop conditions.[80] Evidently the increase in book supply to educated youths in the countryside has not been a one-shot affair but has continued, with a strong focus on the supply of technical manuals.[81]

Finally, some UYs have had opportunities to learn while temporarily in cities. Potentially the most significant of these opportunities has been attendance at an urban college or university for the full three-year course. Assuming that the UYs sent to urban colleges study subjects relevant to agriculture and assuming that they in fact return to the countryside after graduation, they would be qualified to occupy more advanced and more highly specialized posts than the ones this chapter has been describing, such as physician, agronomist, engineer, or commune middle school teacher. Because there are doubts about these assumptions, however, UY study in urban higher schools will be treated in chapter 6 as part of the issue of reassignment. Here let us take note of programs sponsored by cities such as Shanghai to offer short-term training to UYs on home leave. Because many Shanghai youths have been sent to distant provinces such as Heilungkiang, Sinkiang, and Yunnan, they visit their families for longer periods of four to six weeks in the winter months every other year, thereby providing time for the organization of political, cultural, and educational programs. In 1973, borough governments, neighborhood committees, middle schools, and factories held classes in ten subjects ranging from the use of microorganisms to barbering. In 1973–74, colleges and universities offered a series of lectures for UYs, assigning 173 faculty members and reaching 100,000–150,000 UYs. Some 10,000 of them also took brief courses on rural bookkeeping, herbal pharmacology, and acupuncture. And in 1975, industrial enterprises were brought into play with programs to train UYs in various technical skills.[82]

In assessing the worth of all these educational programs, several factors limiting their impact on the UYs should be mentioned. First, with one or two exceptions, these programs are intended for both urban and peasant youths, and the proportion of UYs in them is not known. Preference in favor of local youths may well operate in the selection of trainees.[83] Second, not much is known about the quality of the programs, and obvious questions can be raised about how much can be taught in a short period of time. Even in the case of spare-time study, a proportion of the time available is devoted to politics, thus reducing the time devoted to specialized study. (In a more general sense, opportunities to take part in organized political study in addition to the minimum required of all UYs, as in "political evening schools," are probably greater than opportunities for cultural-technical study.[84]) Thirdly, it is not clear whether those who have been trained actually do the jobs for which they prepared. Only in some instances do accounts refer to prior investigations of needs, and it is possible that coordination between training programs and actual needs is not adequate.

On balance, however, these programs are likely to have a positive impact. First, from the point of view of the modernizing countryside, they reflect a realistic perception that the main quantitative need for specialized manpower is not for full-fledged college or university graduates but for personnel with vocational training who are able to apply knowledge to a limited range of concrete situations. This is not to say that the countryside does not also need highly trained university-level specialists. In China, such specialists can be found at the higher levels of the rural structure, especially the county but also at the commune.[85] But, as studies of the relationship between education and rural modernization suggest, such specialists, in order to be effective in changing agriculture, need to work with technically trained personnel who actually operate the modern inputs and through whom knowledge about them can be diffused to the peasants generally.[86] To the extent that these programs enlarge the pool of village-level technical talent, to that extent modernization of the village is furthered.

Second, UYs who receive training and are assigned specialized tasks are likely to adapt better to the countryside than those who do not. Those able to repair a tractor engine or calculate the proportion of chemical fertilizer to other inputs may derive a sense of satisfaction and achievement from their work. In the case of the "red and expert" schools in the army farm in Heilungkiang described earlier, the UYs' interest in farming reportedly rose as they came to realize that there was more to agriculture than just manual labor: "the more they learned the more they realized how little they knew. . . . The more they learned, the more meaningful they found agricultural work." Opportunity to acquire specialized knowledge and skills enhanced their adaptation: "Evening schools deepened their determination of settling down in border areas and of loving one's own work."[87] If this is so, the outside observer can only wonder why it has taken so long to broaden educational opportunities for the urban youths.

CONTRIBUTIONS TO RURAL DEVELOPMENT

It is the intent of Chinese leaders that the village undergo a variety of fundamental changes which, taken together, may be given the label "development." The changes are political; they aim at the growing institutionalization of socialist forms, values, and practices. They are cultural, aiming at the broadening of the peasants' horizons, increasing their receptivity to learning, rational thinking, and new ideas. They are technical, aiming at the increasingly widespread use of modern inputs and approaches to farming. And they are physical, aiming at the transformation of the "face" (*mien-mao*) of the village, on the model of what has been achieved by the famous Tachai production brigade, which in the course of many years of the most strenuous labor greatly increased the productivity of its formerly largely barren environment. Mao Tse-tung's slogan that "class struggle, the struggle for production, and the struggle for scientific experiment are the three great revolutionary movements for building a mighty socialist country" summarizes these changes.[88]

What contributions have the young urbanites been making to the attainment of these changes? In the spring of 1976, the Chinese press defended the transfer program against Teng Hsiao-p'ing's attacks by praising their role: "The villages need these educated youth who can contribute their knowledge of politics, culture and science to bring about . . . changes and build a socialist new countryside. Experience shows that these young people have revolutionary ideals, culture, and the strong desire to change the outlook of the villages. They are an energetic force in the construction of a socialist countryside."[89] To what extent does reality bear out this positive assessment? This section will assess contributions made by UYs in four capacities: (1) as general leaders and innovators; (2) as scientific and technical innovators; (3) as promoters of education, particularly primary schooling; and (4) as an addition to the rural work force.

Leadership and Influence

Data presented in the previous section show that some urban youths have assumed positions of general leadership. In addition, UYs may play informal leadership roles without holding formal positions. Given the difficulties with adaptation and integration faced by many UYs, however, the proportion of UY leaders is likely to be small. Informants interviewed in 1972–73 knew of no such cases, but the attention that has been paid in the press to this aspect of the transfer since then suggests that the frequency of UYs playing general leadership roles has been increasing. In Hai-ch'eng county, Liaoning, where the authorities had to overcome substantial difficulties in coping with the UYs (see chapter 4), 300 out of 3,000 production teams were headed by sent-down youths as of 1975.[90] Hai-ch'eng is an exceptional case if only because by 1975 it had absorbed 56,000 UYs, whereas the national average of UYs per county is about 5,700. But it is one outcome of the transfer and one that needs to be analyzed. Let us look at individual cases.

The first is that of a young woman from Shanghai, Sung Ai-mei, who settled in a brigade in Hun-ch'un county, Kirin, in March 1969. "Tempered" in the "three revolutionary movements," she joined the party in July 1971 and was elected political team chief (*cheng-chih tui-chang*) of no. 4 production team six months later. Sung displayed leadership initiatives on the issue of village adherence to socialist norms and protected the collective and state interest against encroachments by private, individual interests. In one episode, she opposed a "wind of eating and drinking" (*yi ku ch'ih-ho feng*): class enemies had incited backward team members to slaughter and consume privately owned pigs, rather than sell them to the state as regulations require, and they also demanded that the same be done with team-owned pigs. Sung discussed this with a progressive poor peasant, led the members of her collective household in mobilizing the masses, exposed the enemy's sabotage, and checked this "crooked wind" (*wai feng*). A similar problem arose shortly after she had become a cadre, when, at a membership meeting of the team, some peasants proposed exchanging thirty *mou* of good team land for thirty mou of privately held vegetable land of lesser quality. Sung resolutely opposed this assault on the collective sector. One peasant told her: "You are a sent-down educated youth and you have also been team chief for only a short time. You still haven't learned how to care for people's lives." The proposal evidently had majority support, for the peasant added that "this matter should be settled according to everybody's opinion." A good communist, Sung refused to be bound by mere numbers. She sternly replied that she had been elected by the poor and lower-middle peasants to uphold their (revolutionary) power and that she most definitely would not agree to so retrograde a proposal. She then proceeded to change the views of the peasants, ultimately eliciting self-criticisms from the proponents. Furthermore, Sung was not afraid to criticize severely a team cadre who, in her absence, had diverted 5,000 catties of beans to private use. She used this incident to educate the peasants on the correct relationship between the interests of the state and the individual. In addition to these deeds, Sung also took the lead in spurring production, mobilizing the peasants to enlarge the irrigated portion of the team's crop lands, to make use of river mud as fertilizer, to adapt advanced crop-growing methods to the cold Manchurian climate, and to bring new land under cultivation. Her initiatives helped make it possible for the team to weather a "rather serious" natural disaster and still increase output.[91]

The second case is that of the Red Flag production brigade in Huo-ch'iu county, Anhwei, where 52 youths, mostly from Shanghai, settled between 1968 and 1972. The article about them, authored by the brigade's party branch, depicts the UYs as having played an important role in transforming this small brigade of 800 inhabitants from dependence on the state for grain and loans to a condition in which the brigade not only became self-sufficient but also sold grain to the state even while the income of the members rose. One UY contribution was to strengthen leadership. The quality of the brigade leaders had been low. Four the of seven party branch members had had no education, having been casual laborers or beggars in the old society; two others had gone to primary school. Their grasp of policies and methods had been weak; their work was often characterized by "blindness" (*mang-mu hsing*). In 1970, a female UY became deputy branch secretary. She led the branch in studying Mao's Thoughts. One result was that relations among the local leaders improved. The party secretary had not understood Chairman Mao's approach to cadres who make mistakes but had treated a branch member who committed errors due to infection by Liu Shao-ch'i's revisionist poisons with hostility, rather than seeking to help him change his ways ("cure the illness to save the patient"). The UY's intervention changed the secretary's approach to the errant cadre, who consequently became much more dedicated to his work.

Because leadership in some of the component production teams also was deficient, the brigade party branch assigned UYs to the teams in question. One such team had been afflicted by discord, the roots of which apparently went back to prelibera-tion days. The urban youth investigated the strife, mediated, and resolved it, primarily by injecting a dose of Maoist princi-ples. In this and other teams, a major task of the UYs was to revitalize the class divisions which in theory should divide the village and insure that power is held by the poor and lower-middle peasants rather than by members of the former upper groups. The youths would investigate the history of class struggle in the village, disseminate material about it in the form of posters and meetings, and finally launch mass criticisms of the class enemies. In one team, for instance, a rich peasant who persisted in taking the "reactionary stand" had sowed discord among peasants by playing upon lineage relations (tsung-tzu kuan-hsi). An urban youth who had settled in this village used the case of an old poor peasant who had suffered from exploita-tion in the old society to write an essay entitled "Class Rela-tions or Lineage Relations." He exposed the enemy plot of using crosscutting lineage sentiments to weaken class cleavages and hence undermine the power of the poor.

The enthusiasm and dedication of the Huo-ch'iu UYs gave a "very big impetus" (hen ta ti t'ui-tung) to the transformation of the backward and poverty-stricken brigade. Their determina-tion communicated itself to the party branch, which, after dis-cussion with the peasants, drew up a three-year "all round plan to change the face" of the village. The main projects consisted of construction of water reservoirs and irrigation canals. An-other area where the youths played a key role was in the adoption of innovations in farming practices such as close planting and double cropping of rice. The latter had been tried without success, leading to skepticism about innovation on the

part of the locals. The UY deputy party secretary, while attending a provincial meeting, used her expense money to buy some
new fast-growing rice seeds. These the UYs planted on an experimental plot, and the results convinced the peasants that it
was possible to grow two crops in one season. The UYs similarly demonstrated the advantages of close planting. Finally, the
UYs also took the lead in educational work. The brigade had
not had any middle school students and illiteracy was rife.
The UYs set up eight schools, organized eighteen newspaper
reading groups as well as twenty-six family study assistance
stations, securing the participation of 700 out of 800 persons
in the brigade in cultural or political study.[92]

These two cases in which UYs played active leadership roles
in promoting change are by no means the only ones found in
the press. In understanding them, it is important to note that
the issues on which they exercise leadership are issues of major
concern to the Chinese political system as a whole. The UYs, in
other words, can count on the implicit or explicit backing of
the system. They can invoke its values, principles, or policies,
and they can ask for help from the higher levels. This point
applies with particular force to the issue of erosion of socialist
standards. As policymakers see it, the "struggle between the
two lines" must constantly be waged. Peasants may succumb to
"spontaneous tendencies toward capitalism" that arise from
their very nature as former small-holders, and manifest themselves when a production unit gives preference to individual
over collective interests. Such tendencies occur at all levels of
the commune, but are most threatening at the level of the
production team.[93] As the basic accounting unit of the commune, the team has some autonomy, and it is in the team that
peasant participation is most meaningful. The team often is a
natural village and may be characterized by a high degree of
solidarity. When those villagers who in principle should be the
defenders of socialism—cadres and poor and lower-middle
peasants—fail to uphold the collective interest, the availability
of UYs able and willing to do so constitutes an obvious asset
for the system. Thus *Red Flag* praised the UYs, saying that
"they have grown up to be standard bearers in the effort to
adhere to the socialist road" (my emphasis).[94]

The implicit or explicit backing available to UYs taking the
initiative in upholding socialist standards makes itself felt in

several ways. An urban youth may expose a deviation and bring it to the attention of local leaders, who, realizing that it involves a matter of principle, themselves take corrective action.[95] Or an urban youth may inform the higher levels that a problem exists, for example, that "feudal customs" are reemerging or that the class enemy is launching attacks.[96] In one such case, reported from a village in Yenan prefecture, peasants had taken advantage of a policy of encouraging pig raising by enlarging their private plots, using reclaimed land. A dedicated urban youth reported this threat to the collective interest to the brigade leaders, but they failed to respond. When his appeal to the commune also brought no action, he walked to the county town, where the county party committee finally supported his stand, issuing a corrective edict and calling upon the county to study the youth's "advanced experience."[97] Once support by higher levels has been given, the capacity of a UY to take the lead locally is further enhanced. In some cases, a successful UY becomes a troubleshooter for the higher levels, being sent to a backward team to straighten it out.[98]

In other cases publicized in the press, urban youths may be more on their own, and considerable conflict with local leaders can ensue. In one of these, an urban youth, Sun Yu-wen, waged a year-long struggle with his team chief, a peasant who had held the post for more than a decade but who did not take part in productive labor, did not lead the peasants to improve the village, and embarked on money-making ventures at the expense of grain production. Sun challenged the chief's diversion of the team's large wagon for outside use (that is, to make money pulling loads for county factories) even while it was needed by the team. In one confrontation, he forced its return to the village. Though he incurred the chief's dislike, Sun persevered, opposing other schemes of the chief's such as to enlarge the private sector. Reportedly, poor and lower-middle peasants supported Sun, and in early 1973 they sought to have the team chief recalled and Sun elected in his place. The brigade refused to approve this change as irregular, but it did sanction Sun's becoming deputy chief. Further conflicts developed between the two. The chief tried to come to an understanding with Sun, but the young man refused to compromise with principle and continued to challenge the chief's misbehavior. Finally, during the campaign against Lin Piao and Confucius, the commune

party committee sent cadres to help resolve the team's leadership problem. Sun was elected team chief and later rose to
become brigade party branch secretary.[99]

What motivates such youths to defy local leaders, "daring to
speak, daring to act, daring to struggle"? Confidence that in
the final analysis the political system will back them up is one
factor.* Support from the peasants may be another. Poor and
lower-middle peasants are invariably depicted as encouraging
the UY in question, but in some cases their support is passive
and weak, and the UY may have to stand up to local opinion
as a whole. When this happens, support from the UY's own
collective may be crucial. Sung Ai-mei, for instance, mobilized
her collective household to agitate among the peasants.[100] A
well-organized, well-motivated UY collective provides moral
support for the UY leader. There is safety in numbers; presumably it is much harder for local cadres or peasants to retaliate against a group than against an isolated individual. That
membership in a UY group may supply the confidence needed
to assert oneself in village affairs is indicated by UYs who after
marriage left their collective and then found it "embarrassing
to offend people," becoming less "militant in struggle."[101]
UY collectives, in other words, can act as a pressure group
vis-à-vis the village. The trend noted in chapter 4 of establishing UY collectives more widely may reflect an intent of policy
makers to strengthen the capacity of UYs to act more aggres-
sively as defenders of socialist standards as well as promoters
of change generally. But, as also noted in the previous chapter,
the extent to which UY groups are motivated to support regime
goals varies greatly. Certainly it is not plausible to assume that
more than a minority of such collectives are able and willing to
engage in conflict with peasants.[102]

Whether UYs play roles of assertive leadership thus hinges in
large part on the degree to which support is forthcoming from
higher levels, from the peasants, and from fellow UYs. Such
variables as their own degree of commitment, idealism, persever-
ance, toughness, and ability also strongly influence this matter.

---

*Help from higher level officials may not always have come because of the merits
of a particular local situation. The Politburo members who were purged in October
1976 and labeled the "gang of four" have been charged with cultivating supporters
from among young cadres, encouraging them to oppose established, older officials.
Evidence that such factional ties played a role in the cases here described has not
come to light, but the possibility of the existence of such connections cannot be
excluded. See also chapter 6, last section.

Another personal attribute is class status: coming from a working class or revolutionary cadre background legitimates assertiveness.[103] Because these attributes are not always present, the frequency of assertive leadership on issues such as the erosion of socialist standards is limited. UYs may simply lack the motivation to expose deviations. According to an informant, the peasants in his production team used to cut lumber in a nearby state-owned forest and sell it; the UYs knew about it but did nothing.[104] Or, these variables may not operate in sufficient strength to outweigh pressures to conform. Sam Rayburn's advice, "to get along, go along," is likely to be as compelling for UYs as it has been for freshmen Congressmen in the United States. Sent-down youths who make positive efforts to adapt are likely to do just that—to adapt to local realities, not combat them. A sent-down youth who wants to be recruited—or reassigned to the urban sector—must earn the support of the local community. Offending against local practices is not conducive to achieving either goal, and, besides, locals can retaliate against troublemakers in other ways as well.[105] Given their precarious status, UYs recruited into local leadership groups are thus more likely to reflect local preferences than to mold them. In a production team in Hopei, for instance, the chief, a local cadre, sought to increase the proportion of grain retained in the village rather than sold to the state by providing for fodder for pigs as yet unborn. He secured the assent of the team accountant, an urban youth, in this violation of policy. The UY felt that he had to go along with the chief because he, after all, was in the village to be reeducated. When brigade leaders found out about the deviation, they criticized the young accountant for not daring to struggle against error.[106] In this case, it is worth noting, the policy of reeducation added to pressures on the urban youth to conform, or at least provided the justification for playing it safe. Policy makers themselves, it seems, are ambivalent. They would like UYs to be active in checking erosion of socialist standards but they are also sensitive to the dangers of arousing peasant resentment against self-righteous young urbanites riding roughshod over local sensibilities. "Humbly" receiving reeducation from the poor and lower-middle peasants is the prescription for bossy UY cadres, but one that compounds the competing demands upon them and one that may well contribute to keeping the frequency of assertive leadership low.[107]

Policy makers would also like to see UYs play an active role as promoters of positive change. In many Chinese villages, cadres and peasants have not made the most of the existing potential for development. Tapping this latent potential is a basic part of China's rural development strategy. Youths in villages whose self-help effort has lagged have an opportunity to act as catalysts of change by somehow encouraging, inspiring, and persuading the locals to embark on a project, undertake a scientific experiment, or adopt an innovation. The variables that enable UYs to act as agents of change are not dissimilar to those that enable them to exert leadership on behalf of adherence to socialist practices and values. An additional issue, however, is the attitude of peasants toward UY-initiated innovations. In one village, UYs suggested that their production team adopt new seeds. "Some" cadres and peasants opposed the proposal, fearing that production would decline. A conflict broke out, and, as is usually the case with press accounts, class enemies were allegedly behind the conservatism of the opponents.[108] In another village, when UYs asked to undertake scientific experiments which required allocation of resources such as land, "some were even afraid that the educated young people might fail in their experiments and impede production."[109] Peasants are likely to be cautious and alert to the potential costs of an innovation. Although the commune system offers security against disasters that endanger the minimum needs of a unit, there is no insurance, as far as is known, against moderate drops in income that result from unsuccessful innovations or other risk taking.[110] For locals to respond positively to UY initiatives thus requires a degree of confidence in their competence which cannot be taken for granted, especially in technical matters (see next section), and this is likely to limit the number of cases of UYs' persuading locals to adopt an innovation.[111]

Urban youths can function best as innovative leaders when the backing of the political system is direct and unambiguous, that is, when they are explicitly entrusted by higher-level authority with the mission of acting as a catalyst of change. For instance, a Shanghai UY in a backward team in Erh-yuan county, Yunnan, was approached by the brigade secretary and asked to take the initiative in launching a movement to learn from Tachai. The youth mobilized fellow UYs as well as villagers, including cadres. They first studied politics and class struggle, then worked on several small projects. Their example inspired the village, and an atmosphere of enthusiasm was generated, accompanied, however, by intolerance for slackers. Remarkable results ensued: formerly only 40 to 50 persons would turn out to work during spring planting; now 200 turned out. The UY also led in the introduction of electric power, which enabled the team to till all of its 2,000 mou of arable land, only 1,050 mou having been planted previously.[112] The account does not clarify this youth's relationship with the team chief, who seems to have been effectively bypassed. In other cases in which UYs play the role of catalyst, formal and informal leadership roles converge; an urban youth sent to energize a backward team also becomes its head.[113]

Though most sent-down youths have not played roles of active leadership in their villages—and for good reasons—the young urbanites exert some influence even without directly asserting themselves in village affairs. Their presence, their behavior, their activities, and their interactions with the peasants have an impact on peasant values, customs, and attitudes. Its extent is very difficult to measure, but both press and informants agree that this has been the case. The press depicts young urban women as exerting informal influence by breaking with tradition—marrying less educated peasants, or performing tasks which in the village had customarily not been performed by women, such as planting crops, building houses, cutting firewood, or fishing. The examples set by such female urban youths have been emulated by peasant women.[114] Informants report having widened the horizons of peasants by talking to them about life in Canton, telling them about modern life styles, including husbands doing housework and taking part in child care. Young villagers may be influenced by the example of unmarried youths of both sexes interacting more freely than local custom permits.[115] Sometimes, UYs arouse the envy of local youths by their more citified clothing ("only those dressed like youths in Canton are well dressed"), prompting emulation. In one village, an informant introduced his peasant friends to the urban custom of drinking coffee and beer. Several informants spoke of introducing peasant youths to novels, including forbidden ones. Indeed, the introduction of urban recreational activities designed to break the monotony of village life may well be a significant byproduct of the transfer. Several informants introduced sports to their villages, including table tennis, basketball, and swimming. For its part, the press frequently reports on UY art and spare-time drama groups.[116]

Thus informal contact, particularly in remote villages with poor communications, in which UYs may be the first outsiders with whom peasants have come into sustained personal contact, could well have a significant impact on peasant customs. But the extent to which this is happening is limited since a good many UYs settle in villages close to major cities and in more developed areas that have long felt the influence of urban culture. Furthermore, when UYs do go to backward areas, they often settle on army and state farms, in which contact with peasants is less intense. Contact on communes is also limited since not all UYs are inserted into production teams. From the policy makers' point of view, where opportunities for sustained informal contact exist, undesirable results could ensue, if peasants' expectations were raised or resentment of superior living standards aroused. There is little evidence to show that UY-peasant interactions are producing these results. It is noteworthy, however, that when urban cadres are sent to the villages to take part in manual labor they are told not to flaunt their comparative wealth before the peasants nor to tell them about their salaries.[117]

Technical Innovations

The press has published numerous instances in which urban youths have made technical innovations that have contributed to the modernization of the countryside. The following twelve examples illustrate the range and variety of these reports:

—UYs on an army farm on the banks of the Yellow River in Inner Mongolia learn how to grow paddy rice on land they have reclaimed but which is alkalized. They also grow cotton, in both cases overcoming the belief that paddy rice and cotton could not be grown north of the Great Wall. By engaging in scientific experiment, specifically cross-fertilization, they also solve a problem of the degeneration of potatoes.

—Two female UYs in a brigade in Hsin-kan county, Kiangsi, set up a spare-time weather station and are able to give advance warning of a thunderstorm, thereby helping to avert crop damage. Their forecasting activities make possible a more scientific approach to crop growing.

—A female UY in a brigade in Yung-ning county, Kwangsi, succeeds in growing bacteria that kill insects harmful to paddy rice, using local methods. Now, people from all over the province come to learn from her.

—In Hung-hu county, Hupei, UYs working on a fish-raising farm undertake scientific experiments in order to raise the winter survival rate of fish. The rate increases from 30 percent in 1969 to 80 percent in 1971.

—Virtually all of the 48 UYs in a brigade in Pao-ying county, Kiangsu, participate in scientific experiment groups. They succeed in making bacterial fertilizer "5,406," plant hormone "920," pesticide "4,115," and saccharine feed. They also introduce the use of improved seeds, popularize double cropping of rice, and undertake weather forecasting as well as insect pest prediction.

—The "agricultural science small group" on a company-sized army farm in Heilungkiang breeds improved seeds brought from elsewhere, adapting them through cross-fertilization to the cold northern climate. They succeed in growing wheat, beans, corn, and rice. Moreover, the UYs ask relatives in Shanghai to send them seeds to try raising southern vegetables in the northern environment and they do so successfully.

—A male UY on an army farm in Hainan locates a mountain creek, uses his school knowledge of mathematics and physics to calculate the rate of fall, and proposes to the party committee of his regiment the construction of a hydroelectric station. He draws up the plans, and the party branch of his company assigns him the task of building a hydraulic turbine. Taking the turbines of nearby power stations as models, he succeeds in making the turbine, using material such as a five-millimeter steel plate. He is also assigned the task of making a pressured water pipe (ya-li shui-kuan). Lacking reinforced concrete, he tries using substitutes. At first he fails, but then, again using knowledge acquired in school, he calculates the water pressure, consults older workers, and finds it possible to make a forty-meter-long native water pipe (t'u shui-kuan), using cement made from crushed rocks. Under his leadership, the power station is successfully built.

—A brigade in Li-ling county, Hunan, which specializes in the growing of vegetables, is suffering from drought. The party branch assigns the task of building a sprinkler system (jen-kung chiang-yü ch'i, literally a rain-making machine) to the UYs. The youths are afraid to tackle the task, but branch members encourage them by criticizing Lin Piao's theory of "innate genius." After studying an old model and getting some help from a county factory, and after much trial and error, they succeed in building a sprinkler system able to irrigate seventy-two mou of land and usable for pesticide application as well.

—In a brigade in Yang-kao county, Shansi, livestock fall ill but there are no drugs to treat the animals. Sent-down youths, using crude and simple local methods, set up a shop to manufacture drugs. Within two years, their shop has grown into a factory that supplies the needs of units other than their own brigade, enabling the latter to buy machinery worth 16,000 yuan from the earnings of the factory.

—A male UY in Liang-ch'eng county, Inner Mongolia, who had been interested in electronics, uses his knowledge and enthusiasm for things technical to assist his brigade in its efforts to mechanize. He repairs the motors of threshers, tractors, and water pumps, lays electric lines, repairs radio receivers, and saves the brigade a great deal of money.

—A female UY in a brigade in Tung-t'ai county, Kiangsu, turns 12 mou of alkaline land into productive land. Her brigade applies her experience and reclaims 1,200 mou of alkaline land.
—Three Shanghai UYs in a minority village in Ho-ch'ing county, Yunnan, bring electricity to their village for the first time.[118]

Questions can be raised about these and other cases: What is the long-run worth of some of the contributions? Did the survival rate of fish in Hupei continue to be high in subsequent years? What help or supervision did the UYs get, and, if a contribution was in fact made independently, what enabled the youths to do it? What proportion of UY individuals or groups make contributions of this sort, and how large do they bulk among all cases of local innovation? The answer to the last of these questions is that only a fraction of UYs contributes in these ways. Informants knew of only a few modest innovations made by UYs within their range of acquaintance. In one case, a youth who had worked in a factory in Canton built a water pump. In another, a group of youths constructed a scale for weighing goods, and in still another youths built a wooden water pipe which saved their production team money. With regard to participation in scientific experimentation, a nation-wide evaluation points out that "the ranks of the peasant experimenters and researchers include large numbers of veteran peasants, many young ones who are daring in making break-throughs, and *some* educated urban youths who have settled in the rural areas" (my italics).[119] The same article put total membership in rural scientific experiment groups at 13 million. The highest available aggregate statistics for UY participation in scientific experiments come from Yenan prefecture, where, as of 1971, about a third of the 20,000 Peking youths took part, and from Ssu-hui county, Kwangtung, where in 1974 about 37 percent of UYs participated, constituting a third of the county's spare-time experiment force.[120] If these data were typical and a third of the 10 million UYs in the countryside were involved with scientific activities, UYs would make up about one-fourth of the 13 million members of scientific experiment groups. Undoubtedly the actual number of UY participants is much lower, Yenan and Ssu-hui representing the highs and not the averages. Certainly there are a good many rural units in which few or no UYs have participated. Informants themselves did not take part in such activities, and they knew of only a few UYs who did. Local youths, especially returned educated youths, predominated.[121] That UY participation has not been as high as desired is also indicated by policy statements that have called on UYs to play a more vigorous role in this regard.[122]

The earlier discussion of technical training of UYs suggests that many lack the competence to make the kinds of contributions described here. Informants attributed the paucity of technical contributions by UYs within their range of acquaintance to this factor. One would expect, therefore, a high rate of failure of UY-initiated scientific experiments or other technical innovations. The press does not seem to report complete failure, though a good many of the accounts do depict UYs as failing initially but ultimately succeeding. An instructive case is that of a group of youths from Tangshan, Hopei, who settled in a brigade in Feng-jun county, twenty-five kilometers from their home town. The youths were eager to do scientific experiments. The party branch supported them, allocating twenty mou of good land to them as well as two rooms for laboratory work. The youths borrowed technical books, microscopes, and other equipment from their alma mater in Tangshan and went to work. They set up twenty-six experiments, dreaming of spectacular breakthroughs that would bring them fame (yi-ming ching-jen). One of their projects was growing a cotton tree: by grafting cotton shoots onto a p'ao t'ung tree (Pawlonia imperialis), they hoped to make it unnecessary to plant cotton anew each year. Peasants referred to them as those "foreign scholars (yang hsiu-ts'ai) who plant crops by reading books." Finally, the party leaders stepped in and taught the UYs the importance of integrating with the masses. Three-in-one scientific experiment groups of cadres, peasants, and UYs were formed under the supervision of the deputy party secretary. Proceeding from local conditions and with the cooperation of knowledgeable older peasants, the groups tackled more realistic and feasible tasks, including improving the method of plowing, developing superior strains, and pest control. One youth, who became known as the "scourge of the insects," discovered how to exterminate six kinds of pests. Other achievements included manufacture of plant hormone "920" and of bacterial fertilizer "5,406." Significant gains in output of grain and cotton were said to have resulted from these innovations.[123]

The lesson of this case is the Maoist one that intellectuals—in this case educated urban youths—working in isolation are likely to fail unless their efforts are integrated with those of the masses. Indeed, the case is noteworthy for its reversal of the roles that conventional wisdom assigns to the educated urbanite and the ignorant rustic. Instead of the urbanites introducing the peasants to new ways of altering their environment, it is the peasants who seem to be teaching the urbanites rational approaches to change. Yet, even if it is assumed that Chinese peasants are reasonable judges of what innovations are or are not feasible, the question still arises of whether a "three-in-one" combination of cadres, peasants, and UYs is not a case of the blind leading the blind when it comes to scientific experimentation. In other words, how well integrated are these village-level efforts with those of trained scientists and technicians able to provide supervision and guidance? The fact is that at least a proportion of village-level scientific experimentation is coordinated by "a nationwide network of agricultural science and research organs" that help "the peasant scientists and technicians with their experiments."[124] The close links between the professional agricultural research establishment and the grassroots are described in a report by the American Plant Studies Delegation that visited the PRC in 1974; the report highlights the role of the "basic points" (*chi-tien*) of provincial research institutes:

> These "points" are actually experiment stations attached to selected brigades throughout each province, selected to exemplify particular soil or other environmental conditions. Attached to these stations are scientists from the institutes, sent down in rotation; there are also "peasant technicians" trained by these scientists to carry out experimental work. At any time, one-third to one-half of the scientists at any institute may be serving at the basic points. The scope of this extension effort is impressive: the Shensi Provincial Agricultural Institute, for instance, maintains contact with 100 basic points in 75 counties throughout the province and staffs each one with scientific personnel. . . . Though they adopt a low posture in public, scientists . . . who are sent down to basic point brigades in rotation are obviously playing a major role in the breeding and cultivation work of the experiment stations.[125]

The political climate that causes scientists to adopt a "low posture in public" also inhibits the press from fully recognizing their role.[126] Accounts of scientific experiments of UYs rarely indicate whether and to what degree trained professionals played a part. In one case, specific mention was made of the fact that a brigade in which peasants and UYs were experimenting was an "experimental point" of the Academy of Sciences.[127]

Even if most of the accounts of UY scientific experiments do not refer to professional participation, it can be assumed that in many instances the influence of trained scientists and technicians makes itself felt directly or indirectly. Their influence puts the experimental efforts of UYs and other local people into perspective and enhances understanding of just what it is meant by middle school graduates undertaking scientific work. The point was made earlier that rural modernization requires not only professional scientists but also less well educated people with whom the professionals can work to test and apply new techniques and methods. In other developing countries, as Benedict Stavis, author of a monograph on the green revolution in China, notes, sophisticated high-level research is often carried on, but such countries "have totally inadequate mechanisms for local testing, demonstration, and consultation."[128] In China, by contrast, it is possible to carry out these important functions: "Much of the work of these basic point stations is designed to discover which varieties will do best in a particular area. Other work, though termed experimental, is actually demonstrational; for instance, plantings of improved seeds next to other varieties in order to show peasants the advantages of the new over the old. Much of the experimental work said to be going on at the brigade level must be understood in this sense."[129]

If it is true that many of the scientific-technical contributions made by UYs have been made not by them alone but as subordinate participants in joint efforts, the fact remains that some accounts plausibly depict UYs as making technical innovations largely on their own, and, as far as is known, without benefit of special technical training. A good example would be the urban youth who took the lead in building a small hydroelectric power station (the seventh of the twelve examples cited above). Even if the number of such cases is not great, it is worth dwelling on them as a way of raising a question about the costs and benefits of the transfer. Several factors seem to have contributed to the success of these sent-down youths. One is background and home environment. In one case, a Shanghai UY who went to Yunnan had been an "electricity buff" (tien-mi) in school; he led in the construction of a small hydroelectric station.[130] In another, both parents of an UY who became a midwife were physicians; she had studied with them at home.[131] Time is also an important factor. Some accounts show that UYs sometimes spend many years learning on the job, learning from others, learning from models, or in spare-time self-study before attaining a success.[132] And in still other cases, joint effort by a group of UYs helps explain a successful innovation, attained by dint of collective learning and problem solving. A common factor underlying such cases must be that the UYs in question were highly intelligent and highly motivated. Under different circumstances these talented youths would have continued their education beyond middle school, gone to a college or a university, and become full-fledged scientists or engineers. Instead they were sent to the countryside, where, according to Chairman Mao, "there is plenty of room for them to develop their talents to the full." Yet, had they been allowed to continue their education, would they not have been able to contribute more significantly and lastingly to their country's modernization than they now have with their practical, applied innovations useful for the advancement of a particular locale? Actually, some of these talented UYs have been selected to attend higher schools. In some instances, as in the case of barefoot doctors, a definite link appears to have developed between rural work and higher study.[133] The practical experience accumulated in the village probably enhances the value of higher education, although questions have been raised about the quality of the latter. Undoubtedly, however, a good many of the talented UYs have not been selected for advanced study. For them, the question can be raised of whether their contributions, valuable as they evidently are, do not entail a hidden opportunity cost to the country.

Rural Education

Providing all peasant children with an opportunity to go to school has been a central objective of policy makers. One strategy they have pursued since the Great Leap Forward has been to encourage rural collectives to set up their own community schools, the *min-pan hsüeh-hsiao,* and it is in these that the urban youths have been teaching. Based on the principle of self-reliance, such schools are locally financed and thus save the state money, although some apparently do receive supplemental state assistance. The state lacks the resources to set up primary schools in sufficient quantity to enable all peasant children to attend; hence arose the criticism that, when the state alone was in charge of rural education, schools often were beyond the physical reach of many villages, especially those in mountainous areas.[134] The community schools, conversely, can be set up wherever they are needed, in brigades or in teams (natural villages), and they can be flexibly adjusted to local variations in the agricultural cycle and to local needs. The quality of these schools is necessarily low, since the collectives tend to lack money for adequate equipment and buildings, and the teachers are usually not trained.[135] In fact, their low quality has elicited objections from those who feel that rural education should be "regularized" (*cheng-kuei hua*). As "some comrades" in a brigade in Yunnan put it, "It used to be that when schools were set up, the county sent teachers, the state constructed the buildings, and the higher level met the expenses. In our poor mountain district, how can education be universalized without funds from the state?"[136]

These objections were overcome in the course of such major political campaigns as the Great Leap Forward and the Cultural Revolution, each of which saw a high rate of community school establishment. After these campaigns, community schools either declined in number (as after the Great Leap Forward) or the rate of establishment slowed down (as apparently happened after the Cultural Revolution).[137] Thus it was that another spurt occurred in the recent campaign to criticize Lin Piao and Confucius. In Wu-ch'i county, Szechwan, for instance, only 74 percent of school-age children were attending school in 1972; the proportion had climbed to 98 percent two years later, while nationally, primary school enrollment increased from 127 million in 1972 to 145 million two years later.[138]

As long as the community schools are deemed an appropriate solution to the problem of universalization, the urban youths have a role to play. Accounts in the press depict some of them as setting up schools where there had been none before.[139] In the absence of state aid, a key goal in setting up a school is to minimize the burden falling on the collective. For example, a graduate of a Foochow junior middle school settled in a brigade in Shun-ch'ang county, Fukien, in 1969. A year later he volunteered to teach school in a small village within the brigade. He encountered many difficulties since there was no equipment at all, he and his pupils having to make their own desks and chairs. But frugality paid off, for in a two-year time span the brigade had to appropriate only one *yuan* for the school.[140] Another case is that of an urban girl who opened a primary school in a small village near Taiyuan, Shansi, using an old cave as the building and stones for the pupils to sit on. Although she herself was only a junior middle school graduate, in 1968 she added a year of the middle school curriculum to her five-year primary school, spending Sundays to learn from other teachers in the commune.[141] Still another case is that of a returned educated youth in a Hopei village, who used the holidays to gather medicinal plants in the mountains in order to earn money for her school.[142]

Mention of returned youths serving as teachers serves to recall the point made earlier that UYs are by no means the only source of teachers for the community schools, and that there is a great deal of variation in the extent to which UYs have been used as teachers. Still, while the proportion of community school teachers coming from UY ranks is not known it may well be substantial.[143] The proportion seems to be particularly high in villages inhabited by national minorities, judging by the numerous accounts of urban youths settling in minority villages and setting up schools. The famous model Chu K'o-chia, who taught school in a village of the Ai-ni minority in Yunnan, is only one such example. Another is that of a Peking youth who settled in 1968 in Hsi-wu-chu-mu-ch'in banner (county) in Inner Mongolia, and who established the first team-level school in the banner. Her deed was emulated by others, and in a two-month period the number of such schools in the banner mushroomed to fifty, all staffed by UYs, and making it possible for 90 percent of the school-age children in the banner to get some education.[144] Still other cases have been reported for the Yao nationality in Kwangsi, the Pu-yi in Kweichow, and the Tung-hsiang minority in Kansu.[145] In all of them, the Han youths had to learn the local tongue before being able to teach, since primary education is carried on not in Mandarin but in the tongue of the particular nationality. Learning the local language has been a source of frustration for the UYs. In Yunnan, where a "large number" of UYs have become teachers, "at the beginning, due to the language barrier and different customs and habits, they encountered tremendous difficulties. Therefore, some did not enjoy their work at all." It took study of Chairman Mao's Thoughts to motivate the UYs to learn the local dialects.[146] What is striking is that very rarely does the press mention returned educated youths, who of course would not face a language barrier, in the role of teachers in minority villages.[147] Their absence may be an indicator of the small progress that education had made in many minority villages, particularly those in remote areas with poor communications, at least until recent years.[148] Those UYs who have become teachers of minority children, surmounting the difficulties facing them, have been making an important contribution to the spread of education. It is noteworthy, however, that the UYs apparently do not teach Mandarin to the children, thus limiting their contribution to the furtherance of national integration only to the transmission of basic knowledge and political values.

While some peasants seem eager for education, data from both press and informants show this is not always the case. Community schoolteachers, UYs included, have had to persuade and cajole reluctant parents to send their children to school. One informant, who taught school in Po-lo county, found it necessary to "chase" after poorly motivated children and to visit peasant families in their homes to spur attendance. The returned youth cited above who taught school in a Hopei village found that, of 18 children of school age, only 8 or 9 showed up in the school, and she vigorously criticized the attitude of parents. Several factors account for low interest in education. Cadres often perceive their main task as that of increasing production. Hence they may assign a low priority to such goals as universalization of schooling, failing to undertake the necessary mobilization to arouse peasant interest in educa- tion and to support arrangements that would suit the peasants' needs.[149] From the point of view of many peasants, sending children to school raises problems of cost even in the case of community schools. The objections to state schools had been that often only better–off families were able to afford the school fees as well as the appropriate clothing and board neces- sary when the school was located far from the village. Atten- dance at a community school frees parents from having to meet these expenses, though many of these schools do charge small tuition fees. But many peasant households do need school-age children to care for younger siblings, to work on sideline under- takings, or to earn work points doing light chores for the collective such as herding cattle. Much attention has been paid to these needs since they are quite pervasive and evidently have constituted a significant block to the expansion of rural education. With the encouragement of cadres, community school teachers have invented all kinds of ingenious remedies to enable children to go to school while meeting the needs of their families. Teachers have permitted school children to bring their younger siblings along, thereby providing a kind of rudimentary day care; they have staggered class hours so that pupils could both work and take part in lessons; and they have held classes out on cattle ranges or on fishing boats, the teacher rowing back and forth between the boats giving lessons.[150]

Peasant disinterest in education is also connected with the perception that education has little tangible utility. In the case of girls, the objection is of the traditional kind: "Girls are going to get married sooner or later. What's the use of reading books?"[151] In such cases, UYs serving as teachers, especially when they themselves are female, have tried to change the peasants' attitude of giving preference to males over females (*chung-nan ch'ing-nü*).[152] More broadly, however, peasants have seen the very presence of educated youths in the village as justification for the attitude that "it is useless to study" (*tu-shu wu-yung lun*): "Since graduates from universities and senior middle schools all end up with shovels in their hands, what's the use of children being able to read?"[152] If educated youths, urban and returned, fail to escape from agriculture by securing an official post, and end up working as ordinary peasants, why get an education? Policy makers, who vehemently denounce such attitudes as Liuist revisionism, rightly see education as an essential component of the process of rural modernization. With growing modernization, more and more peasants may in fact come to see the uses of education even if it is not followed by mobility out of agriculture. But it is one of the contradictions of the transfer of educated youths to the villages that some of the effort which they, as teachers, must expend to mobilize peasant children to go to school essentially compensates for the reduced interest in education which their very presence has brought about.

Judging by the accounts of informants, peasants generally do not oppose education as such. That is, they feel it is useful for their children to be able to read and to do simple calculations.

But they are skeptical about the value of more than three or four years of school and conscious of the opportunity cost involved, such as the loss of work points. The result of such attitudes was that many children in the villages in which informants settled failed to complete primary education. All children were able to attend primary schools, and, in a number of cases, brigade-level junior middle schools as well. But informants thought that usually only about half of the youths above primary school age had actually graduated from elementary schools. One informant, together with some fellow UYs, had organized an evening primary school, in which they taught voluntarily, without compensation. At first they had many pupils, but by the end of the year only a few remained.[154] Interest in education, in other words, is not always easy to sustain but requires continuing encouragement and a supportive environment. To the extent that the UYs help arouse interest in education, by teaching in community schools, by teaching adults how to read, or by engaging in other cultural activities, they are making an important contribution to rural change.[155]

Labor

All urban youths sent to the countryside perform manual labor. For those who have not been recruited to major posts—the great majority—labor constitutes their primary activity. Evaluating the contribution of this labor to rural development is a difficult task. One approach is to ask what proportion of the labor force comes from UY ranks. The size of the peasant labor force is not known, but if the peasant population is assumed to be 700 million, the 12 million UYs constitute a mere 1.7 percent. However, UYs are unevenly distributed in the countryside, so they may constitute a much larger proportion of the population in some provinces. The ten suburban Shanghai counties contain 4.4 million inhabitants; the 400,000 UYs living in them thus constitute 8.8 percent. But some of the 4.4 million live in county towns, so the urban youths in fact make up an even larger share of the rural population. For other provincial units, rural-urban breakdowns are not available. Without them, calculating the percentage of UYs in the provincial population—for which estimates are available—can be quite misleading. In Heilungkiang, 1.2 million UYs make up 4.2 percent of an estimated population of 28.3 million; in Liaoning, 1.2 million UYs make up 2.9 percent of an estimated 41.7 million.[156] But Liaoning is much more urbanized than Heilungkiang, so it is possible that the UYs in the former constitute a larger proportion of the rural population than in the latter. Even in the absence of urban-rural population data, the point can be made that some provinces clearly depend much more heavily on UY labor than others. Honan's 360,000 UYs amount to 0.55 percent of the population; Inner Mongolia's 210,000 to 2.6 percent, and Sinkiang's 450,000 to 5.2 percent.[157] All three are predominantly rural or pastoral provinces.

At the local level, evaluation is particularly difficult when UYs are inserted into production teams, their labor merging with that of the peasants. As suggested in chapter 2, UY labor may be contributing in several ways, as by relieving labor shortages in an underpopulated commune or in one in which diversification and multicropping have produced a need for additional laborers. Specific evidence beyond that already cited in chapter 2 does not, however, seem to be available. When UYs are inserted into peasant villages, not only is their labor difficult to isolate from that of the peasants, but it may not in fact be making much of a contribution, given the opportunity which this form of settlement affords for poorly motivated UYs to act out their frustrations (see chapter 4).

In contrast, when UYs are settled separately on state farms, People's Liberation Army (PLA) Production and Construction Corps farms, or as members of youth collectives attached to commune subdivisions, their productive accomplishments can be measured more easily in physical terms, and, as will be noted below, UYs in such units may in fact be working harder. Even in such cases, a given contribution is often not the UYs' alone, since state farms also employ peasants, and army farms may in part be staffed by demobilized servicemen. But when the press describes the accomplishments of UYs on state or army farms, the implication is that the UYs constitute the major component of the labor force. For instance, between 1962 and 1964, 292,000 UYs settled on state-operated agriculture, forestry, livestock, and fishery farms. They reportedly played a key part in the establishment of 185 new state farms and the expansion of 566 old ones. In the two years, they opened up 1,186,000 *mou* of wasteland. In 1963, they planted trees on 346,000 mou of land, while expanding the "marine product cultivation area by more than 557,000 mou."[158]

Urban youth labor groups have typically been engaged in such tasks as land reclamation, afforestation, irrigation, and other construction projects. The scale of separately organized UY efforts varies greatly, ranging from groups of ten to twenty UYs attached to a production team and engaged in reclaiming a hillside,[159] to vast undertakings involving several Production and Construction Corps divisions, as exemplified in the following case from Sinkiang:

During the formidable campaign to harness the Tarim River, the 60,000 educated Shanghai youths became a major assault force. Joining efforts with the veteran military reclamation fighters, they have built a large dam across the upper Tarim River as well as 10 large and medium-sized reservoirs on the plains on its upper and lower reaches, dug more than 1,400 kilometers of irrigation and drainage canals and ditches, and constructed seven hydroelectric power stations. Largely due to their own efforts, they succeeded in harnessing the Tarim River which people used to call an "unbridled horse" and made good fields having irrigation and drainage facilities out of the more than 1.9 million mou of farmland in the Tarim Basin.[160]

Press accounts may be supplemented by those of two informants who served on army farms on Hainan Island and in the Liuchow Peninsula of Kwangtung. Their units were similarly engaged in opening up virgin lands, in these cases for the cultivation of rubber trees. The goal was to help make China less dependent on rubber imports from Malaysia. Progress was rapid, the land was cleared, and, in the space of two years or so, 27,000 mou of land were planted in rubber trees on one of the farms.[161] However, when it is known how much land can potentially be reclaimed in a given area, UY contributions to that cause do not necessarily loom large. As of 1975, "some 300,000" army farm UYs in Heilungkiang, many of whom had been there since 1965, had reclaimed one million mou of land, equal to 67,000 hectares.[162] According to the geographer Theodore Shabad, as of 1971, ten million hectares of land were potentially reclaimable in the three northeastern provinces, mostly in Heilungkiang.[163]

Bringing new land under cultivation is clearly a major purpose of UY labor. Publicity given to the Chu-chou model highlights the importance policy makers have attached to this goal. Hunan's Chu-chou county, it will be recalled, contains a large quantity of mountainous land, some of which could evidently be brought under cultivation. Separate UY farms were set up essentially for this purpose. The Chu-chou example shows that, while the bulk of China's reclaimable land is in the outlying frontier provinces, some land can be reclaimed even in China proper, using collective labor such as that of the urban youths. Scholars have doubted whether much additional land can in fact be brought under cultivation at reasonable cost, suggesting that the main emphasis in China's agricultural development policy is on improvement of yields on existing crop lands.[164] A good many UY collectives are also contributing to the realization of this goal, by taking part in farmland capital construction projects, such as the leveling of fields.[165]

The dominant themes that run through press accounts of the achievements of UY labor groups are self-reliance, endurance of severe hardships, and the surmounting of great obstacles. Indeed, it is fair to say that the celebration of heroic, self-sacrificing labor is perhaps the most prominent of all the themes that run through the press coverage of the transfer. Exemplary heroes abound, such as the "twelve iron girls" who wrested a farm from the desert, defying extremes of heat and cold as well as utterly primitive living conditions.[166] Accounts of how groups of young urbanites carved a settlement out of the wilderness exude a pioneer spirit reminiscent of the settlement of the American frontier, though of course it is a collective pioneer spirit. The following quote, from an article entitled "Founding a New Enterprise through Hard Struggle," describes the deeds of twenty-one Peking youths who were attached to a production team which itself only had twenty-one persons, in P'u county, Shansi:

Having no land, they reclaimed their own . . . having no quarters, they built their own. The thought of founding an enterprise filled their hearts like the rising sun. . . .

For the sake of accelerating the rate of reclamation, the educated young people brought their cooked rice to eat at the work site. When their rations became frozen, they . . . soaked them in hot water. When the skin of their hands cracked in the cold, they . . . bandaged them with adhesive tape, and continued their work. After 12 days of struggle, they reclaimed 54 mou of barren land and harvested more than 9,000 catties of grain that year. . . .

. . . the educated young people . . . built their quarters with their own hands. They felled trees in deep mountains where communications and transportation were difficult. More than ten of the youths, carrying a heavy log, would stagger forward foot by foot.[167]

Descriptions of heroic labor and extreme hardship suggest the presence of an unusually high degree of dedication and commitment, indicating perhaps that collective pioneer labor leads not only to significant productive achievement but also to adaptation. However, the accounts may reflect the newspapers' inspirational goals more than the UYs' actual attitudes. The two informants who served on army farms, for instance, described with some resentment the absolute priority given to the completion of the rubber plantations at the expense of living conditions and cultural life. When the press hails youths who, "fearing neither hardship nor death," insist on working despite sickness or injury, and who risk—in some cases sacrifice—their health for the sake of the cause, the underlying reality may be neglect of medical care or of safety measures rather than youthful heroism.[168]

Still, dedication undoubtedly plays a role in the heroic labor cases. Truly revolutionary youths ask to be sent to places of hardship. Their commitment may be reinforced by the excitement and adventure of the enterprise itself, by the tangible sense of achievement that may come from being a part of a pioneer undertaking, and by recruitment into the party and to leadership positions. (As noted earlier, CCP and YCL membership is particularly high on army farms.) Their dedication may well communicate itself to the rest of the collective, strengthening its solidarity and cohesion. The solidarity of UY groups that score achievements in such tasks as carving a farm out of the wilderness may be further reinforced by such symbolic rewards as conferral of the title of "advanced collective" and attendance at provincial UY congresses.[169] The collective element is clearly very important. As noted above, UYs who are inserted into production teams have often lacked a strong collective spirit, permitting low morale to translate itself into poor work performance, and in turn leading to peasant resentment against lazy urbanites living off the community. In con-

trast, well-organized and well-led UY collectives have the
capacity to mobilize group pressures against laggards, and while
such pressures may not convert them into dedicated activists,
they may at least get them to work harder.[170] For their part,
however, the targets of persuasion and criticism may perceive
the collective's efforts to help them as coercive rather than
normative. This may be the case particularly on army farms,
where horizontal group pressures are extensions of the hierarchical discipline of a quasi-military unit. In such cases, Lin
Piao's alleged charge that the transfer to the countryside
amounted to reform through labor (*pien-hsiang lao-kai*) may
not be too far off the mark. The cement that binds UY labor
groups together is thus likely to contain a coercive element,
in addition to normative and remunerative ones. Whatever the
mix of incentives, separately organized UY labor units undoubtedly contribute in important ways to China's development,
particularly in the remote regions of the country.

ASSESSMENT

In 1975, a major American study of China's economy concluded that "agriculture is benefiting from the broadening of
education and training in the rural areas, the increased experience of the work force with fertilizers and machinery, and the
assignment to the countryside since 1968 of nearly 10 million
middle-school graduates from urban areas."[171] The conclusion
that the transfer of urban youths has benefited the rural sector
is undoubtedly correct. If all of the contributions of the sent-
down youths were added up, the list would be lengthy indeed.
Yet, appraising the extent of this benefit is very difficult. For
example, we do not know what proportion of the increases in
agricultural output attained since 1968 should be attributed to
the efforts of the sent-down youths. We do not even know for
sure whether the benefit the UYs have brought to the countryside is a net benefit, that is, whether the aggregate worth of
their contributions exceeds the costs of the program, assuming
they can both be measured. Because the program is maintained not just in order to spur rural development but for
other reasons as well, however, a net "loss" on the rural side
would not necessarily lead to its demise.

When it is possible to appraise the program against some kind of external standard, however crude, it turns out that the UY contribution is relatively modest. Thus, it appears that UYs provide only a tiny fraction of leadership in the communes, only a small proportion of basic-level scientific experimenters, and, given the data on the returned peasant youths, probably only a small proportion of all community school teachers or barefoot doctors. However, it is important to keep in mind that UYs are unevenly distributed in rural and frontier China. Therefore, in particular locales their contributions are likely to be of great importance.

If the program itself is examined, it is difficult to avoid the conclusion that there is a gap between the actual and potential performance of the sent-down youths. This gap is apparent even if one does not posit some hypothetical optimum, in which every UY is, say, an active modernizing agent busily transforming his village. A good many poorly motivated UYs do not contribute much of anything to their villages, including even labor, leading peasants to resent them as a burden. Furthermore, the discussion in chapter 2 pointed out that some UYs are sent to villages in which the need for them is not all that apparent, but which simply have the capacity to absorb them. The recruitment statistics show that 13–15 percent of UYs occupy political and cultural-technical roles defined as major, but this percentage apparently has not grown much since 1973. Another 20–30 percent occupy roles defined as minor, and undoubtedly others who do not show up in recruitment statistics make their influence felt in informal ways. But, if these statistics are accurate, it means that about half of the youths contribute nothing but their labor. These UYs, in other words, do not combine the roles of "ordinary agricultural producers" with those of "catalysts" of change, as the model would suggest they should.[172]

These findings raise questions about the way the program has been planned. "Up to the mountains and down to the countryside" is a program of sending not just urban youths, but *educated* urban youths to the rural areas. Yet about half do only agricultural labor. If this corresponds to the intent of the planners, why is it necessary for these UYs to have gotten a secondary education? To be sure, it has long been recognized that, as modernization advances, a literate, educated work force is highly desirable, but would primary education not suffice for the performance of most kinds of agricultural labor? Conversely, if the intent of the policy makers is that the transfer should infuse the countryside with educated manpower, why do only about half engage in activities in which their education is likely to be of help? It is worth adding that the "about half" is actually a very generous estimate. Not only does it include all kinds of spare-time activities, but some of the political and cultural-technical roles it includes do not really require a secondary education, as in the case of tractor drivers. Further, some roles require technical training often not provided by urban secondary schools even after the Cultural Revolution, necessitating establishment of short-term training programs in the rural areas.

It is undoubtedly very difficult to develop a transfer program that avoids waste, with regard to education, and one that is carefully designed to maximize the usefulness of the sent-down youths. Indeed, it is fair to say that educational and manpower planning anywhere rarely attains a close fit between formal education and the work that graduates actually do. In China, moreover, planning of the program was disrupted by the Cultural Revolution. To an unknown extent, the utilization of UYs as modernizing agents was frustrated by the fact that the formal education of the Red Guard generation was incomplete. Since the Cultural Revolution, planners and policy makers have learned a great deal about the transfer. New measures have been taken, as in the case of the expansion of opportunities to obtain some technical training. Still, various constraints may limit the extent to which sent-down youths can fill cultural-technical roles. One constraint is the growing availability of educated peasant youths. This constraint is not present when UYs are settled separately, but in that case UYs must do all the physical labor, and hence many of them may end up doing only that, as before. Also, the rate at which cultural-technical roles expand may not be fast enough. However, the country's commitment to the rapid achievement of rural modernization may change this situation.

With regard to adaptation, just as some UYs evaluate recruitment in relation to urban reassignment, so some of them calculate that making a positive contribution may earn them a return ticket to the city. On balance, however, it is likely that both recruitment and contributions increase the probability of successful adaptation to rural life. From the point of view of the peasants, an urban youth who makes a contribution is more acceptable than one who does not, and the extent of successful integration probably varies with this factor. For their part, many UYs in the villages search for activity that gives meaning and significance to their existence. Making a visible contribution to the development of the countryside can provide such meaning, while also enhancing the status of the individual or the group in the rural community. Contributions, however, differ in the degree to which they provide inner satisfaction. Labor may well be the most problematic. Achievements scored by collectives engaged in pioneer labor can bring a sense of worth, but it is doubtful whether over the long run many of the urban youths can be content with leading the life of an ordinary farm laborer. For educated youths who become factory workers in the towns, being in an urban area may compensate for doing blue-collar work, and there may be opportunities to acquire skills and do more complex technical work. But, unless more and more of those UYs who do only farm labor—by my estimate, about half of the total—can take part in meaningful activities in which their education is utilized, a major source of maladjustment to rural life will remain. The point is that for these UYs the transfer has not achieved its stated goal of eliminating the gap between mental and manual labor. These urban youths have ended up on the labor side of the gap; they have not bridged it.

6 THE STABILITY OF THE SETTLEMENT

Although in principle sent-down youths settle in the rural areas for life (*yi-pei-tzu*), in fact some do not stay permanently in the village. The first part of this chapter is devoted to an analysis of reassignment of UYs to urban tasks. Examination of reassignment processes sheds additional light on adaptation and supports the conclusion that many, perhaps even a majority of UYs, have not fully adapted to permanent life in the countryside. The settlement is therefore not self-sustaining. It requires ideological, organizational, material, and coercive resources to make it work. Above all, it requires a stable political system. As far as it is possible to judge, the transfer is not itself a source of political instability. But if for some reason or other the political system were to become destabilized, providing opportunities for dissatisfied groups to voice grievances and articulate interests, sent-down youths would be prominent among them and would constitute a significant force for social unrest. In recent Chinese political history, a destabilizing event in fact occurred in the form of the Cultural Revolution. Many sent-down youths took advantage of that upheaval to return to the cities and to protest against the transfer system. The second half of this chapter is devoted to an examination of UY responses during the Cultural Revolution.

REASSIGNMENT TO THE URBAN SECTOR

"Due to the needs of the socialist revolution and of the development of socialist construction," the Chinese press reports, "each year some (*yi-hsieh*) educated youths are recruited to work in factories, to join the army, and are recommended for entry to higher schools."[1] Factory, army, and university offer the principal ways to leave one's rural unit.[2] However, it is not clear whether assignment to any of the three actually entails permanent departure from the rural sector. In the case of factory work, an individual may be assigned to a state-operated plant in an urban locale, perhaps a county town, or to a commune-operated enterprise. In the latter case, the youth would still be in the rural sector, receiving work points rather than regular wages and fringe benefits.[3] Joining the army also may not lead to permanent return to the urban sector upon demobilization. In the spring of 1973, a classified army document entitled "Outline of Education" asked soldiers to understand that it had become necessary to curtail assignment of retired servicemen to factories, because the state's hiring plan had been exceeded.[4] This curtailment may not have applied to UY service personnel, however, since some kind of regulation apparently gave them a right to city jobs. In 1975, publicity was given to demobilized urban youths who chose to return to the villages to which they had been sent before joining the army, even though they need not have done so. For example, the graduate of a Shenyang middle school had settled in 1968 in K'ai-yuan county, also in Liaoning. He did well in the village and entered the army in late 1970. Upon discharge, he first returned to Shenyang, but, full of ideological fervor, eventually settled in his old production team. He need not have done so, because, he said, "I am a demobilized armyman, and according to regulations, I could return to Shenyang and get a job there."[5] The examples which he and other UY veterans set of volunteering to go back to the countryside were celebrated as repudiating "bourgeois rights." As long as regulations entitle demobilized UYs to a city job, one wonders how widely their examples will be emulated.[6]

Since the Cultural Revolution, graduates of institutions of higher learning have been supposed to return to the units whence they came. The degree to which this in fact has happened is unknown, however. A case in point is that of a young man from Wusih, Kiangsu, who settled in 1963 on a state farm in the northern part of that province. After its conversion to an army farm he joined the Chinese Communist Party (CCP), became company commander, and in 1970 entered Futan University in Shanghai to study biology, graduating in August 1973. The party branch of the biology department asked him to remain as a staff member. This opportunity to live in Shanghai conflicted with his revolutionary values, and he decided to return to the army farm, even though it was located in a poverty-stricken area. Upon his return his regiment entrusted him with the management of a biological control group. Later he became regimental deputy section chief, guiding the scientific experiments of the entire unit, thus assuming a major post in line with his specialized training.[7] His case shows that choice is possible when graduates are assigned. While aggregate data on job assignments are not available, according to members of a delegation of the Academia Sinica visiting Australia in November 1974, "most" of Peking University's first graduating class of January 1974 "had returned to their original posts or original localities"—the latter phrase signifying possible assignment to higher rural levels, such as the *hsien* (county) or the prefecture. However, "students selected from factories mostly returned to factories while students who had been educated youth sent to the countryside were mostly allocated by the central planning agency to various departments," that is, by the Office for Science and Education under the State Planning Commission.[8] The conclusion that many UYs have not returned to their communes, state farms, or army farms is reinforced by articles on reassignment, which have typically implied that leaving one's unit to attend a higher school in the city meant just that—leaving, and permanently.[9]

In 1975 the principle that graduates should return to their units of origin was reiterated in vehement terms under the slogan "from the commune back to the commune." Cases of college graduates who insisted on returning were greeted with enthusiasm: "Upon graduation . . . they took the proletarian initiative to attack the bourgeoisie, displayed the fearless spirit of going against the tide, actually broke with the old, traditional concepts and the force of habit, refused to earn wages, refused to eat marketable grain [that is, lived as ordinary commune members], and went to the countryside to be a new type of socialist peasant."[10] These graduates, in other words, did not acquire the status of state cadres, in sharp contrast to the practice before the Cultural Revolution and apparently also up to 1975.

Widespread application of the principle that college graduates return to the commune and reassume the status of ordinary peasants raises the obvious question of whether they will have opportunities to work in their specialized fields. Thus a Harbin youth who was sent to a village in 1968 was selected to study foreign languages in a higher school in 1971. He graduated in

1975 and volunteered to become a peasant. His application was approved and he returned to his brigade, where he "plunged into the battle of building a socialist countryside." The broadcast made no mention of whether or how this graduate would be able to make use of the knowledge he presumably had gained at considerable expense to the state.[11] Actually, however, it seems that the matter is being handled in a discriminating way, so that those who do return, though they may not be state cadres, at least will work in their specialities. In Sinkiang, for instance, "the principle of 'students who come from communes return there upon graduation' will be carried out as a general policy this year by the agricultural colleges and similar schools in the Sinkiang Autonomous Region. A certain portion of students recruited from medical and teachers' colleges and schools will also return to communes upon completion of schooling. Other colleges and schools will . . . implement this policy on an experimental basis."[12] Higher schools in several provinces have set up "experimental classes for students from communes who will return . . . after graduation," also suggesting that return is not automatic.[13] Assignment of college graduates is a complex matter; it is clearly not easy to reconcile the ideological goal that higher education should not lead to elite status with the manpower needs of an increasingly complex economic and administrative system. Given the small number of current graduates and the long period during which no graduates were produced, the various bureaucracies are likely to be in need of college graduates.[14] Moreover, reducing college graduates to the status of ordinary peasants has provoked conflict among policy makers, some of whom perceived this innovation as irrational from the developmental point of view (see chapter 2). It would thus not be surprising if practice continued to deviate sharply from normative prescriptions.[15] For present purposes, and no doubt at the cost of some distortion of reality, the assignment of UYs to higher schools, as well as to factories and to the People's Liberation Army (PLA), will be taken to mean long-term or permanent return to the urban sector.

The overall extent of UY reassignment to factory work, the PLA, and higher education is not known. One estimate published in the United States in 1975 suggested that 25 percent or 2 million of the 8 million UYs sent to the villages between 1968 and late 1973 had been reassigned. This datum, though not implausible, has not been confirmed.[16] Provinces have not released combined statistics, only occasional statements such as that in Yunnan, as of late 1972, "large numbers" of UYs had joined "the PLA, entered higher schools and factories, or gone to work in the finance, trade and cultural sectors."[17] Drops in the number of UYs reported for some provinces could indicate the magnitude of reassignment, as in the case of Liaoning, where nearly one million UYs were reported in November 1972 but only 710,000 in March of 1973. As previously noted, however, other factors, such as more careful differentiation between UYs and returned educated peasant youths (RYs), could account for the changes. Anhwei reported 500,000 UYs in April 1975 and nearly 400,000 in December; the latter broadcast noted that "many" UYs had refused opportunities to return, thereby lending credence to the conclusion that the drop did reflect reassignment.[18] The UY statistics of most provinces do not show drops, but this cannot be taken to mean absence of reassignment since additional arrivals could have accounted for net increases over time.

Substantial regional differences seem to obtain in rates of reassignment. In 1973 a visitor to Shun-te county, Kwangtung, found that 10,000 of the area's total of 11,000 UYs were still in the villages.[19] In contrast, a visitor to Tsun-hua county, Hopei, learned that virtually all UYs had left the villages as of 1973.[20] In Chi county, Hopei, 2,030 youths had settled since 1965, but as of 1973 only 952 youths were still there.[21] Beginning in 1968, 60,000 UYs settled on state farms under the Chien-san-chiang Farm Administration in Heilungkiang; as of mid-1976, 40,000 were still on the farms.[22] Scattered data on units below the county reinforce the impression of variation. Visitors to Red Star commune outside of Peking learned that 7,200 urban youths had settled there since 1968, but in 1975 their number was put at 5,600, indicating a reassignment rate of 22 percent.[23] In no. 7 commune in Ch'ang-ling county, Kirin, only a "minority" of UYs had been reassigned as of autumn 1972.[24] According to an informant, slightly over 70 UYs out of a total of 800 in one commune in Tseng-ch'eng county, Kwangtung, had returned to the urban sector as of late 1972. Other informants, who usually had specific knowledge of reassignment only for their brigades, reported low rates, well under 10 percent. In one exception, a brigade in Ssu-hui county, 12 out of

50 UYs were transferred, but 8 of them went to commune factories. Occasional references in the press point to much higher rates: in one Liaoning youth point, nearly half of the 60 UYs were sent to factories or higher schools in 1971.[25] In 1964, 30 UYs settled in a village in Yüeh-hsi county, Anhwei; ten years later, 14 were left.[26]

Difficult as it is to generalize, it would seem to be a rare unit in which more than half of the UYs have been transferred. Indeed, many a report has appeared describing long-term settlement without any mention of reassignment.[27] In addition, several indices point to the conclusion that reassignment rates cannot have been all that high. These include the escape every year of several thousand UYs to Hong Kong, including UYs with good class backgrounds (informants stress that they might not have left had urban jobs opened up for them) and the illegal return of UYs to cities, as well as the many stories of morale crises of urban youths resulting from failure to be reassigned (see below).

When higher education, the PLA, and factories are considered separately, it turns out that, in the case of the first, low overall enrollments have precluded more than a small fraction of UYs from going to college. A total of 200,000 students were admitted between 1970 and 1972, 153,000 in 1973, and 167,000 in 1974.*[28] If all had been ex-UYs, they could at most have constituted a mere 6 percent of the sent-down youths. But students have also been recruited from among factory workers, soldiers, and peasants, as well as UYs. Actual percentages of UYs enrolled in higher schools are low indeed. In 1972, 1,738 of 100,000 UYs in Fukien and 6,400 of 800,000 in Szechwan enrolled in higher schools, 1.7 percent and 0.8 percent respectively.[29] Also in 1972, a Heilungkiang Production and Construction Corps (PCC) regiment of 3,400 sent 48 of its UYs, or 1.4 percent, to college.[30] No statistics seem to be available for 1973, but qualitative press reports suggest that the number of UYs sent to higher schools increased.[31] In 1974, Heilungkiang's army

*These statistics refer to enrollment in postsecondary institutions of higher learning, both colleges (hsüeh-yüan) and universities (ta-hsüeh). Apparently they do not include enrollment in the agricultural "universities" that have sprung up in the countryside in recent years (see chapter 5), and whose students do not for the most part undertake a full three-year course of study. The statistics also do not include enrollment in specialized technical and normal secondary schools. Some sent-down youths have been sent to such schools but little has been written about them in the press, and no statistics have been released.

farms sent 8,300 students to higher schools (2.1 percent of 400,000 UYs serving on army farms in that province in 1975).[32] These inadequate data obviously do not permit charting of trends over time.

Paradoxically, however, if these scattered percentages were typical of national enrollments, they would show that an extraordinarily high proportion of college students has actually come from among the UYs. If the three percentages from 1972 are applied to the total number of UYs serving in the countryside that year—around 7 million—the result is as follows: Szechwan's 0.8 percent yields 56,000 students, the Heilungkiang farm's 1.4 percent yields 98,000, and Fukien's 1.7 percent yields 119,000. As noted above, between 1970 and 1972, 200,000 higher school students enrolled nationwide, and, since higher schools reopened quite gradually, the majority probably entered in 1972. If it is assumed that 120,000 new students were recruited in 1972, then, taking the Szechwan percentage (0.8) as typical of national enrollments, 56,000 or nearly half of the new students in 1972 would have been UYs; if the Fukien percentage were applied, virtually all of them would seem to have been UYs. If the Heilungkiang PCC percentage had been typical in 1974, this would mean that 168,000 UYs (2.1 percent of 8 million) entered college, or 1,000 more than the total new enrollment from all sources. These results may be due to imprecise data, or they may indicate the existence of a great deal of regional variation, but it would seem plausible to conclude that UYs must have constituted a very substantial proportion of higher school enrollments, even while the individual UY's opportunity to go to college has been very small.[33] Indeed, disproportionate enrollment of UYs became a political issue at Peking University in late 1973, during the campaign against Lin Piao and Confucius. According to an overseas Chinese student, a big character poster charged that, while 68 out of 85 students who had entered the foreign languages department in 1972 had come from the countryside, only 2 were actually peasants; 66 were UYs originally from Peking.[34] Why this might have occurred will be discussed in the next section.

With regard to the PLA, not even scattered statistics on recruitment are available, and only occasional references to UYs entering the armed forces exist.[35] Similarly, statistics on UYs going to work in industry have not been released. Press references to factory work, however, are far more numerous than references to the PLA, and informants also saw industry as the main way to leave the village. Recruitment to factory work has varied by time and area. Judging by the press and informants, a good many UYs were hired in 1970–72, but at uneven rates.[36] Thus several informants volunteered the complaint that UY reassignment in Kwangtung had been low because of lagging industrialization in that province.[37] These informants had heard that large numbers of sent-down youths were given factory jobs in provinces further north, such as Hupei. In 1973 hiring by industrial enterprises slowed down (see chapter 2), but the rate of hiring of UYs by factories apparently increased again in 1975, judging by denunciations a year later of a "wind of pulling up roots" (pa-ken) allegedly blown by Teng Hsiao-p'ing and his allies.[38] In Hsiang-yang county, Hupei, 160 recently settled UYs were ordered to take up jobs as workers but also as cadres in towns.[39] In Kwangtung, "from July 1975, many factories in Canton were authorised by the Municipal Labour Bureau to recruit youths who performed well in labour and politics to take up vacant posts."[40]

When UYs are given factory jobs, often they are in county factories rather than in a large city or their home town.[41] In long-distance transfers, a Shanghai youth might serve for several years in a commune in Inner Mongolia or Heilungkiang, then become a worker in the county town, rather than returning to Shanghai. If this is a widespread practice, it would mean that UYs are significantly contributing to the industrialization of remote small towns. Particular examples giving the number of factory workers coming from among UYs, however, are not very impressive. Visitors learned that in Hsi-yang county, Shansi (the locale of Tachai), 20 out of 500 UYs were working in a county agricultural machinery plant employing 310 workers, while in Hui county, Honan, 15 of 535 workers in a county chemical fertilizer plant had been sent-down youths.[42] These two instances may not be typical, but, if it is true that perhaps 2 million UYs have been reassigned and that most of them have become factory workers, their impact should be more visible. Some UYs, as noted earlier, have been reassigned not to urban industrial units but to commune or brigade factories, while others have been employed in industrial enterprises run by the PLA's Production and Construction Corps.[43] Lack of statistical

data, however, precludes assessment of the extent to which UYs
are contributing in these ways to China's rural industrialization.

Informal Aspects of Reassignment

In principle, it is the "needs of the state" (*kuo-chia ti hsü-yao*)
that govern reassignment. But whether a particular urban youth
is in fact reassigned not only depends on whether he satisfies
whatever rules and regulations are in effect but hinges very
much on informal factors. Perhaps the most generally applicable
rule is that urban youths must spend a minimum of two years in
the countryside before they can be reassigned. Detailed regulations have been published governing admission to higher schools.
The procedures include voluntary application, recommendation
by the masses of the individual's unit, approval by the leadership, and an academic review by the admitting institution.[44]
Qualifications include graduation from junior middle school, a
good political and work record, as well as a good class background, though regulations call for admission of a few youths
from exploiter families who have done unusually well. Rules
governing recruitment to factories have not been publicized but
apparently include a good conduct requirement as well as preference for those with good class background.[45]

Two informal aspects need to be considered: the behavior of
the UY's rural unit and that of his family in the city. In principle, the rural unit should deny reassignment to troublemakers,
but it is of course in the unit's interest to rid itself of undesirable UYs. Virtually no evidence is available, however, to support the notion that reassignment can be manipulated for this
purpose. Those who consistently misbehave forfeit legal return,
their only recourse being to leave illegally, or drastically to
mend their ways.[46] If a rural unit cannot promote its self-interest by expelling deviants, can it do so by retaining UYs who
have done well? Retention of outstanding performers is clearly
an issue. As noted in the preceding chapter, reassignment has
been denied to "advanced" UYs who contributed to their communities. Some UYs worry that acceptance of a recruitment
offer might adversely affect their chances to return eventually
to the urban sector because they will have become a community
asset. The press has taken approving note of a production team
that selected UYs according to the proper criteria and did not
practice "departmentalism" (*pen-wei chu-yi*).[47] On one army

farm, where UYs were being selected for reassignment, opposition from "some people" who did not want to lose the activists
had to be overcome.[48] However, the degree to which high
achievers have in fact been penalized, resulting in reassignment
of those with middling records, should not be exaggerated. Informants stress that good conduct is a key requirement for reassignment, and also that recognition of this provides a major
motivation for not offending peasants.[49] Peasants have been
known to grumble when those with good records were reassigned, leaving the "dumb ones," those who had not responded
to reeducation, in the village.[50] And sent-down youths who
have been admitted to higher schools have often been described
in the press as having outstanding records.[51]

Do rural decision makers discriminate against UYs when it
comes to reassignment? In the case of higher schools, quotas are
set for each of the country's administrative divisions, and these
may be larger in areas of dense UY settlement.[52] But apparently
quotas are not set for categories such as UYs. The existence of
discrimination is suggested by policy statements that call for
equal treatment for sent-down youths: "Equal treatment must
be given to those who have settled in the countryside and to
those who have returned to the countryside."[53] At the local
level, however, only an occasional complaint of impropriety is
available, as that by an informant who reported that the relative
of a brigade cadre was nominated for higher education, rather
than UYs who were better qualified academically. Indeed, the
finding that UYs have constituted a major proportion of the
student population suggests that discrimination against UYs
must have been playing a minor role in the selection process.

Two factors may have been operating in favor of UYs, or at
least some of them. One is that the academic qualifications of
UYs from the major cities are likely to be higher than those of
educated peasant youths, giving the former an advantage when
academic standards are emphasized, as happened in 1973, when
"some localities pursued such revisionist things as putting emphasis merely on the candidate's cultural record, engaging in the
practice of 'academic education comes first' and putting marks
in command."[54] It is not clear at what level pressure for academic excellence made itself felt, but emphasis on academic
standards could well have resulted in increased admission of
UYs.[55] Since sent-down youths with several years of service in

the countryside apparently are considered peasants, admitting more UYs would still have resulted in meeting the fundamental goal of increasing the proportion of peasants in higher education, at least formally.[56] The greater weight attached to academic qualifications in 1973, however, came under sharp fire as destructive of the results of the Cultural Revolution.[57] Two years later, a new effort was made to raise academic standards, under the auspices of Teng Hsiao-p'ing, but it is not clear whether the enrollment of sent-down youths was affected. The issue of academic preparation is an ongoing one, and informal processes may well be continuing to operate on behalf of bright and well-prepared urban youths.[58]

The second factor that has operated in favor of UYs is that some of them come from families that are able to pull strings on their behalf. Family attitudes, as shown in chapter 3, are a an important influence on the mobilization of urban youths to settle in the rural areas, but they also influence their return. The proper revolutionary family attempts to motivate the UY to stay in the countryside, reinforcing his commitment to do so in letters and during visits.[59] By no means all families, however, play the model role. The press has carried a good many cases of family heads looking for opportunities that would permit their offspring to return. Cadres, particularly high-ranking ones, are in a position to utilize connections for this purpose. Indeed, there are social expectations that cadres will make use of "channels" (ch'u-tao): "everyone thought" or "some people" felt that of course a cadre's child would be able to return.[60] In the case of college admissions, the use of informal influence by high-ranking officials was exposed in 1974 during the campaign to criticize Lin Piao and Confucius, when several students withdrew from higher schools on the grounds that they had entered improperly through the "back door" (hou-men). The most prominent case was that of a Nanking University student, Chung Chih-min. His poignant story, which sheds light on informal networks of influence, on the continuing importance of family ties, and on how ideology can be rationalized, deserves to be spelled out in detail.[61]

Chung is the offspring of a "revolutionary family" with impressive credentials of devotion and sacrifice to the cause. During the period of the Kiangsi Soviet (1928–34), his grandfather served as chairman of a village soviet. He was killed, as was an uncle, on the Long March. His father, also a veteran of that heroic epic, took part in the War of Resistance as well as the Korean War. He stayed in the military and became a high-ranking official in charge of cadre work of the Foochow Military Region. Because of this, Chung Chih-min reflected, "I always felt that I was born into a good family. . . . Being born into a family with such revolutionary merits, I thought there was nothing wrong in receiving a little special care." It is not surprising that during the Cultural Revolution Chung had supported the "theory of blood relations." In 1968, when the mass transfer of Red Guards began, Chung, who had graduated from lower middle school, was slated to be sent down. He was reluctant to go but felt that he had to go along. His parents agreed, given the intensity of the mass campaign, but told him, "You go first and we will have you transferred back later." Chung was sent to Jui-chin county, Kiangsi, the location of the capital of the Kiangsi Soviet—hardly an accidental assignment, given the origins of his family. He stayed in his village for only three months, for the "special care" to which he felt himself entitled was indeed forthcoming. In 1969, when the annual PLA recruitment drive was under way, Chung contacted the political commissar of the county militia and was permitted to enlist by taking the place of a peasant. Chung served in the PLA for three years but wanted to go to university. In April 1972, recalls Chung, "my father, at my insistence, called the cadre department of the military district, saying that I should be selected and sent to the university." Chung was admitted to Nanking University, having bypassed the elaborate procedure designed to give the masses a major voice in this decision.

In due course, however, the contrast between the stated ideals of the system and his own hypocritical conduct gave rise to a crisis of conscience on Chung's part. When he left the PLA unit, there had already been talk of impropriety, and he had felt very "dishonorable." As a student, he repeatedly came into close contact with workers and peasants while doing practical and political work, and from them he "heard many complaints about 'going in by the back door.'" Moreover, as a student of philosophy, that is, Marxism, at Nanking University, Chung was exposed in a concentrated way to the Maoist critique of revisionism and the perpetuation of privilege. He began thinking of withdrawing, and he took his moral dilemma to his family.

The reaction of his family was lukewarm. His relatives agreed that perhaps he had made a mistake, but it would be a pity to leave school after having gotten a good start. One relative justified staying on ideological grounds: "Withdrawal from school may obstruct the implementation of Chairman Mao's revolutionary line from the 'left.' Since many others throughout the country practice 'going by the back door,' your actions may create a disturbance." Similarly, another relative accused him of ultraleftism. When Chung persisted in wanting to leave Nanking University, his mother advised him to turn to the party and let it decide. His father, who had also thought it unnecessary to withdraw, finally agreed that "it was all right for some members of [their] family to become peasants. But [Chung's] action was not accepted by other members of the family."

Chung then turned to the chairman of Nanking University's revolutionary committee, who advised him against withdrawing on the grounds that a Central Committee decision on this question (meaning, improper influence?) had been promulgated after he had been admitted and hence did not apply to him. Besides, Chung was a good student and withdrawing before graduation meant wasting state funds. Chung persisted and finally sent in an application to withdraw, which the *People's Daily* published in January 1974. His application was approved, praised, and widely publicized as a truly revolutionary act. Chung had at first requested permission to rejoin his PLA unit, but in late February 1974 he instead returned to the commune in Jui-chin county, Kiangsi, to which he had been assigned in 1968.[62] Needless to say, his arrival was greeted with acclaim. It is worth adding that Chung has not disappeared among the faceless rural masses. Since his return he has attended provincial UY meetings in Kiangsi and Fukien. In 1976, a *People's Daily* article described his opposition to Teng Hsiao-p'ing's revisionist line. In the same year, he became a deputy secretary of the Jui-chin Young Communist League (YCL) county committee, but he stoutly rejected the state salary that came with the office, insisting on earning work points just like an ordinary peasant.[63]

The most remarkable aspect of this case is the generalizations in which it is couched. Chung himself heard "many complaints" from workers and peasants about the "back door," while a relative noted that "many others throughout the country practice 'going by the back door.'" As his own request to withdraw put it (my italics):

In order to send some of their sons and daughters to the university, some people have relied on position, power, influence, or personal friendship and relations instead of on recommendations by the masses and other valid procedures set by party organizations. Some even regard admission vacancies as "gifts" which they can bestow on others. All this serves to keep out the genuine outstanding worker-peasant-soldier representatives. . . . *Like an epidemic, this unhealthy practice is corrupting our party.* . . . It destroys the ties between the party and the people, damages the fine traditions of our party, and is utterly incompatible with the proletarian party spirit. . . . Why do they [some people] always want to send their children to the university instead of the children of rural families, factory workers, or of PLA members? Because in their opinion, the new socialist universities, like the old ones, are a ladder to fame, and studying in the university will provide a bright future and knowledge.[64]

Chung's example was emulated by other students who had entered higher schools by the back door. Similar cases were publicized in various parts of the country, most of them also involving military families.[65]

If the generalizations in which Chung Chih-min couched his request to withdraw from Nanking University are accurate, one could conclude that the radical goal of ending status transmission, that is, of making it impossible for high-ranking parents to smooth the path to the top for their children, has not been attained.* If this is so, it helps explain the continuing experimentation with college admission and assignment of graduates. The policy stressed in 1975 of "from the commune back to the

*As noted in the discussion of sources in chapter 1, it was alleged after the purge of the "gang of four" that the radicals had publicized the "back door" cases in order to embarrass their opponents in the party and government. If true, this charge might cast doubt on the authenticity of the Chung case, or on his generalization concerning an "epidemic" of influence-peddling within the CCP. Another explanation, however, is that the cases were published not in order to attack the civilian bureaucracy but as part of a broader effort then in progress to reduce the role of the military in society. Before the Cultural Revolution, the PLA had been promoted as a model for Chinese society, and as a result of that upheaval the military's role in the political system rose dramatically. Since then, however, and especially since Lin Piao's fall, the civilian party has been rebuilt and the influence of the PLA reduced. At just about the time that the Chung Chih-min case was publicized, a dramatic reshuffle of powerful regional PLA commanders took place, some of whom had long been entrenched not only in military but also in civilian positions. The Chung Chih-min case could well have been used to show that the military is as susceptible as any institution to "bourgeois" influences, thereby buttressing the case for reduction of the military's role in the civilian sector.

commune," which involves not only return to the agricultural sector but also denying state cadre status to graduates, should lower the incentive to pull strings. Yet, as already pointed out, there are good reasons to doubt whether such a policy can be made to work. Given the continued conflict of values over higher education, it can be assumed that those who are in a position to do so will continue to exercise informal influence in order to facilitate upward mobility of their offspring.

Parents also exert informal influence on behalf of finding city jobs for their children serving in the countryside. In the summer of 1974, wall posters appeared in Peking attacking leading officials who had taken bribes in exchange for securing the reassignment of sent-down youths to "interesting" work in cities.[66] Parents who are cadres are in a position to make use of "private connections" (ssu-li kuan-hsi), to locate job openings and secure them for their children.[67] Legal return is evidently possible if a job has been found for the rural resident, even if official channels, the labor bureaus, were bypassed. In some cases, family members locate jobs in the suburbs of a city, since it is easier to transfer a household registration from one rural unit to another than from a rural to an urban unit. For example, a Shanghai UY who had settled in Sui-yang county, Kweichow, received six letters from her father in early 1974, asking her to return to Shanghai, since he had found her a factory job not far from the city. The father, moreover, had found a husband for her as well. The girl, a true revolutionary, wanted to stay in the village and retain her independence. The father wrote that "the state has its ways and the family has the family's ways" (kuo yu kuo-fa, chia yu chia-kuei). When the girl came home on a visit, a family conference was held, but to no avail. The father severed relations with his daughter. She left home to stay with a classmate's family but wrote a letter to the party committee of the father's work unit, asking that his political consciousness be raised.[68]

Urban youths who make efforts to adapt to rural life may thus be subjected to repeated pressures by relatives to take advantage of opportunities to exchange a life that is deemed "bitter and tiring" (shou k'u shou lei)[69] for a more comfortable one. An urban youth who had settled in Wu-yi county. Chekiang, in 1968, was advised by his parents to take advantage of openings in county town enterprises in 1971. He wrestled with this temptation, asking himself whether one "could leave the countryside after becoming a cadre," and decided to stay. Subsequently, however, new urban opportunities arose periodically, and relatives as well as "social opinion" continued to put pressure on him: "As I grew older, people talked behind my back, saying that if I didn't try to leave the countryside soon, I would get stuck with mud and muck for the rest of my life. When I heard about this, I again wavered ideologically." In the end, his stand firmed up, he married a peasant girl and took root in the village.[70]

The Chinese press, naturally enough, publicizes cases of youths who refuse offers to return to the urban sector. Refusal to return can presumably be taken as an indicator of pure revolutionary motivation. And indeed, some of the cases suggest that true dedication to the cause is a central factor. Idealistic young people who take "bitterness as glory" (k'u wei jung)[71] reject temptations to return, but their faith and commitment may be severely tested by family opposition and societal ridicule.[72] It is not easy to be a true revolutionary, even in China. Other UYs who decide to stay in the countryside may be motivated by less pure considerations. Those who achieve substantial positions, status, and prestige in the village may feel that these are adequate compensations for the deprivations associated with rural life. As suggested in chapter 5, the revolutionary deed of refusing to return may be followed by a further rise in status in the rural hierarchy. A case in point is that of a celebrated young man, Chai Ch'un-tse, who settled in a poor brigade in Weng-niu-te banner, Liaoning, in 1971. Two years later, when Chai had joined the CCP and become deputy branch secretary, his father tried for the second time to entice his son back to the city. Chai responded with a letter admonishing his father to stick to the revolutionary principles which he as a party member of twenty-seven years standing was supposed to have fought for. The letter was published and acclaimed. Several months later, in the spring of 1974, Chai became regular party branch secretary of his brigade.[73]

Youths who refuse to return may harbor still other rationales for so doing. Those who refuse opportunities to enter higher schools may do so because tertiary education has become a less certain path of upward mobility than used to be the case. Youths whose education was shortened by the Cultural Revolution may not feel up to the demands of study in a college or

university. Or, particular circumstances may have reduced or
eliminated the comparative advantage of urban life. One informant knew of sent-down youths in rich Pearl River Delta communes who had no interest in assignment to factory work, since
their incomes were high and they were close to Canton. And, as
the case of the Shanghai father's attempt at arranging his
daughter's marriage suggests, securing independence from family ties may also be a factor causing refusal to return.

While the press carries quite a few cases of rejection of reassignment opportunities, they are likely to be a minority. Such
cases are balanced and outweighed by the persistent theme in
the press of UYs who encounter morale crises because they have
not been reassigned.* Typically, an urban youth who witnesses
the reassignment of compatriots experiences feelings of relative
deprivation. The youth "wavers" (po-tung) in his thinking, becomes less active, feels depressed, loses enthusiasm, and worries
more about the future.[74] This happens to many UYs who have
done well but who calculated that their good performance
would eventually entitle them to return. Thus, a collective of
six youths in a production team in Chung-shan county, Kwangsi,
had compiled an excellent record and, at a prefectural meeting,
was named an advanced unit in the "Living Study and Application of Mao Tse-tung Thought." Seemingly, their values had
been transformed and they had fully adapted to rural life. But
then one of the youths was reassigned, thereby undermining the
commitment of the rest. Disappointed, they regressed, and it
became clear that their reeducation had been rather shallow.[75]
This is by no means the only such example.[76] Reassignment can
rekindle the yearning for city life in UYs who have spent many
years in the villages. A case in point is that of a young woman
who settled in Ch'ien-chiang county, Hupei, in 1965, having
come from Wuhan. She did well, joined the CCP in 1966, and
became YCL branch secretary. Her deeds included running a
school for illiterates as well as struggling with class enemies. In
the early 1970s, the state reassigned UYs and she felt qualified.
As "batch after batch" of her schoolmates left, her morale
buckled. Her party secretary told her that her attitude showed
that she had joined the party outwardly but not really in

*Given the educational role of the press, a refusal case is more likely to be carried
than a case of morale crisis over reassignment. Hence, counting the number of articles
in each category is not likely to be an accurate guide to the frequency distributions
of either set of cases.

spirit.[77] In this as in all the other cases, the solution to the morale crisis was to strengthen political education.[78]

Reassignment and Adaptation

The relationship between reassignment and adaptation is complex. The preceding cases show that the existence of reassignment opportunities has a disruptive effect upon adaptation. It creates uncertainty, arouses expectations that have not been fulfilled, and has a destabilizing impact upon those not reassigned. Therefore, in order to increase the rate of adaptation, policy makers ought perhaps to end reassignment. If the transfer were permanent for all, and not just for the majority, all UYs would be faced with the necessity of coming to terms with their situation, forced to make the best of it, to adapt.

If this line of reasoning is correct, why have policy makers not chosen to end reassignment? One explanation may be that, from the point of view of the state, the "needs of socialist construction" take precedence over problems of individual motivation and hence over the goal of increasing the rate of adaptation. Urban youths are a human resource. They constitute an important pool for the recruitment of college students, and some of them are also needed to work in industrial enterprises. It is a major aspect of the new Chinese value system that the individual ought to subordinate his or her personal interests wholeheartedly to those of the nation, the people, and the collective. A properly motivated sent-down youth, therefore, will serve socialist construction in whatever capacity he or she is called upon to do so, "whether in a factory or on a farm."[79] As long as urban-rural differences persist, however, this ostensibly egalitarian service ethic rationalizes remarkably unequal treatment of individuals. Perhaps it blinds policy makers to the destabilizing implications of inequality.

Another explanation for the continued existence of reassignment, however, is that policy makers consider it essential to the management of the settlement of urban youths in the countryside. They calculate that ending reassignment would prompt some to adapt fully to rural life, but that it would also lead to increased disaffection among others. In this view, reassignment functions as a safety valve: it motivates a good many UYs to try to do well, to adapt—albeit only on the surface—in the hope that good performance (*piao-hsien hao*) will lead to eventual return. This point can be clarified by differentiating between three groups of UYs with regard to adaptation: group 1 includes those who have adapted fully to rural life, group 3, those who have adapted not at all, and group 2, those in between. In terms of return to the urban sector, those in group 1 do not hope for it and may even refuse opportunities to return. Those in group 3 are likely to leave illegally, while those in group 2 hope for eventual reassignment. While precise measurement is not possible, it is reasonable to suggest that UYs in groups 1 and 3 constitute minorities, while those in between are the majority.

Not much needs to be added to the characterization of those in group 1 already given. At the core of this group are the committed revolutionaries, whose values have changed, and who are dedicated to selfless service to their country's cause regardless of personal disadvantage. Among them are also those whose dedication has been reinforced by upward mobility within the rural sector, by personal achievement, and by the satisfactions that come from making tangible contributions. Also among them are those whose personal situation has enabled them to come to terms with rural life, such as those settled on highly prosperous communes. From the viewpoint of policy makers, the existence of this group is extremely important. It provides visible evidence that the transfer to the countryside can be made to work. For radical politicians, this group demonstrates that man can be remolded, that the three great differences can be overcome, and that a new elite of "revolutionary successors" can be recruited not via status inheritance but from the ground up.

At the opposite end of the spectrum are those in group 3. Maladaptation manifests itself in a variety of ways, including passive unhappiness, chronically low morale, poor work performance, long-term dependency on parents, and sexual misconduct.[80] Some in group 3 become troublemakers in the villages, openly displaying their dislike for the peasants and for rural life. They are truculent, disobey cadres, and perhaps commit petty crimes such as theft.[81] The scope for open misbehavior in the rural areas is limited, however, given the relative ease with which organizational controls can be imposed (see chapter 4). Poor work performance rather than overt misconduct is probably the most widespread reflection of membership in group 3 in the village. There is not much plausible evidence that UY collective protest going beyond that mentioned in the section on redress of grievances in chapter 4 has been taking place in the village, with the exception of the Cultural Revolution period (see below).[82] For the authorities, group 3 constitutes a serious problem not so much in the countryside as in the cities. Some of them manage to spend a great deal of time in the cities, alternating between periods at home and in the village, living a kind of semilegal life between town and country.[83] Others leave their rural posts and do not return at all. Judging by various estimates that have been made, there may be several hundred thousand of them.[84] Like those who have failed to go to the countryside in the first place (see chapter 3), they do not have the right to employment or to ration cards for rice and cotton cloth. They must live off relatives and friends, and/or turn to crime to survive. Some display remarkable ingenuity in evading controls, or in forging documents that enable them to get by at least for some time, by obtaining temporary work on a construction project, for instance.[85] Others become petty criminals in order to survive, stealing, picking pockets, and engaging in black market activities. There are strong indications that Chinese cities face a crime problem, and that transfer evaders and illegally returned UYs are a major cause. By United States standards, the problem is no doubt minor; by Chinese standards, it is serious enough for top leaders of the People's Republic to have mentioned it in public.[86] Responses have included tightening of urban social controls, the establishment of urban militias, and meting out of harsh penalties to a few serious offenders.[87] It is one of the costs of the transfer of urban youths to the countryside that some of them have essentially broken with the system, opting to live outside of its constraints and opportunities.

Urban youths in group 2 range in behavior from excellent to fair. By and large, they do not run afoul of the system; they stay within the boundaries of the permissible but vary considerably in the degree to which they work hard or are politically active. What they have in common is that they have adapted only on the surface. They are not reconciled to permanent life in the countryside. Their underlying reservations or dissatisfactions may become visible in the form of periodic morale crises. For the policy makers, those in group 2 are the targets for remedial measures, such as those discussed in chapter 4. It is not clear whether a flow of UYs from group 2 to group 1 has resulted from the remedial campaign of 1973, but circumstantial evidence, particularly the continuing emphasis on the need for more political education, suggests that progress has not been overwhelmingly great.[88]

As long as a large proportion of UYs remains in group 2, as long as remedial measures have not been fully effective and values have not changed, policy makers might well reason that one way of increasing the proportion of those behaving well is to hold out to UYs the prospect of reassignment. Certainly all policy makers must be aware that the single most important objection to the transfer is its permanence, and that the transfer would become acceptable overnight were it based on the principle of rotation. Unquestionably, in a collectivist state such as China, urban youth could readily be motivated to assume the burden of service in the countryside, even under conditions of severe hardship, provided the term were limited.[89] Yet, a full rotation system is not apparently a viable option, for it would constitute an admission—tacit but nonetheless unmistakable, and intolerable for at least some policy makers—that the ideological goal of remaking man cannot be realized. It would also require that the urban sector be able to absorb all its young, which is apparently not possible, at least for the time being. Because of these constraints, policy makers appear to have settled on a partial rotation system, seemingly in affirmation of the proposition that a truly permanent transfer would enlarge the pool of those in group 3, perhaps to unmanageable proportions.

If policy makers in fact feel that a partial rotation system functions as an essential safety valve, they must have decided that it is worth the costs which return for some youths exacts from the program as a whole. As we have seen, those whose expectations to return have been disappointed experience feelings of frustration. Some may join group 3. It is worth recalling from chapter 1 that escapes to Hong Kong increased in 1973 and 1974. Very possibly this was due to the decline in the rate of reassignment that apparently began sometime in 1972 with the curtailment of industrial hiring. Even if those who want to return do not join group 3, their patient wait for a change in policy, one that would enlarge the scope of reassignment, imbues the program with an element of uncertainty and tentativeness that cannot but affect its institutionalization.[90] Moreover, those who hope to return must conceal their true preferences; the resulting pretense would seem to undermine the goal of

changing the values of the young urbanites. The motivational
foundations of the transfer program thus remain shaky.

SENT-DOWN YOUTH IN THE
CULTURAL REVOLUTION

Although many urban youths have not fully adapted to rural
life, most of them operate within the constraints of the political
system, whether from lack of initiative or from the desire to
avoid risking their chance at reassignment. A change must take
place in the political system if their underlying attitudes and
preferences are to find significant public expression. Such a
change occurred with the outbreak of the Great Proletarian Cultural Revolution (1966–68), the hallmark of which was Chairman Mao's mobilization of the masses to rebel against "those
within the Party who are in authority and are taking the capitalist road."[91] During the Cultural Revolution, the masses were
given unprecedented freedom to organize, and as a result student Red Guard and adult "revolutionary rebel" groups mushroomed, first in the cities and later in the countryside. The
groups were permitted to publish their own tabloid newspapers,
in which they criticized "capitalist roaders," polemicized with
rival groups, agitated, and debated. The mass organizations were
also given freedom to oust "capitalist roaders" from power. The
freedom which the masses had was by no means unlimited. For
one, only those upholding the Thought of Chairman Mao and
the Cultural Revolution's goal of overthrowing revisionism had
a legitimate right to take part, and various authorities, central
and local, periodically suppressed "counterrevolutionary"
groups and individuals that did not in their view meet these
criteria. Central and local leaders, moreover, sought to guide
and manipulate the mass movement, and at times some of them
intervened to limit and restrain its scope. Generally, however,
the masses did have considerable freedom, in part because radical leaders at the top succeeded periodically in widening the
scope of the movement, and in part because the Cultural Revolution attained a momentum of its own and was difficult to
control, even when Chairman Mao himself sought to do so. During the upheaval, latent social tensions and conflicts came to the
surface, while groups and individuals had opportunities to behave more in accord with their perceived interests than had

been the case before the Cultural Revolution or has been since.[92]

One of the unanticipated consequences of the Cultural Revolution was that a great many of the 1.2 million urban youths in the countryside as of 1966 returned to their home towns. The central authorities had not sanctioned their return, and the fact that it occurred forced a response from them. Beginning in January 1967, the Central Committee and the State Council (hereafter referred to as "Center") issued directives calling upon the UYs to return to their rural posts and "make revolution" there rather than in the cities.[93] Editorials in the official press and statements by leaders such as Chou En-lai, all insisting that the transfer to the countryside was Chairman Mao's policy and had his full support, lent strength to the official directives.[94] Many UYs, though not all, ignored these official pleas, and it was not until the summer of 1968, when order in the cities was finally and forcibly restored, that all of them returned to the countryside, as part of the mass transfer of Red Guards then getting under way. The Cultural Revolution, in other words, caused the collapse of much of the settlement program.

It would be a gross oversimplification to say that the UYs merely took advantage of the assault on political institutions to return home. The Cultural Revolution did not present itself, certainly not initially, as an opportunity to act on individual interests but rather as a collective enterprise in mass participation. The return must be seen at least in part as a response to the difficulties UYs encountered in asserting themselves against rural "power holders." That is, as the Cultural Revolution spread to the countryside, as UYs learned about events in the cities, they organized themselves into Red Guard units and began to criticize and challenge the rural authorities in charge of their affairs. They did not get very far, however. As a *People's Daily* editorial about the UYs acknowledged, "the handful of Party persons in authority taking the capitalist road . . . carried out all sorts of political suppression against the young intellectuals who rose up in the [Cultural Revolution] to rebel against them."[95] Tactics used by rural cadres to foil UYs included imposition of news blackouts, as in the case of a state farm in Jen-hua county, northern Kwangtung, where the UYs did not learn about the Cultural Revolution until early in 1967.[96] Or, they tried to prevent UYs from "making revolution" on the pretext that production took priority.[97] But the most important tactic was to deny them the right to take part in the Cultural Revolution, or even to make them the target of struggle by pinning on them various class-enemy labels, just as urban party officials had done to suppress criticism from below. Urban youth tabloids publicized cases in which cadres on state farms or work teams coming to organize Cultural Revolution activities in the summer of 1966 would label UYs who dared to criticize them "anti-party elements" or followers of the "black gang" then being denounced, imprisoning and persecuting them. Rural officials could take advantage of the fact that some of the UYs had bad class backgrounds and hence were by definition suspect.[98] Moreover, UYs were often viewed in a suspicious light, as urban rejects and troublemakers, their reputation being further lowered by one of the key themes of the Cultural Revolution, namely, that the schools had been under bourgeois control. As the "highest capitalist roader" of Ling-ling prefecture, Hunan, reportedly remarked: "Educated youths originally were students. Students belong to the petty-bourgeois category. It is possible that they will turn bourgeois and even turn into bourgeois rightists."[99] It follows that UYs should be controlled, reformed, and treated more or less like class enemies. Thus the following notice was posted in early 1967 in a commune in Ning-yuan county, also in Ling-ling prefecture: "During the spring festival, all landlords, rich peasants, bad elements and rightists, as well as educated youths who have gone up to the mountains and down to the villages, must ask for permission if they want to leave. They must not be gone for more than half a day. If they haven't returned by then, they will be handed over to their brigades' poor and lower-middle peasants for struggle."[100] One informant who experienced the Cultural Revolution in a village in Tseng-ch'eng county, Kwangtung, reports that his brigade called a mass meeting from which both UYs and the "five bad elements" (those labeled landlords, rich peasants, counterrevolutionaries, bad elements, and rightists) were excluded. The UYs protested this identification with the class enemy. Their complaints were ultimately heeded by commune officials, but the case illustrates the problem.

Repression of UY activities did not occur everywhere. According to an informant who served on a commune in Tung-kuan county, the 500-odd UYs there organized themselves, put up big character posters, and held a meeting to criticize the commune cadre in charge of UY affairs. They accused him of negligence and indifference, citing the case of an urban youth who had been charged with sabotage in the death of a draft animal. Nothing much resulted from this confrontation but the UYs also did not suffer retaliation. Similarly, on a state farm in Tsun-hua county outside of Canton, UYs criticized local and county cadres for disregarding UY welfare, for bad work style, and for poor attitudes, as well as for lack of concern for the Cultural Revolution. These criticisms were quite mild, however, and the informant contrasted them with the more sustained and violent confrontations on larger state farms about which he had heard. On his state farm, violence between urban youths and local Red Guards did break out in the summer of 1967, but as part of the general armed fighting between rival mass organizations that engulfed Canton and its suburbs at that time. In September, when the Center made a major effort to halt the fighting, the leaders of the UY faction on the farm were arrested and imprisoned for a month by the county organization of poor and lower-middle peasants, with PLA assistance.

When UYs sought to assert themselves against rural cadres, peasants often sided with the latter. As the *People's Daily* editorial quoted earlier charged, "What is especially vicious is the provocation [by capitalist roaders] of friction between young intellectuals and the poor and lower-middle peasants."[101] This point, in fact, was one of the arguments that UYs put forth in defense of their demand that they be allowed to take part in the Cultural Revolution in the cities, a demand consistently refused by the Center. Thus, an appeal by UYs to the people of Canton pointed out that UY rebel forces in the villages were scattered and weak, vulnerable to persecution by conservative forces (*pao-shou shih-li*), whose strength stemmed from the success of the capitalist roaders in "hoodwinking" the peasant masses into supporting them.[102] The Cultural Revolution, in other words, deepened the cleavage between the UYs on the one hand and the rural cadres and peasants on the other. As an informant pointed out, the UYs were radicals who wanted to upset the status quo; the peasants were conservatives who wanted to maintain it. Actually, some peasants did rebel against power holders, but in so doing they did not share the UYs' perspectives and interests.[103] The point is that the UYs were outsiders in a time of rising tension and conflict. During such times, Chinese peasants traditionally become more distrustful and hostile toward outsiders, viewing them as a threat to the local community.[104] During the Cultural Revolution peasants in at least some villages must have reacted in this way, for it would be difficult otherwise to explain some of the more extraordinary incidents that reportedly occurred: "When youths who aided agriculture by coming to work for the Ta-o Agricultural Farm in Hsinhui hsien [Kwangtung] rose up to rebel, they were accused of inciting armed clashes. Peasants who were instigated by capitalist roaders and who were ignorant of the truth encircled and attacked them with fishing forks and bamboo poles, stating that fish ponds were burial places for youths aiding agriculture."[105] In mid-August 1967, mobs of armed peasants in Heng-lan commune, Chung-shan county, Kwangtung, allegedly incited and organized by commune cadres, set upon UYs. These youths had admittedly caused offense by stealing some bananas but had agreed to make restitution. The peasants were not mollified and beat two of them to death, while administering a vicious beating to another urban youth who had intervened on their behalf and who had hitherto maintained good relations with the peasants. The surviving UYs fled in fear of their lives.[106] Such cases may well have been few in number and perhaps the UY tabloids exaggerated them.[107] They do suggest that in a time of turmoil, when rumors fly—the UYs in Heng-lan commune were rumored to have burned down the commune party committee building— when elemental passions are aroused and latent resentments come to the surface, a program that calls for the integration of young urbanites with peasants is not likely to flourish.

The theme of hostility to outsiders is also present in charges that rural officials incited UYs to leave: "Resorting to lies and lures, and even to cruelly withholding rations, they instigated large numbers of young intellectuals . . . to desert their production posts and swarm into the cities and towns."[108] Some power holders told UYs that your "problems cannot be solved locally; they must be solved by your going to Shanghai or Peking." They encouraged UYs as well as other migrants to leave so as to be able to regain their urban residence (hu-k'ou), using slogans such as "Reverse the injustice of moving to the interior."[109] In some areas, including Sinkiang, power holders paid for train fares so that sent-down youths could return to

Shanghai.[110] Use of material incentives to facilitate the departure of UYs from their rural posts was fiercely denounced by
the Central Committee as "counterrevolutionary economism."
Instigating UYs to leave was seen as a way of putting "pressure"
on "Chairman Mao and on the Central Cultural Revolution
Group."[111]

The return of many of the UYs to cities must be appraised
against this rural background. Youths who were frustrated or
suffered repression in asserting themselves against rural leadership concluded that their grievances could find redress only in
the cities, where the "black assignment system" (*hei an-chih*)
and the top power holders responsible for it could be attacked
directly. These UYs thus responded to the Cultural Revolution
in a politicized and participatory way. At the same time, however, other UYs responded in a personally opportunistic manner.
They took advantage of the Cultural Revolution to return home.
In that sense, theirs was also a politically significant act—"voting
with their feet." But these UYs did not expect that they could
have an impact on the transfer policy by taking part in political
activities. For them, "going up to the mountains and down to
the villages" was Chairman Mao's policy and it could and would
not be changed. Urban youths with a low sense of political efficacy were essentially bystanders, curious about the Cultural
Revolution but not involved with it. For them, the upheaval
made possible an extended vacation from the hardships of rural
life, as well as opportunities to travel, ostensibly by taking part
in the "exchange of revolutionary experience" (*ch'uan-lien*).
Some of them evaded the call to return until well into 1968;
others responded earlier to the authorities and returned in
1967.

Data on the number of sent-down youths who returned to the
cities and on the proportion of the returnees who took part in
political activities are few and far between. In November 1967,
Chou En-lai observed in conversation with Canton Red Guards
that about 30,000 UYs had left the countryside, referring apparently only to Canton youths.[112] In the ten years prior to the
outbreak of the Cultural Revolution, about 46,000 Canton
youths had been sent to the countryside;[113] Chou's figure thus
implies that two-thirds returned. Informants report that some
of their colleagues in their rural units did not join the exodus
right away, but that, eventually, virtually all returned home. As

for the rate of participation, one informant, himself active in the UY movement in Canton, estimates that perhaps half of the UYs in Canton took part but that the extent of participation fluctuated.[114] During the height of the armed fighting in Canton in the summer of 1967, for instance, a good many participants withdrew and stayed at home.

Protest Activities and Interest Articulation

Sent-down youths who became politically active upon returning to the cities organized themselves, affiliated with other Red Guard groups, articulated interests, and voiced demands. In Canton, returned UYs organized groups on the basis of the rural units from which they came, such as state farms, and on the basis of common, particularistic interests. One group, for instance, named "6–1,2,3," included Canton UYs sent to the villages between 1961 and 1963, who had been guaranteed, allegedly by T'ao Chu, the right to return after three years. Abrogation of that promise in 1964 or so gave them a common grievance against the capitalist roaders responsible for their plight. Similarly, a "September '66" group consisted of youths of bad class background who had been summarily deported to the countryside as part of an offensive against bourgeois elements during the first stage of the Cultural Revolution. According to one informant, Canton harbored around thirty UY groups, ranging in size from a few dozen youths to several thousand. By the autumn of 1967, a coalition group called Chih-nung Ch'ing-nien ("Youths supporting agriculture"), which published the tabloid *Chih-nung Hung-ch'i* ("Red flag which supports agriculture"), claimed 20,000 members in ten different organizations.[115]

Sent-down youths were also active in Peking, at the national level. Late in 1966 UYs from Canton went to Peking to lobby with the government. One individual claimed to speak for Kwangtung UYs settled on state farms, and another, a member of the "6–1,2,3," for UYs on communes. Activities included visits to the State Council, where they inquired about their right to participate in the urban Cultural Revolution and to the Ministry of Agriculture and Land Reclamation. They were received but politely rebuffed. In January, Canton UYs went to Peking "to bombard the chief of the job placement team, T'an Chen-lin."[116] Changsha UYs sent a "report group" to Peking to tell the Center about the situation of UYs in Hunan, as well as to take part in the "exchange of revolutionary experience."[117] Shanghai youths serving in Sinkiang also came to Peking. The gathering in Peking of UYs from different parts of the country opened up possibilities for the formation of a nationwide UY organization. In December 1966, T'an Chen-lin, himself not yet in disgrace, told UYs: "Your organization should not set up a headquarters on a national scale. The Resettlement Office is your headquarters, the Office of the Premier. Yu Ch'ih-ch'ien and Hsü Li-chih were appointed by the Premier. Can you people replace them? As a matter of fact, you people can in no way control a million people or more."[118] In January, however, Japanese correspondents reported that UYs were organizing the "National Corps of Revolutionary Intellectual Youth in Agricultural Regions."[119] The central authorities moved swiftly to nip such efforts in the bud. All nationwide Red Guard organizations were outlawed, but the UYs were singled out for special attention. The February 17 Central Committee/State Council "circular" ordered that all those UYs "who have gone out to exchange experience, make petitions, and visit people in high places should immediately return to their own units. . . . All liaison stations set up by them should be abolished without exception."[120] A week later, the Peking Military Control Committee published a list of national UY organizations, declared them illegal, and added, "it is decided to repress them."[121] As far as is known, this ended attempts at formation of nationwide groups, but communications between UYs in cities in different provinces such as Changsha and Canton were maintained.[122]

In the cities, a major focus of UY activity was organized denunciation of the "black assignment system." This took the form of wall posters and articles in tabloids which criticized various aspects of the transfer, publicized cases of abuse, and attacked national leaders held responsible for the system, notably Liu Shao-ch'i and T'an Chen-lin. In cities such as Changsha, Canton, and Wuhan, UYs made the local assignment or employment offices the target of attack. In Changsha, a citywide rally of UYs and their parents was held sometime in late 1966 or early 1967, at which a key official in the Changsha assignment system, identified as Yang X X, was subjected to a struggle meeting that reportedly destroyed the "dignity" of this "claws and fangs" (*chua-ya*, meaning "agent") of Liu Shao-ch'i.[123] In

Canton in May 1967, an accusation rally attended by 3,000 denounced provincial and city assignment officials. Their refusal to attend the rally led to a three-day fast and sit-in at the Military Control Commission as well as to the occupation of the Canton assignment office.[124] Apparently, little violence resulted from these confrontations, but a similar one in Wuhan in September 1967 was accompanied by bloodshed. There, UYs had been requested to assemble in a hotel square to receive answers to questions that their representatives had put to the Municipal Population Office. Instead of getting answers, however, UYs were beaten and fired upon by members of mass organizations evidently mobilized by cadres of the Population Office to deal with "rascals and teddy boys." About twelve UYs were killed in this incident which seems to have reflected the massive escalation of urban violence in the summer months.[125] And, finally, UYs also made targets of cadres at the basic level who had been in direct charge of mobilizing youths to go to the countryside. Sent-down youths returning to their schools would struggle against school officials in charge of the selection process, as well as cadres in the neighborhood organizations.[126] In Shanghai, where organizations of parents of youths sent to Sinkiang seem to have played a major role, the street offices of local government were subjected to verbal and physical assault. A Shanghai newspaper complained that some "rebel organizations of revolutionary parents" had "let the brunt of their attack fall on the cadres of the lanes. Some of them even struggled against [them] for the purpose of getting their children back from the frontier region. That was wrong. The mistakes and shortcomings of the cadres . . . and their unconscious execution of the bourgeois reactionary line" should, the paper suggested, be dealt with by reasoning.[127]

Returned sent-down youths pursued targets important to themselves, but often they did so as part of a larger coalition of mass organizations. During the Cultural Revolution, student and adult groups tended to divide into two broad groupings, one popularly labeled "conservative" (*pao-shou p'ai*), the other, radical, leftist, or rebel (*tsao-fan p'ai*). Both claimed to be fighting for Chairman Mao's revolutionary line, but they differed significantly with respect to their orientation, interests, composition, and political ties.[128] Rebel groups tended to have ties to the Cultural Revolution Group in Peking, an ad hoc institution created in the early stages of the movement, whose leaders sought to push the Cultural Revolution as far left as possible. These rebel groups opposed the institutional power of the party, and they wanted a substantial redistribution of political power. Their most radical proposals called for the abolition of hierarchical power and for new, nonbureaucratic institutions on the model of the Paris Commune of 1871. During the "January Storm" of 1967, Shanghai was in fact turned into a commune, but the experiment ended when Chairman Mao, who wanted to purify the hierarchical, Leninist system, not abolish it, condemned anarchism, saying, "there will still always be 'heads.'"[129] Radicals wanted to extend the Cultural Revolution to the People's Liberation Army, and in the later stages of the movement they tended to oppose as premature the newly emerging institutions, the revolutionary committees. Their conservative opponents, in contrast, had little interest in fundamental change. Although they took part in struggles against individual power holders, the conservatives, whose organizations had often originated in defensive maneuvers by local party officials, were more interested in struggling against bourgeois forces in the educational system and in society at large, rather than against the party institution. Conservative groups maintained close ties with order-minded PLA regional commanders.[130]

Conservative groups tended to attract those who had enjoyed advantages in the pre-1966 political system. Youth supporters included children of high-ranking cadres as well as those coming from good class backgrounds, while adults included higher-level cadres, as well as regular and skilled workers in large industrial enterprises. Leftist groupings, on the other hand, found support from among those who felt deprived by the pre–Cultural Revolution system or who had suffered repression by party officials during the first stage of the upheaval. Included among them were students coming from bad class backgrounds, petty cadres, workers in street or cooperative factories, and individuals who had in times past been subjected to rectification. Those with grievances relating to the urban-rural policies of the regime were prominent: demobilized veterans slated to settle in villages but seeking work in cities; temporary and contract workers (that is, peasants hired by industrial enterprises for limited periods and disadvantaged in that they did not receive regular wages or social benefits); urban workers and employees sent to the remote interior or to the countryside, in some cases including regular workers displaced by cheaper peasant labor; and of course, sent-down youths.[131] As one informant put it, those whose status was high joined conservative groups; those whose status was low joined radical groups.

In Canton, UY groups affiliated with the radical "Red Flag" faction, while in Changsha the most prominent UY unit was a "combat regiment" (chan-t'uan) under Hunan's main radical organization, Hsiang-chiang Feng-lei ("Hsiang river wind and thunder"). Sent-down youths in places without UY organizations apparently joined leftist groups as individuals.[132] Thus urban youths experienced the various phases of the upheaval as the rebel movement in general experienced them. They participated in the radical power seizures of January 1967, suffered repression during the "February Adverse Current," when the PLA, told to intervene on behalf of the left, restored order by outlawing many radical groups, and were rehabilitated in the spring and summer when the balance of forces at the Center swung in favor of expanding the leftist drive. They participated in the armed factional fighting that wracked Chinese cities in the summer of 1967, or, as one of the purple prose accounts in Chih-nung Hung-ch'i puts it, "During the black March wind and bloody August rain . . . the heroic youth who had gone to the countryside returned to Canton to face the white terror. They bravely stood up, and openly announced to 'vow to fight together with the Red Flag warriors of Canton.' In the dozens of murderous incidents manufactured by the conservatives in Canton, over 100 intellectuals who had gone to the countryside were killed."[133]

After the August fighting, the Cultural Revolution moved into a demobilization phase and the participation of UYs in the radical movement became problematic. The Center decided to curb factional struggles, ordered all groups to turn in their weapons, empowered the PLA to intervene, and promoted negotiation of "great alliances" among the mass organizations preparatory to the formation of revolutionary committees. The Center also moved vigorously to exclude UY groups from further participation in urban activities. The "Urgent Circular" of October 8 ordered the immediate dissolution of UY organizations and liaison stations in cities and towns, also forbidding urban mass organizations from enlisting UYs as members.[134] Youth groups in

Canton and Changsha, on which data are available, defied the order. Their publications continued to appear as late as January 1968; UY tabloids claimed continued support from sympathetic groups, but it is clear that UY groups were on the defensive and under increasing pressure to dissolve.[135] Probably most of them ceased to function by the end of January 1968. One informant, who had led a small group of thirty UYs from his state farm, resigned his leadership position in January 1968, fearing that otherwise he would be labeled a counterrevolutionary. But he, like a good many UYs generally, continued to participate in Cultural Revolution activities until the summer of 1968, as a member of a radical group otherwise largely made up of legitimate urbanites. Other UYs, however, began returning to their rural posts in the fall of 1967.[136]

During the Cultural Revolution, urban youths articulated three kinds of demands concerning the transfer program. The first called for turning the transfer into a rotation system or abolishing it altogether. The second was for an end to abuses in the implementation of the program. The third was for continuation of the Cultural Revolution until the "black assignment system" had been completely destroyed and a new, truly Maoist mode of integration with the masses had emerged.

Given the point made earlier in this chapter that limiting the term of service would make the transfer acceptable, it is not surprising that this was one of the major demands made by sent-down youths during the Cultural Revolution. In Canton, it was made by groups such as "6-1,2,3," whose members asked that the pledges made to them be redeemed, and by returned UYs who simply put forth the slogan "We want urban household registrations" (yao hu-k'ou), or "It is right to establish residence" (ju hu-k'ou yu-li).[137] While in these cases the demand for limited rural service seemed to be confined to those who had already experienced rural life, other UYs in Canton called for a rotation system of four years service in the countryside for all youths.[138] Rotation was also on the agenda in Shanghai, where power holders in the old party committee "went so far as to agree to the unreasonable demand for demobilization in three to five years presented by some of the befuddled parents of the youths supporting agricultural construction in Sinkiang."[139] In addition, however, UYs also put forth demands for the complete abolition of the transfer. This they did by identifying the transfer policy with power holders such as Liu Shao-ch'i or Teng Hsiao-p'ing. Thus, UYs in Talien (Dairen) announced that "making us educated youth settle in the countryside is nothing but the bourgeois reactionary line."[140] And there were cries for "human rights" (jen-ch'uan), which evidently referred to the right to live in a place of one's choosing.[141]

These demands were not legitimate from the Center's point of view and found no support from anyone in Peking. Abolitionist demands provided the ammunition for attacks on urban youths. In conversation with Canton Red Guard leaders in October and November 1967, Chou En-lai observed that UYs demanding a rotation system had been deceived by the rightist line of T'ao Chu and others. He charged that some UYs were continuing to make illicit demands, going so far as to label as "black" the Center's instructions to return to the countryside, even though Chairman Mao himself had approved them. He cast doubt on the political standpoint of these UYs, whom he accused of making plans to sabotage the Canton trade fair.[142] Chou's charges were magnified by Red Guard groups. One, based on the Canton Fine Arts Academy, published a withering indictment of Chih-nung Ch'ing-nien. It accused that organization of "guild-ism", that is, of functioning as a bourgeois interest group, of having forgotten revolutionary principles, and of opposing Chairman Mao by asserting that the transfer was not a reflection of the "needs of the state" but was purely a product of the capitalist roaders' malevolence:

After they organized youths with guild-ism, they openly announced their political viewpoint, "demand human rights." . . . There have never been . . . abstract human rights. . . . To talk about "human rights" and "families" divorced from . . . revolutionary principle will lead into the snare of . . . counterrevolutionary economism. To preserve one's existence and selfish interest, one would sell out revolution and his comrades, and become a shameful traitor. Under the instigation of the handful of bad eggs, a large number of young people conducted a sit-in at the Military Control Committee and exerted pressure on the proletarian headquarters, openly . . . demanding a solution to their family problem and threatening to wreck the autumn export-commodity trade fair. They attempted to destroy the international reputation of our country and . . . to weaken socialism.[143]

Thrown on the defensive, *Chih-nung Hung-ch'i* proclaimed the UYs' fealty to Chairman Mao's youth program and refuted the charge that bad elements and enemy agents had infiltrated the organization. The paper acknowledged that "primitive slogans" and "low level" demands for household registrations and human rights had been advanced initially, and that these indeed had "not won the support of the people." As the movement gained in experience and understanding, however, these spontaneously generated demands were discarded in favor of a genuinely revolutionary program (see below). One of the articles, published in January 1968, admitted that a "minority" still clung to the old ideas, believing that the main purpose of the struggle was to "establish residence."[144]

Demands for improvement in the management of the transfer were in principle more legitimate than demands for its partial or complete abolition. Remedial demands were implicit in the activities of the UYs, such as the attacks on neighborhood committee cadres who had allegedly accepted bribes, or on assignment offices that had sent UYs to places not prepared to accommodate them or whose officials had sent youths in poor health or of tender age to the countryside.[145] Exposés published in the tabloids charged officials with having used carrot and stick methods to mobilize youths to leave the cities. Exposés of life in in the countryside before the Cultural Revolution complained of inability to earn a living, discriminatory treatment by locals, and brutal abuses.[146] The Center, it is worth noting, did respond to these complaints. T'an Chen-lin, soon to become one of the key targets of UY wrath, acknowledged in late 1966 that there had been "too many errors in specific work and too much rubbish in mobilization work.[147] The October 8 "Urgent Circular" also granted the need for proper treatment: "personnel assigned to the countryside should be treated politically and economically on an equal basis with the old commune members and old workers and staff members. There must not be any discrimination, reduction in work points, and harassment, persecution or attempt to drive them back to cities and towns. . . . Their grain ration must be definitely arranged in the autumn harvest and distribution and their imminent problems of housing . . . should be properly resolved."[148] This document referred not only to conditions before 1966 but also to those brought about during the Cultural Revolution, when relations between

UYs and locals deteriorated. The Center was anxious to facilitate the return of UYs to the countryside and hence warned rural cadres not to retaliate against the returnees.[149] While sensitive to the conditions of the settlement of urban youths, national leaders do not seem to have taken at face value harrowing descriptions in the tabloids of UYs driven to utter despair and even suicide by their wretched and brutalized conditions.[150] Thus, Chou En-lai granted that some "local arrangements had not been appropriate" but thought that the problem could be dealt with locally. For him, the main issue was the faulty ideology of the UYs, which he attributed to the fact that some came from exploiter families, while those from cadre and worker families simply had not gotten used to village life.[151]

Paradoxically, although the Cultural Revolution provided opportunities for groups such as the UYs to demand that specific grievances be remedied, the political climate of the times was not at all propitious for a sympathetic hearing. The Cultural Revolution can be defined as a revitalization movement dedicated to rekindling the values that had animated the Communist revolutionaries before 1949. To this end, the country was flooded with heroic revolutionary rhetoric and inundated with slogans such as "destroy selfishness, establish the public good" (p'o-ssu li-kung). Chairman Mao's "three constantly read articles"—"In Memory of Norman Bethune," "Serve the People," and "The Foolish Old Man Who Removed the Mountain"—gave vivid expression to the spirit of wholehearted service to the people's cause regardless of sacrifice and of never-ending commitment to seemingly unattainable goals.[152] In such a climate, complaints about inadequate work points were likely to be met with indifference; true revolutionaries fight against difficulties and overcome them. When persuading Shanghai youths to return to Sinkiang, Wen-hui Pao responded to fears of retaliation by saying, "Chairman Mao teaches us: 'A thoroughgoing materialist is fearless.' In no way should we refuse to return to Sinkiang because we fear being discriminated against and hit."[153] Several years had to pass before it became possible to focus sustained attention on the concrete difficulties facing the sent-down youths.

Perhaps because of the unfavorable political climate, remedial demands were not made in explicitly programmatic form; they must instead be inferred from the articles describing abuses. The purpose of these materials was not simply to secure redress of specific grievances but to convince the Center and the mass organizations that the UYs had a case for staying in the cities in order to destroy completely the "black assignment system" responsible for these evils.[154] The exposés, in other words, were also designed to support the third demand of the UYs, namely, for continued revolution as the precondition for the emergence of a truly Maoist system of integration with the masses. The third demand, embodied in the crude slogan "revolution yes, assignment no" (*yao ko-ming, pu yao an-chih*), coupled definition of the Liuist transfer as "criminal" with affirmation of Maoist values.[155] As a speaker at a Changsha UY rally held in late October 1967 put it:

> It is a great and longterm strategic directive of our great leader Chairman Mao that intellectuals should go to the village. To do so is urgently required by the socialist revolution and construction. . . . Liu's movement of going up to the mountains and down to the villages is the biggest obstacle preventing intellectuals from so doing. Therefore, it is now the most urgent task of the entire party and people thoroughly to discredit China's Khrushchev, and thoroughly to smash Liu's [transfer system]. On that basis and taking Mao Tse-tung Thought as the guide, a series of concrete political and economic principles, policies, and methods should be adopted. These will open up a bright road for all intellectuals able to go the countryside, and they will all do so most happily.[156]

How would a truly Maoist mode of integrating with the peasants differ from the old transfer system managed by revisionist bureaucrats? Details were not spelled out, but it appears that the plea for an approach in conformity with Maoist values addressed itself to the most basic of the grievances voiced by UYs, namely, that the old system had relegated them to an uncertain but inferior social status. As sent-down youths on a state farm in Hunan complained:

> Which class and which stratum do educated youths in the present society belong to? There are no written rules where the policy for job assignment is concerned. But this is a question in which everyone of us is highly interested. Once a fellow student raised this question with a cadre of the farm XXX. Pulling a long face, this cadre said: "Most educated youths are

landlords or sons of bitches. The sons you will bear will also be landlords, and your sons' sons will be no exception . . ." [Thus], as long as human society exists, landlords will remain, and it will never be possible to eliminate classes. Truly this is the logic of bad eggs.[157]

As noted previously, the tabloids attributed this perception of UYs to generalizations allegedly spread by those in charge of the old transfer system. Thus, Liu Shao-ch'i had reportedly distinguished between "high grade" (*shang-teng*) youths who entered universities, "middle grade" (*chung-teng*) youths hired by urban enterprises, and "low grade" (*hsia-teng*) youths sent to the countryside.[158] A transfer based on Maoist values, then, would obliterate such invidious status distinctions, leading to integration of the educated with the peasants on a truly egalitarian basis.

The demand of urban youths for more revolution on behalf of a truly Maoist transfer was received no better than their blatantly self-interested demand for its abolition had been. In January 1968, Chou En-lai reiterated his conviction that behind all the rhetoric lay the simple desire of UYs to stay in the cities and avoid going to places where "hardships are comparatively great." Sent-down youths, he said, have "come back to Peking, to the large cities, saying that the policy of going up to the mountains and down to the countryside is a policy of Liu-Teng. This is nonsense. [It] is an idea of Chairman Mao, whose aim is to direct our attention to the rural areas and to the masses. . . ."[159] It is worth noting that at about the same time that the sent-down youths were rebuffed, ultraleftist groups appeared, the most famous of which, Hunan's Sheng-wu-lien (an abbreviation of Great Alliance Committee of the Proletarian Revolutionary Faction of Hunan Province) published an indictment of China's "red capitalist class" headed by Chou En-lai, calling for continued revolution and a revival of the commune concept of organizing a nonbureaucratic system. Little is known about the role of UYs in this and similar groups, but it is likely that recalcitrant UYs did participate in them. Sheng-wu-lien's pamphlet, "Whither China," explicitly referred to the "revisionist movement of going up to the mountains and down to the villages."[160] The Center responded by labeling "Whither China" a reactionary document.[161]

The status grievances of the sent-down youths were to some

extent resolved in that the invidious distinction between "rejects" sent to the villages and those who made it into higher schools was eliminated by the more egalitarian post–Cultural Revolution transfer system. At the same time, Chairman Mao's 1968 call on the peasants to "reeducate" urban youths introduced a new status distinction, which has also been resented by a good many sent-down youths. The demand of bad-class youths that they be judged according to behavioral criteria and not by the ascriptive criterion of family origin was not satisfied. The Cultural Revolution Group had encouraged rebellion by youths from bad and average class backgrounds against the "naturally red" pretensions of Red Guards from good backgrounds, whose groups had often been sponsored by party regulars. Yet a purely behavioral approach to class did not emerge from the Cultural Revolution for, as we have seen in various contexts, family background has continued to be a major factor in shaping the treatment of sent-down youths, even while good conduct of those from exploiter families has also received attention.

In evaluating UY protest activities during the Cultural Revolution several factors must be noted that reduced the extent of participation as well as the extent to which frontal challenges to the transfer policy were posed. The first such limiting factor was that the Center's authoritative definitions were in the final analysis backed up by coercive power, a reality that must have exerted a restraining influence on at least some UYs. The eagerness with which UY tabloids disavowed the goal of abolition of the transfer in the fall of 1967 could well be attributed to awareness of the possibility of repression. A second factor reducing participation in anti-transfer activity ran in the opposite direction: some sent-down youths, those defined in the preceding section as belonging to group 1, did not take part simply because they did in fact support the policy.[162] In other cases, the extent of opposition may have been tempered by an ambivalent attitude toward the transfer. Judging from interviews, some UYs understand the reasons for the transfer but reject its application for themselves. Asked why the transfer policy had been adopted, several informants referred to the country's slow rate of industrialization and consequent surplus manpower in the cities, as well as the need to improve agriculture. The transfer, in their view, was an inevitable and necessary response to these conditions. It seems likely that among UYs generally a good many understand, sympathize, or even agree with the economic and ideological rationales for the transfer, but desire and seek personal exemption from its rigors.[163] During the Cultural Revolution, those who separated the interests of the system as a whole from their personal interests probably did not oppose the policy as such but instead demanded urban household registrations for themselves or a rotation system. The latter can clearly be seen as an attempt to reconcile the general with the individual interest, even though it did not find favor with the authorities.

Still another factor limiting UY protests and demands may have been cultural. The dependent political orientations that have been diagnosed as characteristic of Chinese political culture may have inhibited challenges to national authority, and especially to so awesome a figure as Chairman Mao.[164] Belief that it is improper and illegitimate to question the right of the state to make binding decisions about their lives may well have caused some sent-down youths to abstain from political activity altogether, to stay home, to become, as one article put it, non-participating "wanderers" (hsiao-yao p'ai) or to lash out in aimless bursts of violence.[165] Cultural predispositions may account for the fact that some UY groups devoted much time and energy to establishing their eligibility to take part in the Cultural Revolution according to the Center's definitions rather than asserting a general right to do so. One Hunan group of 1966 graduates, who had been sent to the village in October 1966, fought a tenacious battle to return to their alma mater to make revolution, on the grounds that 1966 graduates had been given this right.[166] Some UY groups differentiated among one another according to what they perceived were authoritative rulings. A case in point is "6-1,2,3," whose members felt that they deserved to be treated differently from compatriots sent down in 1964 or 1965, because a seemingly authoritative ruling had once been made for them.[167] Their behavior might seem to be indicative of a subject rather than a citizen political culture, that is, one in which individuals do not feel competent to influence the making of general policy.[168]

Despite these limitations on the extent and nature of UY involvement in the Cultural Revolution, the fact remains that a great many of them did engage in significant protest activity.

Indeed, some of what they did clearly transcended the limits imposed by cultural constraints or fear of the regime's coercive capacities. Demands for the abolition of the transfer openly challenged a policy of the state's, while the appropriation of leftist revolutionary rhetoric to legitimate further assault on the transfer system—a case of "waving the red flag to oppose the red flag"—did so in disguised form. Printed declarations of intent to continue publishing and to maintain urban organizations openly defied the Center's October edict.[169] Whatever the explanation for their willingness to participate, their activities clearly reflected widespread dissatisfaction with the transfer policy.

A full understanding of UY political activities in the Cultural Revolution requires mention of yet another limitation, namely, the relatively minor role of sent-down youths in the mass movement as a whole. There were only 1.2 million UYs as of 1966, and not all of them took part in the upheaval. It is not known just how many middle school students became Red Guards, but 11 million are said to have passed through Peking in the fall of 1966 to be reviewed by Chairman Mao.[170] The overall impact of UY activities was thus necessarily small; indeed, it is possible to read entire books about the Cultural Revolution without coming across more than a few references to them.[171] Moreover, it appears that the issue of transfer of urban youths to the countryside was of little interest to the student movement, as indicated by interviews with Red Guards who had not experienced rural life before 1966. At first glance, this lack of interest seems surprising, since the transfer movement had gained in intensity before the Cultural Revolution. The assignment of the graduating middle school classes of 1966 and 1967 had been postponed, but transfer to the countryside was certainly a possibility.[172] One reason for the disinterest is that Red Guards may have hoped that a good record of political activity and ending up on the winning side in the factional battles would lead to admission to higher schools or to urban jobs.[173] In addition, however, the very purpose of the Cultural Revolution reduced student interest in concrete issues. In launching the movement, Chairman Mao had called upon the country's youth to become involved with "affairs of state" (kuo-chia ta-shih), that is, with fundamental questions of political power. Chairman Mao, the country's great charismatic leader, was thus relying upon the students to defend his revolutionary line against the capitalist roaders. Would power be in the hands of revolutionaries or in the hands of revisionists? For teenagers, hitherto entirely on the receiving end of a hierarchical political system, Mao's call gave rise to an intoxicating sense of importance. Their activities mattered; they held the key to China's future! In this context, the concerns that animated the sent-down youths could not but be perceived as petty side issues. As an informant, himself a returned sent-down youth, concluded, what the UYs wanted was to go back to the cities, but in the Cultural Revolution the big question was political power, and no one cared whether the educated youths would be able to return. Thus, just as the rhetoric of revolutionary sacrifice reduced interest in specific abuses, so the overriding power focus of the Cultural Revolution diverted attention from specific issues such as the transfer program.

Student Red Guards may not have been interested in the transfer, but the transfer was part of a broader bundle of urban-rural policies that created grievances among not only sent-down youths but others as well. Mention was made earlier of the participation in the radical movement of temporary and contract workers, adult urbanites sent to the countryside, demobilized soldiers, and others. All had been affected by a development strategy that emphasized agriculture, one that required urban resources to be sent to the countryside, imposed strict limits on migration to the cities, and sought to keep urban costs low by using cheap peasant contract labor. These policies contradicted the immediate self-interests of the groups concerned, and, when opportunities to protest arose with the Cultural Revolution, they voiced grievances and demands. Their rebellion was implicitly encouraged by radical leaders at the Center, explicitly so in the case of the contract and temporary workers, whose cause was championed in December 1966 by Chiang Ch'ing, Mao's wife.[174] Yet, an aggregated, generalized challenge to the urban-rural strategy responsible for their grievances did not emerge. Many of those adversely affected by urban-rural policies took part in the radical movement, sometimes coalescing into groups as in the case of UYs, sometimes simply as individuals. They assaulted the revisionist establishment, presumably in the hope that a new political structure would somehow resolve their grievances. Conceivably, a coalition of kindred interest groups could have formed, devoted to the cause of jointly, directly, and openly attacking the policies responsible for their plight. Perhaps organization and leadership were inadequate for the formation of a distinctive coalition and the articulation of common interests. It is not in fact clear to what degree members of social categories such as the demobilized veterans or adult urbanites sent to the countryside developed their own organizations, in contrast, say, to the UYs. Failure to do so probably was due in part to intervention by the Center, whose hostility to the articulation of "selfish" economic demands was accentuated by strikes that swept through some cities around the turn of the year 1966–67. Thus, shortly after Chiang Ch'ing championed the grievances of the contract workers, Center enthusiasm for their cause cooled, and in February 1967 they were told not to form organizations of their own.[175] Whatever the cause, the inability or failure of those affected by the country's urban-rural strategy to mount a joint challenge necessarily reduced their impact. Because they remained responsive to the dominant definitions of the goals and purposes of the Cultural Revolution, their energies were diverted from the true source of their grievances. The conclusion that the "performance of the radicals in the Cultural Revolution appears to have been calculated and goal-oriented, resembling that of an 'interest group,'" is thus correct only in a limited sense.[176]

Implications for the Period since the Cultural Revolution

During the Cultural Revolution, sent-down youths protested against the transfer system and contributed to the turmoil that beset China's cities. As this study has shown, the resettlement program implemented since 1968 continues to generate frustrations and dissatisfactions. Were China's political system again to become destabilized as it was from 1966 to 1968, urban youths could be expected to take advantage of the opportunity to organize, voice grievances, and make demands for change.

What forms their participation might take cannot easily be predicted. The experience of the Cultural Revolution is not necessarily an adequate guide. For example, the anger voiced by UY–Red Guards was stimulated by feelings of rejection experienced by those unable to enter higher schools, and resentment felt by those who had been enticed to the villages with promises of return or a happy and pleasant life. Practices have changed to some extent since 1966 and protest would not necessarily focus on these themes. But the fundamental issues raised before the Cultural Revolution persist. These include permanence, equality (with regard to reassignment), status (vis-à-vis the peasants), and, at least to some extent, abuses. Because of these similarities, the themes of protest might well be repeated. At the same time, very little is known about what those who took part in the Cultural Revolution learned from the experience and how this might affect their responses. It has been suggested that Red Guards sent to the countryside in 1968 felt disillusioned, betrayed, and exploited.[177] But it is not at all clear how the process of maturing in the rural areas since the late 1960s has affected their attitudes and hence their potential response to a major new political crisis. Nor is it clear how those who were too young to take part in the Cultural Revolution and who were sent to the villages in the 1970s might act. The nature of the political crisis would itself exert a major influence on the response; it would determine whether UYs openly demand abolition of the transfer or attack the program on leftist or ultraleftist grounds, that is, in the name of true Maoist ideals. Since some support the program, internecine conflict among UYs could well take place. Whatever its shape, the weight of the response would be far greater than it was during the Cultural Revolution, simply because the number of UYs has risen by a factor of ten from 1.2 million in 1966 to 12 million in 1976.[178] If a similar opportunity to protest arose, sent-down youths might well constitute a large force for social disturbance not only in the cities but also in those parts of the countryside where they have settled in large numbers.

Since the Cultural Revolution, the Chinese political system has contained within it a potential for generating new mass upheavals. This potential has existed in Maoist ideology. In 1966, Chairman Mao mobilized the masses to rebel against revisionist power holders. In so doing he introduced into the Chinese political process the principle that revolutionaries could oppose authority on ideological grounds, thereby calling into question the fundamental principle on which Marxist-Leninist parties base their rule, namely, that only the party institution—that is, its regularly constituted leadership—can make binding definitions of right and wrong. After the Cultural Revolution, Mao's principle was reasserted. As Wang Hung-wen, a leader who rose to the top as a result of the Cultural Revolution, put it at the Tenth Party Congress in 1973: "We must have the revolutionary

spirit of going against the tide. . . . When confronted with issues
that concern the line . . . a true Communist must act without
any selfish considerations and dare to go against the tide, fearing neither removal from his post, explusion from the Party,
imprisonment, divorce nor guillotine."[179] A "true Communist,"
seeing evidence of revisionism in the political superstructure,
might well feel it appropriate to mobilize the masses to combat
degenerating bureaucrats. Thus, Wang also quoted Mao's words
from 1966: "Great disorder across the land leads to great order.
And so once again every seven or eight years."[180]

A potential for mass upheaval has also existed because of conflict within the elite. Some contenders for power might see it in
their interests to mobilize mass support in order to advance
their fortunes. After all, mobilization of the masses played a
major role in the toppling of powerful leaders during the Cultural Revolution. In the case of the sent-down youths, the idea
that some leaders have regarded them as a mobilizable political
resource has long been part of the repertoire of charges against
elite opponents. Accusations to this effect were already being
levied during the Cultural Revolution. T'an Chen-lin allegedly
worked out "elaborate plans to turn young intellectuals into a
reserve force for an uprising"; P'eng Chen, the pre-1966 mayor
of Peking, is actually said to have done so.[181] After the Cultural
Revolution, Lin Piao was implicitly charged with having sought
to mobilize the grievances of sent-down youths in his bid for
power; details, however, have not come to light.[182] Even more
obscurely, in 1975, "Teng Hsiao-p'ing and the right deviation-
ists . . . followed the youth and talked such nonsense as 'the
youth will suddenly arrive at a jewelled palace in elfland's hills'
and need not go to the countryside . . . if youth follow them in
a 'new earth-shaking long march' around the 'four modernizations.'"[183] Explicit charges of inciting UYs to violence as part
of their drive to "usurp" power have been made against the
four radical leaders who were purged in October 1976: in
Kiangsi province, the "trusted followers" of the "gang of four"
spread "sinister instructions" among UYs, instigating them to
go against the tide by attacking capitalist roaders, who "actually
were leading party, government, and army cadres at various
levels." Even "more viciously," the gang's followers went to
"intellectual youth locations to instill antiparty ideology among
them, gave them subsidies and instigated some youths to prac-

tice beating, smashing, and looting, to stir up trouble and then to shift the blame onto party committees at various levels."[184]

In addition to inciting UYs to violence, the radicals "established ties everywhere and vainly attempted to make use of the rustication of intellectual youth as a means by which they could engage in intrigues and conspiracies."[185] Specifically, the radical leaders cultivated individual supporters among them. A prime example was that of Chang T'ieh-sheng, who in 1973 had polemicized against restoration of "bourgeois" university entrance examinations.[186] Reportedly, the "gang" sponsored him and used him as one of their agents in the educational system of Liaoning province.[187] Chang was one of nineteen Liaoning UYs who in July 1976 signed a letter vehemently attacking Teng Hsiao-p'ing as well as unnamed "leading comrades" for opposing the lifelong transfer to the countryside. This letter appeared on the front page of the *People's Daily*.[188] After the purge of the radical leaders, Chang was exposed as a fraud who had manipulated his way into a college, and also as a counterrevolutionary.[189] As of early 1977, other UYs famous for their "advanced deeds"—Chung Chih-min, whose withdrawal from Nanking University was discussed earlier in this chapter, comes to mind—have not apparently been mentioned as having had connections with the purged radicals. But it is indeed likely that among sent-down youths eager for advancement there were some who sympathized with or supported the leftist faction. The "gang of four" has been charged with fanning generational tensions by pitting young people against veteran cadres, thereby holding out prospects for more rapid upward mobility should their cause prevail. In Hopei, for instance, the radicals "spread the fallacy that the older one grows, the more revisionist and reactionary one becomes."[190] It has not been established that sent-down youths in fact succeeded in moving into local positions of leadership by espousing radical line. But it is also not accidental that after the purge of the radicals, a group of educated youths who attended the Second National Conference to Learn from Tachai in December 1976 sent a letter to Chairman Hua Kuo-feng pledging to learn from the "older generation of revolutionaries."[191]

Only scattered evidence has thus far come to light to suggest that the political strife involving Teng Hsiao-p'ing, the "gang of four," and the succession to Mao created opportunities for UYs to vent their particular grievances, as they had been able to do in the Cultural Revolution. In March 1976, for example, wall-posters appeared in Canton that dwelt on the miseries of sent-down youths.[192] In January 1977, posters reportedly appeared all over Shanghai in which UYs who had been sent to Heilung-kiang in 1968 described their "ordeal." Taking advantage of the campaign of vilification against Chang Ch'un-ch'iao, one of the "gang of four," they accused Chang of having "deported" to Heilungkiang those Shanghai youths who had opposed him during the Cultural Revolution.[193] Just as during the Cultural Revolution some UYs opposed to the program sought to associate it with Liu Shao-ch'i's "capitalist road," so now UYs who hope to return sought to identify it with the discredited radical leaders.

Judging by evidence available as of early 1977, it seems fair to suggest that institutional restraints continued to operate in 1976, significantly inhibiting the capacity of groups with a high grievance potential such as the UYs from expressing themselves. The existence of these constraints can be linked to the power of those leaders who might be called "institutionalists," who adhere to more orthodox Leninist definitions of party-mass relations, and who eventually succeeded in ousting their radical adversaries.

On the ideological plane, the institutionalists believe that rectification of erroneous trends within the party can be accomplished without destabilizing mass-elite confrontations. They probably believe in the desirability of mass participation, but they are likely to feel that mass political campaigns should take place as they traditionally have, under the leadership and control of the party hierarchy. Their slogan is that the party "leads in everything," that it is the party institution's task to define what is and what is not revisionist.[194] It is worth noting that the institutional point of view also had some support from Mao Tse-tung. Mao thought in terms of contradictory opposites. He desired a "political situation in which there are both centralism and democracy, both discipline and freedom, both unity of will and personal ease of mind and liveliness."[195] He was at times a radical and at times an institutionalist. In early 1975, he issued a slogan calling for "unity and stability," but at the end of the year he complained that unity and stability should not take precedence over class struggle, that is, promotion of radical change.[196] But he did not give support only to the radical viewpoint.

On a practical plane, the institutionalists undoubtedly fear the consequences of relatively unrestrained mass movements such as those of the Cultural Revolution. They are aware of the dangers that could result when latent social tensions, cleavages, and grievances come to the surface. They are conscious of the legacy of factional conflict left by the Cultural Revolution and of the ease with which such conflicts can again burst out into the open.[197] They have sought to maintain preemptive leadership over mass participation, and they tried to keep radical campaigns such as that against Teng Hsiao-p'ing within bounds by proscribing formation of "fighting groups" analogous to those of the Cultural Revolution.[198]

As of early 1977, leaders espousing restoration of discipline, unity, and stability have prevailed. It is not too farfetched to suggest that one reason why they have prevailed is that there is widespread awareness among the Chinese elite of the social disruption that could arise were groups such as the sent-down youths unleashed. If this line of reasoning is correct, it contains an irony. "Up to the mountains and down to the countryside" is one of the "newborn things" of the Cultural Revolution. It is hailed as one of the programs that will prevent revisionism and help achieve the ideological goals of the revolution. Yet the program can be managed successfully only under conditions of political and administrative stability. The transfer of urban youths to the countryside, in other words, itself promotes the very institutional normalcy so suspect to China's ideological radicals.

7   A MODEL FOR THE THIRD WORLD?

One approach to evaluation of the Chinese experience with settling educated young urbanites in the rural areas is to ask what Third World countries can learn from it. Many of them are confronted with major problems of urban unemployment and rural underdevelopment. In recent years observers have been writing about these problems with an increasing sense of urgency and crisis. Cities in the Third World are growing at rates "unprecedented" in history, in part due to high birthrates, and in part due to unchecked migration from the villages, which in turn is rooted both in the attractiveness of urban life and in widespread rural underemployment and poverty.[1] The urban sector, however, is unable to provide employment for all comers; "in many areas, the urban population is growing twice as fast as the number of urban jobs."[2] Unemployment among the educated young, in particular, is taking on "alarming proportions" and is "explosive in character" in countries such as India, Pakistan, and the Philippines.[3] Unemployment of the educated is the product not only of a "mismatch" between type of education and actual labor demand but also of a general shortage of jobs, especially in the cities.[4] As one author puts it, a question that faces "every underdeveloped country" is, "must its youth be idle or engaged in offering services that no one wants?"[5] For the most part, governments have not taken much positive action to cope with this range of problems. The contrast with the Chinese case is stark and compelling. The program examined in this book, under which over 12 million educated young urbanites have been sent to the countryside since 1968, largely for life, is one of the ways in which the Chinese have sought to come to grips with both urban educated unemployment and rural underdevelopment. In comparative perspective, the transfer program stands out as a bold, imaginative, and unique response.

Should the program be emulated by other countries? Before this question can be answered, the issue of capacity must be confronted. Examination of the Chinese case suggests that implementation of the program rests on capacities that may often be lacking elsewhere. The crux of the matter is capacity to enforce the subordination of individual preferences to those of the state. As long as people prefer to remain in cities, and as long as material stimuli, including prospects of upward mobility within the rural sector, are inadequate to motivate many to comply with a rural resettlement program, the state must mobilize its organizational and ideological resources to make it work. Yet, the political institutions of many Third World countries are weak; the web of organizational and institutional restraints and sanctions that enmesh the individual in China is often simply not there. When Tanzania, a country that has sought to emulate the Chinese model in a number of respects, mobilized the urban unemployed to go to work in villages, "the overwhelming majority of those forcibly relocated made their way back to the city within a day or two."[6] It is worth recalling that even China's impressive organizational infrastructure has not prevented evasion on the part of some sent-down youths.

Ideological capacities are as important as organizational ones. In China, ideological values, including those of national construction as well as those of a new, egalitarian society, in which the "three great differences" shall have been overcome, furnish the "energizing myth" that legitimates the sacrifices demanded of the young urbanites by developmental necessity. Ideological values provide the cues for the struggle that sent-down youths and their families must wage against the old values. Ideology is an indispensable functional ingredient in making the program work, for even if only a few have actually internalized the new values, their very existence, as concretely embodied in the models that all UYs study, infuses the program with an essential measure of inspiration, idealism, and dynamism. Moreover, it is the ideology that makes it legitimate to bring to bear those organizational pressures and sanctions without which compliance could not be secured. Yet many Third World countries lack an appropriate legitimating ideology that could generate support for a program such as the transfer. To be sure, ideologies espousing socialism and an ethic of service to the nation and to the people are actually quite prevalent. But not many are oriented to the peasantry while also being linked to organizational capabilities as in China.

China's organizational and ideological capacities are the outgrowth of a unique revolutionary history and are therefore not easily replicable. Even so, it is worth reiterating that the mobilization of these capacities on behalf of the program to send young urbanites to the countryside was not an automatic response to the diagnosis of a problem. It required the generation of powerful political pressures, which are associated with the emergence of Mao Tse-tung Thought as a distinctive variant of Marxism-Leninism relevant for the construction of socialism. As suggested in chapter 2, it appears that the program remained a relatively minor one before the Cultural Revolution because "revisionist" policy makers doubted its feasibility. They regarded it as too radical. They did not believe that deep-rooted values and aspirations could be changed, or they did not feel constrained to behave as if they believed in these possibilities. Hence they sought at least partial alternatives such as employment of urban youths by the emerging street industries. "Pragmatically" oriented development planners, in other words, are likely to look to less revolutionary solutions to problems such as urban employment. In China, the radicalization of thought and society that took place in the 1960s under the leadership of Mao Tse-tung provided the impetus that made it possible to implement the program on a large scale. The transfer movement is thus at least to some degree a distinctive consequence of Maoist ideology. This is not of course to deny that this ideology emerged in the course of a search for a development strategy appropriate to China's needs, but rather to assert that ideologically derived values and goals influenced the emergence of that strategy.

It is not only organizational and ideological capacities to implement the program that must be considered but also the capacity to carry out a wide range of contextual policies and practices. For most Third World governments, programs such as the transfer should in fact be a second-order priority, to be adopted only after certain prerequisites had been met. For example, the logical antecedent of a program of resettling urbanites in the villages in order to relieve unemployment is the curbing of peasant migration to the cities. In China, this was done by the imposition of administrative restrictions in the 1950s and early 1960s. And, indeed, some writers on Asia or Latin America now speak of the desirability of taking authoritarian measures to restrict free movement to the city.[7] But it is also being recognized that fundamental changes must be carried out in the rural sector, changes that would make it possible to provide work for the vast numbers of underemployed, thereby reducing the incentive to migrate.[8] This is precisely what the Chinese have done as a result of a series of institutional reforms in the agricultural sector and of the adoption of a labor-intensive rural development strategy. Judging by the continued existence of migration curbs in China, rural development has not eliminated the attractions of city life, but at least the material conditions have been created that permit peasants to remain in the countryside. Yet, one wonders how many Third World governments have the political, social, and economic capacities to carry out fundamental rural reform.

Policies supportive of the transfer program include also those that aim at reduction of urban-rural disparities. Although the program is itself regarded as contributing to the reduction of urban-rural differences, it can be argued that measures such as those that aim at equalizing urban and rural incomes create favorable conditions that contribute to making the program itself work. To be sure, it is not clear whether such measures have in fact facilitated implementation of the program, or whether they help to keep peasants "down on the farm." But it is reasonable to suppose that failure to manage urban-rural relations, such as failure to take action when the operation of market forces leads to a widening of income disparities, would make implementation of a program such as the transfer far more difficult. And in fact, in many developing countries, there is "a large and often widening gap between urban and rural incomes."[9] Here, too, one wonders how many Third World governments, including nominally socialist ones, possess the requisite redistributive capacities.*

It could also be suggested that the program works as well as it does in China because of cultural factors that may not be present elsewhere. In the traditional Chinese value system, for example, peasants ranked above merchants in the status hierar-

---

*In the case of Marxist-Leninist elites, the mode of coming to power may help determine whether they later adopt redistributive policies favoring the rural sector. Those elites that followed a rural-based revolutionary strategy may be more inclined to adopt such policies than those that followed urban-based strategies. In addition to China, Cuba and Vietnam come to mind as examples.

chy, and peasants were not separated from other classes by barriers such as those of caste. This heritage of comparative openness may to this day facilitate the integration of outsiders as compared, say, to agrarian societies characterized by closed, corporate peasant communities. Similarly, Donald Munro has pointed out that the idea of the malleability of man is rooted in the Chinese tradition; hence the predisposition to accept guidance, to emulate models, may well be greater in China than elsewhere, thereby facilitating acceptance of the program.[10] This of course is not to say that some Chinese traditions may not create distinctively difficult problems for a program such as the transfer. The strength of family bonds comes to mind.*

In evaluating the relevance for other countries of the Chinese developmental model, a distinction must therefore be made between policies and practices that can be applied elsewhere even when the conditions that permitted their application in China are not present or are present only to a lesser extent. Undoubtedly, a careful examination of the rich experience accumulated by the Chinese in fields such as rural development, education, and medicine would yield numerous examples of worthwhile policies and practices that can be fruitfully applied elsewhere. The program to settle urban youths in the countryside, however, is not likely to be among them, simply because its implementation is dependent on distinctive capacities and contextual conditions. Much is to be learned from the Chinese policy of mobilizing urban resources to help the rural areas, but other countries are likely to find it easier to emulate Chinese practices more modest than the transfer program, such as sending doctors or technicians on temporary stints of service to the villages. With regard to the problem at hand—the edu-

---

*Although some undoubtedly oppose the program because they see it as a threat to family continuity, the actual impact of the program on the Chinese family is not as yet altogether clear. The program does not explicitly attack family ties; rather, it seeks to mobilize and utilize family ties on behalf of its goals. Yet, must not the long-run effect of separation inevitably be a weakening of family bonds? Some of the data in this study suggest that the strains to which the program subjects the family actually reinforce family bonds, at least in the short run. But there are also indications that the opposite happens. For some young people, the transfer offers liberation from the authority of parents and relatives; an example is the case of the young woman cited in chapter 6 who refused to return from the countryside, apparently because her father had arranged for her to get married. Indeed, the striking cases of young women playing effective leadership roles in the villages cited in chapter 5 raise the question of whether female UYs perhaps tend to respond disproportionately well to the opportunities to exercise independent initiative which the transfer offers. But the overall impact of the program remains to be determined.

cated unemployed—an approach being tried in some countries such as Iran is formation of a "Literacy Corps" and a "Development Corps" as alternatives to military service.[11] This kind of mobilization of educated youth for national service would also be easier to implement than the Chinese transfer program, but it is of course only a temporary solution.

Should Third World countries emulate the program of resettling urban educated youths permanently in the rural areas, assuming they have the capacity to do so? In view of the data presented in this book showing the difficulties that have plagued the program, the answer can only be an ambivalent one. On the one hand, the program does evidently contribute significantly to the solution of the problem of urban educated unemployment, as well as to such development goals as keeping the cost of the urban infrastructure down. On the rural side, the sent-down youths have also been contributing in various and often substantial ways to the development of the countryside, thus helping in this crucial national effort. On the other hand, the program is a costly one, though, to be sure, neither the benefits nor the costs can be measured very precisely. One of these costs is to the advanced sector, and it comes in the form of wasted talent, in that some of those who ought to be given high-level training do not receive it because they have been sent to the countryside. More broadly, there are costs associated with the effects of the revolution in education. In the rural areas, a gap was found to exist between the actual and potential developmental contributions of the sent-down youths. To some extent, this shortfall can be blamed on inadequate planning and administration. That is, the urban school system could be aligned more closely with rural needs. If adequate resources were allocated, more youths could be sent to places where the need for their education is more pressing than has often been the case in the past, and where there are greater opportunities for mobility within the rural sector. Further remedies can no doubt narrow the gap, but to a significant extent the gap is due to the very premises of the program. A good many of the sent-down youths simply do not accept the idea of lifetime service in the villages. Because of their poor motivation, they do not contribute but instead become a burden on the rural communities. A program less dependent on revolutionary value change might well have avoided this waste of manpower.

When it comes to issues such as upward mobility, family continuity, or urban versus rural life, a gap between official and societal values and preferences is clearly visible. Because of this gap, the costs of running the program are high. Much time and effort must be devoted to the tasks of mobilizing youths to go to the countryside and of keeping them there. Moreover, the gap does damage to the new values, that is, to the attainment of the ideological goals. Thus, there are cadres who publicly affirm allegiance to the revolutionary values of the transfer but privately violate them; there are youths who profess high ideals in going to the countryside but really go to acquire "gold plating," or who volunteer, seemingly from political commitment but really to secure an advantageous destination. By all indications, the discrepancy between outward behavior and private belief is not an insignificant phenomenon. This discrepancy would seem necessarily to lead to distrust in interpersonal relations, to the questioning of motives, and to the suspicion that people are really "waving the red flag to fight the red flag." The resulting social climate can hardly be conducive to the fostering of community and solidarity which the ideology calls for.[12]

It is worth noting that in other sectors of Chinese life a greater balance has been maintained between regime demands and popular preferences. In agriculture, for instance, a small private sector balances the claims of the collective. Similarly, the claims of egalitarianism have been limited by designating the production team as the unit of distribution, thereby avoiding equalization between richer and poorer villages. These compromises have made it possible to increase support for and acceptance of the collective system. The problem with the program of sending urban youths to the countryside is that such a compromise between the demands of the state and popular preferences is less in evidence. Opportunities for some to return to the urban sector can be regarded as such a compromise, but, for many of those who must settle permanently, the gap remains, and so do the costs. Yet permanent resettlement is not simply the product of a failure to compromise utopian visions of a new man; it is rooted in real problems.

In evaluating the transfer, one should keep in mind that no development program, whether motivated by perceptions of necessity or by visions of a new society or by a combination of both, is likely to be free from costs. Certainly it has not been established that a less radical program, such as one involving limited service in the rural areas, would necessarily be more productive or less costly, particularly when it comes to the provision of jobs for the returnees. Even more importantly, what are the costs of taking no action to cope with problems of urban educated unemployment? The frustration of those leading a marginal existence in overcrowded cities must be considered, as must the opportunity costs of their unproductive lives. And there is the potential for violence, which has sometimes become an actuality, as in Sri Lanka's "youth rebellion" of 1971.[13] Thus, it can perhaps be said that China pays the price for seeking solutions and taking action; other nations pay the price for not doing so. In view of the magnitude of the problems facing the Third World, it seems unrealistic to insist that governments must never override individual preferences as drastically as the Chinese have done. Yet, the benefits of so doing ought to be more unambiguously visible in relation to the costs than is the case with the Chinese transfer program.

Because some Chinese policy makers have also drawn ambivalent conclusions about the transfer program, it cannot be taken for granted that it will continue to exist indefinitely. There are three possibilities, namely, that the program will be maintained as is, that it will be turned into a rotation system, and that it will be abolished.

The case for maintenance rests on the assumption that a wide gap will continue to exist between the number of urban young who reach working age and the number that can be given employment within the urban sector. It assumes that industrial growth rates would have to rise above those of the First Five-Year Plan in order to meet the demand for jobs. However, if it is true, as suggested in chapter 2, that urban birthrates have been declining since about 1970, it would seem that by the mid-1980s the number of urban job claimants will also have declined. If the resettlement program is then ended, it could be viewed as part of the Chinese urban demographic transition to low birthrates. And indeed, this seems to correspond to the expectations of at least some Chinese.[14] The rationale for maintenance beyond that stage would have to rest on the contributions of the resettlement program to rural development. Yet, I would rather doubt that the program as it has been run could survive on this basis. Maintenance could also rest on the ideological rationale. But many observers predict that the post-Mao era will see a decline in ideological fervor; it would seem likely that such fundamentalist goals as the remaking of urbanites into peasants would gradually lose their urgency.

As the urban employment rationale for the program declines in significance, it would seem likely that there will be increased emphasis on rotation. As noted, for most of its life, the program has had an element of this, and major ambiguities surround its extent. Asking urbanites to serve in the countryside for a temporary stint is less revolutionary than permanent resettlement, but it is still compatible with the ideological demand that the educated integrate with the masses. It is also congruent with the probable decline in extreme ideological commitments. From the rural point of view, we have seen in various contexts that peasants seem to feel that, if the urbanites do not stay permanently, their usefulness is limited. But a rotation system would make the program much more acceptable to the UYs and hence might lead to substantial increases in their contributions to rural development. Maintenance of the program on a rotating basis would ensure that many urbanites are exposed to the realities of rural life, thereby helping to spread awareness of the country's developmental challenges.

Outright abolition would seem to be the least likely alternative. Even when it does become possible for the urban sector to absorb all its young, the question of the millions of UYs still in the countryside would have to be faced. Abolition would create a major issue of equity for them. To be sure, a rotation system would raise similar problems, but rotation offers opportunities for careful management that could avoid the disruptive impact of open abolition. Abolition would also signify an abrupt and highly visible break with Maoist principles. Post-Mao leaders are likely to legitimate their rule by invoking the Thought of Mao Tse-tung; hence, subtle and not so visible erosion of the more radical tenets of Maoism seems more likely than their abandonment.

As of early 1977, Chinese leaders have made a commitment to continue the transfer program as it has been. Chairman Hua Kuo-feng, who in December 1976 met with a group of sent-down and returned educated youths at the Second National Conference on Learning from Tachai, seems to be determined to make the program work and to raise its developmental significance in the rural areas.[15] The media have spoken of the necessity to "start a new upsurge in the movement to settle educated youths in the countryside."[16] And yet, it would be rash to suggest that these affirmations insure the long-term maintenance of the program to send urban youths "up to the mountains and down to the countryside." New leaders may appear or old leaders reappear whose commitment is less firm and whose doubts are greater. The future of this remarkable program remains to be seen.

NOTES

CHAPTER 1

1. See Samuel P. Huntington, *Political Order in Changing Societies,* pp. 32–59.

2. Ibid., pp. 47–48, 54–59.

3. Pi-chao Chen, "Overurbanization, Rustication of Urban-Educated Youths, and Politics of Rural Transformation."

4. It is not, however, the only political system that has exerted a restraining hand on urbanization and related processes. Both Russia and Japan have at times done so. See Cyril E. Black et al., *The Modernization of Japan and Russia,* pp. 214–16.

5. See, for example, Charles P. Ridley et al., *The Making of a Model Citizen in Communist China,* p. 195.

6. Black et al., *Modernization of Japan and Russia,* p. 215.

7. "Twelve Million School Graduates Settle in the Countryside," *Peking Review* 19, no. 2, 1/9/76, pp. 11–13.

8. See Leo Orleans, *Every Fifth Child,* p. 70.

9. For one such formulation, see *JMJP* 5/12/75.

10. Radio Taiyuan, 4/22/73, *SWB-FE* no. 4283, 5/1/73.

11. Shu Wen, "Maintain the Revolutionary Orientation of the Youth Movement Indicated by Chairman Mao," *KMJP* 5/4/72, in *SCMP* no. 5135, 5/17/72.

12. David Apter, *Choice and the Politics of Allocation,* p. 37.

13. Radio Honan, 3/10/73, *FBIS* no. 50, 3/14/73. See also John W. Lewis, "Political Aspects of Mobility in China's Urban Development."

14. Nicholas R. Lardy, "Economic Planning and Income Distribution in China," pp. 4–6.

15. Martin K. Whyte, "Inequality and Stratification in China," pp. 686–89.

16. William L. Parish, Jr., "Socialism and the Chinese Peasant Family."

17. David M. Lampton, "Performance and the Chinese Political System."

18. See the data on urban-rural consumption cited in H. Yuan Tien, *China's Population Struggle,* p. 93. These data, showing considerable disparities, apply to the 1950s; since then there may well have been some improvement, but there is no question that disparities continue to exist. See, for example, the account by Jack Chen, *A Year in Upper Felicity,* pp. 50–52.

19. This is a point made by informants interviewed in Hong Kong. For discussion of this source, see the next section of this chapter.

20. E.g., Radio Shanghai, 12/24/68, *SWB-FE* no. 2960, 12/30/68.

21. For one of many examples, see Shih Ling, "Chien-ch'ih ch'ing-nien t'ung kung-nung chieh-ho ti cheng-ch'üeh lu-hsien" [Persist in the correct

line of youth integrating with the workers and peasants] *Hung-ch'i,* no. 12, 12/1/75, p. 29.

22. See Zygmunt Bauman, "The Second Generation Socialism."

23. Ezra F. Vogel, *Canton Under Communism,* p. 193.

24. John Gardner, "Educated Youth and Urban-Rural Inequalities, 1958–66," pp. 265–67.

25. These concepts are analyzed in Ted R. Gurr, *Why Men Rebel,* ch. 2.

26. "Counter-Revolutionary Clique Instigating Student Strike Exposed at Hanyang Rally," *NCNA* 8/5/57, in *SCMP* no. 1589, 8/12/57.

27. See the section on students in Michel Oksenberg, "Occupational Groups in Chinese Society and the Cultural Revolution," pp. 14–23.

28. This term was first used by Mao Tse-tung in 1968. See below, chapter 2.

29. For a major reaffirmation of this point, see *JMJP* 5/4/76.

30. Amitai Etzioni, *The Active Society,* esp. ch. 14, "Power, Alienation, and Societal Goals."

31. Ezra F. Vogel's "Voluntarism and Social Control" is the best statement of the problem.

32. Chen, "Overurbanization," pp. 377–78.

33. See Maurice Meisner, *Li Ta-chao and the Origins of Chinese Marxism,* pp. 74–75; Charles Hayford, "The Rural Reconstruction Movement"; and James C. Thomson, Jr., *While China Faced West,* pp. 48–50.

34. Mark Selden, "The Yenan Legacy," esp. pp. 121–30.

35. Maurice Meisner, "Utopian Socialist Themes in Maoism," p. 240.

36. Richard Lowenthal, "Development vs. Utopia in Communist Policy," pp. 50–51.

37. The United States Consulate General in Hong Kong has published a series entitled *Survey of the China Mainland Press*–Supplement, in which articles from the provincial press are translated.

38. Radio Peking, 11/16/76, *FBIS* no. 226, 11/22/76.

39. For two examples of published visitors' reports see *Plant Studies in the People's Republic of China;* and Frederick C. Teiwes, "Before and After the Cultural Revolution."

40. A good example is reported by Derek Davies in "Operatic Duet."

41. *New York Times,* 12/1/74, p. 3.

42. Radio Canton, 5/3/73, *SWB-FE* no. 4304, 5/25/73.

43. A *South China Morning Post* (Hong Kong) editorial on December 13, 1972, reported the figure for 1972, which pertains to the first 11 months of 1972. December chills sharply reduce the rate of influx; hence the number is a fair approximation for the year. The 1970 and 1971 data also come from the *Post.* Data for 1973 and 1974 are in the *New York Times,* 12/1/74, p. 3.

44. *New York Times,* 12/1/74, p. 3. Note the title of the *South China Morning Post* editorial cited in n. 43: "No Room for Other People's Misfits."

45. See, e.g., Joseph Lelyveld, "The Great Leap Farmward."

46. Informants sometimes refer to this punishment as *lao-kai,* short for *lao-tung kai-tsao* or reform through labor in a forced labor camp, but failed escapees are apparently subjected to a milder form of punishment, *lao-tung chiao-yang,* or labor education.

47. While in Hong Kong, I also interviewed a number of ex-cadres, teachers, and overseas Chinese who had lived in the PRC, and in the summer of 1975 a former assistant of mine interviewed four recent es-

capees. In addition, I have had an opportunity to see interview protocols of other researchers, especially those of Professor Bernard M. Frolic, York University. Unless otherwise indicated, however, references in the text to informants refer to those interviewed by myself.

48. For a general analysis, see Richard Kraus, "The Evolving Concept of Class in Post-Liberation China."

49. "On Khrushchev's Phoney Communism and Its Historical Lessons for the World," in A. Doak Barnett, *China After Mao.*

50. Ibid.; also Yao Wen-yuan, "On the Social Basis of the Lin Piao Anti-Party Clique."

51. Mao Tse-tung, "Talk at the Report Meeting, 24 October 1966," in *Chairman Mao Talks to the People,* ed. Stuart Schram, p. 268.

52. While 6 of the 10 bad-class informants interviewed in 1972–73 stayed for two years or less, 4 of 6 good-class informants stayed for more than two years, as did all 6 of those informants whose class background was neither good nor bad.

53. Until 1973, the sum was 230 yuan. In that year it was increased, reportedly to 480 yuan. See chapter 4. One *yuan* equals about US $0.55.

54. One informant, however, did describe abusive cadres on her state farms, in a way reminiscent of Red Guard newspaper accounts.

55. See *Chih-nung Hung-ch'i,* no. 3, 11/1/67, in *JPRS* no. 44052, 1/17/68, *Translations on Communist China: Political and Sociological,* no. 436.

56. *KMJP* 11/2/72, case from Hsin-pin *hsien* (county), Liaoning.

57. For a discussion of Chinese statistics, see Leo A. Orleans, "Chinese Statistics: The Impossible Dream."

58. See for example *JMJP* 2/19/76; also chapter 6, below.

59. Radio Hofei, 3/4/73, *SWB-FE* no. 4243, 3/13/73.

60. For example, Radio Nanchang reported on December 22, 1968 (*FBIS* no. 2, 1/3/69) that 600,000 cadres, teachers, medical workers, and city dwellers had recently gone to the countryside.

61. *KMJP* 9/22/57 and accompanying editorial, in *SCMP* no. 1631, 10/13/57.

62. See *Wen-hui Pao* (Hong Kong), 12/10/63; *Ta Kung Pao* (Hong Kong), 8/28/64; and *JMJP* editorial, 12/9/65.

63. Gardner, "Educated Youth and Urban-Rural Inequalities," p. 268.

64. Radio Sian, 4/29/73, *SWB-FE* no. 4286, 5/4/73; *JMJP* 4/24/74. See also below, table 4. Similarly, one broadcast from Kansu reports that 300,000 educated youth had settled in the countryside; a later one shows that the majority were in fact returned peasant youths. Radio Lanchow, 5/3/73, *SWB-FE* no. 4290, 5/9/73; and Radio Lanchow 12/22/73, *FBIS* no. 249, 12/27/73.

65. *Pei-ching Jih-pao* editorial, 4/25/63, in *SCMP* supp. no. 118, 3/2/64.

66. See above, note 7.

67. *Liaoning Jih-pao,* 10/27/60, in *SCMP* supp. no. 53, 12/13/60.

68. *NCNA,* Peking, 9/27/66.

69. Between mid-October and mid-December 1968, 92,000 youths went to the countryside from Canton, for example. See *Nan-fang Jih-pao,* 1/18/69, in *SCMP* supp. no. 246, 3/12/69.

70. E.g., *JMJP* 12/2/75, reporting on Sinkiang sent-down youths.

71. *KMJP* 9/27/76.

CHAPTER 2

1. *NCNA*, Peking, 8/24/74, *FBIS* no. 166, 8/26/74.

2. John P. Emerson, "Employment in Mainland China," p. 419; and Sung P'ing, "T'an lao-tung chiu-yeh wen-t'i" [The problem of labor employment].

3. Emerson, "Employment in Mainland China," p. 418; Chi-ming Hou, "Manpower, Employment, and Unemployment," pp. 370–75; and note 18, below, on the birthrate.

4. Emerson, "Employment in Mainland China," p. 421; and Christopher Howe, *Employment and Economic Growth in Urban China, 1949–1957*, pp. 36–37, 116.

5. John P. Emerson, "Manpower Training and Utilization of Specialized Cadres, 1949–1968," p. 190.

6. Joel Glassman, "Educational Reform and Manpower Policy in China, 1955–1958."

7. Ibid., p. 29.

8. *JMJP* editorials, 5/12/57, 7/11/57, and 8/22/57; also *JMJP* 5/9/57.

9. As noted in chapter 1, in September 1957, an article entitled "Over Two Million Middle and Primary School Graduates Go to Rural Areas" (*KMJP* 9/22/57, in *SCMP* no. 1631, 10/13/57) mentions urban youth, as does an accompanying editorial, but it is clear that most of the two million were returning peasant youths. It is worth adding that groups of urban youth had gone to rural areas before then, as in 1955, when 91 youths from Shanghai went to settle on a Kiangsi farm. See *Chieh-fang Jih-pao*, 4/23/65, in *SCMP* supp. no. 125, 9/11/65.

10. *JMJP* editorial, 8/22/57. See also the section on "Rural and Frontier Development," below, for more discussion of educated peasant youths returning to their villages.

11. Howe, *Employment and Economic Growth*, pp. 130–31.

12. Emerson, "Manpower Training," p. 190. Emerson puts the overall increase in the number of workers and employees at 21 million. As Emerson also notes (p. 192), the Great Leap Foward saw prodigious mobilization of urbanites to work on rural construction projects for short periods of time.

13. Emerson (ibid., p. 192) cites reports showing that between October and March 1961 "more than ten million peasants" were returned to their villages.

14. Scattered data refer specifically to young urbanites settling in the rural areas, e.g., note 67 in chapter 1. Other articles describe migration by both young and middle-aged people to provinces such as Sinkiang. See the translations from *Sinkiang Jih-pao* in *SCMP* supp. no. 57, 12/29/60.

15. *Ta Kung Pao*, Hong Kong, 1/15/64, in *Communist China Digest*, no. 118, *JPRS* no. 24464, 5/4/64.

16. See Central Intelligence Agency, "People's Republic of China: Handbook of Economic Indicators."

17. *Chih-nung Hung-ch'i*, no. 3, 11/1/67, in *JPRS* no. 44052, 1/17/68, *Translations on Communist China: Political and Sociological*, no. 436.

18. Sung Ping, "The Problem of Employment," *Lao Tung* no. 21, 10/4/57, quoted in Glassman, "Educational Reform," p. 28.

19. John S. Aird, "Population Policy and Demographic Prospects in the People's Republic of China," pp. 302–04.

20. Ross Terrill was told in Wuhan that during the Cultural Revolution birth planning lapsed and the birthrate rose again from an unspecified level to 15 per 1,000; see Terrill, *Flowers on an Iron Tree*, p. 295.

21. The 1956 data are in Aird, "Population Policy," pp. 272–73; the 1975 data are in Harlan Cleveland, *China Diary*, p. 47.

22. To Aird, a demographer, such low birthrates "make little sense except as the product of grossly defective birth registration systems." See his "Population Policy," p. 316. Concerning smaller towns, see below in this chapter.

23. John W. Lewis, "China Trip Notes," p. 164.

24. Chun Pu, "How China Popularizes Education," p. 9.

25. In 1955, about 25 percent of primary school students came from urban households, as reported in Emerson, "Manpower Training," p. 193, while total primary school enrollment was about 53 million. See Leo A. Orleans, *Professional Manpower and Education in Communist China*, p. 32.

26. "Wrathfully Condemning Liu Shao-ch'i," *Ko-ming Ch'ing-nien*, no. 2, 11/10/67, in *SCMP* no. 4093, 1/5/68.

27. *Chieh-fang Jih-pao*, 2/27/64, in *SCMP* supp. no. 125, 9/11/65.

28. Radio Peking, 12/22/75, *FBIS* no. 248, 12/24/75.

29. "T'an Chen-lin's Speeches on Resettlement Work," *Chih-nung Hung-ch'i*, no. 7, 1/68, in *SCMP* no. 4123, 2/21/68.

30. "Outline of Education on Situation for Companies (Lesson Five)," prepared by Propaganda Division, Political Department, Kunming Military Region, 4/6/73, pp. 99–104, translation slightly modified to improve wording.

31. It is a common practice for the Chinese masses to be informed at meetings or in study groups about decisions or events that are not published in the media. See Michel Oksenberg, "Methods of Communication within the Chinese Bureaucracy," p. 1.

32. Radio Shihchiachuang, 4/28/73, *SWB-FE* no. 4286, 5/4/73.

33. See chapter 4 for a discussion of remedial measures; also *JMJP* editorial, 8/7/73.

34. Radio Changsha, 9/25/73, *FBIS* no. 192, 10/3/73. According to informants, a national directive called for the formulation of such plans.

35. I am indebted to Professor Nicholas Lardy of the Economics Department, Yale University, for bringing this point to my attention.

36. For one case from Dairen, see Terrill, *Flowers on an Iron Tree*, p. 132.

37. Howe, *Employment and Economic Growth*, p. 127.

38. Ibid., p. 43; and Cleveland, *China Diary*, p. 46.

39. Shanghai officials told this to a delegation of the National Committee on U.S.-China Relations in late 1972. See Lewis, "China Trip Notes," p. 307.

40. On temporary workers, see Editor, "Sources of Labor Discontent in China: The Worker-Peasant System," pp. 3–7; and *Rural Small-Scale Industry in the People's Republic of China*, report by an American delegation sent by the Committee for Scholarly Communications with the PRC in 1975, chapter 3.

41. Lewis, "China Trip Notes," p. 307.

42. *Rural Small-Scale Industry*, chapter 9.

43. Gur Ofer, *Industrial Structure, Urbanization, and Growth Strategy*

of Socialist Countries. I am indebted to Professor Nicholas Lardy for bringing this source to my attention.

44. Data on Shanghai comes from Lewis, "China Trip Notes," p. 307, and Cleveland, *China Diary*, p. 45; data on Hsin-hsiang from *Rural Small-Scale Industry*, chapter 9.

45. *Rural Small-Scale Industry*, chapter 9.

46. *JMJP* 10/17/74.

47. The article on San Ming refers to such worker-migrants; see *JMJP* 10/17/74. See also Howe, *Employment and Economic Growth*, pp. 36–37.

48. The economist Dwight Perkins asserts that, "despite the hsia-fang or down to the countryside movement, the cities have probably received a net inflow of migrants." See his "Constraints Influencing China's Agricultural Performance," p. 354.

49. Specific data on Tsinan to support this hypothesis do not, however, seem to be available.

50. "Chairman Mao on Revolution in Education," *CB* no. 888, 8/22/69, p. 6.

51. Lewis, "China Trip Notes," p. 170.

52. Liu Wei-hsien, "T'an chung-hsiao-hsüeh pi-yeh sheng sheng-hsüeh chiu-ye wen-t'i" [The problem of graduates of secondary and primary schools continuing their education or going to work], *JMJP* 4/5/57. However, Liu treated universalization, particularly of college education, as a matter for the distant future, when the transition from socialism to communism would be made. In 1960, Lu Ting-yi, director of the Central Committee's Propaganda Department, mentioned a goal of basically univeral primary education by 1962 and junior middle school education by 1966. See his speech "Our Educational Work Must be Reformed," in *Second Session of the Second National People's Congress of the People's Republic of China—Documents*, p. 137.

53. Chun Pu, "How China Popularizes Education," p. 9. As will be noted in chapter 5, however, the dropout rate in rural primary schools is probably substantial.

54. Ibid.

55. Specialized secondary schools, which have provided an additional avenue of opportunity for primary school graduates, enrolled 778,000 students in 1957, i.e., nearly as many as were enrolled in senior middle schools. See John P. Emerson, *Administrative and Technical Manpower in the People's Republic of China*, p. 91. On planning, see ibid., pp. 76–77. Planning has, however, often been quite ineffective. See Emerson, "Manpower Training," pp. 195–213.

56. Lu Ting-yi, *Education Must Be Combined with Productive Labor*, p. 8.

57. Liu Wei-hsien, "T'an chung-hsiao-hsüeh pi-yeh sheng," *JMJP* 4/5/57.

58. Emerson, "Manpower Training," p. 199.

59. *JMJP* editorial, 4/8/57.

60. Chang Hsi-jo, "Kuan-yü chung-hsiao-hsüeh pi-yeh sheng chiu-yeh ho hsüeh-ling erh-t'ung ju-hsüeh wen-t'i" [The problems of graduates of primary and secondary schools continuing their education or going to work and compulsory schooling], *JMJP* 3/19/57.

61. The downturn in educational opportunities affected both urban and rural youth but the former disproportionately so, since the majority of higher school students came from the urban sector. Thus in 1955,

50 percent of middle school students and 75 percent of higher school students came from the urban sector. See Emerson, "Manpower Training," p. 193.

62. Editors, "Kuan-yü ju-ho k'an-tai tzu-nü ti ch'ien-t'u wen-t'i hsiang chia-chang-men hai yi yen" [Another word for heads of families on how to treat the question of the future of their children], *Chung-kuo Ch'ing-nien*, no. 14 (1954), pp. 1–3.

63. *JMJP* editorial, 8/22/57.

64. *JMJP* editorials, 4/8/57 and 5/12/57.

65. *JMJP* 5/9/57.

66. See Oskar Anweiler, "Educational Policy and Social Structure in the Soviet Union."

67. John W. Lewis, "Party Cadres in Communist China," p. 427. The precommunist educational system differed from the new one in not being as strongly oriented to science and technology.

68. See note 60, above.

69. In 1958 Khrushchev promoted a radical educational reform the purpose of which was to prepare students for "life" by including manual labor in the curriculum and requiring a period of work between graduation from secondary school and admission to higher schools. Khrushchev's reform proposals were diluted even before their legal adoption in December 1958 and were essentially repealed in later years. Observers have suggested that pressure exerted by institutional interest groups as well as by elite parents was responsible for the failure of Khrushchev's reforms to have a lasting impact. See Joel S. Schwartz and W. R. Keech, "Group Influence and the Policy Process in the Soviet Union"; and Philip D. Stewart, "Soviet Interest Groups and the Policy Process."

70. See Donald J. Munro, "Egalitarian Ideal and Educational Fact in Communist China," pp. 256–304.

71. Emerson, *Administrative and Technical Manpower*, p. 95.

72. Emerson, "Manpower Training," p. 201.

73. Quoted in Orleans, *Professional Manpower*, pp. 63–64.

74. Based on the figure cited by Emerson in "Manpower Training," p. 201, and data cited in Orleans, *Professional Manpower*, pp. 38, 61.

75. Leo A. Orleans, "Communist China's Education," p. 516.

76. Table 8 showed that as of 1965 the ratio between students in senior secondary and higher schools was about 3:1. Greater precision cannot be attained in the absence of data on the size of graduating and entering classes. According to information given a visitor, only 25 percent of senior middle school graduates were actually able to enter higher schools in 1964, while another official source puts the annual rate of university admissions as ranging between 120,000 and 150,000 which would suggest an even lower percentage of 17–21 percent, when calculated against one-third of 2.1 million students attending senior middle schools. See Barry M. Richman, *Industrial Society in Communist China*, p. 142; and "Remarks at the Spring Festival—Summary Record, 13 February 1964," in Stuart Schram, ed., *Chairman Mao Talks to the People*, p. 202.

77. Post-Leap changes in education are discussed in Gardner, "Educated Youth and Urban-Rural Inequalities, 1958–66" pp. 253–68; Munro, "Egalitarian Ideal," p. 268 ff.; and Susan Shirk, "The 1963 Temporary Work Regulations for Full-Time Middle and Primary Schools."

78. "Selected Edition on Liu Shao-ch'i's Counterrevolutionary Crimes," Nankai University, April 1967, in *SCMM* no. 653, 5/5/69, p. 22.

79. Susan Shirk, "The Middle School Experience in China." See also Michel Oksenberg, "Getting Ahead and Along in Communist China."

80. See Gardner, "Educated Youth and Urban-Rural Inequalities," esp. p. 253 ff.

81. *Hsiao-ping,* no. 20, 12/24/67. It is worth adding that administrators and teachers who take "the percentage of students promoted to a higher school as the only criterion measuring the quality of school education" were criticized even before the Cultural Revolution. *Wen-hui Pao,* Shanghai, 7/4/64, in *SCMP* supp. no. 130, 12/17/64, p. 24.

82. *Chiao-yü Ko-ming,* no. 5, 5/10/67, article on Ching-shan school in Peking.

83. *Peking Wen-hua Ko-ming T'ung-hsün,* no. 12, 5/67, in *SCMP* supp. no. 200, 8/31/67. On funding, see "What Are Such Schools Meant For?" *Peking Chung-hsüeh Tou-P'i-Kai,* no. 1, 6/19/67, in *SCMP* supp. no. 200, 8/31/67.

84. "Smash the Revisionist System of 'Attached Middle Schools,'" *Peking Chung-hsüeh Tou-P'i-Kai,* no. 1, 6/19/67, in *SCMP* supp. no. 200, 8/31/67.

85. "Selected Edition on Liu Shao-ch'i's Counterrevolutionary Crimes," pp. 26–27.

86. See the lengthy indictment by Shih Yen-hung, "Down with the Chief Backer of the Revisionist Educational Line," *JMJP* 7/18/67, in *CB* no. 836, 9/25/67.

87. A concise summary of Mao's views is in Stuart Schram, "Introduction: The Cultural Revolution in Historical Perspective," pp. 57–58, 82–85.

88. "Talk at the Hangchow Conference, 12/21/65," in *Long Live Mao Tse-tung Thought, CB* no. 891, 10/8/69.

89. See for example *Ko-ming Ch'ing-nien,* no. 2, 11/10/67, where UYs depict themselves as "societal scrap not accepted by the schools and not wanted by factories" (*hsüeh-hsiao pu shou, kung-ch'ang pu yao ti she-hui cha-tzu*).

90. See "On Khrushchev's Phoney Communism and Its Historical Lessons for the World," in A. Doak Barnett, *China After Mao,* pp. 192–94.

91. *Hsin-min Wan-pao,* 1/16/65, in *SCMP* supp. no. 134, 3/11/65.

92. *Chung-kuo Ch'ing-nien Pao,* 9/8/64, in *Communist China Digest,* no. 132, 11/10/64, *JPRS* no. 27303.

93. "On Khrushchev's Phoney Communism," p. 194.

94. See, e.g., Ezra F. Vogel, *Canton Under Communism,* p. 337.

95. John Gittings, "Stifling the Students," pp. 377–78. Gittings quotes Mao as having said: "You have let me down. . . . And what is more, you have disappointed the workers, peasants, and armymen of China." But this is apparently not authentic.

96. Radio Peking, 12/23/68, *FBIS* no. 250, 12/24/68.

97. Allegedly he did so in his "Outline for 'Project 571'," a plan to oust Mao from power. See Michael Y. M. Kau, ed., *The Lin Piao Affair,* p. 84.

98. Keesing's Research Report, *The Cultural Revolution in China,* p. 20.

99. The main changes are summarized in John Gardner and Wilt Idema, "China's Educational Revolution." See also William Kessen, ed., *Child-*

hood in China, a report by an American delegation investigating early childhood education in the PRC.

100. Educational policy was central to the conflict that led to the ouster of Teng Hsiao-p'ing in April 1976. See, for instance, "What Type of 'Top-Notch Scientists' Should be Raised?" *KMJP* 2/23/76, in *FBIS* no. 45, 3/5/76.

101. Radio Tsinan, 10/14/74, in *FBIS* no. 205, 10/22/74. See also *JMJP* editorial, 8/7/73.

102. *Chung-kuo Ch'ing-nien Pao,* 9/8/64, in *Communist China Digest,* no. 132, *JPRS* no. 27303, 11/10/64.

103. *JMJP* editorial, 8/7/73; and Yen Chih, "Be Promoters in Helping Educated Young People Settle in the Countryside," *Red Flag,* no. 11 (1973), broadcast by Peking Radio, 11/19/73, *FBIS* no. 224, 11/20/73.

104. Lewis, "China Trip Notes," p. 164. Junior middle schooling at the brigade level, it is worth noting, has expanded greatly in recent years as well, making it less necessary to leave the village. See *JMJP* 6/1/76.

105. *Socialist Upsurge in China's Countryside,* pp. 378, 383. See also Teng Tzu-hui, "Mobilize All Peasants and Rural Youth to Struggle for Cooperativization of Agriculture," *Chung-kuo Ch'ing-nien Pao,* 4/1/54, in *CB* no. 305, 11/18/54, as well as *JMJP* editorial, 5/20/55, in *SCMP* no. 1059, 6/1/55.

106. Teng Tzu-hui, "Certain Problems concerning Intellectual Youths Who Are Going to the Rural Villages," *KMJP* 7/4/62, in *JPRS* no. 14779, 8/9/62, *Translations on Communist China: Political and Sociological,* no. 5.

107. *JMJP* editorial, 4/8/57.

108. Teng Tzu-hui, "Certain Problems."

109. M. C. Yang's pre-1949 village study has an interesting illustration of community attitudes: "A member of the Yang clan . . . had a very good reputation as a student when he was in the market-town school. He was praised by the teachers, the community leaders of the whole market-town area, and also by the senior members of the P'an clan, so that great hope was roused among all the people of the clan. . . . The young man was very unconventional. Even after he became a college student, he still came home to work on his father's farm during the summer vacations. He dressed like an ordinary farmer. This gave the kinsmen and the villagers the impression that he was not going to be a scholar or a gentleman or an official, and they became indifferent to him." See Martin C. Yang, *A Chinese Village,* pp. 140–41.

110. See H. Yuan Tien, *China's Population Struggle,* pp. 326–27.

111. "Should Educated Youth Dirty Their Hands With Cow Dung?" *Chung-kuo Ch'ing-nien Pao,* 2/8/64, in *Communist China Digest,* no. 119, *JPRS* no. 24610, 5/14/64. Similar articles have appeared in *Pei-ching Jih-pao,* 6/7/62, *SCMP* supp. no. 105, 3/14/63. The issue of the propriety of peasant youths' returning to their villages to take up farming has not disappeared since the Cultural Revolution. See *KMJP* 4/16/75, story from Feng-jun *hsien* (county), Hopei, and an article authored by the YCL branch of Tachai brigade, "Educate Young People with Communist Ideas," *Red Flag,* no. 5 (1975), broadcast by Radio Peking, 5/20/75, *FBIS* no. 100, 5/25/75.

112. The press often quotes enthusiastic UYs as "demanding to be sent to the most difficult places . . . where we are most needed by the party and the people" (Radio Canton, 5/29/76, *FBIS* no. 108, 6/3/76).

113. I am indebted to Professor Roy Hofheinz for processing these county lists.

114. Data on this variable were available for 1,870 counties not mentioned and for 299 that were mentioned. In the case of the former, the average distance from the capital was 248 kilometers; in the case of the latter, 217 kilometers. $F = 6.73574, P < 0.01$.

115. Using a scale in which 1 = sea level and 11 = 6,000 meters above sea level, it turns out that 1,675 counties not mentioned averaged 3.028 on the scale (3 = 250 to 500 meters above sea level), and 275 mentioned counties averaged 2.356 (2 = 50 to 250 meters). $F = 32.4725, P < 0.001$.

116. A scale in which 1 = railroad construction since 1949 and 5 = construction prior to 1903 yielded the finding that 477 counties not mentioned and on which data were available ranked 2.817 and 100 counties that were mentioned ranked 3.170. $F = 5.30228, P < 0.025$.

117. It is a well-known fact that there is considerable inequality among rural units with respect to income in much of rural China. For a recent summary of the evidence, see Martin K. Whyte, "Inequality and Stratification in China."

118. Chi-square = 2.3448, $DF = 1$; not significant at 0.10 level of probability.

119. However, another of the Parish-Whyte findings deviates from the pattern of urban youths tending to settle in more modernized villages. A communications scale, based on 35 villages and made up of data on primary school attendance, type of radio network, and frequency of movie team visits, shows fewer UYs in villages that ranked high on the scale. Chi-square = 2.9132, $DF = 1$; $P < 0.10$. Still another of their results, in contrast, reinforces the finding from the county comparison that UYs have tended to settle in villages closer to their provincial capitals. That is, the percentage of UYs tended to exceed 3 the closer the village was to either of the two major cities of Kwangtung, Canton or Swatow. Chi-square = 3.6728, $DF = 2$; not significant at 0.10 level.

120. See Dwight Perkins, "Development of Agriculture," pp. 61–64. The diversion of manpower to nonagricultural has caused controversy, since it is often more profitable to engage in nonagricultural enterprises. Restrictions on the amount of manpower have been applied. See CNS no. 500, 1/10/74.

121. Rural Small-Scale Industry, chapter 10.

122. As far as informants knew, UYs tended not to be sent to the most densely populated villages. One informant served in a brigade in Tung-kuan hsien, Kwangtung, with a population of 4,000 and 25 UYs (0.6 percent), while a second informant served in another brigade in Tung-kuan which had 69 UYs and a population of 1,600 (4.3 percent). United States visitors to a commune in Honan also were told that UYs could not be accommodated because of the low land-labor ratio; see Rural Small-Scale Industry.

123. Chi-square = 3.0283, $DF = 1$; $P < 0.10$.

124. Martin K. Whyte, personal communication.

125. Informants make this point, as does the press, e.g., KMJP 1/16/74.

126. This point is made in the section on the transfer in Rural Small-Scale Industry, chapter 10.

127. Informants knew only that their school had certain destinations to which they could go; see chapter 3.

128. Radio Nanchang, 12/29/75, SWB-FE no. 5104, 1/10/76; China News Analysis, no. 1031, 2/20/76; and Ch'i Chien, "Kung-ku ho fa-chan

shang-shan hsia-hsiang ti ch'eng-kuo" [Consolidate and develop the effectiveness of up to the mountains and down to the countryside], esp. p. 8. Sometimes the press prints accounts of UYs sent to grain-deficient brigades but without mentioning how they managed, e.g., *KMJP* 1/3/74, from Ai-hui hsien, Heilungkiang.

129. During and after the Cultural Revolution, the PLA took control of many state farms that had hitherto been operated by the Ministry of State Farms and Land Reclamation or its subdivisions. Since then, however, some of these army farms have reportedly reverted to state farm status, probably under the Ministry of Agriculture and Forestry. For a discussion of state farms, see Audrey Donnithorne, *China's Economic System*, ch. 4; on army farms, see Chang Yun-t'ien, "The Establishment and Expansion of Communist China's 'Production-Construction Corps.'"

130. Radio Shanghai, 1/21/74, *FBIS* no. 17, 1/24/74.

131. Radio Harbin, 9/18/75, *FBIS* no.183, 9/19/75. However, another report puts the number at "over 300,000." See *NCNA*, Peking, 9/10/75, *FBIS* no. 183, 9/19/75.

132. *NCNA*, Peking, 6/14/74, *FBIS* no. 116, 6/14/74.

133. See Radio Hu-ho-hot, 12/22/72, *FBIS* no. 251, 12/29/72; Radio Peking, 5/9/73, *SWB-FE*, no. 4302, 5/23/73; Radio Urumchi, 2/17/76, *FBIS* no. 34, 2/19/76; and George Moseley, *A Sino-Soviet Cultural Frontier*.

134. Radio Kunming, 12/21/75, *FBIS* no. 6, 1/9/76.

135. Leo Orleans, *Every Fifth Child*, ch. 4.

136. Saifudin, "Advance Victoriously under the Guidance of Chairman Mao's Revolutionary Line." For Yunnan, references to manpower shortages can also be found, e.g., *Shanghai Wen-hui Pao*, 2/17/69, in *SCMP* supp. no. 249, 5/2/69.

137. *Chih-shih ch'ing-nien tsai pei ta-huang* [Educated youths in the great northern wilderness], ed. Heilungkiang Sheng-ch'an Chien-she Pu-tui Cheng-chih pu [Heilungkiang PCC Political Department], p. 132 ff., shows some of the UYs' military activities.

138. *NCNA*, Peking, 5/3/76, *FBIS* no. 88, 5/5/76.

139. "'T'an Chen-lin's Speeches on Resettlement Work"; and "Chung-yang an-pan wen-chien chai-p'ien" [Excerpts from Central Assignment documents], *Chih-nung Hung-ch'i*, no. 7, 1/68. Chou Jung-hsin became minister of education in 1975 but fell under a cloud in 1976 (see below). In 1977, it was revealed that the State Council unit had already been established in 1962. See *NCNA*, Peking, 1/31/77, *FBIS* no. 21, 2/1/77.

140. See *KMJP* 6/6/72, in *SCMP* no. 5159, 6/22/72.

141. Radio Changsha, 6/29/76, *FBIS* no. 127, 6/30/76. This broadcast identified Yu Chu-chien as being in charge of the office. The broadcast transcript is in English and is possibly faulty. In 1966, T'an Chen-lin had referred to Yu Ch'ih-ch'ien as one of two cadres appointed by Chou En-lai to run the Resettlement Office; see "T'an Chen-lin's Speeches on Resettlement Work." If the two names refer to the same person, it would indicate remarkable continuity in the administration of the transfer.

142. For mentions of provincial-level offices, see, e.g., *KMJP* 12/24/70, and Radio Harbin 3/4/76, *FBIS* no. 46, 3/8/76.

143. "Wrathfully Condemning Liu Shao-ch'i" (note 26, above); "Chung-yang an-pan wen-chien chai-p'ien"; "Traveller's Report," app. A, *China Topics*, no. 465, 2/26/68.

144. "Premier Chou's Important Speech," *Hsiao-ping*, no. 22, 2/17/68, in *SCMP* no. 4134, 3/8/68. An article commemorating Chou En-lai's

death, published in 1977, described several instances of Chou's direct participation in the management of the program from 1962 on. See *NCNA,* Peking, 1/31/77, *FBIS* no. 21, 2/1/77.

145. *JMJP* 11/23/76 and 12/28/76.

146. Tan Wen, "Take the Road of Integrating with Workers and Peasants, Be Vanguards in Combating and Preventing Revisionism," translation slightly modified to improve wording. Liu Shao-ch'i's "theory of going to the countryside to make a name" has often been translated more expressively as the "theory of gold-plating" (*tu-chin lun*).

147. *JMJP* 1/4/77; Radio Nanchang, 1/10/77, *FBIS* no. 10, 1/14/77; and Radio Nanking, 12/4/76, *FBIS* no. 238, 12/9/76.

148. *JMJP* 5/3/76.

149. Chou En-lai, "Report on the Work of the Government," p. 23.

150. For a summary of these criticisms, see Robert A. Scalapino, "The Struggle over Higher Education: Revolution vs. Development." For some specific materials, see the reference cited in note 100, above; also Radio Peking, 12/17/75, *FBIS* no. 245, 12/19/75; George Biannic, Agence France Press, in *FBIS* no. 248, 12/24/74; and "Black Talks by Chou Jung-hsin," *Free China Weekly,* 5/23/76. The need for basic research has also been noted by American specialists; see *Plant Studies in the People's Republic of China,* p. 119.

151. *JMJP* 5/3/76 and 5/10/76.

152. Radio Shenyang, 6/20/76, *FBIS* no. 121, 6/22/76. See also chapter 6.

153. *KMJP* 12/12/76, in *FBIS* no. 252, 12/30/76.

154. For a stimulating and pertinent analysis, see Michel Oksenberg and Steven Goldstein, "The Chinese Political Spectrum"; for a recent analysis of foreign trade and self-reliance, see Alexander Eckstein, "China's Trade Policy and Sino-American Relations."

155. During the Cultural Revolution, a Red Guard article criticized T'an Chen-lin for having wanted to send UYs to frontier and mountainous regions, presumably because that is where he felt they were needed, even though this violated Mao's dictum that the entire countryside was a "broad arena" for the educated young. This is one of the few hints of possible cleavages over the placement of UYs. See "T'an Chen-lin's Speeches on Resettlement Work."

156. Ch'i Chien, "Kung-ku ho fa-chan shang-shan hsia-hsiang ti ch'eng-kuo," pp. 7, 9.

157. "Black Talk of the Demons," *Chih-nung Hung-ch'i,* no. 3, 11/1/67, in *JPRS* no. 44052, 1/17/68, *Translations on Communist China: Political and Sociological,* no. 436.

158. See Gardner, "Educated Youth and Urban-Rural Inequalities," p. 269.

159. Peking wall poster, as reported by *Mainichi,* 1/20/67, in *Daily Summary of the Japanese Press,* 1/25/67.

160. Radio Shenyang, 6/20/76, *FBIS* no. 121, 6/22/76; and *JMJP* 7/14/76.

161. *JMJP* 7/14/76.

162. "A Few Examples of the Crimes Committed by T'an Chen-lin against the Thought of Mao Tse-tung," *K'e-chi Hung-ch'i,* 3/26/67, in *SCMP* supp. no. 181, 5/8/67. For Liu's views, see "Selected Edition on Liu Shao-ch'i's Counterrevolutionary Crimes," pp. 29–30.

163. "T'an Chen-lin's Speeches on Resettlement Work."

164. Ibid.

165. T'an's statements about crime and the transfer as a solution were made in 1963 and 1964; his skeptical statement about becoming peasants was made in 1966. Not enough is known about T'an to tell whether he changed his views.

166. Radio Chengchow, 3/10/73, *FBIS* no. 50, 3/14/73.

167. Tan Wen, "Take the Road of Integrating with Workers and Peasants."

168. Robert Scalapino, "The Struggle over Higher Education," p. 9.

169. Radio Nanchang, 1/15/77, *FBIS* no. 11, 1/17/77; *JMJP* 1/4/77.

170. Radio Nanchang, 1/15/77, *FBIS* no. 11, 1/17/77.

171. "A Hundred Examples of Liu Shao-ch'i's Speeches Opposing the Thought of Mao Tse-tung," *Ching-kang-shan*, 2/1/67 and 2/8/67, in *SCMP* supp. no. 173, 4/4/67, p. 12.

172. *Nung-ts'un Ch'ing-nien*, no. 20, 10/25/67, in *SCMM* no. 612, 1/29/68.

173. "Wrathfully Condemning Liu Shao-ch'i"; "Chung-yang an-pan wenchien chai-p'ien."

174. Kuo Ch'ing, "Show Concern for the Life of the Educated Young People," *KMJP* 6/22/73, in *SCMP* no. 5406, 7/2/73.

175. E.g., *KMJP* 8/8/74; and Radio Hofei, 6/4/76, *FBIS* no. 110, 6/7/76.

176. Informants interviewed by Professor Frolic and by my assistant in 1975 reported having heard about Mao's letter, but it has also been referred to in the press. See Radio Foochow, 4/25/74, *FBIS* no. 92, 5/10/74; and Radio Foochow, 5/4/74, *FBIS* no. 88, 5/6/74.

177. Radio Nanchang, 1/15/77, *FBIS* no. 11, 1/17/77.

178. Theoretical Group of the General Office of the State Council, "In Commemoration of the First Anniversary of the Passing of Our Esteemed and Beloved Premier Chou En-lai," p. 15.

CHAPTER 3

1. Radio Nanchang, 7/26/75, *FBIS* no. 147, 7/30/75.

2. Radio Canton, 10/2/74, *FBIS* no. 201, 10/16/74.

3. Radio Changchun, 6/5/75, *FBIS* no. 110, 6/6/75.

4. *JMJP* 8/8/70; Radio Shanghai, 8/21/72, *FBIS* no. 165, 8/23/72; and informant's report.

5. For examples, see *Shanghai Wen-hui Pao*, 5/26/65, in *SCMP* supp. no. 141, 7/27/65, on visiting UYs reporting on their deeds; *KMJP* 5/22/69, for a case of peasant cadres reporting to family heads on the UYs in their charge; and *JMJP* 1/3/72 for a report on a group sent by Yenan prefecture to Peking. Between 1969 and 1972, Peking sent ten study and comfort missions and seven study teams to investigate the life of Peking UYs, according to Radio Peking, 2/25/73, *FBIS* no. 41, 3/1/73. For a report on a group of parents that went from Peking to Yenan, see *KMJP* 5/13/72.

6. Radio Shanghai, 10/18/72, *FBIS* no. 205, 10/20/72.

7. T'an Wen, "Youth Should Stand at the Forefront of the Revolutionary Ranks," *Hung-ch'i*, no. 5, 5/1/73, in *SCMM* no. 753, 6/4/73.

8. Radio Shanghai, 10/20/72, *FBIS* no. 208, 10/26/72.

9. *Chieh-fang Jih-pao*, 7/7/62, in *SCMP* supp. no. 100, 11/21/62.

10. *JMJP* editorial, 8/7/73.

11. *JMJP* 5/26/73, in *SCMP* no. 5389, 6/7/73. See also Yen Chih, "Be Promoters in Helping Educated Young People Settle in the Countryside,"

Red Flag, no. 11 (1973), broadcast by Peking Radio, 11/19/73, *FBIS* no. 224, 11/20/73.

12. The Canton example comes from interviews conducted by Martin K. Whyte in 1968/69. See *KMJP* 7/28/69 for a criticism of pre–Cultural Revolution appeals in a Tientsin school, where students were told about the beautiful scenery in the borderlands, the good climate, and other attractions.

13. The Heilungkiang Party Committee allegedly lured UYs to that province with promises of quick entry into the YCL and the CCP; see *JMJP* 2/20/67.

14. Shih Ling, "Chien-ch'ih ch'ing-nien t'ung kung-nung chieh-ho ti cheng-ch'üeh lu-hsien," p. 30.

15. Based on the data supplied by informants interviewed by my assistant in 1975.

16. Information from Professor Steven Goldstein of Smith College, who visited a Chengchow school in 1973.

17. *NCNA,* Peking, 1/7/74, in *FBIS* no. 6, 1/9/74 (Liaoning story); and *JMJP* 1/7/72, a story from Loyang, Honan, characteristically entitled "T'ung-kuo she-hui tiao-ch'a p'i-p'an 'tu-shu wu-yung lun'" [Criticize the theory that it is useless to study by making a social analysis]. See also next section.

18. *Pei-ching Jih-pao,* 9/14/68, *SCMM* no. 659, 6/16/69; *Nan-fang Jih-pao,* 1/18/69, in *SCMP* supp. no. 246, 3/12/69; informants' reports.

19. Radio Shanghai, 8/13/72, *FBIS* no. 159, 8/15/72; and *JMJP* 5/3/75.

20. Radio Shenyang, 8/8/75, *FBIS* no. 158, 8/14/75.

21. *KMJP* 6/1/69 and 7/23/69; Radio Shenyang, 8/8/75, *FBIS* no. 158, 8/14/75.

22. *Chih-nung Hung-ch'i,* no. 3, 11/1/67, in *JPRS* no. 44052, 1/17/68, *Translations on Communist China: Political and Sociological,* no. 436.

23. *JMJP* 12/22/73.

24. *JMJP* 1/18/73. The 3 percent excludes those who were sick or exempted for special reasons.

25. Radio Changchun, 5/4/74, *FBIS* no. 89, 5/7/74; Radio Changchun, 5/8/75, *FBIS* no. 92, 5/12/75.

26. In Liaoning, high compliance rates are reported, however, in recent years. Thus, in Ying-k'ou, Chaoyang, and other places, over 98 percent of those "who should have gone" did so in 1974, and in Lü-ta 99 percent of those who should have gone did so in 1975. See Radio Shenyang, 9/22/74, *FBIS* no. 208, 10/25/74; and *JMJP* 10/26/75.

27. Radio Canton, 7/19/75, *FBIS* no. 141, 7/22/75. Peking is credited with having pioneered political evening schools as well as literary and art propaganda activities in residential areas. For a case of emulation in far-off Urumchi, see Radio Urumchi, 7/20/75, *FBIS* no. 146, 7/29/75.

28. Based on data supplied by informants to my assistant in 1975.

29. Radio Harbin, 7/31/75, *FBIS* no. 150, 8/4/75.

30. In Lü-ta, the militia rendered "energetic assistance" in transfer mobilization, but so did other organizations, including PLA units, the YCL, trade unions, the women's associations, and public security organs. See Radio Shenyang, 8/8/75, *FBIS* no. 158, 8/14/75. This all-out mobilization may well have insured the 99 percent compliance rate reported in *JMJP* 10/26/75. See also *JMJP* 6/19/75 for articles on the role of the Shanghai and Peking militias in youth work. Whether the transfer has

resulted in increased delinquency is of course very difficult to establish, but there can be no doubt but that youthful misbehavior has become a source of concern. According to an informant, for instance, a document was read in Canton work units in late 1972 complaining of delinquency, while the public media have also spoken of crime in connection with youths. In addition to the militia articles, see Radio Tsinan, 5/28/75, *FBIS* no. 107, 6/3/75, and also chapter 6, below.

31. Radio Nanking, 11/14/76, *FBIS* no. 224, 11/18/76; Radio Nanning, 11/13/76, *FBIS* no. 221, 11/15/76.

32. *Pei-ching Jih-pao* editorial, 4/25/63, in *SCMP* supp. no. 118, 3/2/64.

33. *Chung-kuo Ch'ing-nien Pao*, 7/25/64, in *Communist China Digest* no. 132, *JPRS* no. 27303, 11/10/64. Wording slightly modified to improve grammar.

34. *Chieh-fang Jih-pao*, 5/11/64, in *SCMP* supp. no. 126, 9/18/64.

35. *Chieh-fang Jih-pao*, 7/7/62, in *SCMP* supp. no. 100, 11/21/62.

36. *Chieh-fang Jih-pao*, 5/18/63, in *SCMP* supp. no. 113, 8/12/63.

37. *Shanghai Wen-hui Pao*, 7/4/64, in *SCMP* supp. no. 130, 12/17/64.

38. Ibid.; also *KMJP* 4/24/69, 11/20/69, and 1/30/72.

39. *Chung-kuo Ch'ing-nien Pao*, 1/11/64 and 2/29/64, in *Communist China Digest* no. 119, *JPRS* no. 24610, 5/14/64. The arguments were of course refuted.

40. Radio Peking, 1/7/74, *FBIS* no. 6, 1/9/74. The reaction against revival of entrance examinations was spearheaded by publication of a letter from a sent-down student, Chang T'ieh-sheng. See chapter 6, note 57.

41. Radio Harbin, 2/15/74, *FBIS* no. 37, 2/22/74. The quote is from the letter of a student who complained about harassment by this revisionist teacher. For another case, from a school in Taiyuan, Shansi, where antitransfer sentiment was voiced, see *KMJP* 2/26/74.

42. *KMJP* 8/16/72 and 9/6/72.

43. *JMJP* 3/17/73.

44. *KMJP* 12/2/72; and *JMJP* 2/13/75. See also the discussion below of cadre influence on assignments.

45. Professor Ezra Vogel has suggested that in a society as thoroughly penetrated by politics as China personal communication changes from "friendship to comradeship", i.e., from the expression of private views to the expression of official views. In the case of the transfer, however, in which the official values are not congruent with popular expectations and aspirations, such a transformation has evidently not taken place, at least not completely. See Ezra F. Vogel, "From Friendship to Comradeship."

46. *KMJP* 1/16/71.

47. *Pei-ching Jih-pao*, 9/14/29, in *SCMM* no. 659, 6/16/69. See also *Shanghai Wen-hui Pao*, 6/30/65, in *SCMP* supp. no. 142, 8/27/65 ("When I heard people talking about how things were in Sinkiang, I was restless and disquieted"); *Kuang-chou Kung-tai Hui*, 8/6/69, in *SCMP* supp. no. 258, 9/16/69; and *JMJP* 5/26/73, in *SCMP* 5389, 6/7/73.

48. *JMJP* 2/13/75.

49. *Pei-ching Jih-pao*, 9/14/68, in *SCMM* no. 659, 6/16/69; *KMJP* 10/23/69; *JMJP* 1/6/69, 1/12/69, and 2/17/72.

50. *JMJP* 4/17/74.

51. *JMJP* 5/26/73, in *SCMP* 5389, 6/7/73.

52. "Chih-ch'ih ho chiao-yü tzu-nü shang-shan hsia-hsiang kan ko-ming" [Support and educate our sons and daughters in making revolution

by going up to the mountains and down to the villages], *Hung-ch'i*, no. 8, 8/1/72, p. 66. Actually, in this case these sentiments were voiced by the grandparents; the father refuted them.

53. *Kuang-chou Kung-tai Hui*, 8/6/69, in *SCMP* supp. no. 259, 9/16/69.

54. For cases, see *Pei-ching Jih-pao*, 6/5/68, in *SCMM* no. 654, 5/12/69; *JMJP* 11/13/69; *KMJP* 9/6/72, 12/20/72, and 6/13/73.

55. Radio Peking, 12/28/72, *FBIS* no. 6, 1/9/73. For a similar case, see *KMJP* 12/29/72.

56. For cases, see *JMJP* 1/5/69, 1/15/69, 2/13/69, 2/27/73, 3/27/73, and 8/20/73.

57. For one such case, from Yangchow, Kiangsu, where parents discouraged their children from going, see *JMJP* 12/21/71.

58. This was essentially the situation of most informants, especially those from bad class backgrounds.

59. This is how mobilization in a Shanghai enterprise was described; see *JMJP* 6/8/75.

60. Radio Shenyang, 7/28/74, *FBIS* no. 149, 8/1/74; and Radio Wuhan, 10/9/74, *FBIS* no. 198, 10/10/74.

61. See especially *Pei-ching Wan-pao*, 6/5/65, in *SCMP* supp. no. 142, 8/27/65; and *Pei-ching Jih-pao*, 6/6/65, in *SCMP* supp. no. 144, 10/11/65.

62. *Kuang-chou Kung-tai Hui*, 8/6/69, in *SCMP* supp. no. 258, 9/16/69. Professor Gordon Bennett of the University of Texas, who has made an extensive study of finance and trade in China, suggests that low-level trade jobs have also gained in attractiveness since migration to the rural areas began.

63. Of course, many ambiguities remain. For instance, are school dropouts included in the recent statistics, which for the most part focus on graduates of middle schools?

64. Radio Shenyang, 11/22/72, *FBIS* no. 235, 12/5/72, reports on 1971 but defines the 99.5 percent sent as "educated youths." Data for 1972 are apparently not available. For the remaining years, see Radio Shenyang, 11/22/73, *FBIS* no. 249, 12/27/73; *NCNA*, Peking, 11/23/74, *FBIS* no. 228, 11/25/74; and Radio Shenyang, 9/14/75, *FBIS* no. 192, 10/2/75.

65. Radio Wuhan, 7/11/74, *FBIS* no. 135, 7/12/74; and Radio Wuhan, 8/8/74, *FBIS* no. 156, 8/12/74.

66. Radio Shenyang, 9/22/74, *FBIS* no. 208, 10/25/74; Radio Shenyang, 9/14/75, *FBIS* no. 192, 10/2/75.

67. *JMJP* 8/4/75.

68. Radio Canton, 8/24/75, *FBIS* no. 168, 8/28/75. The broadcast spoke of a plan to send 80,000 in 1975. As of August, 20,000 had actually gone and 30,000 had sent "letters of resolution to go," which represented more than half of the recent secondary school graduates, hence the 80,000 must be in the neighborhood of 80 percent. The datum for 1972 is reported in *Hong Kong Standard*, 7/30/73.

69. William Shawcross, "City Children and Peasants: Not Quite Equal," *New York Times*, News of the Week, 2/15/76.

70. Reported by an informant interviewed by my assistant in 1975.

71. As far as is known, bribery does not play a significant role in these decisions, although during the Cultural Revolution, charges that officials of neighborhood administrations had accepted bribes were voiced. See Lynn T. White III, "Shanghai's Polity in the Cultural Revolution," p. 339.

72. *Pei-ching Jih-pao*, 7/13/68, in *SCMM* no. 655, 5/19/69.

73. Information from Professor Michel Oksenberg, University of Michigan, 1973; and William Kessen, ed., *Childhood in China*, p. 170.

74. *Hong Kong Standard*, 7/30/73.

75. Information from members of a Yale University group that visited China in May 1974.

76. Various observers have suggested that these paths to advanced training exist, but specific evidence for them does not seem to have come to light.

77. Information obtained by members of a Yale group that visited China in May 1974.

78. Such a role is played apparently by the system of children's palaces, the most prominent of which, in Shanghai, has been seen by many visitors, including myself. See the report by Frederick C. Teiwes, "Before and After the Cultural Revolution," pp. 343–44.

79. This and other officials, it should be noted, pointed to the mass nature of swimming in China, as popularized by Chairman Mao. South China's many rivers and lakes, for instance, have made it possible to popularize the sport far beyond the major cities.

80. Teiwes, "Before and After the Cultural Revolution," pp. 343–44.

81. Of course there are exceptions, as at least one informant reported.

82. One informant, a worker's son, had a poor political record; another, the son of a revolutionary cadre, had a good record, but he did not try to get out of the transfer.

83. Teiwes, "Before and After the Cultural Revolution," p. 344.

84. These reports come from senior middle schools in 1968, when not just the graduating class but the other classes were subject to the transfer. An informant from a lower middle school reports that about 25 percent of students were permitted to continue schooling.

85. See above, notes 42 and 43.

86. *JMJP* 3/17/73; story entitled "Hsien-wei chu-hsi sung nü hsia-hsiang" [The chairman of a county party committee sends his daughter to the countryside]. The article cited in note 43 appeared in the same issue but is a different one, entitled "Tso shang-shan hsia-hsiang ti tsu-chin p'ai" [Be a promoter of up-to-the-mountains-down-to-the-country-side].

87. *KMJP* 8/16/72.

88. *JMJP* 8/29/73.

89. Radio Lanchow, 9/14/73, *FBIS* no. 182, 9/19/73; Radio Nanchang, 9/14/73, *FBIS* no. 183, 9/20/73; and Radio Hofei, 1/24/74, *FBIS* no. 20, 1/29/74 (emphasis added). A similar charge was made by Radio Hang-chow, 9/20/73, *FBIS* no. 188, 9/27/73, for Chekiang.

90. Sources for this case (involving Chung Chih-min) can be found in note 61, chapter 6.

91. For cases, see *JMJP* 12/22/72, 8/20/73, and 10/29/73.

92. *JMJP* 11/23/76.

93. See the second part of chapter 6 and also the discussion in chapter 2 of advantages enjoyed by high-ranking cadre children in pre–Cultural Revolution elite schools.

94. See *JMJP* editorial, 8/7/73; also *JMJP* 10/26/75.

95. *JMJP* 12/22/73. For another case where a party committee acted to forestall favoritism, see *KMJP* 7/3/72.

96. Hence massive publicity is devoted to cases of leading cadres sending their children to the countryside. For examples, see *KMJP* 4/21/74

(military cadres); *KMJP* 4/22/75 (Peking government officials); and *JMJP* 5/3/75 (Tsinghai Military District cadres).

97. "To combat and prevent revisionism . . . they should not try to prevent their sons and daughters from going to settle in the countryside and make revolution there." "They," however, referred not only to party members, cadres and staff members but also to workers. Radio Shih-chiachuang, 4/26/75, *FBIS* no. 84, 4/20/75.

98. *JMJP* 4/22/75. Except for those wanting to settle in Yenan or in Pao-ti hsien, Hopei, where a famous model settlement is located, the 30,000 Peking youths described in the story settled in the suburbs.

99. *Nan-fang Jih-pao*, 1/18/69, *SCMP* supp. no. 246, 3/12/69.

100. An American schistosomiasis delegation that visited this farm in the spring of 1975 was told that the disease had been wiped out in 1971 (information from Professor Myron Cohen, Columbia University). *JMJP* 2/9/72 ran a story hailing a youth from Canton who conquered her fears of schistosomiasis with the aid of Chairman Mao's Thought, plunging barefoot into snail-infested waters.

101. In other parts of the country, the practice of permitting relatives to follow one another to the same destination still prevails. See *Je-ch'ing kuan-huai hsia-hsiang chih-shih ch'ing-nien ti ch'eng-chang* [Be enthusiastically concerned about the growth of sent-down educated youth], pp. 28–38, story about Shanghai youths in an Anhwei village.

102. *JMJP* 2/13/75.

103. Committee of Concerned Asian Scholars, *China: Inside the People's Republic*, p. 215; Kessen, *Childhood In China*, pp. 152, 170; and information from Professor Martin Whyte, University of Michigan, who was a member of the Kessen delegation.

104. Information from Professor Ross Terrill, Harvard University.

105. As noted in chapter 2, however, there is a question about the extent to which urban middle schools equip their students with technical knowledge and skills useful in the villages. See chapter 5.

106. Radio Canton, 10/12/74, *FBIS* no. 201, 10/16/74.

107. "Yi-ke hen hao-ti tien-hsing" [A very good model], *JMJP* 6/12/74. *KMJP* carried the article a day later, and Radio Peking broadcast it: 6/11/74, *FBIS* no. 115, 6/13/74.

108. *JMJP* 6/12/74.

109. For articles on educational work with parents see *KMJP* 9/23/71 (Shanghai's Huang-p'u district); *JMJP* 12/21/71 (a district in Yangchow, Kiangsu); and *KMJP* 9/6/70 (Tsingtao, Shantung). While the effort to influence parental communications with children in the countryside often takes the form of despatching group letters, there is little evidence that letters are censored, as alleged in *China News Analysis* no. 919, 5/11/73, p. 6. Thus, in 1975 a broadcast complained: "However, some parents worried that the daily life of their sons and daughters would be rough. Some wrote to their children, not encouraging them to settle in the countryside, but spreading the incorrect idea of becoming 'gold plated.'" Radio Nanning, 5/27/75, *FBIS* no. 103, 5/28/75.

110. For two examples of the numerous reports on activities for visiting UYs, see *KMJP* 12/23/71, and Radio Shanghai, 1/16/73, *FBIS* no. 13, 1/18/73.

111. Sometimes accounts appear of schools that not only seek to buck up the morale of their graduates in the countryside but also render concrete assistance. For one case from Anshan, Liaoning, see *JMJP* 9/5/65.

112. *JMJP* 7/25/75.
113. *JMJP* 6/12/74.
114. *JMJP* 2/13/75.
115. Radio Shanghai, 3/30/76, *FBIS* no. 64, 4/1/76.
116. See *KMJP* 4/29/74, and *JMJP* 4/22/75. Volunteers going to such places as Yenan were the exception.

CHAPTER 4

1. "Chih-ch'ih ho chiao-yü tzu-nü shang-shan hsia-hsiang kan ko-ming," *Hung-ch'i,* no. 8, pp. 66–68. That UYs "waver" most a few months after arrival is a common theme in the press. See, for instance, *KMJP* 12/5/68, case from Lai-yang *hsien,* (county) Shantung; and Radio Shen-yang, 11/22/72, *FBIS* no. 230, 11/28/72.
2. Informants report this.
3. For some examples see *KMJP* 7/8/70 (pig falling into nightsoil pit repels UY); *KMJP* 7/27/70 (San-ho hsien, Hopei); *KMJP* 11/15/70 (UY is afraid of leeches); *JMJP* 1/10/72, (returned educated peasant youth is afraid of contact with nightsoil); *JMJP* 2/25/72 (Ho-ch'ing, Yunnan).
4. *JMJP* 6/27/69.
5. D. Gordon White's "The Politics of Hsia-Hsiang Youth" stresses this point. The press also refers to this attitude (e.g., *KMJP* 5/22/69).
6. One informant made this point specifically in relation to friends of his in Canton. The press also refers to the awareness of the advantages that *t'ung-hsüeh* (schoolmates) not sent down enjoy, which contributes to wavering among UYs; see, e.g., *KMJP* 7/25/73.
7. *JMJP* 12/20/70, case from Fu hsien, Liaoning; *KMJP* 8/10/73, from Lung hsien, Shensi; and *Je-ch'ing kuan-huai hsia-hsiang chih-shih ch'ing-nien ti ch'eng-chang* [Be enthusiastically concerned about the growth of sent-down educated youth] pp. 28–38, case from Huo-ch'iu hsien, Anhwei. References to this collection of articles on the transfer will henceforth be abbreviated as *Je-ch'ing kuan-huai.*
8. Radio Hofei, 11/1/72, *FBIS* no. 214, 11/3/72.
9. Cases where this has been done very well include one from Tung-t'ai hsien, Kiangsu, *KMJP* 6/27/69, and one from Hui-ning hsien, Kansu, where a party secretary took a UY home and studied with him more than twenty times, *KMJP* 12/22/70.
10. Because the press tends to accent the positive, a count of articles on the subject would undoubtedly show a majority of cases fulfilling the norm.
11. For examples, see *KMJP* 7/25/73, and *JMJP* 8/18/74, as well as Radio Nanchang, 12/22/72, *FBIS* no. 4, 1/5/73, ("All Rural Comrades in Various Localities Should Welcome These Educated Young People and Should Never Regard Them as Mere Passersby").
12. *JMJP* 6/15/74. This point was made by authorities in Chu-chou, Hunan, which, as noted in chapter 3, has become a model case for urban-rural linkages in the transfer movement.
13. *KMJP* 12/24/70, article by the Graduates' Office of the Liaoning Revolutionary Committee (Pi-yeh Pan-kung-shih).
14. *KMJP* 12/17/70, article by Revolutionary Committee of Hung-ho Ha-ni Tzu Yi-Tzu Autonomous Chou, Yunnan.
15. Radio Changchun, 1/2/73, *FBIS* no. 7, 1/10/73.

16. Letter by an unnamed UY, "Kuan-yü chung-shih tui ch'ing-nien ti ssu-hsiang chiao-yü kung-tso ti t'ao-lun" [Discussion on emphasizing thought education work for youth], pp. 71-73.

17. See Martin King Whyte, *Small Groups and Political Rituals in China,* p. 11.

18. For some cases, see *KMJP* 7/11/69; also, *KMJP* 12/24/70, case from Hu-lin hsien, Heilungkiang; and *JMJP* 4/10/70, case from Ho hsien, Kwangsi.

19. *KMJP* 1/24/72, case from Ch'ang-ling hsien, Kirin.

20. *JMJP* 1/11/71, case from Lung-hua hsien, Hopei, (also reported in *KMJP* 11/20/70).

21. *JMJP* 6/13/69; the case is from An-t'u hsien, Kirin, but it is one in which subgroups among the schoolmates developed.

22. This point is made in Richard Kraus, "The Evolving Concept of Class in Post-Liberation China." See also White, "Politics of Hsia-hsiang Youth."

23. See chapter 6 for a discussion of UY behavior during the Cultural Revolution.

24. See below in this chapter.

25. The press does mention occasionally discord arising from Cultural Revolution membership in different organizations; see for instance *KMJP* 4/7/70. In other instances, UYs are charged with having "anarchist" or liberal ideas; see, e.g., *JMJP* 4/14/70, and *KMJP* 12/6/70, case from Yai hsien, Hainan, Kwangtung.

26. See "Using Mao Tse-tung Thought to Reeducate Educated Youths Coming to the Countryside," *Hung-ch'i* no. 9, 8/27/69, in *SCMM* no. 665, 9/22/69.

27. *JMJP* 12/14/72, case from Pei-chen hsien, Liaoning.

28. *KMJP* 6/30/73 and 10/15/70.

29. *KMJP* 6/30/73, case from Feng-jun hsien, Hopei. This article is in *Je-ch'ing kuan-huai,* pp. 39-50.

30. Radio Shenyang, 11/26/72, *SWB-FE* no. 4160, 12/2/72.

31. *JMJP* 7/5/73, reprinted in *Je-ch'ing kuan-huai,* pp. 13-19.

32. See *JMJP* 8/29/73 and 8/18/74. A case of UYs in a brigade in Huo-ch'iu hsien, Anhwei, reported in *Je-ch'ing kuan-huai,* pp. 28-38, shows variation among the UYs as well. "Last year," presumably 1972, the average number of days put in was 280, but the largest number ever was 324; see p. 37.

33. Chi hsien case, in *Je-ch'ing kuan-huai,* pp. 13-19.

34. E.g., *KMJP* 2/17/70, where UYs are reported as eating cold food in order not to hold up the work; also *KMJP* 7/20/70 (case from Lung hsien, Shensi); *KMJP* 8/10/73 (case from Ssu-hui hsien, Kwangtung); and Radio Nanchang, 9/16/73, *FBIS* no. 189, 9/28/73.

35. For one such example, see *KMJP* 11/3/69; for another, which stresses peasant leadership, *KMJP* 12/21/72.

36. *KMJP* 7/25/73 (case from Ch'ang-yi hsien, Shantung), and 12/24/70. The idea that UYs constituted an extra burden was still around in 1975; see Ch'i Chien, "Kung-ku ho fa-chan shang-shan hsia-hsiang ti ch'eng-kuo," p. 7.

37. For one example of fears of UY rebellion, see *KMJP* 11/23/69, case from Ling fu-yuan hsien, Liaoning.

38. *JMJP* 12/6/68.

39. *Lao-tung,* no. 3, 1964, pp. 6-7 (I am indebted to Chongwook Chung of Yale University for this reference).

40. State and army farms are not, however, homogeneous in composition. Regular and demobilized soldiers served on the two army farms described by informants. In Sinkiang, a great many Nationalist units were incorporated into the PCC after the communist takeover; see George Mosely, *A Sino-Soviet Cultural Frontier*, p. 35. It is not clear how much ex-soldiers mingle with UYs. One army farm company in Inner Mongolia was made up of 80 percent sent-down youths (see *JMJP* 11/9/73); who the others were was not revealed. State farms may also have a considerable mix of locals and newcomers. Ta-wang state farm near Canton is composed of 50 percent UYs and 50 percent peasants (information from Professor Myron Cohen, Columbia University, 1975). Another such Kwangtung state farm mentioned in the press (*KMJP* 4/22/75) was composed of 70 percent UYs.

41. *KMJP* 3/17/70 reports the case of a Peking girl who lived with a Mongol family; *KMJP* 3/17/71 describes a similar case involving a Tientsin girl. In still another press case, *KMJP* 5/5/71, a single individual, a girl from Shanghai, lived with a family in a small brigade of thirteen households in Hun-ch'un hsien, Kirin.

42. For a case of a Peking UY who settled by herself in a Mongol village and had great difficulty adjusting because of language and cultural differences, see *KMJP* 3/17/70. For another concerning a girl who went from Honan to an army farm in Tibet and did have problems of getting along with natives, not speaking Tibetan and not being accustomed to Tibetan food, see *KMJP* 11/1/68.

43. *JMJP* editorial, 11/11/57. This editorial dealt with returning educated peasant youths also.

44. Several informants reported this. For an important article acknowledging this, see Kuo Ch'ing, "Show Concern for the Life of the Educated Young People," *KMJP* 5/22/73, in *SCMP* 5406, 7/2/73.

45. Feng-jun hsien case, in *Je-ch'ing kuan-huai*, p. 40; and *KMJP* 5/6/71, Luan-nan hsien, Hopei, where UYs attributed their warm welcome to the labor shortage.

46. *JMJP* 1/24/73.

47. Victor Li, Stanford University Law School, reports that peasants he talked to often took pride in pointing to UYs who had found rural life very difficult at first, being unable to do hard agricultural labor, but who gradually got used to it and have been doing very well.

48. For examples of altruistic acts performed by peasants for UYs, see *KMJP* 1/4/70 (UY gets sick, team chief and peasant walk 8.5 kilometers to take him to a hospital); *KMJP* 2/17/70 (team chief rescues UY from water); and *KMJP* 3/22/70 (peasants care for sick UY). Conversely, an example of UYs caring for sick peasants is given in *KMJP* 7/3/72.

49. For examples, see *KMJP* 6/30/73 and 10/15/70.

50. *JMJP* 3/9/70.

51. Informants say they have heard of such cases.

52. S. Shum, "Living Conditions Still Backward in the Villages," *South China Morning Post*, 2/15/73.

53. For an example, see "The Heng-lan Tragic Incident," *Chih-nung Hung-ch'i*, no. 3, 11/67, in *JPRS* 44052, 1/17/68, *Translations on Communist China: Political and Sociological*, no. 436, pp. 16–23.

54. See *JMJP* 1/24/69, case from a small state farm in Kiangsu.

55. *JMJP* 4/22/72, case from Han-chiang hsien, Kiangsu.

56. Howard Chao of Yale University, who visited Hopei villages, similarly reports cadres as referring to UYs as "them." Still, it is worth noting

that the press does describe poor and lower-middle peasants who invite UYs to their homes, as in Ai-hui hsien, Heilungkiang, where the purpose, however, was reportedly to "recall past bitterness and compare it with present sweetness" (*Chieh-fang Jih-pao*, 2/10/70, in *SCMP* supp. no. 272, 5/21/70). *KMJP* 7/3/72 carries a case from Mu-ling hsien, Heilungkiang, where peasants invited UYs to New Year's feasts.

57. E.g., Radio Canton, 1/18/72, in *CNS*, no. 403, 1/20/72.

58. *Je-ch'ing kuan-huai*, pp. 13–19.

59. I am indebted for this story to Professor W. Parish, University of Chicago.

60. *KMJP* 1/8/69, case from Wu-yang hsien, Honan.

61. *KMJP* 12/21/72, case from Nan hsien, Hunan.

62. *KMJP* 5/6/71, case concerning UY participation in a post–Cultural Revolution campaign called *tou-p'i-kai*, "struggle, criticism, transformation."

63. "Taking the Revolutionary Path of Going to the Countryside," *Peking Review* 17, no. 19, 5/10/74, p. 21.

64. *JMJP* 11/7/73 (see also chapter 5).

65. Kuo Ch'ing, "Show Concern for the Life of the Educated Young People." Girls' physiological conditions apparently refers to the practice on PLA farms of assigning girls work as heavy as that for males, as reported by an informant. On medical care, *KMJP* 11/21/73 reports a case of equal treatment of UYs, who pay 70 *fen* per year for cooperation medical care. *JMJP* 12/23/73, has a story on UYs in E-chi-na banner (county), Kansu, on assistance to those who are sick.

66. Radio Nanchang, 1/15/77, *FBIS* no. 11, 1/17/77.

67. Radio Kweiyang, 9/11/73, *FBIS* no. 178, 9/13/73.

68. *JMJP* 4/30/73, reprinted in *Je-ch'ing kuan-huai*, pp. 5–12.

69. Radio Changsha, 9/25/73, *FBIS* no. 192, 10/3/73.

70. *Je-ch'ing kuan-huai*, p. 32, case from Huo-ch'iu hsien, Anhwei.

71. Ch'i Ch'ien, "Kung-ku ho fa-chan," p. 7.

72. Radio Wuhan, 10/22/75, *FBIS* no. 212, 11/3/75. For a similar exhortation, see Radio Hangchow, 4/27/75, *FBIS* no. 82, 4/28/75.

73. Radio Shihchiachuang, 4/26/75, *FBIS* no. 84, 4/30/75.

74. Radio Hofei, 11/1/75, *FBIS* no. 216, 11/7/75.

75. *NCNA*, Peking, 12/22/75, *FBIS* no. 248, 12/24/75.

76. Radio Peking, 1/18/75, *FBIS* no. 14, 1/21/75. It is possible, however, that the 40,000 included cadres sent not only in 1974 but earlier as well.

77. *NCNA*, Peking, 12/22/75, *FBIS* no. 248, 12/24/75.

78. *NCNA*, Shanghai, 5/5/70, in *SCMP* no. 4656, 5/14/70; and Radio Chengtu, 7/20/74, *FBIS* no. 141, 7/22/74. For another reference to Shanghai cadres having accompanied UYs, see *KMJP* 12/23/71.

79. Radio Wuhan, 10/8/74, *FBIS* no. 199, 10/11/74; and *NCNA*, Peking, 8/22/75, *FBIS* no. 165, 8/25/75.

80. *JMJP* 2/13/75; Radio Wuhan, 7/29/74, *FBIS* no. 148, 7/31/74; and Radio Sian, 10/15/74, *FBIS* no. 201, 10/16/74.

81. Radio Wuhan, 7/29/74, *FBIS* no. 148, 7/31/74. In the Sian case, 84 percent of 516 urban cadres were CCP members. In Chu-chou, 176 of 193 urban or 91 percent, cadres, were CCP members, and 13 of them were members of party committees. See *KMJP* 6/13/74.

82. *JMJP* 12/20/74, story on Sian cadres working with UYs.

83. Radio Wuhan, 7/29/74, *FBIS* no. 148, 7/31/74. Mention of "unified leadership" is in the Sian article, *JMJP* 12/20/74.

NOTES TO PAGES 147–154

84. This is implied in a story about the Chu-chou model, *KMJP* 6/13/74.

.85. Radio Lanchow, 2/17/75, *FBIS* no. 36, 2/21/75. A similar formulation broadcast from Wuhan speaks of national regulations. See Radio Wuhan, 7/29/74, *FBIS* no. 148, 7/31/74.

86. Radio Foochow, 1/4/75, *FBIS* no. 4, 1/7/75.

87. Radio Chengtu, 7/20/74, *FBIS* no. 141, 7/22/74.

88. Radio Canton, 8/24/75, *FBIS* no. 168, 8/28/75.

89. Radio Peking, 10/13/75, *FBIS* no. 201, 10/16/75. The broadcast also mentions other farms, including orchards, herb farms, and fish and livestock farms.

90. *JMJP* 6/12/74.

91. For examples of UY units that are separate accounting units, see Radio Nanking, 11/22/74, *FBIS* no. 231, 11/29/74.

92. For examples, see *KMJP* 6/30/73 and 10/15/70.

93. Ch'i Chien, "Kung-ku ho fa-chan," p. 8.

94. See, e.g., *JMJP* 1/24/73, case from Huai-te hsien, Kirin. Later in 1973, another report from the same county described a peasant *hu-chang* (household head) as teaching his charges to economize by cutting grass for fuel rather than buying coal with their living allowance. See *JMJP* 8/29/73.

95. Radio Nanking, 11/22/74, *FBIS* no. 231, 11/29/74. In Chu-chou, Hunan, one-third of the personnel of UY settlements are local peasants and cadres; see *KMJP* 6/13/74.

96. Radio Shenyang, 11/26/72, *SWB-FE* 4160, 12/2/72.

97. Radio Peking, 11/23/74, *FBIS* no. 229, 11/26/74.

98. E.g., *JMJP* 12/23/74.

99. Radio Nanking, 11/22/74, *FBIS* no. 231, 11/29/74. Also, larger collectives permit allocation of appropriate tasks to physically weaker youths, a point made by Ch'i Chien, "Kung-ku ho fa-chan," p. 8.

100. Ibid. Other stories on self-sufficiency appear in *KMJP* 8/10/73 (Lung hsien, Shensi); *KMJP* 7/20/73; and Radio Nanchang, 9/16/73, *FBIS* no. 189, 9/28/73.

101. *JMJP* 8/18/74. In 1973 they worked an average of 335 days.

102. Labor checks were instituted in the Huo-ch'iu, Anhwei, case; see *Je-ch'ing kuan-huai*, pp. 28–38 (there also was a system of asking for leave, rather than just taking it). The 22-day-per-month work requirement is reported by Radio Hofei, 11/1/72, *FBIS* no. 214, 11/3/72.

103. *JMJP* 12/23/74.

104. *JMJP* 8/29/73.

105. Ch'i Chien, "Kung-ku ho fa-chan," p. 8.

106. *CNS*, no. 494, 11/22/73.

107. Informants' reports, as well as that of Professor Myron Cohen, Columbia University, who visited Ta-wang State Farm outside Canton in 1975.

108. Radio Changchun, 6/5/75, *FBIS* no. 110, 6/6/75.

109. See, for instance, Radio Shenyang, 11/3/73, *FBIS* no. 216, 11/8/73, which describes work done in Hai-ch'eng hsien, Liaoning, to prepare sent-down youths for the winter.

110. Informants interviewed in 1975 by an assistant.

111. In Liu-ling, Shensi, it cost 600 *yuan* to build a new house, according to Jan Myrdal (quoted in William L. Parish, Jr., "Socialism and the Chinese Peasant Family," p. 621). If four youths occupy one house, the old state settlement fee would presumably have sufficed but would not

have left much for the other purposes for which the grant was intended. My informants, who left before the onset of remedial action, experienced a variety of housing conditions. In a good many cases housing does not seem to have been a problem, because the UYs were able to move into vacant houses formerly occupied by peasants who had migrated to Hong Kong or other places. Thus, one informant had been assigned to a team with ten other youths. They occupied three houses, of which only one had been newly built. In other cases, however, informants lived in villages in which new housing was not built and they had to make do with run-down, crowded accommodations.

112. *KMJP* 8/25/73.

113. *Je-ch'ing kuan-huai*, Feng-jun hsien case, pp. 48–49.

114. Radio Chengtu, 7/20/74, *FBIS* no. 141, 7/22/74.

115. Radio Chengtu, 10/29/73, *FBIS* no. 209, 10/30/73.

116. *JMJP* 8/15/73.

117. Radio Lanchow, 10/27/73, *FBIS* no. 210, 10/31/73. One *li* equals a third of a mile.

118. Radio Peking, 6/11/74, *FBIS* no. 115, 6/13/74.

119. *JMJP* 12/15/74, case of Lu-chai hsien, Kwangsi, where a county fertilizer plant supplied trucks. See Radio Canton, 8/24/75, *FBIS* no. 168, 8/28/75, for a story about the Canton Construction Work Bureau which sent technicians to 14 counties to help with the building of hostels.

120. See *KMJP* 10/28/73 for a description of a youth collective in Lu-feng county, Kwangtung, that had accumulated a common fund of 4,000 yuan which was apparently used for housing and other construction.

121. *Je-ch'ing kuan-huai*, Chi hsien case, p. 15.

122. Radio Hofei, 9/29/74, *FBIS* no. 197, 10/9/74.

123. *JMJP* 11/28/75. For other articles on housing problems, see *JMJP* 11/5/74, case from Ch'ung-li hsien, Hopei; and *JMJP* 12/20/74, Shansi urban cadre article.

124. Radio Foochow, 8/29/73, *FBIS* no. 172, 9/5/73. See also Radio Changchun, 9/10/73, *FBIS* no. 180, 9/17/73; and Radio Lanchow, 9/14/73, *FBIS* no. 182, 9/19/73.

125. Radio Hofei, 9/20/73, *FBIS* no. 188, 9/27/73; and Kuo Ch'ing, "Show Concern for the Life of the Educated Young People."

126. Radio Foochow, 8/29/73, *FBIS* no. 172, 9/5/73.

127. One example is a set of 29 sentences pronounced by the Tientsin Intermediate Level People's Court, dated August 5, 1973, and posted for public reading. Of the 29 sentences, 17 were for rape or seduction of girls sent to communes in the suburban areas of Tientsin. In 11 out of the 17 cases, the culprits had held official positions in the communes, primarily at the team and brigade levels. Cadres who took advantage of their official positions to engage in illicit relations with urban girls were punished severely. Sentences ranged from death to 15–20 years in prison. I am indebted to Professor Randle Edwards of Columbia University Law School for a copy of the Tientsin sentences. For a set of similar cases from Yunnan, see "Deal a Hard Blow to the Crimes Undermining the Program of Sending Educated Youths to Rural Areas," *Issues and Studies* 11, no. 3, 3/75, pp. 111–15. Questions can of course be raised concerning the authenticity of the cases, but they do appear to be genuine.

128. "Wrathfully Condemn Liu Shao-ch'i," *Ko-ming Ch'ing-nien*, no. 2 11/10/67, in *SCMP* 4093, 1/5/68.

129. E.g., *KMJP* 2/12/71.

130. Informants report this. See also *Wen-hui Pao*, 2/25/68, *SCMP* no. 4146, 3/26/68, which exhorts UYs to return to Sinkiang despite their fears of being "hit" in retaliation.

131. *JMJP* 3/8/70. One informant reports that in his production team, when the cadres diverted the state settlement fee to pay for chemical fertilizer instead of such basic supplies as chopsticks and bowls needed by the UYs, the sent-down youths expressed their "opinion" about this to the team chief. When the team chief did not respond, they took their complaint to the brigade cadre in charge of UY work, and the problem was resolved in favor of the UYs.

132. In the case of a Heilungkiang army farm, peasants reportedly criticized neglect of living conditions of UYs, evidently leading to redress; see *JMJP* 12/6/72. Also letters to higher levels can have some effect: *JMJP* 11/23/74 reports on an investigation launched upon receipt of a letter from married UYs in Hai-ch'eng, Liaoning.

133. For a comprehensive discussion, see Michel Oksenberg, "Methods of Communication within the Chinese Bureaucracy," pp. 21–28.

134. *JMJP* 8/9/72.

135. *JMJP* 11/5/74.

136. Urban youths did not have free access to such national documents. In this case they were not permitted to take notes.

137. It was this informant who was quoted earlier as reporting the remark of a county cadre to the effect that he could not understand why so many UYs were infected with bourgeois ideology.

138. Radio Kweiyang, 9/11/73, *FBIS* no. 178, 9/13/73.

139. Story on Hsiangyang commune, T'ien-ch'ang hsien, Anhwei, *KMJP* 5/21/73, in *SCMP* no. 5387, 6/4/73.

140. In chapter 3 it was noted that parents were happy with the Chu-chou innovation of establishing urban rural linkages, including utilization of urban cadres in UY settlement. Parents may well be reassured by the presence of these cadres, given the existence of abuses.

141. *JMJP* 12/20/74.

142. Radio Changchun, 12/19/75, *FBIS* no. 247, 12/23/75; and Radio Nanning, 6/29/76, *FBIS* no. 127, 6/30/76. See also Radio Wuhan, 10/22/75, *FBIS* no. 212, 11/3/75.

143. Radio Hu-ho-hot, 12/22/72, *FBIS* no. 251, 12/29/72. For a story about UY girls in Ho hsien, Kwangsi, some of whom thought about premature marriage, see *JMJP* 10/16/72; and for one from Honan where an "early marriage wind" blew, see *JMJP* 1/30/71. Both were apparently reactions to settlement difficulties.

144. Kuo Ch'ing, "Show Concern for the Life of the Educated Young People"; *JMJP* 7/9/76.

145. *KMJP* 5/6/74.

146. Martin Whyte, personal communication.

147. *People's Daily*, 3/22/75, in *FBIS* no. 62, 3/31/75; and *People's Daily*, 1/28/75, in *FBIS* no. 45, 3/6/75. The first case is about a Shanghai girl who wanted to marry a peasant in the suburbs; the second about a Tientsin girl who wanted to marry a peasant in a Mongol area of Kirin. In both, contemptuous views of peasants are voiced. See *KMJP* 12/21/73 for a contrasting case concerning an industrial plant party secretary in Chu-chou, Hunan, who encouraged his daughter to marry in the rural areas, even though doing so foreclosed return possibilities.

148. On Pai Chi-hsien, see *Peking Review* 17, no. 8, 2/22/74; *JMJP* 3/19/74; and *NCNA*, Peking, 5/30/74, in *FBIS* no. 107, 6/3/74.

149. *KMJP* 4/21/74.

150. Radio Shenyang, 11/15/74, *FBIS* no. 229, 11/26/74.

151. *JMJP* 11/23/74. The broadcast, cited in the preceding note, gives the same quote but in a more general sense, without mentioning a specific commune.

152. Radio Changchun, 12/27/75, *SWB-FE* no. 5104, 1/10/76; *JMJP* 5/10/76.

153. *JMJP* 7/9/76. Of course, the Hai-ch'eng report dates from 1974.

154. *NCNA,* Peking, 7/4/73, *FBIS* no. 131, 7/9/73.

155. Radio Shenyang, 12/22/73, *FBIS* no. 249, 12/27/73.

156. *JMJP* 7/9/76.

157. Radio Changchun, 1/15/75, *FBIS* no. 11, 1/16/75.

158. *KMJP* 5/21/73, story on Hsiangyang commune, T'ien-ch'ang hsien, Anhwei, in *SCMP* no. 5387. Study by locals includes teaching them to take a more nurturing and tolerant attitude toward UY shortcomings and errors. Thus, in Ming-shui hsien, Heilungkiang, instead of disdaining and looking down on the backward youths, the locals were encouraged to unite with them and encourage them to make progress; see Radio Peking, 3/30/73, *FBIS* no. 87, 5/4/73.

159. See *KMJP* 12/16/71, case from Lung-men hsien, Kwangtung; and *KMJP* 12/16/71, case from Pao-ying hsien, Kiangsu.

160. *KMJP* 5/5/74 and 4/25/74.

161. *Wen-hui Pao,* Shanghai, 2/17/69, in *SCMP* supp. no. 249, 5/2/69.

162. See Martin K. Whyte, *Small Groups and Political Rituals,* pp. 164–66.

163. Informants point to the low quality of study meetings, in which those who knew lots of quotations from Chairman Mao were able to distinguish themselves. Attendance was reportedly spurred by incentives such as work points and free meals.

164. E.g., *JMJP* 12/20/74, Sian urban cadre article.

165. Radio Shenyang, 11/15/72, *FBIS* no. 226, 11/21/72.

166. E.g., *JMJP* 1/24/69.

167. *JMJP* 12/20/74, op. cit.

168. *Wen-hui Pao,* Shanghai, 2/17/69, *SCMP* supp. no. 249, 5/2/69.

169. Cf. the concept of "strict political atmosphere" in Whyte, *Small Groups and Political Rituals.*

170. Two informants who came from working-class backgrounds reported this.

171. See, e.g., *KMJP* 4/22/75, for a story about a sent-down youth on a state farm in Kwangtung whose adjustment difficulties were aggravated because he came from a well-off family.

172. Cf. *KMJP*, 1/16/74, in which special educational efforts are described as having been designed to promote adjustment among UYs from Yangchow, Kiangsu, sent to a very difficult and poverty-stricken place.

CHAPTER 5

1. No job at the team or brigade level exempts the incumbent from manual labor. The team chief, for instance, is not exempt (*t'o-ch'an*), although he does receive work points for the meetings he attends. The brigade party secretary and chairman of the brigade's revolutionary committee used to be exempt on a half-time basis, but more recently the demand has been voiced that brigade cadres should work 300 days per

year. Commune officials do full-time administrative work, but they too should, according to the principle of cadre participation in labor, labor in the fields, formerly for at least 60 days; more recently for 200 days. Barefoot doctors and accountants may be half-exempt; teachers in daytime schools may teach full time during the busy season. At the team and brigade levels, compensation is in the form of work points; state salaries begin at the commune level. For an overview of rural office holding, see A. Doak Barnett, *Cadres, Bureaucracy, and Political Power in China*, pts. 2 and 3. For a statement of recent policy on labor participation, see "Ch'en Yung-kuei Report," *NCNA*, Peking, 12/24/76, *FBIS* no. 249, 12/27/76.

2. These distinctions are based on my judgment, as influenced by informants, the press, and secondary literature.

3. For articles about Hsing Yen-tzu, see *JMJP* 7/26/68; *KMJP* 3/30/70; and Radio Peking, 4/30/74, *FBIS* no. 94, 5/14/74.

4. *Cha-ken nung-ts'un kan ko-ming* [Take root in the village to make revolution], articles by and about Chu K'o-chia, pp. 51–61; Chu K'o-chia, "I Am Deeply in Love with Every Blade of Grass and Tree in the Border Region"; *KMJP* 5/5/72; *JMJP* 9/12/72, 5/20/73, and 10/18/75; "A Young Man's Wish," *Peking Review* 16, no. 34 8/24/73, p. 23; "Proclamation of National People's Congress of PRC," *Peking Review* 18, no. 4, 1/24/75, p. 10; Chung Hua-min, "A Preliminary Evaluation of the Tenth National Congress of the CCP," p. 22; and *JMJP* 1/22/74.

5. *KMJP* 3/8/70; *KMJP* 12/20/72 (also in *JMJP* 12/22/72).

6. *JMJP* 12/22/73.

7. Radio Harbin, 8/22/72, *FBIS* no. 169, 8/29/72; and *KMJP* 12/21/73. The diary of her brother Chin Hsün-hua was published in *Hung-ch'i*, no. 12, 11/29/69, and translated in *SCMM* no. 669, 12/29/69.

8. *JMJP* 2/13/75.

9. "Educated Shanghai Youths from Rural Areas and Frontiers Meet and Report on Their Achievements," *Chieh-fang Jih-pao*, 4/23/64, in *SCMP* supp. no. 125, 9/11/64. For a similar story, see Shanghai *Hsin-min Wan-pao*, 8/15/65, in *SCMP* supp. no. 145, 11/8/65.

10. "Selected Edition on Liu Shao-ch'i's Counterrevolutionary Revisionist Crimes," 4/67, in *SCMM* no. 653, 5/5/69, p. 5.

11. Radio Peking, 10/16/72, *FBIS* no. 204, 10/19/72; and Radio Hu-ho-hot, 12/22/72, *FBIS* no. 251, 12/29/72.

12. Radio Kweiyang, 9/8/73, *FBIS* no. 178, 9/13/73.

13. Radio Foochow, 12/23/75, *FBIS* no. 3, 1/6/76.

14. For an analysis of rural party membership at different levels of the hierarchy, see Michel Oksenberg, "Local Leaders in Rural China, 1962–1965," pp. 170–80.

15. *JMJP* 8/28/74, describing a commune in Ninghsia Hui Autonomous Region. For a story about a commune in Pao-ying *hsien* (county), Kiangsu, where reluctance to recruit UYs was based on their youth, see *JMJP* 8/23/73.

16. Cultural-technical recruitment is overstated since extraneous categories are included; membership in leading groups may be understated since a level of the hierarchy may not have been included.

17. Quoted in Byung-joon Ahn, "The Political Economy of the People's Commune in China," pp. 639–40.

18. Radio Changchun, 1/7/75, *FBIS* no. 7, 1/10/75; and Radio Changchun, 12/27/75 *SWB-FE* no. 5104, 1/10/76.

19. In January 1973, the cultural-technical jobs were listed as teacher, barefoot doctor, agricultural technician, accountant, and tractor driver. Two years later the same jobs were mentioned, along with livestock keeper, public health worker, and theory guide. Because of these additions the number should if anything have increased, not decreased. For Inner Mongolia, see below, table 15.

20. Liaoning is the only province in table 14 to show a temporary decline in the number of UYs. This drop may reflect reassignment or perhaps a more careful differentiation between UYs and RYs.

21. Radio Wuhan, 10/22/75, *FBIS* no. 212, 11/3/75.

22. It is noteworthy that Liaoning's 1974 recruitment data do not include UYs who settled in the countryside that year, of whom there were 220,000. Radio Peking, 12/23/74, *FBIS* no. 249, 12/26/74.

23. Some sent-down youths join the YCL before they are sent to the countryside. For an example, see Radio Shanghai, 3/19/75, *FBIS* no. 62, 3/31/75.

24. Victor C. Funnell, "The Chinese Communist Youth Movement, 1949–1966," p. 116.

25. "Integrating with Workers and Peasants," *Peking Review* 16, no. 19, 5/11/73, p. 7.

26. Radio Shihchiachuang, 3/8/75, *FBIS* no. 52, 3/17/75.

27. For example, in Tientsin prefecture, Hopei, 12,600 of 40,000 UYs, or 31.5 percent, had been recruited to major political and cultural-technical roles as of 1973, while Hopei's total stood at 20.8 percent. See *Cha-ken nung-ts'un kan ko-ming*, p. 24, and table 13. In Hui-ning county, Kansu, 1,620 of 5,000 UYs had become teachers, 1,500 instructors in Mao Tse-tung's Thought, and 1,265 scientific experiment group members. Although some individuals undoubtedly took part in more than one job or activity, the combined rate of major and minor recruitment could have reached 88 percent, far exceeding the national maximum estimate for both of 45 percent. See *JMJP* 5/4/73. Li-lin commune, Lo-p'ing county, Kiangsi, admitted 39 of its 200 UYs, or 17 percent, into the party, even while Kiangsi's overall party membership rate stood at 0.4 percent. See *KMJP* 8/10/73, and table 13.

Informants did not report high rates of recruitment. In those instances in which informants were able to cite specific figures for their production brigades, the percentage of major recruitment was under 10 percent. Thus in one brigade with 53 UYs, 2 became teachers, 3 became cadres. The exception was a brigade with 30 UYs in which 13.1 percent were recruited: 2 became teachers, 1 a midwife and a fourth a carpenter. One informant also knew of a neighboring brigade with about 20 UYs, whose commitment was high; about half of them became teachers, cadres, or workers in local factories. Virtually no one knew of UYs who had joined the CCP; one informant thought that, because of the proximity of Hong Kong, special care was taken in party recruitment. Yet, as the data on Kwangtung in table 13 show, that province's CCP recruitment is slightly above the national average. Many of the informants, it should be noted, had left China before the increased emphasis on UY recruitment.

28. In 1973, recruitment statistics were published for Kwangchow Production and Construction Corps units but the total number of UYs was not given. Since 1969, 7,200 UYs had joined the CCP and 55,000 the YCL; 2,080 had become company or administrative cadres (*chi-kuan kan-pu*); 190 had become deputy secretaries of YCL committees; and 78

members of party committees of regiments or divisions (see *JMJP* 6/25/73). Presumably these statistics apply to UYs on army farms in the three provinces in Kwangchow Military Region, i.e., Hunan, Kwangsi, and Kwangtung.

29. *China News Analysis*, no. 910, 2/16/73, p. 3, argues that UYs on army farms are a specially selected elite. But there is evidence of adjustment problems on army farms too (see chapter 4). Also, as noted in chapter 3, highly motivated young people might choose to go to communes in places such as Yenan prefecture. Recruitment statistics for the 20,000 UYs in the Yenan area are substantially higher than for Shensi as a whole. In 1973, 1.5 percent of Yenan's UYs had joined the CCP, but only 0.28 percent of Shensi's; 15 percent of Yenan's UYs had entered the YCL but only 5 percent of Shensi's, and 11.5 percent of Yenan's UYs had become cadres, but only 6.3 percent of Shensi's. For the provincial data, see table 13; for Yenan, *NCNA*, Peking, 11/15/73, *FBIS* no. 221, 11/15/73.

30. An informant who served on an army farm reports that UYs could rise to the level of company commander, but that in fact this happened very rarely. UY mobility above the level of deputy company commander tended to be blocked by the regular and demobilized military men that staff the upper echelons of the Production and Construction Corps. Because data concerning membership on leading groups are incomplete, it is difficult to verify this point. Still, tables 15–17, as well as the data on Kwangchow Military Region (see note 28) all show that more UYs joined the party than became army farm cadres, in contrast to the opposite finding presented earlier for the provinces. With regard to state farms, a report on 100,000 UYs serving on Yunnan state reclamation farms also shows more CCP members than leading group members: 2.7 percent joined the CCP, 33 percent the YCL, and 2.5 percent leading groups. See Radio Kunming, 12/21/75, *FBIS* no. 6, 1/9/76. Quite possibly, successful UYs on state and army farms are rewarded with CCP membership but only to a lesser extent with administrative positions.

31. "Using Mao Tse-tung Thought to Reeducate Youths Coming to the Countryside," *Hung-ch'i*, no. 9, 8/27/69, *SCMM* no. 655, 9/22/69. See also *KMJP* 8/22/72, for a story from a Fukien village where it was thought that UYs could not be cadres even after two or three years in the village.

32. *JMJP* 7/23/73. One of the reasons was that UYs came from afar; hence it was difficult to check on their family and social relationships, as is done when party members are recruited.

33. *JMJP* 7/25/73.

34. Informants stressed this point strongly. It should, however, be recalled that RYs do have an adjustment problem in that they too have urban aspirations strengthened by their educational experience. For one case, see *JMJP* 5/12/75.

35. *KMJP* 1/20/74, Chung-shan hsien, Kwangsi.

36. "Yi-ke she-hui chu-yi ti chiao-yü p'u-chi wang" [A socialist network for the universalization of education], *Hung-ch'i*, no. 6, 6/1/71, p. 40. P. J. Seybolt's *Revolutionary Education in China* carries this article but omits the word "returned" (*hui-hsiang*) in the phrase "31 percent are educated youths . . ." (p. 221).

37. Nan-an hsien does not show up in transfer articles published by *KMJP* and *JMJP* between 1968 and 1972.

38. Graham Johnson, "Rural Economic Development and Social

Change in South China"; and *JMJP* 5/4/73. It is possible that returned youths are included in the Hui-ning data.

39. This informant served in the progressive Po-lo county (see chapter 4).

40. William L. Parish, Jr. "Political Participation in Rural China." See also Oksenberg, "Local Leaders in Rural China," pp. 183–84.

41. *KMJP* 1/7/74. The cultural-technical jobs broke down as follows: 14 teachers, 4 tractor drivers, 6 heads of scientific experiment groups, and 1 agricultural technician.

42. In individual categories, UY recruitment can be higher, as in the commune in Lo-p'ing hsien, Kiangsi, where 39 out of 200 UYs, or 17 percent, joined the CCP. See note 27.

43. *JMJP* 2/13/75.

44. *JMJP* 7/9/76.

45. *JMJP* 4/30/73.

46. *KMJP* 8/29/72, San-ho hsien, Hopei.

47. *KMJP* 8/18/73, Kuei hsien, Kwangsi.

48. For other cases of UY reluctance to serve, see *JMJP* 7/25/68, 4/23/71, and 2/25/72; and *KMJP* 9/19/70.

49. This informant left China in 1970. Since then, a pattern has apparently developed of recruiting medical school students primarily from among barefoot doctors (information from Professor Myron Cohen, Columbia University, 1975). However, the odds are against an individual barefoot doctor making it to medical school; there are about one million of these paraprofessionals, while medical students make up only a fraction of China's three or four hundred thousand college and university students. See Chou En-lai, "Report on the Work of the Government," p. 21. In 1957–58, 54,800 out of 434,600 students were in the health field; see Leo Orleans, *Professional Manpower and Education in Communist China,* p. 69.

50. Informants' reports. The same point about the difficulties of reconciling pressures from above and below was made by an informant who became company commander on an army farm.

51. See *JMJP* 3/2/70 for the case of a UY in K'ai-p'ing hsien, Kwangtung, who became an accountant but feared making mistakes.

52. See *KMJP* 5/5/68, for the story of a UY in Hsin-chin hsien, Liaoning, who volunteered to go to the village but was disappointed in not being recruited. Also see *KMJP* 11/22/71, which describes the goals of UYs on an army farm in Shenyang Military Region.

53. This informant was eligible for major political recruitment since he came from the working class, but he spurned the opportunities available to him, disliking village life.

54. One informant resigned her teaching job after one semester because of the poor conditions under which she worked. See also below, section on rural education.

55. The activist in Mao Thought study mentioned above came from a bad class background. Her rise to higher political status was frustrated, but, interestingly, she was permitted to serve as a teacher. Another informant knew a UY in her village who was selected to attend a county-level training course for teachers of lower middle schools, but discovery of his bad class background caused him to be sent back to the village. Most informants from bad backgrounds perceived their status as an essentially ascriptive barrier to mobility. When queried about recruitment, they

would shrug and respond that only those with good backgrounds were eligible. See *Cha-ken nung-ts'un kan ko-ming*, pp. 117–23, for a story about a UY from an exploiter family, who settled in Ling-ling hsien, Hunan. Initially, he was full of resentment but he was educated in class struggle, became a propagandist, was then put in charge of insect extermination and machinery repair, and became leader of a youth group. Another such case is reported in *JMJP* 8/23/73, Pao-ying hsien, Kiangsu.

56. Hua Kuo-feng, "Mobilize the Whole Party, Make Greater Efforts to Develop Agriculture, and Strive to Build Tachai-Type Counties throughout the Country," p. 10.

57. The press, however, has reported shortages of trained personnel. In one brigade in Tseng-ch'eng county, Kwangtung, no one could repair any of twenty pieces of machinery. See "Four New Kinds of Schools," in Seybolt, *Revolutionary Education in China*, p. 182.

58. Leo Orleans, "Communist China's Education," p. 507.

59. *JMJP* 12/14/73.

60. E.g., *Pei-ching Jih-pao*, 5/4/63, in *SCMP* supp. no. 118, 3/2/64.

61. *KMJP* 7/1/73.

62. *JMJP* 5/5/74.

63. See "Shanghai reemphasises educational reform," *CNS* no. 573, 7/2/75.

64. For one such criticism, which charged that students knew so little that some "even applied cement to the fields, thinking that it was insecticide," see Radio Foochow, 1/15/74, *FBIS* no. 14, 1/21/74. For cases of promotion of vocational knowledge, see *KMJP* 4/22/75 (Peking) and *CNS* no. 573, 7/2/75 (for Shanghai).

65. *JMJP* 8/27/74.

66. See the broadcast cited in note 64 which dealt with a school in a county town. For discussion of a major effort to make education in a county town relevant to rural needs, see *KMJP* 5/11/75.

67. In articles in the press that appeared between 1968 and 1972, mention of UYs serving as barefoot doctors or health officers (*wei-sheng yüan*) totaled 62, the largest single item in the category of major cultural-technical recruitment. Teaching in locally run schools followed with 37 references, accountants were next (35), followed by mechanics (23) and agricultural technicians (15).

68. "A Hundred Examples of Liu Shao-ch'i's Speeches Opposing the Thought of Mao Tse-tung," *Ching-kang-shan*, 2/1/67 and 2/8/67 in *SCMP* supp. no. 173, 4/4/67, p. 12.

69. Radio Peking, 10/16/72, *FBIS* no. 204, 10/19/72; and Radio Hu-ho-hot, 12/13/72, *FBIS* no. 243, 12/15/72.

70. *JMJP* 6/15/74, Chu-chou, Hunan.

71. For an example of a county-operated training system, see *JMJP* 6/15/73 (also in *KMJP* 7/17/73), Ch'ang-ling county, Kirin. For an example of a commune-level spare-time school established in Lo-ch'eng county, Kwangtung, see *JMJP* 8/17/74.

72. *KMJP* 12/29/72, in *SCMP* no. 6296, 1/16/73.

73. "Schools Should Be a Tool for the Dictatorship of the Proletariat." *Red Flag* no. 5, broadcast by Radio Peking, 5/29/75, *FBIS* no. 105, 5/30/75.

74. Radio Shihchiachuang, 7/5/74, *FBIS* no. 131, 7/8/75.

75. *JMJP* 12/25/74. See *JMJP* 3/10/75 for a story on a college organized by nine Shanghai communes.

76. Radio Harbin, 11/2/73, *FBIS* no. 215, 11/7/73; and *KMJP* 6/16/74. For additional cases, see *JMJP* 6/7/74; "Correspondence Courses for Educated Youth in the Countryside," *Peking Review* 17, no. 30, 7/26/74, p. 23; and *CNS* no. 521, 6/12/74. See also Radio Kunming, 7/4/75, *FBIS* no. 133, 7/10/75; *JMJP* 5/12/75 on Wuhan correspondence schools; *JMJP* 7/3/73 for those in Chengtu; and *KMJP* 3/12/75 for a report on a correspondence school run by Shansi's Agricultural College.

77. In August 1973, a provincial book supply conference was held in Heilungkiang; see *KMJP* 1/9/74.

78. *Ta Kung Pao*, Hong Kong, 6/27/73.

79. *KMJP* 1/9/74; Radio Harbin, 11/25/73, *FBIS* no. 232, 12/3/73. This broadcast mentioned "revolutionary works" designed to combat bad habits and customs.

80. *JMJP* 8/10/73 (or *KMJP* 8/10/73).

81. *JMJP* 7/3/75; also *NCNA*, Peking, 7/18/75, in *FBIS* no. 140, 7/21/75.

82. Radio Shanghai, 1/16/73, *FBIS* no. 13, 1/18/73; *KMJP* 1/17/74; Radio Shanghai, 1/17/74, *FBIS* no. 18, 1/25/74; Radio Shanghai, 2/20/75, *FBIS* no. 40, 2/27/75; and *JMJP* 5/3/75.

83. The only informant who took part in a hsien training program—one for barefoot doctors—reports that most of his classmates were local youths.

84. The press reports intensively on UY political study, but the impression thus created may be more of an artifact of "politics in command" than of the real situation; see chapter 4.

85. One informant reports that his commune's machine repair station employed two graduates of an engineering college. But since skilled workers were able to do all the work, the two were transferred to the hsien. See Benedict Stavis, *Making Green Revolution,* esp. ch. 4, "Strengthening Agro-Technical Services." See also below, section on "Technical Innovation."

86. Clifton R. Wharton, Jr., "Education and Agricultural Growth."

87. *KMJP* 12/29/72, in *SCMP* no. 6296, 1/16/73.

88. "On Khrushchev's Phoney Communism and Its Historical Lessons for the World," in A. Doak Barnett, *China After Mao,* p. 191.

89. *NCNA*, Peking, 5/3/76, *FBIS* no. 88, 5/5/76.

90. *JMJP* 10/31/75. It is possible that some of these are independent youth teams.

91. *JMJP* 11/7/73, second of two stories under the same headline, p. 3.

92. *JMJP* 4/22/72. Other stories on these UYs appear in *Je-ch'ing kuan-huai hsia-hsiang chih-shih ch'ing-nien ti ch'eng-chang,* pp. 28–38; and *JMJP* 7/18/74.

93. Chi Yen, "Going in for Agriculture in a Big Way," esp. p. 7.

94. Yen Chih, "Be Promoters in Helping Educated Young People Settle in the Countryside."

95. See *KMJP* 11/3/73, about a UY in Ch'ien-chiang hsien, Hupei, who reported to the party branch on capitalist deviations and got the leaders' support in struggling against them. In the case cited in note 51, the UY, once he had become a cadre, exposed improprieties, in this instance advocacy by "some people" of increasing distribution to villagers (*to ch'ih to fen*).

96. *KMJP* 1/20/74, case from Chung-shan hsien, Kwangsi.

97. *JMJP* 11/7/73, the first of two stories under the same headline,

p. 3; and *JMJP* 6/8/74. These articles describe a Peking youth in Yen-ch'uan hsien, Shensi, who engaged in a series of conflicts with local leaders.

98. *KMJP* 2/5/72, Wei-ch'ang hsien, Hopei; *KMJP* 10/4/72, Chi hsien, Hopei. In both cases, the UY cadre troubleshooters were women.

99. *JMJP* 7/15/75, Hsin-pin hsien, Liaoning.

100. The role of the UY collective was also important in the case of Sun Yu-wen.

101. *JMJP* 11/23/74, Hai-ch'eng, Liaoning.

102. *JMJP* 1/11/71. In a brigade in Yuan-chiang hsien, Hunan, where "some people" in a team tried to pressure the accountant into distributing more to the members, a female UY, reportedly with the support of poor and lower-middle peasants, came to the aid of the accountant, but fellow UYs, believing that this was none of her business, failed to support her.

103. Sun Yu-wen, note 99, was a miner's son. The Peking youth in Yen-ch'uan hsien, note 97, also had a revolutionary background.

104. A UY cadre may also come under pressure from his peers to misuse his powers on their behalf. In one case, UYs wanted to borrow money from a UY accountant, knowing the team had earned some from the sale of cotton. The accountant refused on principle. *JMJP* 2/9/70.

105. During the Cultural Revolution, the following example was publicized from Hsin-hui county, Kwangtung: "Chang X-x (female), an aid-agriculture youth in Huangpu brigade . . . disclosed that cadres of her village had distributed grain among themselves privately. The cadres incited the commune members to denounce her and did not allow her to work in that production team. With tears in her eyes she was forced to move to another village." See *Chih-nung Hung-ch'i,* no. 7, 1/68, in *SCMP* no. 4125, 2/26/68.

106. *KMJP* 12/17/70, Ku-an hsien, Hopei.

107. See *JMJP* 9/11/71 for an interesting case of a UY from K'o-tso-hou banner (county), Kirin, who became a cadre and lost his *kan-ch'ing* (relations based on good feelings) with the peasants. Another case, of a female UY who became team chief and failed to practice the mass line, is in *JMJP* 1/30/70, from Huan-jen hsien, Liaoning.

108. *KMJP* 11/22/71, Lung-lin hsien, Kwangsi.

109. *JMJP* 10/16/72, in *SCMP* 5244, 10/30/72, Pao-ying hsien, Kiangsu.

110. In this connection, see Clifton R. Wharton, Jr., "Risk, Uncertainty and the Subsistence Farmer."

111. At the very least, UY proposals may be scrutinized carefully. For an example, see *JMJP* 1/18/73, case of a group of UYs in Lung hsien, Shansi, who proposed construction of a hydroelectric power station.

112. *JMJP* 5/26/73, Erh-yuan hsien, Yunnan.

113. *KMJP* 5/30/75, case of a UY girl in K'ai-yuan hsien, Liaoning, who was sent to a team to transform it and almost immediately, apparently, became its team chief. See also *KMJP* 1/3/74, for a case from Inner Mongolia. A major article on the transfer published in late 1975 spoke of the growing practice of "planned assignment of educated youths to backward teams." It mentioned K'ai-yuan county, Liaoning, which in 1974 sent 200 "outstanding educated youths" to shoulder heavy burdens "in the county's backward teams, where they scored significant successes." See "Yi-ch'ien-erh-pai-wan chih-shih ch'ing-nien kuang-jung wu-nung," [Twelve million educated youths are gloriously serving the peasants], *JMJP* 12/23/75.

114. For one example, from Yen-ch'ing hsien, Peking suburbs, see *KMJP* 9/12/74. A famous model, Hsing Yen-tzu, a returned youth who has become a Central Committee member, pioneered a "women's fish-catching team," which some people looked down upon, since women were not supposed to be able to do that kind of work. *JMJP* 7/26/58.

115. Personal communication from Professor William L. Parish, Jr., University of Chicago.

116. See, e.g., *KMJP* 6/12/72, Shang-hang hsien, Fukien.

117. Jack Chen, *A Year in Upper Felicity*, p. 26.

118. The sources for the twelve cases are, in the order in which they were listed: *JMJP* 1/24/72; *JMJP* 8/23/73; *KMJP* 8/16/72; *JMJP* 12/25/72; *JMJP* 10/16/72, in *SCMP* 5244, 10/30/72; *JMJP* 2/9/72; *KMJP* 7/25/73; *KMJP* 3/28/74; *JMJP* 8/23/73; *KMJP* 11/20/72; *KMJP* 12/16/72; *JMJP* 2/25/72.

119. "Mass Scientific Experiments Yield Fresh Results in China's Countryside," *NCNA, Daily News Release*, Peking, 12/29/74.

120. Yenan: *New York Times*, 7/3/71, p. 2; Ssu-hui hsien: Radio Canton, 10/10/74, *FBIS* no. 199, 10/11/74.

121. For one of many cases of RYs, see *KMJP* 10/27/72, in *SCMP* 5252, 11/9/72, concerning the deeds of Liu Ch'ang-yin, who returned to his Korean mountain village in An-t'u hsien, Kirin, in the 1950s and spent many years experimenting with the cultivation of rice in the mountains.

122. Jen Wei-nung, "Chia-ch'iang nung-yeh k'e-hsüeh yen-chiu" [Strengthen study of agriculture science].

123. *Je-ch'ing kuan-huai*, pp. 44–46.

124. See note 119.

125. *Plant Studies in the People's Republic of China*, pp. 163–64.

126. Jen Wei-nung, "Chia-ch'iang nung-yeh k'e-hsüeh yen-chiu," p. 32, writes that "it is wrong to disregard the role played by special agricultural research organs and scientists and technicians."

127. *KMJP* 2/21/71, Nei-huang county, Honan. There are also cases of young people who learn informally, score some successes, and then develop a relationship with professional scientific bodies. For a well-publicized case, that of Cheng Yu-chih, who settled in a Hopei village in 1964, see *JMJP* 5/15/72, and *NCNA*, Peking, 5/29/74, in *FBIS* no. 106, 5/31/74. Cheng also became party secretary of his brigade.

128. Dr. Benedict Stavis, Cornell University, personal communication.

129. *Plant Studies in the People's Republic of China*, p. 164.

130. *JMJP* 9/17/73; perhaps he had benefited from the facilities in Shanghai's famous Children's Palace.

131. *KMJP* 12/7/73; during the Cultural Revolution, a good many nonparticipating youths stayed home, and some studied on their own.

132. The UY who turned alkaline land into productive land had been sent down in 1964; her success was reported in 1972 (the 11th of the 12 examples). Similarly, Cheng Yu-chih, a fruit specialist, came to the village in 1964; his successes were reported in the 1970s; see note 127.

133. See note 49, this chapter.

134. For material on these problems, see Seybolt, *Revolutionary Education in China*, pt. 7, "Elementary Education, Rural Schools."

135. Some efforts to provide training for village teachers have been made. See Seybolt, pp. 166–77, and *CNS* no. 386, 9/16/71, for a description of mobile teams sent by Kwangtung Normal College. Most of the effort is probably devoted to training teachers for lower middle school

classes attached to village primary schools. See *KMJP* 10/29/74, in *FBIS* no. 241, 12/13/74, for training programs run by Peking Teachers' College.

136. *JMJP* 2/18/75, Li-chiang Na-hsi autonomous hsien.

137. See Donald J. Munro, "Egalitarian Ideal and Educational Fact in Communist China," pp. 256–304.

138. *JMJP* 2/18/75. For the national data, see John W. Lewis, "China Trip Notes," p. 156; and Chun Pu, "How China Popularizes Education," p. 9. In 1976, primary school enrollment was reported as 150 million; see *JMJP* 6/1/76.

139. *JMJP* 7/9/70, Yi-ch'uan hsien, Shensi.

140. *JMJP* 11/27/73.

141. *JMJP* 8/10/72.

142. *KMJP* 2/18/73.

143. Transfer articles that appeared in *JMJP* and *KMJP* between 1968 and 1972 mentioned UYs becoming teachers 37 times, the second most frequently mentioned major cultural-technical recruitment. See note 67, this chapter.

144. *KMJP* 2/21/73.

145. For the Yao, see *JMJP* 1/11/73, Chung-shan hsien, Kwangsi, and *JMJP* 8/23/73, Pa-ma Yao autonomous hsien; for the Pu-yi, *KMJP* 12/16/72, Ts'e-heng Pu-yi autonomous hsien, Kweichow; for the Tung-hsiang, *JMJP* 5/4/74, Tung-hsiang autonomous hsien, Kansu.

146. Radio Kunming, 9/14/72, in *FBIS* no. 181, 9/15/72, Hung-ho Hani and Yi autonomous prefecture, Yunnan.

147. For one case, see *KMJP* 5/12/70, A-erh-k'e-sun minority, Sinkiang.

148. *JMJP* 5/25/75, K'ang-lo hsien, Kansu.

149. *JMJP* 2/18/75, Wu-ch'i hsien, Szechwan. An informant who had been a teacher complained that cadres in her village failed to repair desks and chairs and were generally indifferent.

150. *KMJP* 12/15/73, Yen-ch'eng hsien, Kiangsu. The cases cited in note 145 also contain descriptions of makeshift arrangements, such as permitting children to bring their younger siblings to class. See also *JMJP* 5/4/74, Chia hsien, Honan.

151. "The Poor and Lower-Middle Peasants Have Acquired Socialist Culture," in Seybolt, *Revolutionary Education in China*, p. 202. The article is an investigation report from Lin-t'ao hsien, Kansu.

152. *JMJP* 1/11/73, Chung-shan hsien, Kwangsi.

153. "Poor and Lower-Middle Peasants," p. 202.

154. Thus, when the dropout rate is unknown, it is difficult to evaluate claims of extremely great progress in the universalization of education, such as the claim that in 1973, "93 percent of all school-age children were in school." See Chun Pu, "How China Popularizes Education," p. 9.

155. UYs have also taught literacy classes for adults. See, e.g., *JMJP* 11/27/73, Shun-ch'ang hsien, Fukien, and the Red Flag production brigade case cited earlier, note 92.

156. John S. Aird, *Population Estimates for the Provinces of the People's Republic of China*, p. 22. The estimates are for 1974. The UY data are from table 9.

157. Ibid., p. 22. Honan: 65.8 million (1974); Sinkiang: 8.6 million (1974); Inner Mongolia: 7.7 million (1974).

158. *Kung-jen Jih-pao* 3/22/64, in *Communist China Digest*, no. 122, *JPRS* 25108, 6/16/64.

159. *JMJP* 7/28/69, Kai hsien, Liaoning. See also *KMJP* 7/24/73, T'ung-hsü hsien, Honan, for a similar case.

160. Radio Peking, 5/4/74, *FBIS* no. 91, 5/9/74. For similar stories, see *JMJP* 5/13/74; and Radio Peking, 5/9/74, *FBIS* no. 93, 5/14/73. For an example of a more modest undertaking, see *KMJP* 6/25/71, which describes an army farm set up in the winter of 1969 near Wu-liang-su Lake in Inner Mongolia. The youths of this regiment-sized unit of 2,500 to 3,000 came from such cities as Peking, Tientsin, and Shanghai. Within two years, they had reclaimed nearly 10,000 mou of land, built factories, planted more than 10,000 fruit trees, caught 380,000 catties of fish, and harvested an enormous quantity of reeds and rushes from the swamps of the lake.

161. "More Tropical Crops on Hainan Island," *Peking Review* 17, no 23, 6/7/74, p. 31, mentions progress in establishing new rubber estates.

162. Radio Harbin, 12/29/75, *FBIS* no. 3, 1/6/76.

163. Theodore Shabad, *China's Changing Map*, p. 243.

164. See the discussion by Dwight Perkins, "Constraints Influencing China's Agricultural Performance," p. 353.

165. The theme of UY participation in farmland capital construction was stressed after the national conference on multiplying the number of Tachai-type counties. See, e.g., Radio Changchun, 12/19/75, *FBIS* no. 247, 12/23/75.

166. Radio Lanchow, 5/1/72, *FBIS* no. 87, 5/3/72. There are numerous cases of very difficult living conditions. For another example see *KMJP* 5/9/72, which tells of eight girls on a horse farm in the Northwest. Their grass house had holes in it, letting in wind and rain. They got up at 3:00 AM and returned late at night; they cut their own firewood, etc.

167. *KMJP* 6/12/73, in *SCMP* no. 5399, 6/21/73. It is worth noting that three years earlier a story had appeared on these UYs in which it was said that some of them had been reluctant to build permanent houses. They felt that they would be leaving in a few years, once having been reeducated. *KMJP* 6/22/70.

168. *KMJP* 5/13/70 carries a story about UYs in Sinkiang engaged in sinking a well. For lack of oxygen, the lamps went out, but several UYs kept on working in the well for another 40 minutes. The case of a female UY on an army farm in Inner Mongolia who kept on working despite sickness is in *KMJP* 4/4/72. For a case of a male UY in Ch'ien-kuo hsien, Kirin, who got liver disease while repairing water irrigation works but kept on working for 20 days before being sent to a hospital see *KMJP* 4/7/70. *JMJP* 11/22/72 describes two female UYs on an army farm who died trying to save grazing animals. And, for a case of a female UY whose hand got caught in a grass-cutting machine and who, for the sake of saving the machine, asked that her arm be amputated, see *KMJP* 6/29/69, Shuo hsien, Shansi.

169. For mention of such "advanced collectives," see Radio Nanking, 2/23/75, *FBIS* no. 40, 2/27/75; Radio Canton 8/11/75, *FBIS* no. 156, 8/12/75; Radio Chengtu, 11/6/75, *FBIS* no. 220, 11/13/75; and *JMJP* 6/22/76.

170. An interesting illustration comes from a commune in Ming-shui hsien, Heilungkiang. After a group of UYs complained about the poor living conditions, local leaders settled them separately, but with peasant supervision. The separate UY collective subsequently undertook land reclamation in very difficult circumstances, prevailing even though the "thought of some people wavered." See *KMJP* 7/10/70.

171. Arthur G. Ashbrook, Jr., "China: Economic Overview, 1975," p. 30.

172. Pi-chao Chen, "Overurbanization, Rustication of Urban-Educated Youths, and Politics of Rural Transformation," pp. 377-78.

CHAPTER 6

1. *JMJP* 5/6/75, editorial note appended to story on reeducation of UYs in Ch'ang-ling *hsien* (county) Kirin.

2. Individuals may also be allowed to return to alleviate family hardships. In 1974, for instance, Ch'ang-chou city, Kiangsu, sent out a notice (*t'ung-chih shu*) according to which an only child could return to be with his parents. See *JMJP* 4/4/75. It is not clear whether nationwide regulations have been issued to this effect, which would amount to the practice of permitting one child per family to stay in the city, or whether local administrative units draw up their own rules, perhaps in the light of national guidelines. Informants referred to regulations (*kuei-ting*) that permitted one sibling to return if two were also in the countryside, or for a child to return if needed to care for sick parents. The press, it is worth adding, praises those who do not take advantage of such regulations but insist, because of their pure ideology, on staying in the village despite the consequent hardships for the family. See, e.g., *KMJP* 2/21/71, story of Nanking cadre daughter who refused to return from Inner Mongolia, despite her mother's sickness.

3. For some examples of UYs working in commune factories, see *KMJP* 8/22/72 and *JMJP* 11/17/75. In the latter case, UYs started a factory by themselves in a commune in Lin-ch'uan county, Anhwei. According to one report, UYs "may also be settled in factories run by communes or production brigades." See Radio Lanchow, 2/17/75, *FBIS* no. 36, 2/21/75.

4. "Outline of Education on Situation for Companies (Lesson Five)," prepared by Propaganda Division, Political Department, Kunming Military Region, 4/6/73.

5. Radio Shenyang, 4/6/75, *FBIS* no. 67, 4/7/75. One informant who had served on an army farm thought that UYs joining the regular PLA would of course return to the army farm on demobilization.

6. For other examples, see Radio Lanchow, 6/15/75, *FBIS* no. 118, 6/18/75; and Radio Shanghai, 3/31/75, *FBIS* no. 63, 4/1/75.

7. *JMJP* 1/18/75.

8. Frederick C. Teiwes, "The Assignment of University Graduates in China, 1974," pp. 308-09. It is not clear, however, whether the statement applied only to Peking University or to all higher schools.

9. See, e.g., *JMJP* 8/29/73, Hsia hsien, Shansi.

10. Radio Shihchiachuang, 2/26/75, *FBIS* no. 40, 2/27/75.

11. Radio Harbin, 8/14/75, *FBIS* no. 160, 8/18/75.

12. Radio Urumchi, 8/15/75, *FBIS* no. 161, 8/19/75. In the case of the college graduate who insisted on leaving Shanghai in order to return to his Kiangsu army farm, he was given a position in accord with his training. See above, note 7.

13. Radio Harbin, 7/6/75, *FBIS* no. 132, 7/9/75; and Radio Tsinan, 7/10/75, *FBIS* no. 135, 7/14/75.

14. University presidents from the United States who visited China in November 1974 were told that the number of college graduates was clearly too low. See "Report of the Delegation of University and College Presidents to the People's Republic of China."

15. As of early 1977, the new leaders do not seem to have taken action on this issue.

16. Peter J. Seybolt, "Editor's Introduction." This figure was supplied by a North American professor of Chinese origin who obtained it in Peking but regards it as a highly preliminary estimate. He does not wish to be named.

17. Radio Kunming, 12/21/72, *FBIS* no. 248, 12/22/72.

18. See table 14, chapter 5; Radio Hofei, 4/10/75, *FBIS* no. 71, 4/11/75; and Radio Peking, 12/10/75, *FBIS* no. 240, 12/12/75.

19. Graham Johnson, "Rural Economic Development and Social Change in South China" p. 41.

20. Information from Howard Chao, Yale University, 1973.

21. *JMJP* 7/5/73; and *NCNA*, Peking, 7/4/74, *FBIS* no. 131, 7/9/74.

22. Radio Harbin, 5/21/76, *FBIS* no. 106, 6/1/76.

23. *Rural Small-Scale Industry*, chapter 10.

24. *KMJP* 10/4/72.

25. *KMJP* 12/21/73.

26. *JMJP* 12/22/74.

27. For example, between 1963 and 1966, 60,000 Shanghai youths settled in the Tarim Basin, Sinkiang. A story about them that appeared in 1974 is written as if they were all still there. See note 160, chapter 5.

28. *Wen-hui Pao*, Hong Kong, 11/26/73, quoted in *CNS* no. 495, 11/19/73; and *JMJP* 10/15/73.

29. Radio Foochow, 11/22/72, *FBIS* no. 228, 11/24/72; and Radio Chengtu, 12/21/72, *SWB-FE* no. 4178, 12/23/72. The Szechwan figure includes students admitted to specialized middle schools.

30. Radio Peking 12/6/72, in *FBIS* no. 240, 12/12/72.

31. Radio Foochow, 9/27/73, *FBIS* no. 191, 10/2/73.

32. *JMJP* 10/15/74; and Radio Harbin, 9/18/75, *FBIS* no. 183, 9/19/75.

33. Informants who experienced the enrollment periods of 1970 to 1972 stress the very small numbers involved. Typically, they speak of only individual cases. One informant's production brigade had absorbed about 50 UYs as of 1970 and 1971; not one was chosen for higher study. In a neighboring brigade with 20 UYs, however, 2 were chosen in 1971.

34. Erica Jen, Yale College, 1974. Ms. Jen spent some time at Peking University.

35. See, e.g., *KMJP* 12/24/69.

36. *KMJP* 12/21/74 refers to a "part" (*yi pu-fen*) of Yunnan UYs as having been hired by factories in 1971.

37. The complaint that Kwangtung has lagged with regard to industrialization is not new. See Ezra F. Vogel, *Canton Under Communism*, p. 130.

38. *JMJP* 7/14/76.

39. Radio Wuhan, 7/24/76, *FBIS* no. 145, 7/27/76.

40. *CNS* no. 582, 9/10/75.

41. The informant who reported that in her commune 70 UYs out of 800 were reassigned also reported that 30 were sent to Canton and 40 to hsien factories, as well as to commercial units.

42. *Rural Small-Scale Industry*, chapter 10.

43. *Chih-shih ch'ing-nien tsai pei ta-huang*, a book of photos about UYs on Heilungkiang army farms, contains pictures of young people, presumably sent-down youths, working in a mine and an oil refinery; see pp. 111, 112.

44. See, e.g., Radio Kunming, 2/6/72, *FBIS* no. 29, 2/10/72; and Radio Shenyang, 3/2/72, *FBIS* no. 45, 3/6/73.

45. Interview data. Good health is obviously also important, especially in the case of the PLA.

46. Of course, those who commit crimes are subject to arrest and hence leave the rural unit by that route. One informant, it is worth noting, knew of a schoolmate who had failed in escaping to Hong Kong and who then was assigned to factory work, much to the informant's puzzlement.

47. *KMJP* 7/27/72.

48. *JMJP* 3/4/72.

49. However, one informant who served on an army farm, reports that in 1970 it sent to higher schools five UYs whose records were all right but not outstanding. For the case of a sent-down youth who feared that causing offense would jeopardize his chances to return, see *KMJP* 2/12/71, Li-shu hsien, Kirin.

50. *JMJP* 5/6/75, Ch'ang-ling hsien, Kirin.

51. See, e.g., *KMJP* 5/17/72, for an article on three high achievers who were sent to the Peking Industrial College. One, from Yenan, had been a Yenan hsien party committee member; another had been a member of the standing committee of Sun-wu hsien, Heilungkiang; and the third was a commune party committee member in Yün-ch'eng hsien, Shansi. For other examples, see note 7, above, and Radio Shenyang, 3/2/72, *FBIS* no. 45, 3/6/72.

52. In Fukien, special attention was paid in 1953 to enrollment of sent-down youths: "more students of this category have been enrolled in schools from places settled by large numbers of educated youths." See Radio Foochow, 9/27/73, *FBIS* no. 240, 12/12/72.

53. Radio Wuhan, 7/20/74, in *CNS* no. 527, 7/24/74; and Radio Tsinan, 7/10/75, in *FBIS* no. 135, 7/14/75.

54. Radio Wuhan, 7/6/75, *FBIS* no. 130, 7/7/75. The broadcast seems to refer to Hupei only.

55. The complex process whereby local and intermediate-level bodies make selections is described in *CNS* no. 480, 8/16/73, for Hupei, in which it is noted that the initial list of candidates approved by communes and factories should be three times as large as the number of students ultimately enrolled. See also Frederick C. Teiwes, "Before and After the Cultural Revolution," pp. 362–63. He reports that two to five times as many candidates are recommended as there are places.

56. Visitor's report by Professor Steven Goldstein, spring 1973.

57. These attacks centered on the issue of entrance examinations. Although such tests have been formally abolished, academic institutions review the candidate's record and conduct tests to measure his or her degree of preparation and ability to solve problems. In 1973, the tests were administered in a rather rigorous manner. One candidate, Chang T'ieh-sheng, spearheaded the attack against this restoration of "bourgeois" examinations. A junior middle school graduate, Chang had settled in a commune in his home county of Hsing-ch'eng, Liaoning, in 1968. In 1969, he transferred to his native village, located in the same county. He did well, was elected team leader, and compiled a highly progressive record. Nominated for higher education, Chang had to take examinations in physics and chemistry. Instead of answering the questions, he wrote a denunciation of the academics-in-command approach. He complained that his work had left him no time to prepare and he assailed those youths who failed to do well in the countryside because they thought only of

getting into a high school. His denunciation was published, and a discussion of the issues he had raised began. Chang, it should be noted, was admitted anyway, to Liaoning Agricultural College, and his leftist views continued to be publicized. See *JMJP* 8/10/73 and 9/10/73; Radio Shenyang, 7/19/74, *FBIS* no. 143, 7/24/74; and *CNS* no. 480, 8/16/73. After the purge of the "gang of four," Chang also got into trouble; see the last section of this chapter.

58. Dr. B. Osadczuk of the Free University, Berlin, visited Nanking University in 1975 and was told that the student body composition was as follows: 28 percent came from the working class, 20 percent from among employees, 10 percent from the PLA, and 42 percent from the countryside, but no breakdowns of the true origins of the latter were given. He was told that the 20 percent employees figure was too high and the worker component was too low.

59. For cases, see *JMJP* 8/9/72 and 8/31/72.

60. "Channels" are mentioned in *JMJP* 5/6/75, Ju-tung hsien, Kiangsu. For the other quotes, see *KMJP* 11/2/72, Mao-ming hsien, Kwangtung; and *KMJP* 12/21/73, Shenyang, Liaoning.

61. The case is based on the following sources: Radio Peking, 1/18/74, *FBIS* no. 15, 1/22/74 (broadcast of *JMJP* 1/18/74 story); Radio Nanking, 1/20/74, *FBIS* no. 15, 1/22/74; Radio Peking, 1/26/74, *FBIS* no. 20, 1/29/74; Radio Peking, 1/28/74, *FBIS* no. 22, 1/31/74.

62. Radio Nanking, 1/20/74, *FBIS* no. 15, 1/22/74, reports his request to return to the PLA unit; Nanking Radio 3/1/74, *FBIS* no. 50, 3/13/74, reports that Chung returned to his production team.

63. See Radio Nanchang, 10/30/74, *FBIS* no. 213, 11/4/74, which reports Chung attending a UY rally sponsored by the Kiangsi Military District, and also Radio Foochow, 9/18/75, *FBIS* no. 183, 9/19/75, and *JMJP* 7/17/76. It is possible that Chung had ties to radical leaders; since the October 1976 purge of the "gang of four" he has not been heard from.

64. Radio Peking, 1/18/74, *FBIS* no. 15, 1/22/74, my italics.

65. In one case of a youth who was admitted to the Kirin Chemical Industry Research Institute, admission was due to "consideration given by the higher level to take care of sons and daughters of troop units." See Radio Changchun, 2/9/74, *FBIS* no. 31, 2/13/74. For other withdrawal cases involving military families, see Radio Changchun, 2/9/74, *FBIS* no. 30, 2/12/74; Radio Changchun, 2/9/74, *FBIS* no. 31, 2/13/74; Radio Shenyang, 2/9/74, *FBIS* no. 31, 2/13/74; Radio Tsinan, 2/16/74, *FBIS* no. 39, 2/26/74; and Radio Lanchow, 2/21/74, *FBIS* no. 39, 2/26/74.

66. Rene Flipo, Agence France Press, 6/20/74, in *FBIS* no. 120, 6/20/74; and Jonathan Sharp, Reuters, 6/24/74, in *FBIS* no. 122, 6/24/74.

67. *JMJP* 5/6/75, Ju-tung hsien, Kiangsu.

68. *JMJP* 8/18/74.

69. *JMJP* 5/6/75, Ju-tung hsien, Kiangsu. A case of similar pressure from relatives was reported at the same time from P'u-ch'eng hsien, Fukien.

70. Radio Hangchow, 8/12/75, *FBIS* no. 157, 8/13/75. This is a rare case of a marriage of an urban male to a local woman.

71. *KMJP* 10/28/73, Lu-feng hsien, Kwangtung.

72. For another, detailed case of family opposition, see the story of the son of Kunming intellectuals, *JMJP* 12/21/74, also broadcast by Peking Radio, 12/21/74, *FBIS* no. 247, 12/23/74. See *JMJP* 3/15/73

for the case of a UY who turned down offers to enter higher school or factory, and who was ridiculed by "bad men," leading to a hsien committee drive against sabotage of the transfer movement.

73. *JMJP* 1/5/74; *KMJP* 1/6/74; and "Rupture with Traditional Ideas," *Peking Review* 17, no. 5, 2/17/74, pp. 6, 23. Chai could apparently have returned legally to become a miner, following in his father's footsteps; see Ross Terrill, *Flowers on an Iron Tree*, pp. 151-52. In fact, there may be something of an hereditary principle in urban job assignments. That is, as vacancies arise in an urban enterprise, priority in filling them may be accorded to the offspring of the unit's work force, even when they are serving in the countryside. When urban units take part in the management of UY settlements, implementing a preferential job allocations system may be further facilitated, as suggested in chapter 3 in the discussion of the Chu-chou model. This could well be the case particularly when an urban unit or set of units sends its youths to a particular set of rural destinations, as in the case of Canton's "textile system" (*fang-chih hsi-t'ung*) which has several places of settlement for the children of the system's workers and employees. See *JMJP* 2/13/75.

74. For cases, see *KMJP* 10/18/71, Inner Mongolia Production and Construction Corps unit; *JMJP* 4/23/71, Wu-ch'ing hsien, Hopei; 2/17/72, Han-chiang hsien, Kiangsu; *KMJP* 1/24/72, Lung-chi hsien, Fukien; *KMJP* 8/16/72, Wu-lan-ch'a-pu League, Inner Mongolia; *KMJP* 8/16/72, Canton Military Region army farm; *KMJP* 11/22/72, Lung-lin autonomous county Kwangsi; *KMJP* 1/16/74, about sent-down graduates of a middle school in Yangchow, Kiangsu; and *KMJP* 4/21/74, Ning-yuan hsien, Hunan.

75. *JMJP* 1/30/71, Chung-shan hsien, Kwangsi.

76. An informant told about a group of 20 UYs in a neighboring brigade who had made important contributions, many also becoming cadres and teachers. But after the Cultural Revolution when reassignment prospects receded, their morale was adversely affected and their performance deteriorated.

77. *KMJP* 11/3/73.

78. For educational measures, see the preceding cases, but also Radio Harbin, 12/22/72, *FBIS* no. 2, 1/3/73; *KMJP* 10/4/72, Ch'ang-lin hsien, Kirin; and *JMJP* 3/22/72, letter to editor by UY from Wu-ch'iang hsien, Kiangsu, calling for more education to combat wavering over reassignment. Also, reassignment is viewed as an issue involving class enemies whose incitement must be combatted. See, e.g., *KMJP* 12/16/71, Lung-men hsien, Kwangtung; and *JMJP* 5/3/75, Yen-ch'ing hsien, Peking.

79. "Chih-ch'ih ho chiao-yü tzu-nü shang-shan hsia-hsiang kan ko-ming," *Hung-ch'i*, no. 8, 8/1/72, p. 67.

80. Sexual misconduct is not reported in the press. Informants mention having heard of cases of premarital sex, leading to births of illegitimate children. According to an overseas Chinese migrant from Peking interviewed in Hong Kong in 1973, Peking cadres were informed in 1971 through the internal communications system of poor morale among UYs in Yenan prefecture, one manifestation being sexual promiscuity. The press does occasionally speak about marriages involving UYs taking place before the approved ages. See, e.g., *JMJP* 10/16/72, case from Ho hsien, Kwangsi.

81. Two informants report having known of arrests of UYs for theft. Reference to UYs stealing chickens, picking fights with peasant youths,

etc., also crop up in press reports, as do cases of undisciplined, defiant behavior. See, e.g., *JMJP* 11/18/69, Tzu-t'ung hsien, Szechwan.

82. For reports of such occurrences, see "Yi-chiu ch'i-yi nien ti ta lu jen-min fan-kung k'ang-pao huo-tung" [The mainland people's anticommunist violent resistance activities in 1971], sec. 2, pp. 330–47. This Nationalist article describes organized oppositional activity, including formation of resistance groups and violent incidents involving UYs. These data have not been confirmed. One informant had heard of a UY guerrilla band in northern Kwangtung but was unable to provide concrete details.

83. Most of the informants overstayed leaves, but some of them actually spent months at a time in Canton. The press mentions this; see e.g., Radio Peking, 12/18/70, *FBIS* no. 250, 12/28/70, on Heilungkiang UYs from Shanghai: "some . . . feel that since it is now the slack winter season, they can leave for the cities to pass the winter season." For the case of a UY influenced by "anarchist thought" who returned home illicitly but was subsequently mobilized to go back to his Inner Mongolian Production and Construction Corps unit, see *JMJP* 2/22/70.

84. Newspaper correspondents, diplomats, and visitors have made various estimates of the number of youths living illegally in the cities. In 1974, journalist Mark Gayn quoted Western diplomats stationed in Peking as estimating the number at 400,000 in the country as a whole. See Mark Gayn, "A View from the Village," p. 15. John Burns, then the Peking correspondent for the *Toronto Globe and Mail*, estimated that 50,000 UYs had illicitly returned to Peking as of early 1974; see *New York Times*, 1/11/74. Ross Terrill estimates that "maybe tens of thousands" of UYs had "slipped back without authorization to Wuhan," as of the summer of 1973; see his *Flowers on an Iron Tree*, pp. 274–75. Of course, such estimates are only that—estimates. Also it is not in fact clear whether these numbers include those who have failed to respond to the demand that they go to the countryside in the first place. The Chinese press does occasionally refer to illegal returnees. A year after the mass transfer began, a Canton newspaper wrote: "On various excuses they have returned to the city and stay in the city for several months and some of them even resolve not to go back to the countryside. . . . If you go on wandering about the city, you are likely to fall into the trap of the class enemy. . . . [S]ome youths love ease, hate labor and seek enjoyment of life after returning to the city; tempted by the class enemy they have embarked upon the criminal road and become tools of the class enemy." See *Kuangchou Kung-tai Hui*, 9/1/69, in *SCMP* supp. no. 265, 2/2/70. When visiting the "Sino-Albanian Friendship Commune" in rural Peking in June 1973, I was told that some sent-down youths had returned to the city on their own.

85. Interview data.

86. See Yao Wen-yuan, "On the Social Basis of the Lin Piao Anti-Party Clique." Yao spoke of crimes committed by young people but did not mention sent-down youths. For crime in Canton, see *New York Times* 8/15/72; and *CNS* no. 407, 2/24/74. In 1976 *China News Analysis*, no. 1046, 7/9/76, published an issue devoted to discussion of prostitution in Canton (based on interviews) in which returned female UYs played a role. According to an informant, at the end of 1972, an internal document was discussed in Canton factories and street organizations which singled out illegally returned UYs as a source of robberies, black market activities, and gambling. This same document, already mentioned in note 30, chap-

ter 3, reportedly asserted that a great many youths who were not UYs had committed errors of varying kinds, though not necessarily crimes. For a discussion of crime in Peking, see *New York Times,* 1/11/74, story by John Burns; for Wuhan, see Terrill, *Flowers on an Iron Tree,* p. 275.

87. For material on the urban militia, see chapter 3, and *China News Analysis,* no. 1005, 7/5/75. For punishments, see Paul Strauss, "Public Executions Authorized," *Boston Globe,* 1/13/74, story based on conversations with officials held in Canton.

88. For some statements about an ongoing struggle between "taking roots" and "pulling up roots," see Radio Nanning, 6/29/76, *FBIS* no. 127, 6/30/76.

89. Informants make this point. See also the next section of this chapter.

90. In the summer of 1975, when some policy makers apparently favored a rotation system—chapter 2 reported accusations against Teng Hsiao-p'ing to this effect—some youths apparently heard about this and responded with alacrity, returning home on their own. See *JMJP* 7/9/76, story about a Heilungkiang state farm.

91. "Decision of the Central Committee of the Chinese Communist Party concerning the Great Proletarian Cultural Revolution," August 8, 1966, in *CCP Documents of the Great Proletarian Cultural Revolution,* ed. Union Research Institute, p. 46 (cited hereafter as *CCP Documents of the CR*).

92. For an excellent analysis, to which the preceding paragraph is much indebted, see Hong Yung Lee, "A Theoretical Framework for the Analysis of the Great Proletarian Cultural Revolution," chapter 2 of a forthcoming study of the Cultural Revolution. For a detailed history of that upheaval, see Stanley Karnow, *Mao and China.*

93. See the directives on economism and on sent-down youths promulgated by the national authorities on January 11, February 17, and October 8, 1967, all in *CCP Documents of the CR,* pp. 165–67, 301–02, and 560–63.

94. *JMJP* editorial, 7/9/67, in *SCMP* no. 3983, 7/19/67; and remarks by Chou En-lai, reported in Hai Feng, *Kuang-chou ti-ch'ü wen-ko li-cheng shu-lüe* [A brief account of the Cultural Revolution in the Canton area], pp. 268, 286–87.

95. *JMJP* editorial, in *SCMP* no. 3983, 7/19/67.

96. Interview data; also "Three Years of Blood and Tears," *Chih-nung Hung-ch'i,* no. 7, 1/68, in *China Topics,* no. 483, 5/27/68. Henceforth titles of stories appearing in Red Guard tabloids will often be supplied, since this section relies heavily on the few available numbers.

97. *Wen-hui Pao,* Shanghai, 2/9/67, in *SCMP* supp. no. 167, 3/14/67.

98. For one such case, see "Chih-shih ch'ing-nien ying-hsiung Kuo Chia-hung lieh-shih yung-chui pu hsiu" [Eternal glory to Kuo Chia-hung, a fallen hero-educated-youth], *3211 Chan-pao,* no. 2, 10/30/67. Kuo, who served on a Kiangsu state farm, was labeled and imprisoned but became a hero when, having gone to Peking to seek rehabilitation, he sacrificed his life trying to save socialist property. *People's Daily* devoted an editorial to him on March 18, 1967, which the tabloid also reprinted. The same issue ran two other such cases.

99. "Chih-shih ch'ing-nien pu k'e-wu" [Educated youths cannot be insulted], *Ko-ming Ch'ing-nien,* no. 2, 11/10/67.

100. Ibid.

101. *JMJP* editorial, 7/9/67, in *SCMP* no. 3983, 7/19/67.

102. "Kao ch'üan shih ko-min jen-min shu" [Open letter to the revolutionary people of the city], *Chih-nung Hung-ch'i,* 1/6/68.

103. For an analysis, see Richard Baum, "The Cultural Revolution in the Countryside."

104. G. William Skinner, "Chinese Peasants and the Closed Community."

105. "Three Years of Blood and Tears," *Chih-nung Hung-ch'i,* no. 7, 1/68.

106. "The Heng-lan Tragic Incident," *Chih-nung Hung-ch'i,* no. 3, 11/1/67, *JPRS* no. 44052, 1/17/68. *Translations on Communist China: Political and Sociological,* no. 436.

107. See also the case reported by *Pi-hsüeh Huang-p'o,* 7/68, quoted in Martin Singer, *Educated Youth and the Cultural Revolution in China,* p. 63. Reportedly, peasants attacked UYs on a state farm in Ying-te hsien, Kwangtung, and tortured some; five deaths resulted, including that of a cadre. As noted previously, informants did not experience this kind of violence.

108. *JMJP* editorial, 7/9/67, in *SCMP* no. 3983, 7/19/67.

109. *Wen-hui Pao,* 2/12/67, in *SCMP* supp. no. 167, 3/14/67.

110. In addition to inciting UYs to return to Shanghai, the officials of Sinkiang and of the Sinkiang Production and Construction Corps allegedly subjected UYs who tried to rebel against power holders to a "reign of white terror," involving "political and bodily oppression." Wang En-mao, Sinkiang's leading official, mobilized the PLA against Red Guards from Peking who traveled to Urumchi to ignite local rebellions, and armed forces evidently suppressed UYs who sought to participate. Because of the delicate situation of Sinkiang, which borders on the Soviet Union and is inhabited by sometimes restive minority nationalities, a joint "Regulation" issued by the Central Committee, the State Council, and the Military Affairs Commission in February 1967 sharply restricted Cultural Revolution activities within the PCC. The Center confined the formation of mass organizations to specific units and forbade seizures of power, noting that officials could be dismissed but only with the sanction of higher party committees. See *Wen-hui Pao,* 1/25/67, in *SCMP* supp. no. 166, 3/13/67; Karnow, *Mao and China,* pp. 250–52, *Wen-hui Pao* editorial, 1/18/67, in *SCMP* supp. no. 164, 2/28/67, which incites UYs to rebel against Sinkiang capitalist roaders. For the Center regulations, see *CCP Documents of the CR,* pp. 258–61. See also Lynn T. White, "The Road to Urumchi," and June T. Dreyer, "Go West Young Han."

111. *Chieh-fang Jih-pao* editorial, 2/2/67, in *SCMP* supp. no. 178, 4/24/67; Center "Circular" on economism, in *CCP Documents of the CR,* pp. 165–67; *Wen-hui Pao* editorial, 2/12/67, in *SCMP* supp. no. 168, 3/17/67; and *JMJP* 1/26/67 and 2/1/67, in *CB* no. 818, 3/6/67. In some places in Hunan, however, UYs had to break through "blockades" allegedly set up by capitalist roaders in order to be able to return to the city of Changsha. Changsha UY organizations sent a "rehabilitation investigation team" in November 1966 in order to extricate comrades in Ling-ling prefecture who had been labeled rightists by party officials during the summer and who were supposed to have been rehabilitated by order of the Center. See "Hsiung-kuan man-tao chen ju t'ieh," *Ko-ming Ch'ing-nien,* no. 2, 11/10/67. The title of the article is a line from Mao's poem "Lou Mountain Pass": "Tough pass, long trail, like iron." See Hua-ling Nieh Engle and Paul Engle, trans., *Poems of Mao Tse-tung,* p. 63.

112. Quoted in Hai Feng, *Kuang-chou ti-ch'ü wen-ko,* p. 287.

113. *Nan-fang Jih-pao,* 1/18/69, in *SCMP* supp. no. 246, 3/12/69.

114. Of four informants who had been sent to the countryside before the Cultural Revolution, only one took part in activities during the upheaval.

115. *Chih-nung Hung-ch'i,* no. 2, 10/7/67. There was also a "Kwangtung chih-shih ch'ing-nien tsao-fan tsung-p'u," or general headquarters of Kwangtung educated youth rebels; see *Ko-ming Ch'ing-nien,* no. 2, 11/10/67.

116. Interview data; also "Is It a Movement of Crooks or a Movement of the Revolutionary Vanguard?" *Chih-nung Hung-ch'i,* no. 3, 1/11/67, in *JPRS* no. 44052, 1/17/68. *Translations on Communist China: Political and Sociological,* no. 436.

117. "Hsiung-kuan man-tao chen ju t'ieh."

118. "T'an Chen-lin's Speeches on Resettlement Work," *Chih-nung Hung-ch'i,* no. 7, 1/68, in *SCMP* no. 4123, 2/21/68.

119. *Mainichi,* 1/20/67, in *Daily Summary of the Japanese Press,* 1/25/67.

120. *CCP Documents on the CR,* pp. 301–02.

121. "Bulletin of the PLA Military Control Committee of the Peking Municipal Public Security Bureau," 2/25/67, in *CCP Documents on the CR,* pp. 670–71.

122. For instance, UYs from Kwangtung and from Hsien-ning prefecture, Hupei, attended a UY rally in Changsha on October 22, 1967; see *Ko-ming Ch'ing-nien,* no. 2, 11/10/67.

123. "Hsiung-kuan man-tao chen ju t'ieh."

124. "Traveller's Report," app. A, *China Topics,* no. 465, 2/26/68.

125. "Factual Account of 'September 7' Bloodshed in Wuhan Municipality," *3211 Chan Pao,* no. 2, 10/30/67, in *SCMP* no. 4909, 1/2/68.

126. Interview data; see also Editor, "Sources of Labor Discontent in China."

127. *Wen-hui Pao,* 2/11/67, in *SCMP* supp. no. 168, 3/17/68. See also Lynn T. White III, "Shanghai's Polity in the Cultural Revolution," pp. 334–41.

128. See Hong Yung Lee, "A Theoretical Framework."

129. Mao Tse-tung, "Talks at Three Meetings with Comrades Chang Ch'un-ch'iao and Yao Wen-yuan," in Stuart Schram, ed., *Chairman Mao Talks to the People,* p. 277. See also Schram, "Introduction: The Cultural Revolution in Historical Perspective," esp. pp. 85–108.

130. Hong Yung Lee, "A Theoretical Framework."

131. Ibid. See also Vogel, *Canton Under Communism,* pp. 339–45; "Sources of Labor Discontent in China"; and Hong Yung Lee, "The Radical Students in Kwangtung during the Cultural Revolution."

132. However, Chou En-lai claimed that UYs were to be found in all groups, not just radical ones; see Hai Feng, *Kuang-chou ti-ch'ü wen-ko,* p. 287.

133. "Is It a Movement of Crooks?"

134. See *CCP Documents of the CR,* pp. 560–63. It is worth noting that this "Urgent Circular" was addressed not just to UYs but to all personnel serving in the countryside who had originally been city dwellers.

135. See "Hsiung-kuan man-tao chen ju t'ieh," in which supporting groups are listed, thus showing that "our cause is just and that we have friends everywhere." See also "Po chih-shih ch'ing-nien tsao-fan wu-li" [Refute the notion that educated youths don't have the right to rebel], *Chih-nung Hung-ch'i,* no. 7, 1/68.

136. In November 1967, Chou En-lai said that only 10,000 of the 30,000 UYs who went back, apparently to Canton, had failed to respond to the October order to return to the countryside. See Hai Feng, *Kuang-chou ti-ch'ü wen-ko,* p. 287. If true, this would show a remarkably high rate of compliance, but the claim is disputed by informants.

137. "Po chih-shih ch'ing-nien tsao-fan wu-li."

138. Hai Feng, *Kuang-chou ti-ch'ü wen-ko,* p. 268.

139. *Wen-hui Pao,* 1/25/67, in *SCMP* supp. no. 166, 3/15/67.

140. "Growing Up in the Storm of Class Struggle," *Peking Review* 11, no. 30, 7/26/68, pp. 22-25.

141. "Whither the Agriculture-Supporting Youth?" *Chih-nung Hung-ch'i,* no. 3, 11/1/67, in *JPRS* 44052, 1/17/68. *Translations on Communist China: Political and Sociological,* no. 436.

142. Hai Feng, *Kuang-chou ti-ch'ü wen-ko,* p. 287. Chou En-lai refers to a notice by the Center specifically on Chih-nung Ch'ing-nien.

143. "Whither the Agriculture-Supporting Youth?" This article, a vehement attack, was published by the UY tabloid *Chih-nung Hung-ch'i* but accompanied by a rebuttal entitled "Is it a Movement of Crooks or a Movement of the Revolutionary Vanguard?" For another attack on UYs following the bourgeois reactionary line, see *Nung-ts'un Ch'ing-nien,* no. 20, 10/25/67, in *SCMM* no. 612, 1/29/68.

144. "Is It a Movement of Crooks?" and "Po chih-shih ch'ing-nien tsao-fan wu-li."

145. Interview data; White, "Shanghai's Polity," p. 339.

146. "What We Saw and Heard on T'ung-shan Ridge," in *Ko-ming Ch'ing-nien,* no. 2, 11/10/67, in *China Topics,* no. 465, 2/26/68; and "Three Years of Blood and Tears."

147. "T'an Chen-lin's Speeches on Resettlement Work."

148. *CCP Documents on the CR,* pp. 560-63.

149. *JMJP* editorial, 7/9/67, in *SCMP* no. 3983, 7/19/67.

150. See citations in note 146; also "The Case of Ch'en Shui-ch'un," *Chih-nung Hung-ch'i,* no. 6, 1/6/68, in *Chinese Sociology and Anthropology* 2, nos. 3-4 (spring-summer 1970): 140-48; and "T'a wei-shemo tzu-sha?" [Why did she kill herself?], in *Chih-nung Hung-ch'i,* no. 6, 1/6/68.

151. Hai Feng, *Kuang-chou ti-ch'ü wen-ko,* p. 287.

152. These three articles can be found in Mao Tse-tung, *Selected Works,* 3:104-05; 4:219-20, 316-18.

153. *Wen-hui Pao,* 2/25/68, *SCMP* no. 4146, 3/26/68.

154. Martin Singer, *Educated Youth and the Cultural Revolution in China,* p. 50.

155. The slogan was shouted at a Changsha rally held on September 3, 1967; see "Hsiung-kuan man-tao chen ju t'ieh." "Criminal" is the characterization used in "Letter from Ch'a-ling," *Ko-ming Ch'ing-nien,* no. 2, 11/10/67, in *China Topics,* no. 465, 2/26/68.

156. "Wrathfully Condemning Liu Shao-ch'i," *Ko-ming Ch'ing-nien,* no. 2, 11/10/67, in *SCMP* no. 4093, 1/5/68; quote rewritten using the original.

157. "What We Saw and Heard on T'ung-shan Ridge"; quote rewritten using the original.

158. "Chih-shih ch'ing-nien pu k'e-wu."

159. "Premier Chou's Important Speech," *Hsiao-ping,* no. 22, 2/17/68, in *SCMP* no. 4134, 3/8/68.

160. "Whither China," *Kuang-yin Hung-ch'i*, no. 5, 3/68, in *SCMP* no. 4190, 6/4/68. See also Singer, *Educated Youth and the CR*, pp. 54–56. In Canton, similar ultraleftist groups appeared, calling for "more disorder" and opposing the revolutionary committees; see Singer, p. 60. According to informants, one of these, the "August 5 Commune," was composed of students in a nominally higher school, the Agricultural Labor University. See also Hai Feng, *Kuang-chou ti-ch'ü wen-ko*, p. 330.

161. *Chung-kung Wen-hua Ta Ko-ming tzu-liao hui-pien* [Collection of materials about the Chinese Communist Great Proletarian Cultural Revolution], ed. Ting Wang, 6: 43–54. It should be noted, however, that another leftist upsurge did take place in the spring of 1968. Some leaders were evidently lukewarm in their condemnation of these ultraleftist groups. See Karnow, *Mao and China*, p. 420 ff.

162. One such group was celebrated in the article "Growing up in the Storm of Class Struggle," cited in note 140.

163. Informants who sympathized with transfer policy did so on economic grounds, except for one, a former Red Guard militant who reported that he supported the ideological reasons for the transfer as well, initially at least. Professor Ying-mao Kao of Brown University talked in 1973 with sent-down youths in China who told him that preventing revisionism was an important reason for the transfer.

164. The major work is Richard Solomon, *Mao's Revolution and Chinese Political Culture.*

165. "Mu-ch'ien chih-ch'ing yün-tung ti shih-chü ho jen-wu" [The present situation and tasks of the movement of educated youths], *Chih-nung Hung-ch'i*, no. 6, 1/6/68. Red Guard violence during the Cultural Revolution could perhaps be explained by Richard Solomon's hypothesis that dependence on hierarchical authority generates resentments and anxieties that at times burst forth into chaotic violence (*luan*). In the case of the sent-down youths, both informants and Center documents allege that some of them engaged not just in armed factional fighting but also in anomic, random violence, and in criminal behavior such as "smashing, snatching, ransacking." See *CCP Documents of the CR*, p. 561. However, if it is in fact true that UYs engaged disproportionately in violence, a proposition not easy to test, their behavior could well be explained more simply by frustration over the hopeless situation in which they found themselves.

166. "Letter from Ch'a-ling."

167. Interview data; one informant attributed the fragmentation of UY groups to this perception that some were more qualified to participate in the Cultural Revolution or to return to the cities than others, in terms of the Center's policies or rulings.

168. For an elaboration of these concepts, see Sidney Verba and Gabriel Almond, *The Civic Culture*, ch. 1.

169. "Kao ko-ming tu-che" [To the revolutionary reader], *Chih-nung Hung-ch'i*, no. 7, January 1968.

170. Keesing's Research Report, *The Cultural Revolution in China*, p. 20.

171. Karnow's book, *Mao and China*, devotes little attention to their activities. Neither does the important account by Jean Esmein, *The Chinese Cultural Revolution*. One informant thought that UYs made up perhaps 10 percent of the Red Flag faction in Canton.

172. Interview data. Cf. Vogel, *Canton Under Communism*, p. 341.

173. Interview data; informants of good class background not sent down before 1968 also thought that the transfer was mainly for bad class elements.

174. Karnow, *Mao and China,* p. 264. Editor, "Sources of Labor Discontent in China," p. 8 ff. Reportedly, Mao termed the use of temporary workers a disgrace. But they have continued to be used since the Cultural Revolution. See *Rural Small-Scale Industry*, chapter 3.

175. Editor, "Sources of Labor Discontent in China," p. 16.

176. Hong Yung Lee, "Radical Students in Kwangtung," p. 681.

177. This point was also reportedly made by Lin Piao: "During the early stages, the Red Guards were cheated and used, and they served as cannon fodder; during the later stages, they were suppressed and made into scapegoats"; see Michael Y. M. Kau, ed., *The Lin Piao Affair,* p. 84. See also Miriam and Ivan D. London, "China's Lost Generation."

178. Of course, not all of the 12 million are still in the countryside, given partial reassignment.

179. Wang Hung-wen, "Report on the Revision of the Party Constitution," p. 31. Wang was purged in October 1976.

180. Ibid., p. 30.

181. "T'an Chen-lin's Speeches on Resettlement Work." T'an spoke at a resettlement meeting held on February 8, 1965, when China was greatly concerned over the threat posed by United States intervention in Vietnam.

182. Speech by William Hinton, the American farmer-writer and head of the U.S.-China Friendship Association, who has close contacts in Peking, at Princeton, N.J., March 15, 1975. In his "Outline for Project 571," Lin Piao had said that the transfer "is really a disguised form of labor reform"; see Kau, *Lin Piao Affair,* p. 84.

183. Tan Wen, "Take the Road of Integrating with Workers and Peasants."

184. Radio Nanchang, 1/10/77, *FBIS* no. 10, 1/14/77.

185. Radio Nanchang, 1/12/77, *FBIS* no. 12, 1/18/77. The charge is worded so as to make it appear that the "gang" carried on these activities everywhere, not just in Kiangsi.

186. See above, note 57.

187. *JMJP* 11/30/76.

188. *JMJP* 7/14/76.

189. *JMJP* 11/30/76. It is not clear what has happened to the other 18 signers of the July letter denouncing Teng Hsiao-p'ing. Among them was Chai Ch'un-ts'e, mentioned earlier in this chapter, who refused opportunities to return to the urban sector.

190. Radio Shihchiachuang, 12/7/76, *FBIS* no. 240, 12/13/76.

191. *JMJP* 1/4/77. The group of 208 educated youths also included returned educated youths, i.e., locals.

192. "Campaign to Repulse the Right Deviationist Wind to Reverse Previous Verdicts: Posters For and Against," *Issues and Studies* 12, 11/76, pp. 105–06.

193. *New York Times,* 1/19/77, p. 8.

194. "Tang shih ling-tao yi ch'ieh-ti" [The party leads in everything], *JMJP* editorial, 7/1/74.

195. This formulation originally appeared in Mao's 1957 speech on contradictions among the people but is now widely quoted, e.g., in the new state constitution adopted in early 1975.

196. See his directive, quoted in "Nothing Is Hard in This World If You

Dare to Scale the Heights," joint New Year's editorial of the *People's Daily, Red Flag,* and *Liberation Daily,* in *Peking Review* 19, no. 1, 1/2/76, p. 9.

197. Factional disputes with a Cultural Revolution background have occurred in a number of industrial and mining enterprises. Hangchow, in Chekiang province, has had particularly serious problems of this nature. See *JMJP* 7/14/75, 8/8/75, 8/15/75, and 9/11/75. On conflict in Anhwei mines, see *JMJP* 11/3/74.

198. This prohibition appears in the joint New Year's editorial cited in note 196, p. 8.

CHAPTER 7

1. Derek T. Healey, "Development and Unemployment," p. 10, quoting World Bank president Robert S. McNamara.

2. Robert S. McNamara, *One Hundred Countries, Two Billion People,* p. 54.

3. Muhammad Shamsul Huq, *Education, Manpower, and Development in South and Southeast Asia,* p. 16.

4. Ibid. Healey, "Development and Unemployment," p. 20, cites a study on Sri Lanka that shows the level of unemployment rising with the level of education. Thus, in 1971, 29 percent of those aged 20-24 who had no schooling were unemployed, as compared to 45 percent of those in the same age group who had passed the "0" level examination.

5. Nathan Keyfitz, "The Youth Cohort Revisited," in *Population, Politics, and the Future of Southern Asia,* ed. W. Howard Wriggins and James F. Guyot, p. 255. I am indebted to Howard Wriggins for drawing this source to my attention.

6. *New York Times,* 1/17/77, p. 3. For a review article of literature on socialist transformation there, see Michael F. Lofchie, "Agrarian Socialism in the Third World: The Tanzanian Case."

7. Healey, "Development and Unemployment," p. 42 ff. See also Frederick C. Turner, "The Rush to the Cities in Latin America," pp. 14-15.

8. This point is stressed in McNamara, *One Hundred Countries, Two Billion People,* ch. 3.

9. Ibid., p. 63.

10. Donald J. Munro, "Man, State, and School."

11. Huq, *Education, Manpower, and Development,* p. 121.

12. For a perceptive analysis of the consequences of this gap, see Kenneth Jowitt, "An Organizational Approach to the Study of Political Culture in Marxist-Leninist Systems."

13. W. Howard Wriggins and C. H. S. Jayewardene, "Youth Protest in Sri Lanka (Ceylon)."

14. At a meeting held by the Canton CCP Committee in February 1977, the "gang of four" was attacked for "preaching that when urban birth control is managed well there will be less pressure to send young people to settle in the countryside." Radio Canton, 2/20/77, *FBIS* no. 35, 2/22/77.

15. *JMJP* 12/28/76.

16. Radio Nanking, 12/4/76, *FBIS* no. 238, 12/8/76.

BIBLIOGRAPHY

A. BOOKS, ARTICLES, AND UNPUBLISHED PAPERS

Ahn, Byung-joon. "The Political Economy of the People's Commune in China: Changes and Continuities." *Journal of Asian Studies* 34, no. 3 (May 1975): 631–58.

Aird, John S. *Population Estimates for the Provinces of the People's Republic of China: 1953 to 1974.* International Population Reports, ser. P–95, no. 73. Washington, D.C.: U.S. Department of Commerce, 1974.

――――. "Population Policy and Demographic Prospects in the People's Republic of China." In *People's Republic of China: An Economic Assessment,* edited by the Joint Economic Committee, 92d Congress, pp. 220–334. Washington, D.C.: U.S. Government Printing Office, 1972.

Anweiler, Oskar. "Educational Policy and Social Structure in the Soviet Union." In *Social Change in the Soviet Union,* edited by Boris Meissner, pp. 173–210. South Bend, Ind.: University of Notre Dame Press, 1972.

Apter, David. *Choice and the Politics of Allocation.* New Haven: Yale University Press, 1971.

Ashbrook, Arthur G., Jr. "China: Economic Overview, 1975." In *China: A Reassessment of the Economy,* edited by the Joint Economic Committee, 94th Congress, pp. 20–51. Washington, D.C.: U.S. Government Printing Office, 1975.

Barnett, A. Doak. *Cadres, Bureaucracy, and Political Power in China.* New York: Columbia University Press, 1967.

Baum, Richard. "The Cultural Revolution in the Countryside: Anatomy of a Limited Rebellion." In *The Cultural Revolution in China,* edited by Thomas W. Robinson, pp. 367–476. Berkeley: University of California Press, 1971.

Bauman, Zygmunt. "The Second Generation Socialism." In *Political Opposition in One-Party States,* edited by Leonard Schapiro, pp. 217–40. New York: John Wiley & Sons, 1972.

Black, Cyril E., et al. *The Modernization of Japan and Russia: A Comparative Study.* New York: The Free Press, 1975.

"Campaign to Repulse the Right Deviationist Wind to Reverse Previous Verdicts: Posters For and Against." *Issues and Studies* 12, no. 11 (November 1976): 100–14.

CCP Documents of the Great Proletarian Cultural Revolution. Edited by Union Research Institute. Hong Kong: Union Research Institute, 1968.

Central Intelligence Agency. "People's Republic of China: Handbook of

Economic Indicators." Research aid made available by Document Expediting Project, Library of Congress. Washington, D.C., August 1975.

Cha-ken nung-ts'un kan ko-ming [Take root in the village to make revolution]. Peking: Jen-min Ch'u-pan She, 1973.

Chang Yun-t'ien. "The Establishment and Expansion of Communist China's 'Production-Construction Corps': A Study of Its Conditions and Functions." *Chung-kung Yen-chiu,* no. 3 (March 1970): 31–40. In *Translations on Communist China,* no. 108, *JPRS* no. 50719, 6/11/70.

Chen, Jack. *A Year in Upper Felicity.* New York: Macmillan, 1973.

Chen, Pi-chao. "Overurbanization, Rustication of Urban-Educated Youths, and Politics of Rural Transformation." *Comparative Politics* 4, no. 3 (April 1972): 361–86.

Ch'i Chien. "Kung-ku ho fa-chan shang-shan hsia-hsiang ti ch'eng-kuo" [Consolidate and develop the effectiveness of up to the mountains and down to the countryside]. *Hung-ch'i,* no. 7, (July 1, 1975): 6–9.

"Chih-ch'ih ho chiao-yü tzu-nü shang-shan hsia-hsiang kan ko-ming" [Support and educate our sons and daughters in making revolution by going up to the mountains and down to the villages]. *Hung-ch'i,* no. 8 (August 1, 1972): 66–68.

Chih-shih ch'ing-nien tsai pei ta-huang [Educated youths in the great northern wilderness]. Edited by Heilungkiang Sheng-ch'an Chien-she Pu-tui Cheng-chih Pu [Heilungkiang Production and Construction Corps Political Department]. Peking: Jen-min Mei-shu Ch'u-pan She, 1973.

Chi Yen. "Going in for Agriculture in a Big Way." *Peking Review* 18, no. 23 (June 6, 1975): 5–9.

Ch'i Yung-hung. "Hua pei-t'ung wei li-liang" [Turn grief into strength]. *Hung-ch'i,* no. 10 (September 28, 1976): 26–29.

Chou En-lai. "Report on the Work of the Government." *Peking Review* 18, no. 4 (January 24, 1975): 21–25.

Chu K'o-chia. "I Am Deeply in Love with Every Blade of Grass and Tree in the Border Region," *Hung-ch'i,* no. 5 (May 1, 1973). In *SCMM* no. 753, 6/4/73.

Chung Hua-min. "A Preliminary Evaluation of the Tenth National Congress of the CCP." *Chung-hua Yüeh-pao,* no. 697 (October 1, 1973). In *Chinese Law and Government* 7, nos. 1–2 (spring-summer 1974): 6–35.

Chung-kung Wen-hua Ta Ko-ming tzu-liao hui-pien [Collection of materials about the Chinese Communist Great Proletarian Cultural Revolution], vol. 6. Edited by Ting Wang. Hong Kong: Ming-pao Yueh-k'an She, 1972.

"Chung-yang an-pan wen-chien chai-p'ien" [Excerpts from Central Assignment documents]. *Chih-nung Hung-ch'i,* no. 7 (January 1968).

Chun Pu. "How China Popularizes Education." *Peking Review* 18, no. 29 (July 18, 1975): 9–11.

Cleveland, Harlan. *China Diary.* Washington, D.C.: Center for Strategic and International Studies, Georgetown University, 1976.

Committee of Concerned Asian Scholars. *China: Inside the People's Republic.* New York: Bantam Books, 1972.

"Correspondence Courses for Educated Youth in the Countryside." *Peking Review* 17, no. 30 (July 26, 1974): 23.

Davies, Derek. "Operatic Duet." *Far Eastern Economic Review* 80, no. 18 (May 7, 1973): 21–24.

"Deal a Hard Blow to the Crimes Undermining the Program of Sending Educated Youths to Rural Areas." *Issues and Studies* 11, no. 3 (March 1975): 111–15.

Donnithorne, Audrey. *China's Economic System*. New York: Praeger, 1967.

Dreyer, June T. "Go West Young Han: The Hsia Fang Movement to Minority Areas." Paper delivered at the 27th Annual Meeting of the Association for Asian Studies, March 24–26, 1975, San Francisco.

Eckstein, Alexander. "China's Trade Policy and Sino-American Relations." *Foreign Affairs* 54, no. 1 (October 1975): 135–54.

Editor. "Sources of Labor Discontent in China: The Worker-Peasant System." *Current Scene* 6, no. 5 (March 15, 1968): 1–28.

Editors. "Kuan-yü ju-ho k'an-tai tzu-nü ti ch'ien-t'u wen-t'i hsiang chia-chang-men hai yi yen" [Another word for heads of families on how to treat the question of the future of their children]. *Chung-kuo Ch'ing-nien*, no.14 (July 16, 1954): 1–3.

Emerson, John P. *Administrative and Technical Manpower in the People's Republic of China*. International Population Reports, ser. P-95, no. 7 Washington, D.C.: U.S. Department of Commerce, 1973.

――――. "Employment in Mainland China: Problems and Prospects." In *An Economic Profile of Mainland China,* edited by the Joint Economic Committee, 94th Congress, pp. 403–70. Washington, D.C.: U.S. Government Printing Office, 1967.

――――. "Manpower Training and Utilization of Specialized Cadres, 1949–1968." In *The City in Communist China,* edited by John W. Lewis, pp. 183–214. Stanford: Stanford University Press, 1971.

Engle, Hua-ling Nieh, and Engle, Paul, trans. *Poems of Mao Tse-tung*. New York: Dell, 1972.

Esmein, Jean. *The Chinese Cultural Revolution*. Garden City: Anchor Books, 1973.

Etzioni, Amitai. *The Active Society*. New York: The Free Press, 1968.

Fan Kang. "Capitalist-Roaders are the Bourgeoisie inside the Party." *Peking Review* 19, no. 25 (June 18, 1976): 7–10.

"Four New Kinds of Schools." *Hung-ch'i,* no. 8 (July 21, 1970). In Peter Seybolt, *Revolutionary Education in China: Documents and Commentary,* pp. 181–88. White Plains, N.Y.: International Arts and Sciences Press, 1973.

Funnell, Victor C. "The Chinese Communist Youth Movement, 1949–1966." *China Quarterly,* no. 42 (April-June 1970): 105–30.

Gardner, John. "Educated Youth and Urban-Rural Inequalities, 1958–66." In *The City in Communist China,* edited by John W. Lewis, pp. 235–88. Stanford: Stanford University Press, 1971.

――――, and Idema, Wilt. "China's Educational Revolution." In *Authority, Participation and Cultural Change in China*, edited by Stuart Schram, pp. 257–90. Cambridge: Cambridge University Press, 1973.

Gayn, Mark. "A View from the Village." *Problems of Communism* 23, no. 5 (September-October 1974): 10–15.

Gittings, John. "Stifling the Students." *Far Eastern Economic Review* 61, no. 35 (August 25, 1968): 377–79.

Glassman, Joel. "Educational Reform and Manpower Policy in China. 1955–1958." Paper presented to the 27th Annual Meeting of the Association for Asian Studies, March 24–26, 1975, San Francisco.

"Growing Up in the Storm of Class Struggle." *Peking Review* 11, no. 30 (July 26, 1968): 22–25.

Gurr, Ted R. *Why Men Rebel.* Princeton: Princeton University Press, 1970.

Hai Feng. *Kuang-chou ti-ch'ü wen-ko li-cheng shu-lüe* [A brief account of the Cultural Revolution in the Canton area]. Hong Kong: Yu-lien Yen-chiu-so, 1971.

Hayford, Charles. "The Rural Reconstruction Movement: Notes and Implications." Paper delivered to the University Seminar on Modern East Asia: China, Columbia University, January 27, 1972.

Healey, Derek T. "Development and Unemployment: The Asian Experience." Paper no. 1, Centre for Asian Studies, University of Adelaide (1975?).

Hou, Chi-ming. "Manpower, Employment, and Unemployment." In *Economic Trends in Communist China,* edited by Alexander Eckstein et al., pp. 329–97. Chicago: Aldine, 1968.

Howe, Christopher. *Employment and Economic Growth in Urban China, 1949–1957.* New York: Cambridge University Press, 1971.

Hua Kuo-feng. "Mobilize the Whole Party, Make Greater Efforts to Develop Agriculture, and Strive to Build Tachai-Type Counties throughout the Country." *Peking Review* 18, no. 44 (October 31, 1975): 7–10.

Huntington, Samuel P. *Political Order in Changing Societies.* New Haven: Yale University Press, 1968.

Huq, Muhammad Shamsul. *Education, Manpower, and Development in South and Southeast Asia.* New York: Praeger Publishers, 1975.

"Integrating with Workers and Peasants." *Peking Review* 16, no. 19 (May 11, 1973): 7–10.

Je-ch'ing kuan-huai hsia-hsiang chih-shih ch'ing-nien ti ch'eng-chang [Be enthusiastically concerned about the growth of sent-down educated youth]. Peking: Jen-min Ch'u-pan She, 1973.

Jen Wei-nung. "Chia-ch'iang nung-yeh k'e-hsüeh yen-chiu" [Strengthen study of agriculture science]. *Hung-ch'i,* no. 12 (December 1, 1972): 29–33.

Johnson, Graham. "Rural Economic Development and Social Change in South China." Unpublished paper, December 1973.

Jowitt, Kenneth. "An Organizational Approach to the Study of Political Culture in Marxist-Leninist Systems." *American Political Science Review* 67, no. 3 (September 1974): 1171–91.

Karnow, Stanley. *Mao and China.* New York: Viking Press, 1972.

Kau, Michael Y. M., ed. *The Lin Piao Affair.* White Plains, N.Y.: International Arts and Sciences Press, 1975.

Keesing's Research Report. *The Cultural Revolution in China.* New York: Charles Scribner's Sons, 1967.

Kessen, William, ed. *Childhood in China.* New Haven: Yale University Press, 1975.

Keyfitz, Nathan. "The Youth Cohort Revisited." In *Population, Politics, and the Future of Southern Asia*, edited by W. Howard Wriggins and James F. Guyot, pp. 231–58. New York: Columbia University Press, 1973.

Ko Chu-p'o and Liu Ts'un. "Kuan-yü wo kuo chung-hsiao-hsüeh chiao-yü fa-chan chi-hua wen-t'i" [On planning the development of our country's primary and secondary education]. *Chi-hua Ching-chi*, no. 10 (October 9, 1957): 20–22.

Kraus, Richard. "The Evolving Concept of Class in Post-Liberation China." Ph.D. diss., Columbia University, 1974.

"Kuan-yü chung-shih tui ch'ing-nien ti ssu-hsiang chiao-yü kung-tso ti t'ao-lun" [Discussion on emphasizing thought education work for youth]. *Hung-ch'i*, no. 11 (1971): 71–78.

Lampton, David M. "Performance and the Chinese Political System: A Preliminary Assessment of Education and Health Policies." Paper delivered at the annual meeting of the American Political Science Association, September 2–5, 1975, San Francisco.

Lardy, Nicholas R. "Economic Planning and Income Distribution in China." *Current Scene* 14, no. 11 (November 1976): 1–12.

Lee, Hong Yung. "The Radical Students in Kwangtung during the Cultural Revolution." *China Quarterly*, no. 64 (December 1975): 645–83.

——. "A Theoretical Framework for the Analysis of the Great Proletarian Cultural Revolution." Chapter 2 of a forthcoming study of the Cultural Revolution.

Lelyveld, Joseph. "The Great Leap Farmward." *New York Times Magazine*, July 28, 1974, pp. 6–7, 56–62.

Lewis, John W. "China Trip Notes." Unpublished manuscript, 1973.

——. "Party Cadres in Communist China." In *Education and Political Development*, edited by James S. Coleman, pp. 408–36. Princeton: Princeton University Press, 1965.

——. "Political Aspects of Mobility in China's Urban Development." *American Political Science Review* 60, no. 4 (December 1966): 899–912.

Liu Ai-feng. "Chieh-chüeh an-chao Mao Chu-hsi chih-shih pan-shih pa chung-hsiao-hsüeh ti t'i-yü kung-tso tso ti hen hao" [Decisively do a good job in primary and middle school sports according to Chairman Mao's instructions]. *Hsin T'i-yü*, no. 3 (March 20, 1966): 8–11.

Lofchie, Michael F. "Agrarian Socialism in the Third World: The Tanzanian Case." *Comparative Politics* 8, no. 3 (April 1976): 479–99.

London, Miriam, and London, Ivan D. "China's Lost Generation: The Fate of the Red Guards since 1968." *Saturday Review*, November 30, 1974, pp. 12–19.

Lowenthal, Richard. "Development vs. Utopia in Communist Policy." In *Change in Communist Systems*, edited by Chalmers Johnson, pp. 33–116. Stanford: Stanford University Press, 1970.

Lu Ting-i. *Education Must Be Combined with Productive Labor*. Peking: Foreign Languages Press, 1964.

McNamara, Robert S. *One Hundred Countries, Two Billion People*. New York: Praeger Publishers, 1973.

Mao Tse-tung. *Selected Works*. 4 vols. New York: International Publishers, 1954, 1956.

Meisner, Maurice. *Li Ta-chao and the Origins of Chinese Marxism*. Cambridge: Harvard University Press, 1967.

——. "Utopian Socialist Themes in Maoism." In *Peasant Rebellion and Communist Revolution in Asia*, edited by John W. Lewis, pp. 207–52. Stanford: Stanford University Press, 1974.

"More Tropical Crops on Hainan Island." *Peking Review* 17, no. 23 (June 7, 1974): 31.

Moseley, George. *A Sino-Soviet Cultural Frontier: The Ili-Kazakh Autonomous Chou*. Cambridge: Harvard East Asian Research Center Monographs, 1966.

Munro, Donald J. "Egalitarian Ideal and Educational Fact in Communist China." In *China: Management of a Revolutionary Society*, edited by John M. H. Lindbeck, pp. 256–304. Seattle: University of Washington Press, 1971.

——. "Man, State, and School." In *China's Developmental Experience*, edited by Michel Oksenberg, pp. 121–43. New York: Praeger, 1973.

"Nothing Is Hard in This World If You Dare to Scale the Heights." Joint New Year's editorial of the *People's Daily, Red Flag*, and *Liberation Daily*, in *Peking Review* 19, no. 1 (January 2, 1976): 8–10.

Ofer, Gur. *Industrial Structure, Urbanization, and Growth Strategy of Socialist Countries*. Research Report no. 53, Department of Economics, Hebrew University of Jerusalem, March 1974.

Oksenberg, Michel, "Getting Ahead and Along in Communist China: The Ladder of Success on the Eve of the Cultural Revolution." In *Party Leadership and Revolutionary Power in China*, edited by John W. Lewis, pp. 304–50. Cambridge: Cambridge University Press, 1970.

——. "Local Leaders in Rural China, 1962–1965: Individual Attributes, Bureaucratic Positions, and Political Recruitment." In *Chinese Communist Politics in Action*, edited by A. Doak Barnett, pp. 155–215. Seattle: University of Washington Press, 1969.

——. "Methods of Communication within the Chinese Bureaucracy." *China Quarterly*, no. 57 (January-March 1974): 1–40.

——. "Occupational Groups in Chinese Society and the Cultural Revolution." In *The Cultural Revolution: 1967 in Review*, pp. 1–37. Ann Arbor: Michigan Papers in Chinese Studies no. 2, 1968.

——, and Goldstein, Steven. "The Chinese Political Spectrum." *Problems of Communism* 23 (March-April 1974): 1–13.

"Old Ideas of Looking Down on Peasants Criticized." *Peking Review* 17, no. 8 (February 22, 1974): 3, 21.

"On Khrushchev's Phoney Communism and Its Historical Lessons for the World." In A. Doak Barnett, *China After Mao (with Selected Documents)*, pp. 123–95. Princeton: Princeton University Press, 1967.

Orleans, Leo A. "Chinese Statistics: The Impossible Dream." *American Statistician* 28, no. 2 (May 1974): 47–52.

——. "Communist China's Education: Policies, Problems, and Prospects." In *An Economic Profile of Mainland China*, edited by the Joint Economic Committee, 90th Congress, pp. 499–518. Washington, D.C.: U.S. Government Printing Office, 1967.

———. *Every Fifth Child.* Stanford: Stanford University Press, 1973.

———. *Professional Manpower and Education in Communist China.* Washington, D.C.: U.S. Government Printing Office, 1961.

"Outline of Education on Situation for Companies (Lesson Five)." Prepared by Propaganda Division, Political Department, Kunming Military Region, April 6, 1973. In *Issues and Studies* 10, no. 10 (July 1974): 94–105.

Parish, William, Jr. "Political Participation in Rural China." Unpublished paper, December 1973.

———. "Socialism and the Chinese Peasant Family." *Journal of Asian Studies* 34, no. 3 (May 1975): 613–30.

———, and Whyte, Martin K. *Village and Family in Contemporary China* (forthcoming).

Perkins, Dwight. "Constraints Influencing China's Agricultural Performance." In *China: A Reassessment of the Economy,* edited by the Joint Economic Committee, 94th Congress, pp. 350–65. Washington, D.C.: U.S. Government Printing Office, 1975.

———. "Development of Agriculture." In *China's Developmental Experience,* edited by Michel Oksenberg, pp. 55–67. New York: Praeger, 1973.

Plant Studies in the People's Republic of China: A Trip Report of the American Plant Studies Delegation. Washington, D.C.: National Academy of Sciences, 1975.

"The Poor and Lower-Middle Peasants Have Acquired Socialist Culture." *Hung-ch'i,* no. 8 (July 21, 1970). In Peter Seybolt, *Revolutionary Education in China: Documents and Commentary,* pp. 200–09. White Plains, N.Y.: International Arts and Sciences Press, 1973.

"Proclamation of National People's Congress of PRC." *Peking Review* 18, no. 4, (January 24, 1975): 10.

"Report of the Delegation of University and College Presidents to the People's Republic of China." Prepared by the National Committee on U.S.-China Relations, New York, n.d.

Richman, Barry M. *Industrial Society in Communist China.* New York: Vintage Books, 1969.

Ridley, Charles P., et al. *The Making of a Model Citizen in Communist China.* Stanford: Hoover Institution Press, 1971.

"Rupture with Traditional Ideas." *Peking Review* 17, no. 5 (February 17, 1974): 6, 23.

Rural Small-Scale Industry in the People's Republic of China. Berkeley: University of California Press, forthcoming (cited from second draft).

Saifudin. "Advance Victoriously under the Guidance of Chairman Mao's Revolutionary Line." *Red Flag,* no. 10 (1975). Broadcast by Radio Urumchi, 10/6/75, *FBIS* no. 197, 10/9/75.

Scalapino, Robert. "The Struggle over Higher Education: Revolution vs. Development." *Issues and Studies* 12, no. 7 (July 1976): 1–8.

"Schools Should Be a Tool for the Dictatorship of the Proletariat." *Red Flag,* no. 5. Broadcast by Radio Peking, 5/29/75, *FBIS* no. 105, 5/30/75.

Schram, Stuart. "Introduction: The Cultural Revolution in Historical Perspective." In *Authority, Participation and Cultural Change in China,* edited by Stuart Schram, pp. 1–109. Cambridge: Cambridge University Press, 1973.

———, ed. *Chairman Mao Talks to the People.* New York: Pantheon Books, 1974.

Schwartz, Joel S., and Keech, W. R. "Group Influence and the Policy Process in the Soviet Union." *American Political Science Review* 62, no. 3 (September 1968): 840–51.

Second Session of the Second National People's Congress of the People's Republic of China—Documents. Peking: Foreign Languages Press, 1960.

Selden, Mark. "The Yenan Legacy: The Mass Line." In *Chinese Communist Politics in Action,* edited by A. Doak Barnett, pp. 99–154. Seattle: University of Washington Press, 1969.

"Selected Edition on Liu Shao-ch'i's Counterrevolutionary Crimes." Nankai University, April 1967. In *SCMM* no. 653, 5/5/69.

Seybolt, Peter J. "Editor's Introduction." *Chinese Education* 8, no. 2 (summer 1975): 3.

Shabad, Theodore. *China's Changing Map.* New York: Praeger Publishers, 1972.

Shih Ling. "Chien-ch'ih ch'ing-nien t'ung kung-nung chieh-ho ti cheng-ch'üeh lu-hsien" [Persist in the correct line of youth integrating with the workers and peasants]. *Hung-ch'i,* no. 12 (December 1, 1975): 25–30.

Shirk, Susan. "The Middle School Experience in China." Paper presented to the 27th Annual Meeting of the Association for Asian Studies, March 24–26, 1975, San Francisco.

———. "The 1963 Temporary Work Regulations for Full-Time Middle and Primary Schools: Commentary and Translation." *China Quarterly,* no. 55 (July-September 1973): 511–46.

Singer, Martin. *Educated Youth and the Cultural Revolution in China.* Michigan Papers in Chinese Studies, no. 10. Ann Arbor: Center for Chinese Studies, 1971.

Skinner, G. William. "Chinese Peasants and the Closed Community: An Open and Shut Case." *Comparative Studies in Society and History,* 13, no. 3 (July 1971): 270–81.

Socialist Upsurge in China's Countryside. Peking: Foreign Languages Press, 1957.

Solomon, Richard. *Mao's Revolution and the Chinese Political Culture.* Berkeley: University of California Press, 1971.

Stavis, Benedict. *Making Green Revolution: Politics of Agricultural Development in China.* Rural Development Committee Monograph no. 1. Ithaca, N.Y.: Cornell University Press, 1974.

Stewart, Philip D. "Soviet Interest Groups and the Policy Process: The Repeal of Production Education." *World Politics* 22, no. 1 (October 1969): 29–50.

Sung P'ing. "T'an lao-tung chiu-yeh wen-t'i" [The problem of labor employment]. *Hsüeh-hsi,* no. 12 (June 18, 1957): 25–28.

"Taking the Revolutionary Path of Going to the Countryside." *Peking Review* 17, no. 19 (May 10, 1974): 19–21.

"T'an Chen-lin's Speeches on Resettlement Work." *Chih-nung Hung-ch'i,* no. 7 (January 1968). In *SCMP* no. 4123, 2/21/68.

T'an Wen. "Take the Road of Integrating with Workers and Peasants, Be Vanguards in Combating and Preventing Revisionism." *People's Daily,* 5/4/76. Broadcast by Radio Peking, 5/3/76, *FBIS* no. 89, 5/6/76.

T'an Wen. "Youth Should Stand at the Forefront of the Revolutionary Ranks." *Hung-ch'i*, no. 5 (May 1, 1973). In *SCMM* no. 753, 6/4/73.

Teiwes, Frederick C. "The Assignment of University Graduates in China, 1974." *China Quarterly*, no. 62 (June 1975): 308–09.

———. "Before and After the Cultural Revolution." *China Quarterly*, no. 58 (April-May 1974): 332–48.

Terrill, Ross. *Flowers on an Iron Tree.* Boston: Little, Brown, 1975.

Theoretical Group of the General Office of the State Council. "In Commemoration of the First Anniversary of the Passing of Our Esteemed and Beloved Premier Chou En-lai." *Peking Review* 20, no. 3 (January 14, 1977), pp. 8–21.

Thomson, James C., Jr. *While China Faced West.* Cambridge: Harvard University Press, 1969.

Tien, H. Yuan. *China's Population Struggle.* Columbus: Ohio University Press, 1973.

Turner, Frederick C. "The Rush to the Cities in Latin America: Government Policies Have More Effect Than We Recognize." Unpublished paper, University of Connecticut, Storrs (1976?).

"Twelve Million School Graduates Settle in the Countryside." *Peking Review* 19, no. 2 (January 9, 1976): 11–13.

"Using Mao Tse-tung Thought to Reeducate Educated Youths Coming to the Countryside." *Hung-ch'i*, no. 9, (August 27, 1969). In *SCMM* no. 665, 9/22/69.

Verba, Sidney, and Almond, Gabriel. *The Civic Culture.* Boston: Little, Brown, 1963.

Vogel, Ezra F. *Canton Under Communism.* New York: Harper Torchbooks. 1971.

———. "From Friendship to Comradeship: The Change in Personal Relations in Communist China." In *China under Mao: Politics Takes Command,* edited by Roderick MacFarquhar, pp. 407–24. Cambridge: MIT Press, 1966.

———. "Voluntarism and Social Control." In *Soviet and Chinese Communism: Similarities and Differences,* edited by Donald W. Treadgold, pp. 168–84. Seattle: University of Washington Press, 1967.

Wang Hung-wen. "Report on the Revision of the Party Constitution." *Peking Review* 16, nos. 35–36 (September 7, 1973): 29–33.

Wharton, Clifton R., Jr. "Education and Agricultural Growth: The Role of Education in Early-Stage Agriculture." In *Education and Economic Development,* edited by Arnold Anderson and Mary Jean Bowman, pp. 202–28. Chicago: Aldine, 1965.

———. "Risk, Uncertainty and the Subsistence Farmer." In *Economic Development and Social Change,* edited by George Dalton, pp. 566–74. Garden City, N.Y.: Natural History Press, 1971.

White, D. Gordon. "The Politics of Hsia-Hsiang Youth." *China Quarterly,* no. 59 (July-September 1974): 491–517.

White, Lynn T., III. "The Road to Urumchi: Rustication from Shanghai through the Cultural Revolution." Paper delivered at the 27th Annual Meeting of the Association for Asian Studies, March 24–26, 1975, San Francisco.

———. "Shanghai's Polity in the Cultural Revolution." In *The City in*

Joint Publications Research Service—Translations on Communist China: Political and Sociological. Springfield, Va.: National Technical Information Service, United States Department of Commerce.

Selections from China Mainland Magazines (renamed in 1973: *Selections from People's Republic of China Press*). Hong Kong: United States Consulate General.

Summary of World Broadcasts—Far East. Reading, Eng.: British Broadcasting Corporation.

Survey of the China Mainland Press (renamed in 1973: *Survey of the People's Republic of China Press*). Hong Kong: United States Consulate General.

*Survey of the China Mainland Press—*Supplement. Hong Kong: United States Consulate General.

C. RADIO STATIONS CITED

Canton, Kwangtung
Changchun, Kirin
Changsha, Hunan
Chengchow, Honan
Chengtu, Szechwan
Foochow, Fukien
Hangchow, Chekiang
Harbin, Heilungkiang
Hofei, Anhwei
Hu-ho-hot, Inner Mongolia
Kunming, Yunnan
Kweiyang, Kweichow

Lanchow, Kansu
Nanchang, Kiangsi
Nanking, Kiangsu
Nanning, Kwangsi
Peking
Shanghai
Shenyang, Liaoning
Shihchiachuang, Hopei
Sian, Shensi
Tsinan, Shantung
Urumchi, Sinkiang
Wuhan, Hupei

D. CHINESE NEWSPAPERS CITED

1. Regularly Published Papers

Chieh-fang Jih-pao, Shanghai
Chung-kuo Ch'ing-nien Pao, Peking
Hsin-min Wan-pao, Shanghai
Jen-min Jih-pao, Peking
Kuang-ming Jih-pao, Peking
Kung-jen Jih-pao, Peking
Liaoning Jih-pao, Shenyang

Nan-fang Jih-pao, Canton
Pei-ching (Peking) *Jih-pao*
Sinkiang Jih-pao, Urumchi
Ta kung Pao, Hong Kong
Wen-hui Pao, Hong Kong
Wen-hui Pao, Shanghai

2. Cultural Revolution Tabloids

Chiao-yü Ko-ming, Peking
Chih-nung Hung-ch'i, Canton
Ching-kang-shan, Peking
Chung-hsüeh Tou-P'i-Kai, Peking
Hsiao-ping, Canton
K'e-chi Hung-ch'i, Peking

Ko-ming Ch'ing-nien, Changsha
Kuang-chou (Canton) *Kung-tai Hui*
Nung-ts'un Ch'ing-nien
3211 Chan-pao, Changsha
Wen-hua Ko-ming T'ung-hsün, Peking

INDEX

"Foolish Old Man Who Removed the Mountain, The" (Mao Tse-tung), 277

"Founding a New Enterprise through Hard Struggle," 236

"Four modernizations, The," 74

Frontier provinces: UY settlement in, 63, 68–70

Frustration of expectations: in education, 47–49, 53

Fukien, 43, 182; UYs and RYs in, 61; cadre/UY ratio, 146; youth points in, 148; percentage of UYs in higher education, 247, 248

"Gang of four," 14, 76, 176n, 218n, 255n, 288; purged, 74; and urban militias, 95–96; incited UYs to violence, 286–87

Graduates, 21–22, 38n, 175

Great Leap Forward, 35–36; led to economic depression, 36, 52, emphasized female employment, 41; educational reform during, 50–52, 58; school establishment in, 229

Great Proletarian Cultural Revolution. *See* Cultural Revolution

Grievances (UYs), redress of, 128, 156–61

Guidance and supervision of UYs, 124–32; 151–52

Hai-ch'eng county, Liaoning: settlement patterns in, 128, 150–51; UY marriage statistics, 163–64, 165; UY leadership in, 213

Hainan Island, 88, 113, 114, 223, 235; army farms on, 69; national minorities in, 70; Red Guards sent to, 115

Hakka village, 134

Hangchow, 29

Harbin: urban militia in, 95; higher schools offer correspondence courses, 209

Heilungkiang, 112, 199, 223, 235, 288; UY settlement in, 29, 63, 114, 119, 246; army farms in, 69; recruitment in, 190, 192; "red and expert" schools, 211; proportion of UYs in population, 233–34

Heilungkiang Production and Construction Corps, 207; companies set up reading rooms, 209; UYs enrolled in higher education, 247–48

Heng-lan commune (Chung-shan county, Kwangtung): Cultural Revolution violence in, 267

Hofei: compliance rate for transfer mobilization, 93

Hofei City Party Committee, 111

Honan: cities, 43; major recruitment in, 185, 186–87, 188; proportion of UYs in population, 234

Hong Kong: illegal immigrants, 15–16, 247; settlements close to, 135

Hopei, 145, 158, 182, 219, 230; "communist labor universities" in, 208; generational tensions fanned in, 287

Hou Chin: model youth, 176–77

Housing: for UYs, 135, 154–56, 157–58; for UY married couples, 164

Hsiang-chiang Feng-lei, 273

Hsiang-yang commune (Tien-chang county, Anhwei), 124

Hsin-hsiang, Honan: population, 43

Hsin-hua Bookstore network, 209

Hsinhui hsien, Kwangtung: peasant/UY clashes during Cultural Revolution, 267

Hsi-yang county, Shansi: UY factory employment in, 249

Hsü Li-chih, 270

Huai-an county, Kiangsu: settlement patterns, 150; youth collectives in, 151

Huai-te county, Kirin, 136; UY income in, 152

Hua Kuo-feng, 82, 144, 287; supported transfer program, 73; set example sending daughter to countryside, 110; quoted, 203; determined to make transfer program work, 298–99

Hui county, Honan: UY factory employment in, 249

Hui-ning county, Kansu: UYs recruited as teachers, 195

Hui-t'ung county, Hunan: UY contributions, 205

Hunan, 41, 273, 281; major recruitment in, 185, 186–87, 188; Sheng-wu-lien (Great Alliance Committee of the Proletarian Revolutionary Faction of Hunan), 279

Hun-ch'un county, Kirin, 213; UY leadership in, 213–14

Hung-ch'i ("Red flag"), 12

Huo-ch'iu county, Anhwei: UY leadership in, 214–16

Hupei province, 145; cadres to accompany UYs, 146; UY reassignment, 249

Incentives, 9, 178; material, 81–82, 88–90; to adaptation, 198–203

Income: per capita, 47; in villages, 64; UY, 152

India: unemployment of educated young, 290

Industrial growth, 35–36, 43, 76; labor requirements for, 41; capital-intensive techniques, 42